CRUCIFIED WISDOM

Comparative Theology / Thinking Across Traditions

SERIES EDITORS

Loye Ashton and John Thatamanil

This series invites books that engage in constructive comparative theological reflection that draws from the resources of more than one religious tradition. It offers a venue for constructive thinkers, from a variety of religious traditions (or thinkers belonging to more than one), who seek to advance theology understood as "deep learning" across religious traditions.

CRUCIFIED WISDOM

Theological Reflection on Christ
and the Bodhisattva

S. MARK HEIM

Fordham University Press NEW YORK 2019

Fordham University Press has no responsibility for the persistence or accuracy of
URLs for external or third-party Internet websites referred to in this publication
and does not guarantee that any content on such websites is, or will remain,
accurate or appropriate.

Fordham University Press also publishes its books in a variety of electronic
formats. Some content that appears in print may not be available in
electronic books.

Visit us online at www.fordhampress.com.

Library of Congress Cataloging-in-Publication Data available online
at https://catalog.loc.gov.

Printed in the United States of America

21 20 19   5 4 3 2 1

First edition

For my son,
Jacob Lewis Heim
Courageous and Cherished

Freedom is the freedom to say that two plus two
makes four. If that is granted, all else follows.

Winston Smith, from his diary in *1984*
—GEORGE ORWELL

CONTENTS

PREFACE AND ACKNOWLEDGMENTS

Christian readers will readily discern the particularities of my own Christianity. They may not so readily perceive the limitations of the approach to Buddhism involved in this book. Between *Theravāda* and *Mahāyāna*, often regarded as the two primary branches of Buddhist tradition, I focus exclusively on the latter. Within the universe of *Mahāyāna* texts, I focus on Śāntideva's *Bodhicaryāvatāra*. In the interpretation of Śāntideva, I largely follow Tibetan commentators. These commentators belong to the *Vajrayāna* tradition, which some scholars and practitioners regard as a third primary branch of Buddhism.[1] A Buddhist-Christian reflection focused on the *Theravāda* tradition might draw some sharper contrasts and limit attention to the role of bodhisattvas. But this study aims to engage the full *Mahāyāna* vision of these figures and to take account of its understanding of Buddha nature.

In the realm of practice, I have had some general experience of *vipassanā* and mindfulness meditation. But I have been most strongly influenced by the Tibetan Rimé tradition (specifically, by teachers from both Nyingma and Kargyu lineages). Of particular importance for my thinking has been the teaching of adapted practices from this tradition within the Natural Dharma Fellowship and the Foundation for Active Compassion.[2] One of the most notable aspects of that teaching is the way that traditional Tibetan meditations, which involve detailed visualizations of deity figures, have been transposed into forms of "benefactor" meditation, in which students draw upon figures or moments from their own life history as objects of focus.

I am deeply grateful for the hospitality and the instruction of the Natural Dharma Fellowship. Its leadership makes clear that they welcome practitioners with identities or commitments that bind them to other religious communities. This made it possible for me to enter fullheartedly into participation in their *margha* program. My thanks also go to Lama John Makransky, Lama Willa Miller, Liz Monson, Bob Morrison, my *margha* group, and the staff of the Wonderwell Mountain Refuge. Their teaching and practice were a living commentary on Śāntideva's *bodhicitta*. I am only a beginner on the path they embody, a fact that should alert readers that failings in interpretation or understanding are not the fault of any of these teachers. My thanks to John Makransky extend equally into the academic realm, where he has been a cherished colleague and friend in many settings. He was gracious enough to review the manuscript of this work and to share his comments. In the area of Buddhism, specifically of Buddhist-Christian study, Paul Knitter, Ruben Habito, Maria Reis Habito, John Keenan, Robert Jonas, and Mark Unno have each greatly enriched me over past years through their writings, presentations, and personal conversation.

I would like to thank the leadership at the Kwan Um Zen Center in Cumberland, Rhode Island, and at the Barre Buddhist Study Center in Barre, Massachusetts, (particularly its resident teacher, Mu Soeng) for the hospitality extended to me and my classes over a number of years. I am grateful to Hiutung Chan, past director of the Tao Fong Shan study center in Hong Kong, for inviting me to lecture and teach there, and for guiding me on visits to Buddhist monasteries in China. Appreciation is also due to the abbot and assistant abbot of the Chanmyay Yeiktha meditation center at Hmawbi, Myanmar, for the hospitality and instruction there. The cover art for this book is "The Risen Christ at Emmaus" by Jyoti Sahi, who is not only an extraordinary artist but an insightful author on topics similar to those treated in this book. I am deeply appreciative for his permission to use the painting here. It is not only thematically apt, but a very happy reminder of our acquaintance in India a good many years ago.

My colleagues at Andover Newton Theological School have been a constant support and inspiration in my work. To our librarians, Nancy Lois and Diana Yount, and to our dean, Sarah Drummond, I extend particular gratitude for their personal and institutional support. My colleagues Sze-kar Wan, now of the Perkins School of Theology at Southern Methodist University, and Brita Gill-Austern contributed much that informed this book, though their gifts are by no means limited to that content. Sze-kar has taught me much about China and the riches of cross-cultural readings of the Bible. Brita has established connections between Andover Newton and Christian seminaries and Buddhist centers in Myanmar, which allowed me to travel there twice in recent years. I treasure them both as colleagues and friends.

The length of time it has taken me to complete this project testifies partly no doubt to my own sloth. But it also reflects both the difficulty in finding an understanding that seems adequate to the topic, and the way in which the horizons of the project tend to expand with each new source. On that score, I can complain only of the excessive richness of the stimulation I have received from others along the way. Service on the faculty of the American Academy of Religion summer Luce seminars on comparative theology and theologies of religious pluralism brought me into extended conversation with other faculty leaders and three cohorts of outstanding participants. I am especially grateful to Anand Rambachan, John Thatamanil, Frank Clooney, Jeannine Hill Fletcher, Peter Ochs, Maria Hermanson, Najeeba Syeed Miller, John Makransky, and Devorah Schoenfeld. I also deeply appreciate Frank Clooney's invitation to give a talk on some of this material at the Harvard Center for the Study of World Religions.

I received a Henry Luce III Fellowship in Theology that allowed me to devote a year from 2009 to 2010 to this project. I am deeply grateful for that support and for the wonderful inspiration that came from the yearly conferences that were part of that fellowship. Special thanks to Michael Gilligan and Stephen Graham for their leadership in the Luce program. Max Stackhouse organized a three-year consultation on mission through the Center of Theological Inquiry that allowed me to develop earlier versions of some ideas involved in this book. Likewise, I would like to thank Terry Muck and Frances Adeney for including me in their project on mission and religious pluralism.

One benefit of the delay in producing this book was the opportunity to read Joseph O'Leary's *Buddhist Nonduality, Paschal Paradox: A Christian Commentary on The Teaching of Vimalakirti*, from which I learned much. My thanks to Catherine Cornille of Boston College for inviting me to take part in a symposium on the book as well as for her own scholarship and friendship, and to Professor O'Leary for sharing an advance copy of the text. I also thank Terrence Tilley for the opportunity to read his unpublished manuscript on Śāntideva, and Frank Clooney for making me aware of it. I am sorry that Perry Schmidt-Leukel's major work, *Buddha Mind—Christ Mind: A Christian Commentary on the Bodhicaryāvatāra*, had not yet appeared at the time I completed this text.

No source could be more relevant to this project. I am grateful to have been able to benefit from his preliminary summary of some of the themes in his commentary.[3]

During the completion of this book, I relocated—along with my entire institution, Andover Newton Theological School—from Massachusetts to affiliate with Yale Divinity School. I regret the resulting delay for the project and the need to part with many in the Boston area who contributed so much to it. But I deeply appreciate the hospitality and support of Dean Gregory Sterling and the Yale Divinity School staff. In particular, I want to thank both Rona Gordon for her editorial assistance and the students who have participated in my seminar titled Christ and the Bodhisattva over recent years for their insights and enthusiasm.

Finally, to Melissa, for her wisdom on the path of this project, my thanks; for her partnership and grace in all, my love.

In Christ,
S. MARK HEIM
Andover Newton Seminary at Yale
New Haven, CT
August 2017

Linguistic note: I have treated "Buddha," "bodhisattva," and "karma" as words that have essentially become part of the English language. I have italicized other technical Buddhist terms and titles. Scholars will note that I have not been consistent on the linguistic source for the transliteration, usually using a Sanskrit-derived version (e.g., *saṃsāra*) but for some terms using a Pāli-derived version (e.g., *anattā*), guided simply by which I believe more familiar to a general reader.

Introduction: The Bodhisattva Path and the Christ Path

This book experiments with a conviction: the conviction that there is a comparative dimension in confessional theology. It illustrates how a Christian theologian studies another religion's sources not for the primary purpose of addressing an interreligious question, but in order to better understand and interpret her own tradition. In this case, that means reflecting on reconciliation and self-giving in Christian theology, particularly in regard to the cross, by reference to Buddhist teaching. The book focuses on specific Buddhist traditions, texts, and practices. It approaches them not as phenomena whose very existence requires an apologetic justification but as wells of constructive wisdom that invite theological insight.

Theologians have grown accustomed to turning to the very best they can find in philosophy, history, and science for use in their work, regardless of whether authors in these disciplines may either assume or accept Christian faith. Attention to these perspectives is not just a requisite for serious intellectual argument; it is often the entry point for any effective discussion of religious faith in wider culture. I believe that sources from various religions will increasingly become key elements in Christian reflection, though privileged access to those sources lies outside the Christian tradition.[1] Primary expertise about these sources rests among those in their own tradition, and theologians will turn to that expertise to guide their understanding.[2] This dependence, whether personal or textual, is an appropriate Christian stance. It reflects not only a warranted humility in the face of profound wisdom and our own limitations but a deep consonance with the Christian hope of salvation as a communion enriched by diverse gifts and diverse participations in the divine life.

Kenneth Cragg responds to Wilfred Cantwell Smith's statement that "Islam is what Muslims say it is" by asking "Why only Muslims?"[3] If the

Qur'an and its message are addressed in principle to an unrestricted audience, then one might respond to it religiously even if not "owning" it in the manner in which Muslims typically do. In a similar way, Jesus is not only who Christians say Jesus is; he is also the one who figures in the living faith of Sufis, Hindus, and many others who encounter him at least in part from Christian sources. I am not arguing that those outside a community get a vote in that community's self-understanding. I am talking about the outflow of religious wisdom to those willing to place themselves at least partially within a tradition's sphere of influence and instruction. Thoughtful exploration of these relations may be viewed as "part of a global religious *resourcement* and re-foundation."[4]

Thinkers within one religious communion typically hone their work through engaging the views of major predecessors in that tradition.[5] Christian faith genuinely seeking understanding widens this circle of dialogue to include figures in other religions as teachers and critics. If God is the subject, other people's religious testimony, arguments, and experiences are relevant data. Wendy Farley notes that without "neo-Platonism and Aristotle there could hardly have been anything we recognize as Christian theology. Without pre-Christian Irish religion, there would be no Saint Brigit or Celtic Christianity. . . . The dialogue with Buddhism might be seen as a contemporary example of Christianity's openness to exchange with other ways of thinking that broadens and deepens its best insights."[6]

I believe that Buddhist wisdom uniquely grasps a dimension of the way things are (as Buddhists would say) and a dimension of God's relation to and presence in the world (as Christians would say). This truth is relevant to theological topics in a way that is up to Buddhist-attentive theologians to discern. It is not related in the sense that it can simply be transcribed into Christian discourse or that one can see beyond the Buddhist and Christian frameworks to something better or more adequate in their place. At least that is not my expectation. Contemplation of a fully Buddhist way of understanding things can have an effect on a holistic way of understanding Christian faith.

Comparative Theology as Christian Theology

This experiment could hardly exist if it were not for the history of Buddhist-Christian dialogue and the more recent history of comparative theology. But it is not quite one or the other. Just as the theologians who take account of history and science are not necessarily by trade professional historians or scientists, so those who take account of multiple religious perspectives need not be professional scholars of other traditions. In fact, the significance of these areas for theology is reflected precisely in the extent to which they move beyond the concern of an esoteric circle. Comparative theology, like biblical studies or social history, need not be every theologian's research vocation. Our role is to be avid and informed consumers.

Contemporary work in comparative theology illustrates the major modes of learning that are operative in it.[7] One is intensification, a deepening of the existing meaning in one text by juxtaposition with another, in which the two magnify each other along similar trajectories. One might for instance explore arguments for the existence of God that are advanced by great Hindu writers as, in large measure, part of a common project, with important variations on the nature of the God subject to the argumentation.[8] An example specific to Christian study of Buddhism would be the common cause that can be made in deconstructing the pernicious projections in a self-centered worldview.[9] A second mode of comparative learning is rediscovery, in which study of another faith throws new light on undervalued strands in one's own. Dialogue with Buddhism has led many Christian thinkers to renewed encounter with their own apophatic traditions and with mystics.[10] A third kind of learning is reinterpretation, where key theological elements are reformulated in light of categories and insights from other religious sources. An example would be John Keenan's pioneering work in reading Christian doctrine through the lens of *Mahāyāna* Buddhist thought in place of Hellenistic philosophy.[11] The fourth mode is adoption or appropriation, the direct borrowing of elements from one religious context for another. Such would be the widespread undertaking of Buddhist forms of mindfulness and other forms of meditation.[12] The fifth form of learning we could call reaffirmation, a clarification by difference, in which elements in one's tradition that have been highlighted by contrast are grasped with renewed conviction. For some Christians, an enhanced appreciation for the significance attributed to social transformation in the biblical tradition flows from engagement with alternative Buddhist perspectives.[13]

Buddhist-Christian dialogue has provided variations on all these types of learning. This means there is a great deal of existing work that bears on my topic. The subjects of Christology and Trinity have been significant themes in Buddhist-Christian dialogue.[14] In that context, the topic of Jesus's crucifixion and death has been explored as well. Sometimes these studies have proceeded through exploration of somewhat parallel terms such as, for instance, *kenosis*, the Christian term used to interpret God's incarnation and particularly the death of Jesus, and the Buddhist term *Śūnyatā* (emptiness), used to describe the inner character of reality.[15] Some Christians seek a rapprochement between the two traditions by identifying the Trinitarian God with emptiness. How far might these describe the same thing, and how would Christian (or Buddhist) thought be altered by recognition of this convergence? At times, Christian scripture is interpreted through Buddhist lenses.[16] At other times, the dialogue is enriched by reformulations of tradition on both sides. Examples would be Paul Knitter's proposal to think of God and emptiness under the categories of process thought, and Thich Nhat Hanh's reconception of emptiness as "interbeing," a definition that itself stretches Buddhist thought toward Christian categories.[17]

My approach is indebted to all of these conversations. However, it is somewhat less flavored by direct interest in Buddhist-Christian relations than by the interest in integrating sources and perspectives from another religion into the normal practice of "faith seeking understanding." My comparative interest is in bodhisattvas and the bodhisattva path on the one hand, and Christ and the Christ-disciple path on the other. One may find many parallels between Christ and Buddha. But Buddhists generally view it as more a virtue than a problem that their teaching offers no framework for some of the key problems that Christ is presumed to resolve—issues of atonement, for instance. A whole complex of questions regarding reconciliation, forgiveness, and transformation is central in Christian faith while absent in that form in Buddhism. The same is true in reverse perspective: a complex of questions regarding selves, compassion, truth, and wisdom is central in Buddhism and missing in Christianity. When juxtaposed with each other, these complexes are a rich field for all the modes of interreligious learning described above.

Buddhist sources have found a place in my practice of Christian theology, particularly in reshaping my vision of the Trinity. The theology of religious pluralism I outline below, and specifically its delineation of a dimension of emptiness in God's relation with the world, would not have taken the shape it has without study and knowledge of Buddhist teaching and traditions. That theology sets the stage for this book by affirming that there are nonpersonal dimensions in God's life and relations (and so of all other life and relations) that require apprenticeship to Buddhist wisdom. It is one thing to suggest the importance of such apprenticeship but another to actually exemplify it. This book seeks to follow my own advice.

My project is unapologetically intellectual in nature. Buddhists and Christians both have much to say about the limits of language and reason. But so long as both remain key elements in the lived reality of these traditions, there is value to such study. "Theology" is a loaded word, but if it stands for reflection on the coherence and practice of Christian faith, then there is no doubt a parallel history of profound reflection on the understanding and practice of the Buddhist *dharma*.[18] The appropriate uses for these intellectual formulations are themselves a topic for debate, as we will have occasion to see. In choosing this focus, I mean no disrespect to those who focus their Buddhist-Christian encounter in the realm of practice, any more than the work of Christian theology disrespects the profound attainments and contributions of Christians who put their energy elsewhere.

Both the religious practitioner and the scholar run the risk of misappropriation, of thoughtlessly bending religious sources to purposes they were never intended to serve or twisting them to fit one's own ideological insistence. That danger is real. But I think the greater danger is the long-standing assumption that the breadth and depth of sources like these are simply irrelevant to Christian theology. We rectify that omission by paying them the serious attention they deserve. The challenge requires a balance between, on one side, dealing with Buddhist sources in their Buddhist integrity while on the other side acknowledging that my task is a Christian one.

Some Historical Background

This interaction with Buddhist sources is not entirely novel. It revisits a conversation, even a mutual influence, that existed much earlier. Christian theological interaction with Buddhism has a history, a recent and well-documented one and a much older and only recently uncovered one. The recent one could be dated from Paul Tillich's 1960 visit to Japan, late in his life, and the subsequent pioneering of Buddhist-Christian dialogue by John Cobb and others in particular connection with the Kyoto School of Buddhism.[19] The ancient one involves the interaction of Christianity and an emerging *Mahāyāna* Buddhism across the span of the Silk Road over the early centuries of the Common Era. It includes the planting of an Assyrian Christian church in China in the seventh century, one that was in clear dialogue with Buddhism and Taoism and that survived down to the time of Marco Polo. Between these periods, most notably from the sixteenth to nineteenth centuries, there were significant encounters and Buddhist responses largely driven by Western missionary movements and colonialism.[20]

The Indian Buddhist emperor Aśoka sent out Buddhist missionaries to other lands in the third century BCE. The Hellenistic kingdoms that Alexander the Great established a century earlier on his march into India provided a conduit for influence to run in both directions. It appears that the anthropomorphic representations of the Buddha that are now common everywhere among Buddhists originated in this Hellenized setting and spread from there. Lines of communication clearly existed between India and the Mediterranean, and Buddhists were present in Alexandria, Egypt, by at least the third century CE. This leaves room for speculation on ways that Buddhism might have affected early Christianity (even Jesus), but it remains speculation.

Buddhism originates around the fifth century BCE, but its *Mahāyāna* branches date roughly from the same time as the development of Christianity. The origins and development of *Mahāyāna* are complex issues. It is not until the fifth century CE that the tradition can be historically grounded, though texts that are key for *Mahāyāna*, like the Lotus Sutra, appear centuries earlier.[21] For our topic, the rise of *Mahāyāna* is of crucial interest, since bodhisattva convictions are at the heart of that tradition. Early Buddhism as represented in the Pāli canon and, arguably, by the *Theravāda* tradition long antedates Christianity and presumably was the substance of the Buddhism that spread down to the time of Christ and beyond. *Mahāyāna* presents a much more complicated picture; it developed in a time frame that was somewhat parallel with Christianity's, so that sources in each of the traditions may have had an effect on developments in the other.

Among the crucial areas for development of *Mahāyāna* were Northwest India (today's Pakistan and Afghanistan) and the Silk Road of central Asia, areas of known interaction among Buddhists, Manichaeans, Zoroastrians, Christians, and, later, Muslims. In 635, a delegation of Christians from the church in what is now Iraq and Iran, arrived in Tang-dynasty China, established a monastery, and began translating scripture and Christian texts into Chinese. Just some five years earlier, the Chinese Buddhist monk Xuanzang had traveled the same route in the opposite direction, headed to central Asia and India on his famous search for Buddhist texts to bring back and translate.[22]

In this book, I will focus on a classic *Mahāyāna* text describing the path to enlightenment, the *Bodhicaryāvatāra*, written by an Indian Buddhist monk named Śāntideva.[23] During the same eighth century, when Śāntideva lived and wrote, a stele was erected near Xian in China bearing a text produced by the Christian community that had arrived a century before. The content of that text reflected the community's growth and deep engagement with Buddhism and Taoism.[24] We cannot say what those so-called Nestorian Christians of China would have made of an encounter with Śāntideva and his way of the bodhisattva, but they had already gone much farther along this path of engagement than we have.

Just as the Qumran and Nag Hammadi discoveries shed new light on Jewish and Christian history, similar finds in central Asia have had a similar, if much less publicized, impact on the histories of several traditions. Three different archaeological finds frame this picture. One was in and near Turfan in central Asia in the years immediately prior to the First World War. It uncovered manuscripts from Manichaean, Buddhist, and Christian writers. Slightly earlier, around 1900, a monk in Dunhuang, China, discovered a sealed cave with a rich collection of scrolls, mainly from Buddhist authors but also from others, including Christians. These texts date from the fifth to the eleventh centuries CE.[25] In the past twenty years, a collection of Buddhist birchbark texts dating from the first century CE to the eighth century CE came to light. These were found in Pakistan and Afghanistan in an area that belonged to an ancient Buddhist kingdom, Gandhara.[26] These include the oldest Buddhist manuscripts of any sort yet discovered and stem from an area that was pivotal in the dissemination of Buddhism to central Asia and China. The three archaeological discovery sites are spread along the Silk Road from Gandhara in the west to Turfan in central Asia to Dunhuang in the east, each site having been a bustling stop on that route. The texts give us a clear glimpse into a context in which religious groups were using other's sources in reflection and interpretation of their own.

One of the texts recovered from the Dunhuang caves appears to be a Chinese translation of an Indo-Greek Christian source that reflects Christian encounter with Buddhism in the Afghanistan region from between the third and fifth centuries CE.[27] It follows the pattern of an earlier, Hellenized Buddhist text, the *Milindapañha*. Thus, we can see that in the seventh century, Christians in China were bringing to bear in their setting texts that had already developed in dialogue with Buddhist ideas farther west and centuries earlier, where those Buddhist ideas had themselves been contextualized to a new setting. Among the other Dunhuang materials are Christian writings composed in China that are reflective of a Chinese church in the Tang dynasty period that was deeply transformed by engagement with Buddhism and Taoism.[28]

The Gandharan Buddhist texts cover the time period and the location in which *Mahāyāna* was developing and spreading, as Christianity was, thereby raising the possibility of mutual influence. For instance, the earliest instance of a bodhisattva (in this case, Avalokiteśvara) descending into hell to assist those there is found in a text originating in northwest India around the second or third century CE. It appears that on this point, the text was influenced by the Gospel of Nicodemus' account of Christ's descent into hell.[29] In the opposite direction, scholars have traced the way in which stories of the Buddha were misapprehended and transmitted as the life of a Christian saint, Josaphat, whose name in fact was taken from the title "bodhisattva."[30] On one distant end of this chain of transmission is the story of the Buddha/saint who became central to Russian novelist Leo Tolstoy's conversion to Christianity.[31] All of this indicates a longer history and more intimate contact between Buddhism and Christianity than might have been thought.

One case of special interest for us is that of Manicheanism.[32] Known primarily today as an early rival to the church, Manicheanism spread widely in the East, going deeper and surviving longer than Christianity did in certain places, not disappearing entirely until around the fourteenth century. Hans Jonas says of its founder, Mani, that it was he alone who made the Gnostic religious system a broad historical force.[33] Previously known almost entirely through the writings of its opponents, Manichaeism was illuminated by the discovery in the twentieth century of original sources both in Egypt and in Central Asia.

One of the things those sources demonstrate is that in addition to direct relations between Buddhists and Christians, Manicheans had profound connections with both and may well have been a bridge between the two. According to Manichean sources, Mani himself traveled to the Indus Valley region, in the heart of the exchange zone that we have described, in 241/242. Mani grew up in a third-century Jewish-Christian sect in the Persian Empire, and he always maintained his Christian roots, referring to himself as, among many other things, an "apostle of Jesus Christ." As Jonas says, Mani seems to have been the first to deliberately fuse Buddhist, Zoroastrian, and Christian elements, making them explicit tributary streams to his own teaching.[34]

Manichaeans in central Asia and farther east could at times adopt a completely Buddhist vocabulary. In one hymn celebrating the "root doctrine of noble Jesus," salvation is a realm of light: "the good *nirvāna*" and "the realm of the Buddhas."[35] The world from which one is saved is "terrifying *samsāra*." The hymn addresses Mani:

> After the four Buddhas [i.e., Seth(?), Jesus, Zoroaster, and Śākyamuni]
> You also descended [to earth]
> And attained complete incomparable Buddhahood
> Many myriads of living beings did you redeem
> You freed them all from dark hells.[36]

The writer has not hesitated to make Mani one in a succession of Buddhas. In ritual invocations, Mani was also referred to as a "bodhisattva."[37] Just as Manichaeans viewed Mani as the comforter promised by Jesus in the Gospel of John, so they could view him as Maitreya, the future Buddha.[38]

Another hymn has the Manichean Jesus dialogue with a boy who represents the soul that seeks salvation. Jesus speaks of three gods sent to save the soul—Zarathustra, Buddha, and Jesus—and of all three in turn sending Mani. The soul says that fortunate souls in India had the door of salvation opened by the Buddha, and Jesus responds:

> Because of the (skillful) means and wisdom that you received from the Buddha, Dibat, the great Virgin, envies you. When he [Buddha] entered into Nirvāna, he commanded you "Await Maitreya here."[39]

So extensive is this assimilation, that one can well imagine some Manichean texts (with their emphasis on Jesus) being mistaken by Buddhists as Christian and others (with their pervasive Buddhist language) being mistaken by Christians as Buddhist. In fact, this mediating function of Manicheanism may have been exactly the mechanism by which the Buddha was transmuted into a Christian saint in the example given above.[40] If we bracket for a moment Manicheanism's legitimate claim to be a major religious tradition in its own right and view it in line with Mani's own insistence that it is a Christian tradition, albeit one deemed heretical by opposed Christian groups for its radical dualism, then we could say that the data recovered from Manicheanism documents the earliest and most extensive Christian engagement with Buddhism.

Manichaeism had a threefold Christology. Most important was "Jesus the Splendor," a divine emanation whose role was to descend into the world and communicate with the true spiritual nature of humans, delivering them from their entanglement with matter. Jesus would also appear as an eschatological judge at the end of the world, when the opposing substances of spirit and matter, good and evil, would be finally separated as they had rightly been at the beginning. Alongside these two there is "Jesus the Messiah," or the historical Jesus. This figure is understood so as to be consistent with the first two images, in a docetic sense. Jesus's suffering and death were not important events to Manichaeans. Unlike many Gnostics, they believed that these events had actually taken place for a human Jesus. But this fleshly person was only a kind of crude metaphor, a shadow of a heavenly being. What was important was the symbolic meaning of that metaphor.

They readily mixed the language of different traditions, referring to Jesus as "the Messiah-Buddha." When Manichaeans referred to "the suffering Jesus," they meant this as an omnibus reference to the sad state of all divine spirit or light that had fallen into the world of matter. They could take a somewhat similar view of the life of the Buddha, seeing his teaching on the nature of suffering as wisdom about the inherent unsatisfactory state of a world in which spirit and matter are unfortunately mingled. "Crucifixion" is a word for what is always and everywhere the case for elements of true divinity so long as they remain in the impure world where the proper dualism between light and darkness has been compromised. Resurrection is similarly understood as the release of the spirit from the physical world, and has nothing to do with the renewal of the body or human beings, historical persons being, like all of creation, artifacts of a definitive "fall" into a material world.[41]

Among the recovered Manichaean materials are liturgical texts, called the *parinirvāṇa* hymns. Apparently, a new such hymn was composed and sung each year on the anniversary of Mani's death and entry into the realm of spirit. The Manichean community had adopted the Buddhist term for the Buddha's death, *parinirvāṇa*, and applied it both to Mani and to Jesus. Other texts were crucifixion hymns, in which Jesus's death on the cross was taken as a sign of the entry into the pure world of *nirvāṇa/* eternal spirit. These liturgical pieces include an account of Jesus's death, apparently based on two Syrian gospel harmonies, the *Diatessaron* of Tatian, used by the Syrian Christian church, and another melding canonical and apocryphal gospels such as the Gospel of Peter, which support a docetic reading of the cross. The term "crucifixion" and the Buddhist term *parinirvāṇa* come to be used interchangeably. Here is the first verse from one of these texts:

> Awake, brethren, you chosen ones, on this day of the salvation of souls, the fourteenth [day] of the month of Mihr, on which Jesus, the Son of God, entered Parinirvāṇa![42]

Whether applied to Jesus or Mani, this term signifies the departure of the divine spark from the material world for its eternal home in the realm of light.

Manichaeans were ready to adopt not only Buddhist vocabulary but also much of Buddhist cosmology. So, for instance, they spoke of three types of judgement. The first two involved a dualistic resolution of substances, with souls destined either to permanent damnation or full eternal spiritual life. The third involved the continuation of an intermediate mixture of spirit and flesh in the world, in which one took rebirth in line with one's prior behavior. In this way, the entire structure of Buddhist hells and heavens, karma and rebirth, could be assimilated. Since the essential constants of Mani's teaching involved only cosmic events and allowed historical matters to be viewed in the nature of parables, he and his followers could make linguistic adjustments to the point that Manichaean texts in different contexts seem almost indistinguishable from a *Mahāyāna* sutra or a Christian gospel. Two bodhisattvas regularly seen on either side of the Buddha in artistic representations common on the Silk Road were Avalokiteśvara and Mahāsthāmaprāpta. Chinese Manichaeans could simply substitute them for two other deities ("Call" and "Answer") in their cosmology. The names were unimportant so long as the grammar of the myth remained the same.[43] Manichaeism seems to have had a precept of "wisdom and skillful means" that positively encouraged this mixing of media for effective communication, similar to the idea of skillful means in *Mahāyāna* tradition.

All this adaptation still preserved a Manichaean kernel in the husks of Buddhist language. The kernel that was maintained was radical dualism, a belief in both eternal natures and substances that seem antithetical to Buddhist wisdom. For instance, Chinese Manichaeans speak freely of humans' "Buddha nature." But what they designate by this term is the divine spark imprisoned in matter, an eternal chip off an eternal substance, quite at odds with Buddhist ideas of impermanence.[44] Manicheans and Buddhists both found the Christian idea of resurrection

objectionable because of the value it placed on the body. This commonality smoothed the way for Manicheans to equate Christ's death with the
Buddha's. The Buddha's death was an entry into *nirvāṇa*, and so it had
lost the qualities that attach to normal death. It was no longer a portal to
rebirth; it no longer required special practices to minimize its karmic li-
abilities. It simply marked a final transition to the state that perfectly
transcends the world of suffering. For Mani, the essential thing was likewise a transition, the departure of the spirit from entanglement in the
world for its true, eternal home. From the Buddhist side, the stark dualism would in principle be rejected. But the Manichaean reading of the
language of Jesus's suffering as emblematic of the struggle and corruption of humanity's universal condition, not in terms of an actual event,
would be intelligible and welcome.

In Manicheanism, we have the first Buddhist-informed, Christian-
derived theology. It incorporated the realities of karma and rebirth,
readily applied Buddhist labels (e.g., "Buddha," "bodhisattva") to its own
savior figures (i.e., Jesus and Mani), adopted *saṃsāra* as a term to apply
to the fallen material world from which spirit must be freed, and identified the return of eternal souls to their eternal source with the Buddhist
nirvāṇa. To the pure nondualism of emptiness, it paralleled the literal
fragmentation and then reunification of an eternal spirit. Beside the
Buddhist distinction of conditioned and unconditioned perspectives,
it advanced a rigid dualism, ontologically dividing sprit and matter.
Measured on an historical scale, this approach was a notable accomplish-
ment. Manicheanism survived another thousand years, often in continued contact with evolving Buddhism. The label of "heresy" need not
block us from considering that achievement on its merits. But the fact
that this approach could not survive as a living presence alongside Buddhism and other religious options cautions that it may not model the
way forward today.

Theology of Religious Pluralism

It is not obvious to all that this Christian study of extra-Christian religious sources is a task that needs doing.[45] I have written extensively about
why I believe it is.[46] I will sketch that vision here, as it summarizes my
rationale for this work at the same time as it indicates the matrix into
which we might incorporate what we learn in the process.

The truth that Christians recognize in other religious traditions can be all the more concrete and extensive when we acknowledge that it may correlate to ends that are not the Christian one.[47] The extent to which, say, Christianity and Buddhism are both teaching, telling, and living the truth is expanded when they need not be telling the truth about exactly the same human state of religious fulfillment. The complexity of the inner divine life finds echoes in different modes of relation with creation. Within the divine, what theology traditionally describes as the relations of the "persons" of the Trinity already includes three dimensions: nonpersonal, personal, and communion. These dimensions are manifest in relation with creation and are engaged by various religions in distinct ways.[48]

I understand God to relate to the world in multiple dimensions, and understand the religions to constitute differentially receptive sensitivity for these dimensions. That diversity is rooted in the way things are, from a Christian view, the relation at every point of the created world with the life of the Trinitarian God. The internal experiential and relational complexity in God underwrites an authentic variety in the relations of God with the world.

The three dimensions of *koinonia* in the Trinitarian life have three human analogies.[49] In regard to the first aspect, we can note the biblical epiphanies in which God manifests in a nonpersonal form, as wind or fire. God and fire, light, or wind are indistinguishably one. The reality that these epiphanies express is a raw energy or dynamic in which the divine suffuses elements of creation. Within the Trinity, this could be likened to the divine life that is shared in an undifferentiated way by all the "persons," what Western Trinitarian theology called the divine "substance." A human analogy to this might be the shared chemistry or physiological process at the root of all human (and other) life, reflected in forms of nonpersonal interchangeability like that which is manifest in blood transfusion or immunization. These are processes of life, but not of particular consciousness. Insofar as consciousness is constituted by the distinction from others or awareness of self, it emerges against the backdrop of these preconscious or nonconscious continuing realities that have no such dualism within themselves. This is a key point to which we will return shortly.

Secondly, within the Trinity, each of the three persons encounters the others in freedom, with its own unique character. The relations are asymmetrical because each person has its own identity and is no rote copy of another. In human beings, we see a likeness to this in the dimension of direct personal encounter in which we exchange ideas, intentions, and emotion. We meet as distinctive others, honoring and enacting our identities in exchange. We do this face to face or through a medium such as writing or art, so that it is possible for us to have a "personal" relation with someone whom we have never met.

The triune God as a whole also encounters humanity in this dimension. The first, nonpersonal dimension makes this personal dimension possible. God's undifferentiated immanence (or apophatic absence) everywhere sets the stage of creation as a theater for a free and historical encounter of humans with God as a single "Thou." This is the God of the biblical and Qur'anic traditions, an agent who speaks and acts with humanity.[50] Faithful response to this encounter builds an authentic personal relation with God and leads to distinct religious fulfillments that are in line with the nature of that relation. A Trinitarian perspective suggests that what is apprehended in these cases of encounter with a divine "Thou" is the external unity of the Trinity, its cooperative unity in willing the good for creation. Christianity characteristically extends its grasp of this dimension in two ways: in the conviction that the icon for this personal God is also a living person, Jesus Christ, and in the understanding of God as Trinity, which finds this single divine "I" grounded in the unity of the divine persons.

The third dimension, that of communion, points to the fact that the divine persons do not only share one seamless life process and encounter each other in uniqueness. They also indwell each other precisely as different persons.[51] If the first dimension senses God's presence as a universal background radiation virtually impossible to detect as a separate signal, and the second dimension reflects God's presence as an historical encounter, then the third realizes God's presence as an active indwelling. We know some shadow of this in our human relations when empathy and intimacy with a person give rise to a vicarious capacity to share his or her inner life. That person's characteristic responses and feelings begin to arise in us also, as a kind of second nature. They do not replace our own reactions but become part of those responses, complementing and in some cases even transforming them.

Relations of deep love or friendship are marked by this dynamic. The typical feature of this communion is the discovery in ourselves of an openness or response to a third person or to others that we can hardly credit as coming from us except by virtue of the indwelling of a second.

But it is manifest above all for us in our incorporation into Christ by faith through the indwelling of the Holy Spirit. In this way, we can share in Christ's love for others. Christian captivation with this communion dimension accounts for most that is distinctive about Christian faith and constitutive of the Christian understanding of salvation. The incarnation is a window into this Trinitarian communion, and the path to participate in it. A fundamental feature of this dimension of relation with God is defined by the fact that we can only have it by sharing it with others. It is innately social. We can have koinonia with God only through koinonia with others, Christ being central among these others. The characteristic sign of our communion with Christ is that we discover a new openness and love toward neighbors and enemies, things hard to explain apart from Christ's dwelling in us. The effect of communion is openness to more communion.

Salvation is constituted by relation with Christ, an instance of communion that opens into a condition in which relation with God is realized in all three of the dimensions we have discussed and in which one shares that realization with others. Salvation is a *complex* state, for in it a person is open to each of the dimensions of the divine life that we have described. That is why it requires sharing with others: no individual can or could realize the complete fullness of possible relation with God in all of these dimensions in a self-contained way.[52] But she or he does approach that fullness through communion with other persons and creatures, each of whom in their relations with God and with others fill out aspects that would be lacking for any one individual. Eschatological fulfillment is marked by the depth and breadth of this communion. We can picture its extent and intensity crossing new thresholds of emergence, just as is true of biological or physical systems.

Each of these three dimensions conditions the understanding of the others. In God's relation with creation, God manifests in a proportionate way the modes of relation present in the divine life itself. They are present in our human lives as part of the image of God that is given in creation and broken by sin. The validity of human responses to each of these dimensions of the complex divine life grounds the worthy claims of alternative traditions and so supports religious pluralism. Christians can understand the distinctive religious truth of other religions as rooted in connections with dimensions of the living, triune God. On the one hand, this provides a rationale for the Christian inclusive hope that such truths might lead people toward salvation, since the ends sought through such relations have an intrinsic ground in the triune God. On the other hand, this perspective also recognizes the reality of alternative religious ends on their own terms, and the validity of religious claims to their ultimacy. Persons may navigate through other traditions toward the salvation Christians seek, but those traditions are ordinarily the primary means of attaining their own unique ends, not salvation. From perspectives defined by such ends, other traditions reasonably interpret the Christian aim as secondary or preliminary.

Rather than posing it as a flat opposition to the distinctive religious claims of all other religions, we should situate belief in the Trinity among them. If Trinity is real, then many of these specific religious claims and ends must be real also. Communion cannot function as an identity of contradiction. As a paradigm of complex relations, Trinity is a blueprint that allows, indeed invites, concrete truth from other religions. The distinctive religious ends of various traditions correspond to relations with God constituted by limitation or intensification within particular facets of the Trinitarian relations with creation. This understanding of Trinity provides the basis both to affirm the reality of these religious ends and to distinguish them from the Christian end, which is salvation.

That perspective is far from suggesting that religious traditions are homogenous, "one-note" projects. Major traditions take clear account of the various dimensions we have described. Their differences stem from the ways in which they coordinate these dimensions.[53] Each tends to take one dimension as fundamental for interpretation of the others. This is no less true of Christians, who grasp the entire set of dimensions through the mode of communion. The peculiarity of this dimension is that it depends upon the continuation of the other two within the divine life and within salvation itself. Communion includes the other dimensions *as other*, in a kind of coinherence.

Buddhism has its own profound account of these dimensions. In most cases, Buddhist teaching views all of them except the nonpersonal dimension (in the form of emptiness) as realities at the level of conventional discourse only, not at the level of ultimate truth. A powerful spiritual and intellectual analysis examines all the alleged subjects and objects of our experience and finds them without any grounding in entities either enduring or distinct. They have their relative places and uses, which Buddhist thought expounds with great care. Emptiness is the characteristic that applies most profoundly across the board, and this makes it absolute in an ironic, self-canceling sense. To put it another way, Buddhism has a defining insight experience that orders the dimensions in a particular way, privileging a nonpersonal dimension that is often described as nonduality (we will say more about nonduality in a moment).

In this connection, it is important to expand on the earlier, brief discussion of what I called a "nonpersonal" dimension in the divine life and in God's relation to the world. From a Christian perspective, there are two sides to this nonpersonal dimension: emptiness and immanence. The three divine persons each "empty themselves" to allow the indwelling of the others, and they each have an immanent presence within the others. These two faces of the nonpersonal dimension are also expressed in God's relation with creation. Indeed, the act of creation reflects both. On the one hand, God "withdraws" or makes space for creatures to have their own character and freedom distinct from God. God ordains a divine absence, a distance between creator and creature that makes freedom and identity possible. And on the other hand, God practices a universal immanence, sustaining every being by the presence of divine power and order.

These relations are not obtrusive but universal and hidden. God practices an active absence and an anonymous identity in creation. In both cases, we can say that God's presence is nondual: there is no perceivable distinction between God and the emptiness or between God and the phenomena as they appear on their own in the natural order. This nonduality is not the complete story, as Christians hold that God is not exhausted in this identity but exceeds it. Both the personal and communion modes of God's relation with the world witness to this excess.

Humans can tune in to this nonpersonal and nondual dimension of God's life and manifestation in either an apophatic or immanent form. In either case, just as human personhood is not discernible at the level of the molecular interactions in our bodies, so God has neither personal or communion attributes when encountered solely in this dimension. God's contraction to make way for creation makes possible human insight into the insubstantiality of all being. If creation is analyzed rigorously on this frequency—through meditation or science—then we find emptiness at its base. Enduring, distinct identities dissolve. Such insight, and rigorous practice based on it, results in a religious fulfillment essentially as described in Buddhist understanding of *nirvāṇa*. Such emptiness clings to nothing, not even an identity, and realizes freedom from suffering, estrangement, and relationship. This religious end is quite distinct from salvation in its firm exclusion of any enduring participation in the other dimensions of relation with God and creatures.

This wisdom is far more developed in Buddhism than in any facet of Christian tradition.[54] Buddhist visions of emptiness provide an accurate, indeed unsurpassed, account of this dimension of God's relation with the world. Christians will incline to read that dimension as a creative absence conditioned by the equal ultimacy of God's personal and communion reality, while Buddhists will incline to read it as the true nature of things, the final deliverance of analytical insight. Even if the Buddhist religious realization and many assumptions grounding it cannot be fully shared by Christians, the data of Buddhist insight are still primary sources for Christian thought. In fact, we most fruitfully apprentice ourselves to Buddhist interpretation of Buddhist sources precisely at those points where they differ from Christian assumptions.

In Buddhist-Christian conversation, nondualism is always a central topic. Nondualism has several levels of application in Buddhist thought and practice. Our discussion of the dimensions of God's relation with creation illustrates that there are several forms of nondualism in Christian life and thought. David Loy identifies three types or applications of nonduality: the negation of dualistic thinking, the nonplurality of the world, and the nondifference of subject and object.[55] The apophatic and immanent forms of the nonpersonal dimensions that we have just discussed arguably meet all three of Loy's measures, while the personal dimension does not meet any. The communion dimension meets the first but not the second and, at best, only partially the third. To put it another way, the nonpersonal dimension, in both emptiness and immanence modes, is a type of identity nondualism, while the communion dimension is an achieved type of nondualism, a mutual indwelling.

In Buddhism, nondualism appears most often as a consistent metaphysical truth, while in Christianity it is typically a special class of relation. The nondualism/identity relation is a primordial, unchanging not-twoness. It is similar to the Buddhist nondualism in that its nature can be misperceived or forgotten but it cannot be altered. We will have occasion to think particularly about the Christian apophatic nonpersonalism in connection with Buddhist emptiness, as well as the Christian immanent nonpersonalism in connection with Buddha nature. We will consider the communion dimension, which deals in a unity-in-difference rather than an identity oneness, primarily in connection to the bodhisattva's melding of *saṃsāra* and *nirvāṇa*.

Loy identifies two further nondualities: the identity of phenomena with the absolute (characteristic of *Mahāyāna* Buddhism) and a mystical unity between God and humanity (characteristic of Christianity).[56] He views these nondualities as additional types. But I would rather say that each represents the perspective of one of these two religious traditions, cross-cutting and specifying the first three nondualities he describes. So what he calls mystical unity of God and humanity, I call a special case of communion. What he calls identity of phenomena with the absolute I see as the *Mahāyāna* vision of the coincidence of *saṃsāra* with *nirvāṇa*. In this sense, Loy's categories track closely with my own, and they illustrate the similarities and tensions that characterize nonduality as a meeting place for *Mahāyāna* Buddhism and Christianity. Though the word conjures up an erasure of all distinctions, "nondualism" not only stands out from views that commend differences, but also stands in as an umbrella term covering a range of possible interpretations. In Joseph O'Leary's words, in Buddhist-Christian contexts, we are invited to let the theme of nonduality "lay claim on our minds in such a way that we are both haunted by its elusive resonances with what some in the Christian tradition have glimpsed and at the same time challenged by its constant friction with inherited Christian ways of thinking."[57]

At the level of diagnosis (i.e., no-self) and at the level of fulfilment (i.e., Buddha nature), nonduality is central to the Buddhist outlook. Christian scholars have labored diligently to reclaim currents of nonduality in the Christian theological tradition.[58] Prescriptions for Christian learning from Buddhism understandably lean heavily on reappropriation of those sources to bring deeper resonance between the two traditions.[59] I have benefitted greatly from these studies. While I will not recapitulate them in this text, I will note when I draw upon them explicitly in my own constructive efforts.[60]

I have given a brief summary of the perspective on Buddhism expressed in my theology of religious pluralism. I state it here not as the necessary condition for the discussion that follows, but as acknowledgement of the framework that guides it. Without Buddhist wisdom, there are dimensions of God's relation with the world and with us (to put it in Buddhist terms, dimensions of the true nature of things) that cannot be fully grasped by Christianity alone. These are not simply transient or instrumental truths, but truths that remain relevant for understanding what Christians regard as the ultimate reality and the final state of humans. Mine is a minority view among Christians. The majority view likely is that Buddhist insight is a preliminary view that must be superseded in full by a Christian one, if it is not simply error. I believe that the majority Buddhist view would be that Christianity, or theistic devotional faith like it, may be a more or less permanent option in ages when the *dharma* does not flourish.[61] It can be beneficial for those at preliminary stages of practice or knowledge on the way to true enlightenment, but a snare for those who might remain within it indefinitely.[62] Christians may differ over how much value to grant Buddhist tradition as a preparatory path toward Christ, just as Buddhists may differ over whether to stress the distance separating Christian notions and true wisdom or, like the Dalai Lama, to stress the skillful means by which this path can foster spiritual growth.

My primary concern is not to change these global judgements but to demonstrate the scope for mutual learning and appreciation that is possible within them. The rest of this book is an implicit test to see whether the paradigm I have suggested above stands up to more detailed interaction with Buddhist wisdom. It is an experiment to see whether that interaction can yield learnings that will enhance the trajectory of Christian theology.

Plan of This Book

This book has three parts, which follow this Introduction. In Part I, Chapter 1, I summarize the substance of the bodhisattva path as a theme and teaching in *Mahāyāna* Buddhism, and similarly summarize the Christian themes of incarnation, atonement and reconciliation. I highlight the ways in which the bodhisattva path and the Christ/disciple path each embody and resolve tensions constituted by their distinctive understandings of our condition. And I give a preliminary assessment of some of the contrasts and similarities between the paths, of their respective problems and solutions.

In Part II, Chapters 2 and 3, I first trace some of the historical background in the development of the bodhisattva path and then turn to a reading of Śāntideva's *Bodhicaryāvatāra* for a concrete exposition of that path. In interpreting Śāntideva, I have leaned heavily on Buddhist commentaries and particularly on commentaries from Tibetan traditions. I do not suppose that this is a definitive Buddhist perspective any more than the version of Christian theology that I engage here is a definitive one. But this seems the best approach to assure that I treat a more consistent and specific form of the teaching. In Part III, Chapters 4, 5, and 6,

I reflect on topics in Christian theology in light of key aspects of the bodhisattva paradigm as we have seen it. Chapter 4 deals with the bodhisattva from an "ascending" or aspirant perspective, the path that one follows from our ordinary human condition. The theological learning focuses primarily on the understanding of the created self in light of the teachings of impermanence and emptiness. Chapter 5 deals with the bodhisattva from a "descending" or attainment perspective, with the bodhisattva as Buddha. The Christian topics most dramatically engaged here are Trinity and creation. Chapter 6 deals with the bodhisattva in a soteriological mode, with the bodhisattva as helper. The Christian topic that is our focus here is the work of Christ and the life of the disciple. In Chapter 7, I briefly review all of these elements and sketch the conclusions of the study.

PART I

Two Paths

1 Two Problems, Two Miracles

For as long as space endures and for as long as the world lasts,
May I live dispelling the miseries of the world.
Whatever suffering there is for the world, may it all ripen upon me.
May the world find happiness through all the virtues of the
Bodhisattvas.

—ŚĀNTIDEVA, *A Guide to the Bodhisattva's*
Way of Life 10:55–56

What to Study?

Productive interreligious learning of the type we have described in the
Introduction must attend to specific Buddhist teachings and reflect on
specific Christian teachings. But which ones? The scope of any single religious tradition is vast, and the number of possible connections between
two traditions even larger. A natural tendency draws us to compare subjects that seem most similar. One might, for instance, explore Buddhist
and Christian understandings of scripture, beginning with a recognition that the category figures centrally if not identically in the two traditions. But there are important topics for which correlatives are anything
but obvious.

The cross is one of those resistant knots of otherness between religions.
There is no cognate for it in most traditions. One could look to elements
of purely formal similarity, which in the Buddhist-Christian context
might mean investigating accounts of the Buddha's death. One learns a
good deal in considering the ways in which Buddhist tradition represented the last days of the Buddha and the ways in which Christian tradition represented the last days of Jesus. But in formally comparing the

same thing, we would really be comparing very disparate things, different in their respective locations and importance in the two traditions. Plainly these events have nothing like the same role in their settings. We could pick something thematic about Jesus's death, such as its characterization as sacrifice, and then look for parallels in the *Jataka* tales of the prior lives of the Buddha, in which he sometimes gave up his life for the benefit of others. Here is self-sacrifice to the point of death that strongly parallels the cross. But we are talking of a handful of cases amid hundreds of tales. Even with this explicit correspondence, we are not engaging at the same level in the two faiths.

I am interested in studying elements that have a similar functional or structural place in the two traditions, however disparate they may be in formal terms. The cross stands at the center of a distinctively Christian complex of issues around evil and guilt, mortality and nature, estrangement from and reconciliation with God. Its best interreligious illumination might come from a similarly situated central complex at the heart of another tradition, even if the elements do not line up one to one. If we were to think of a parallel in Buddhist tradition to Christian themes of incarnation and salvation, to something that is unique, at least in this eon, and that is of ultimate transformative value, then we might look to the Buddha's own enlightenment and his initiation of teaching, the first turning of the wheel of *dharma*.

Christians believe that the incarnation has an intrinsic cosmic character, but at the same time its burning importance has to do with the way in which it is saving for us. Buddhists see the importance of the Buddha's achievement of enlightenment in the sharing of that insight and achievement as accessible to others. So we can regard the Buddha's awakening and turning the wheel of the *dharma* as structurally though not necessarily substantively similar to the incarnation and redemptive activity of Christ, and focus our reflection accordingly. The features picked out for comparison would then be something like what Raimon Panikkar refers to as "homeomorphic" elements in different traditions.[1] But whereas Panikkar seems to be thinking of individual homeomorphic elements, I am thinking of homeomorphic complexes.

Kathryn Tanner discusses Pierre Bourdieu's attempts to avoid reductionism when comparing subjects in different semantic fields, say those of religion and economics. Each element in religion cannot be neatly mapped onto an element in a market economy, and each relation between religious elements does not mirror a relation between cognate economic factors. Such simple translation distorts rather than clarifies. Bourdieu avoids reductionism primarily "by allowing each field to define its own distinctive interests and ends."[2] Eternal life and capital accumulation are not the same thing. Not only are the practices leading to one different from those leading to the other, but the interrelations within one set of practices may not match the pattern of interrelations within the other. Tanner pushes beyond Bourdieu at this point, arguing that all fields need not have the same functional principles. Bourdieu assumes that all fields will be marked by competition for goods; it is simply that the goods are defined differently and the supporting practices need not be organized in the same pattern. Tanner suggests that difference between fields can extend to difference in their very operative processes. In the case of the fields of economics and theology, this is manifest in the difference between a noncompetitive process for the distribution of goods and a competitive distribution process.[3] This same argument applies, I believe, to comparison of religious traditions. Not only do goods and relations differ, but so do the functional modes of transformation.

I am interested in sites where tensions or internal stresses are at play. Such tensions are key to the nature of religion. Stresses intrinsic to human life instigate religious responses, responses to the tension in nature between continuity and disruption, the experiential tension between joy and suffering in human life, the unresolved intellectual tension in the terms by which we understand the world, the ongoing social tension in the interactions among people, the existential tension in our suspension between life and death. Religious forms of transformation and realization hold out the promise of resolution to these tensions.

Religious outlooks not only respond to these existing stresses. They distinctively *constitute* their own tensions. They subsume those presenting conflicts in human life within a novel overarching description and diagnosis, pointing to a prescribed remedy. To see the world as a theater of relation between humans and God is to redefine the world and set up an additional set of tensions that would not exist apart from these assumptions. The same is true if we see the world as a cycle of birth and rebirth fed by ignorance and craving. Between my attachment to the reality of my own self and its happiness, on the one hand, and the suffering that inevitably attaches to desires based upon that attachment, on the other, an apparently irresolvable tension exists. I want the first and not the second, yet liberation from suffering is not possible as long as that attachment remains.[4] So Buddhism might define its tension. There is a solution—enlightenment and the path toward it—in which this tension is overcome. Similarly, between my desire to put the value of my own existence first, to make the world as I want it, on the one hand, and the reality that I am made by God to find joy in communion with others on the other, a profound tension exists. As long as I hold to the first, I cannot realize the second. So Christianity might define its tension. There is a solution—transformation of my desire and reconciliation with God and neighbor, achieved on the way of Christ—in which the tension is overcome.

In addition to the empirical tensions of life that compose the soil of religion and the constituted tensions in whose terms religions frame their diagnoses, there is yet another tension embodied in the paradigm events of redemption or liberation. Religious communities actually *heighten* the terms in which they express their particular tension in the mode of analysis, even as they revere the maximal value of the events or practices that overcome it. We may say that the Buddha attained an unconditioned liberation from the suffering of birth and rebirth and taught the way for others to do the same, so bridging the two realms. But the teachings of the Buddha in which we might take refuge all lie on this side of enlightenment, and enlightenment itself is a realm where none of the terms of the teaching applies. There is something paradoxical, miraculous, about the turning of the wheel of *dharma* itself, a worldly vehicle of transmundane truth. It resolves the tension but contains it. So also is Christ the one in whose person and actions the tension between God and humanity is resolved, the solution. But Christ's person and actions are for that very reason themselves a paradoxical unity of divine and human, miraculous, a distilled tension. In both cases, we might say the founding events address the problem precisely because they embody it.

This tension is replicated one more time within the pursuit of the path these traditions lay out, in the realization of the hopes that they mediate. The tensions exist in the devotees or disciples themselves, as the point of departure, the existential reality of the problems. The tensions recur as part of the solution, in a replication of the paradox found in the founders. The divine-human tension of Jesus's nature is reflected in the tension of the interplay between God's action and individual response in the life of the believer. The contrast between the Buddha's ineffable enlightenment and the conventional terms in which it must be conveyed is reflected in the tension between the truth of emptiness and the centrality of the self as the instrument of practice. The intellectual treatment of these questions is never simply an analysis of something that happened in the past. In a living religious tradition, that analysis is always also a running commentary on the lives of disciples and followers as they seek to participate in the realizations.

In looking at things from this perspective, we focus more on the drama or the complex patterns in each tradition rather than on the one-to-one correspondence of particular elements such as Christ-Buddha or God-emptiness. We consider a complex of elements in motion. There are methodological benefits to this focus. Comparing complexes in this way requires us to retain a good deal of nuance in describing the traditions. It is hard to essentialize when one focuses on those moments when faith expresses its most powerful attainments in terms that are also deeply paradoxical. And it is hard to draw overly simple equivalences between religions when one attends not only to the specific ideas but also to the multiple articulations of these elements in reflection and practice. Attending to the complex articulations within the bodhisattva path, for instance, keeps us in touch with the differences at play within that tradition as well as in contrast with other traditions.

When interpreting texts or ideas within two religious contexts, we can always find options that will bring them most fully into agreement or conformity. If done consistently, this can only collapse the tension within each tradition so as to minimize the tension between them. To do so seems pointless, since presumably these tensions have to do with the transforming dynamism present in each side. And such a strategy has rapidly diminishing returns when attempted in parallel conversations with more than one tradition.[5]

In reading a close study of a group of prominent "dual belongers," those who have gone far in simultaneous participation in Buddhist and Christian practice, I was particularly struck by one observation from the author. Rose Drew notes that her subjects agreed that it was essential to each of them that the distinctions between the traditions be maintained.[6] Even though in their own lives they sought a deeply personal harmony of the two, they felt a tension between a too-full or settled integration and a constant, resistant divergence. Only when those differences were maintained, like the opposite ends of a battery, could they conserve the power that provided the rationale for the dual participation in the first place. Drew observes, "It is precisely *in virtue* of the distinctiveness of each that they belong to both."[7] I believe that this holds true for theological learning as well.

Accordingly, my experiment sought a topic in Christian theology that presents contrast as well as similarity. The atonement—the reconciling work of the incarnation, and particularly of Christ's passion—is a peculiarly Christian matter.[8] By that I mean that it is a topic that arises at the intersection of a set of questions constituted by Christian assumptions about God, incarnation, sin, and resurrection, for instance. In my past work on Christian theologies of atonement, it struck me that the cross is an intersection point, a locus where various basic assumptions about God and human nature come into play and, often, into tension with each other.[9] This complex is not replicated in other religions. It has the appearance of an intensely intra-Christian question. Christ's death and resurrection mark a common point of confession across widely disparate Christian groups, a point which is the subject of a rich variety of theological interpretations. This crucial intra-Christian topic is the subject of intense debate today.[10] To seek light from Buddhist sources is thus no mere academic exercise, but one that fits easily into an existing conversation. For these reasons, I have chosen to think about reconciliation and the cross in association with Buddhist teaching about the bodhisattva path.

As I studied texts related to the way of the bodhisattva, I saw that the bodhisattva also sits at the intersection of basic assumptions in Buddhist teaching and practice, likewise expressing and resolving certain tensions in the working out of those assumptions. "Theories" of atonement and "theories" of awakening mind are not only intellectual issues but are also closely tied to devotional and spiritual practice. The bodhisattva tradition is not simply one element in Buddhism. As the kind of complex we have described, it is one way of talking about the whole teaching, just as passion and resurrection are not just elements in Christianity but can be a short representation of the entire gospel message.

In one sense, this comparison is intuitive. Contemporary Buddhists who reach for a positive category in which to interpret Jesus often see him as a bodhisattva.[11] When Christians encounter famous bodhisattvas such as Avalokiteśvara, characterized by their selfless concern to relieve the suffering of others, it is hard for them not to see something like the self-sacrifice of Jesus. At its extremes, this parallel would simply understand Christ as a bodhisattva, or bodhisattvas simply as images and prefigurations of Christ. Such views have their place within each of the traditions, but in the end they collapse too much real difference.

Christ is a historical and salvific singular event, constitutive of salvation and the believer's practice but not fully replicable by the believer.

Bodhisattvas are plural, and their path lies open to others to duplicate in its entirety. These differences go with the territory of belonging to different religious complexes to begin with. My interest is in comparing the dynamic that is embodied in Christian views of Christ's self-giving and the dynamic that is embodied in Buddhist views of the bodhisattva's benevolence. They do not address the same problem, but they address the same kind of problem. Each preserves and resolves tensions within a wider system, not just an abstract system of thought, but a structure of devotion and practice. O'Leary states this succinctly: "If many of the paradoxes of Christianity center on Jesus Christ, who is both true [human] and true God, those of Buddhism often center on the bodhisattvas, in whom *samsaric* and *nirvanic* existence are conjoined."[12]

As intersection points, the cross and the bodhisattva way have a similar focus: an orientation "for others." Christ died for all. The bodhisattva vows to attain enlightenment for the sake of all sentient beings. In both cases, these statements are foundational, rooted in the New Testament texts on the one hand and in *Mahāyāna* sutras on the other. Yet on their face they also manifest tensions in that foundation. How can God be human and die? And how can that death be "for us"? How can enlightenment be for the sake of anything mundane or conventional? And in what sense are there "others" for whose sake to seek enlightenment? In each tradition, such questions lie at the heart of practice and reflection. As a Christian theologian, I find that much is learned from exploring these paths together.

Bridging Gaps

Care for others is the most evident similarity between the path of Christ/ disciples and the path of Buddha/bodhisattvas. In both cases, it is a matter not of normal altruism or concern simply amplified in degree but of a radical recasting of the basis for this care. Care for others may be normal for humans within a certain circle of kin and community. But extension of that circle to the point of a universal benevolence is not natural at all. Each tradition therefore traces a profoundly counterintuitive foundation for the compassion or love it commends.

It is not obvious that there is a transcendent God behind or alongside all the reality we know nor that there is a deathless, spacious, Buddha nature underneath that reality. Nor is it plain either that God took on human nature at the turn of our Common Era and remains a living presence through relation with that person, or that all human conscious-ness is systematic illusion with the exception of that achieved by an as-cetic from the fifth century BCE and which was evoked in his teaching and replicated in the experience of some later followers. The world-views of the two traditions—the creation/history/eschatology complex of Christianity and the spacious cosmic cycle of eons and realms in Buddhism—differ from each other and from many of our normal per-ceptions. The same can be said of the expectation that humans live trans-formed lives in community after death or that person-shaped successions of events continue in a stream of rebirths until they reach a nondual realization.

The pictures of the world painted in these two traditions conflict with each other at many points, though they agree in important respects in their diagnosis of the human situation and their practical prescriptions to address it.[13] My concern at the moment is only to point out that to ground the kind of care for others that we are talking about here, each tradition voyages far from our prosaic field of view. The extraordinary attainments in each case relate to a problem already reconceived in a dra-matic way. The solution to the presenting concern (e.g., suffering, mean-inglessness, guilt, or estrangement) comes only through the resolution of another, initially far-from-obvious dilemma, in which that concern is understood to be embedded. Faith practices arise because we find our-selves in human dilemmas that have no resolution within our common perspective. For such dilemmas, religions offer first of all a different perspective.

Joseph O'Leary proposes that "nonduality always begins from an ap-parent impossibility, and the overcoming of it can be a paschal break-through."[14] Nondualisms are different, odd as that sounds, depending on the apparent impossibilities they overcome. We sketched this in the Introduction and now can say more now about these distinctive impos-sibilities and their respective breakthroughs.

The initial, counterintuitive move of Christian wisdom or practice is the extension of the personal beyond its apparent relevant application in order to interpret things like the origin of the universe, the meaning of the natural order, the existence of evil, and the nature of human history in terms not of mindless causation but of persons and intentions. The ma-terial and efficient causality operative in everything is somehow bound up in a relational story. The key insight is the presence of what is appar-ently absent: an ultimate relational reality.

The initial counterintuitive move of Buddhist wisdom or practice is the extension of nonpersonal causal analysis beyond its obvious relevant application, to interpret things like self-consciousness, relations, and morality in terms not of persons but of conditioned effects. The agents and identities apparently at the root of our experience of the world are in fact products of factors in which those subjective entities have no ground.[15] The key insight is the absence of what is apparently present: an emptiness that liberates.

These first paradoxes are the basis for subsequent, derivative counterintuitive steps in each case. The Christian hyperextension of personal qualities yields conundrums formulated precisely in those personal terms, questions of theodicy, justification, freedom. Christ and Christ-disciples accomplish something that is at least partly counterintuitive to ground-level Christian teaching. They bring the holiness and eternity of God into intimate communion with the corruption and contingency of creatures. The Buddhist hyperextension of conditioned suchness yields conundrums formulated in precisely those causal terms, which pose questions of what constitutes the subject of transmigration or how the wisdom of emptiness may be married to compassion for beings. Bodhisattvas, aspirant and realized, accomplish something that is at least partly counterintuitive to ground-level Buddhist teaching. They connect the unconditioned with the conditioned and wisdom with compassion.

It is at these points of paradoxical resolution within each tradition that forms of nondualism come most strongly into play. The mystical union or indwelling of human and divine is the solution to first-order conundrums. That solution is, in turn, the basis for the amazing qualities of the incarnate Christ and of those who belong to the same communion body with Christ. It is because reality is this way that God can heal human sin and infirmity, and humans can share divine life and power in community. Such Christian nondualism is an overflowing of persons, a blurring of the boundaries between them and between God and creation. The very attachment to these distinctions depends closely on the ability to soften and suspend them in crucial respects.

The identification of *nirvāṇa* and *saṃsāra* is the solution to first-order conundrums and so, in turn, the basis for the amazing qualities of bodhisattvas. It is because reality is this way that the bodhisattva can paradoxically care for the suffering of beings that do not exist. This Buddhist nondualism is an emptying of misperceived solidities. It comes to realization through insight into the coincidence of emptiness with dependent

co-arising, the mode by which appearances are built up without foundational entities. It is the identity of emptiness and dependent co-arising
that forms the foundation of the miraculous character of the bodhisattva. The understanding and practice of this identity seem to depend
closely on the continuing distinction between conventional and ultimate
truth.[16] O'Leary notes that neither Buddhist nor Christian teaching is primarily a cognitive matter. In each case, the question is resolved not with
a philosophical conclusion but with a deeper vision (Buddhism) or a concrete event (Christianity) in which dualism need not arise.[17] If defined
by the gaps they are filling, these nondualities are not the same.

Let us consider a simple, transient moment of spiritual awe, as experienced by a person under a night sky on the ocean.[18] This phenomenal
experience has different aspects. On the one hand, it expresses heightened difference: I am so small, the universe is so vast. On the other hand,
the experience is shot through with blurred boundaries, a literally "oceanic" sense of silenced egoism or unity with the entire universe.

Neither Christian nor Buddhist will leave that moment of experience
undisturbed as a sufficient instantiation of enlightenment or salvation.
It stands in need of interrogation, teaching, or deconstruction. Buddhists
tend to regard the strong sense of contrast in the first aspect under the
heading of conventional appearance and the second unitive dimension
as something more like a glimpse into reality. Christians tend to regard
the first aspect as insight into the character of creatures and the second
as a taste of a possible communion with God. Of course, in the experience itself, conscious distinction between the two dimensions may be
missing, the absence being what gives this experience its peculiar character and power. My point is simply that the experiencer comes from and
returns to a certain field of interpretation for the phenomenon. There
seems to be some way of apprehending whether it was a true ultimate or
some experiential facsimile or precursor. Even where all discursive
thought is to evaporate in a crowning silence that ends debate, it remains
the case, in O'Leary's words, that "it was that debate that enabled us to
hear the silence."[19]

Nonduality for Buddhism is a teaching, actively advanced and applied,
to lead one to the right kind of silence. It is also a perspective on teaching,
with a kind of self-canceling effect, to avoid intruding on or substituting
for that true silence once it is achieved. It is, in sum, a skillful exercise.
O'Leary shows that Christian attention to Buddhist teaching invites

the development or recognition of comparable exercises on specifically Christian themes such as the nonduality of love of God and love of neighbor.[20]

This chapter sketches the way in which the bodhisattva path and the Christ path constitute two miracles in relation to two distinct visions of the dilemma of human existence. Their extraordinary individual textures come from the way in which they address tensions that have been revealed or constituted by these religious approaches themselves. Grappling with these internal tensions is part and parcel of life within these paths.

The way in which the founding events themselves are described—the Buddha's attainment of enlightenment and God's indwelling in Jesus— already express distinct approaches to our situation. In the Buddha's case, the issue is an ignorance about the true nature of things that results in constant captivity to suffering through cycles of birth and rebirth. In Jesus's case it is a relational brokenness in the connections between humans and nature, humans and each other, and humans and God that manifest in physical, moral, and spiritual suffering. In both cases, these prototypical events have an integral meaning. They address the core problem for all people. The Buddha's realization may have been his alone to begin with, but the decision to turn the wheel of *dharma* and teach the path to others made it a universal event. The presence of God in Jesus may have been located in one person, but it happened to the humanity shared by all and took place in a social community that is part of the whole of history.

Each of these events bridges a gap. For the Buddha, that gap lies between the state of enlightenment and the world of deluded perception and causal continuity from which it is the release. The enlightenment event itself has a paradoxical character. Under the conditions of ignorance, it is extraordinary that the Buddha is able to realize the true nature of things. It even seems contradictory that an impermanent mind, dependently co-arisen, could know the permanent and ultimate nature of things, as it would be paradoxical for a character in a novel to know he is a character in a novel. In any event, the sharp divide between awakening and the ignorant state it dispels could mean that each is left to its own side of a chasm. But the teaching of a way from one to the other sets up a bridge, the teaching, which cannot be made wholly of the materials from either side of the gap that it spans. The first (i.e., enlightenment) is the basis for the second (i.e., teaching), but their relation is problematic in a way that is recognized from the beginning, because of the incommen-surability between the unconditioned realization itself and the conven-tional language pointing toward it.

Likewise, in the Christian origin, the event of the incarnation is on its face a paradoxical union of the divine and the human, the infinite and the finite. There is an intrinsic distinction between the creator and the created. That gap becomes a starker divide when the relations between the two and among the creatures are broken or corrupted by sin, evil, and death. The challenge for transformation bears on this distinction (and, in sin, near opposition) between the two and the need for them to be reconciled, the relations healed on both ends, so to speak. The event of incarnation is not the same thing as the redemption that it produces. The first is unique to Jesus and is the basis for the second, which occurs for those with their own distinctive personhood. The gap between the divine and human is paralleled by the gap between savior and disciple, the question being not so much how teaching can be communicated as how the reality of divine-human communion can be shared.

All that we have reviewed so far—the gaps bridged in the original events, the tensions distinctively resolved in the bodhisattva path or Christ path—is reflected again in the concrete struggle of living practice within each tradition. The follower of the Buddha or the follower of Je-sus asks, How do I participate in these events and their benefits? For the Buddhist, one can replicate the realization of the Buddha by following the path of instruction that he left. For the Christian, participation in re-lation with Christ and his body is the basis for other relations to be transformed and reconciled in communion. Theories of awakening mind or theories of redemption are not only intellectual issues but also closely tied to devotional and spiritual practice.

The Miracle of the Bodhisattva

The Buddha's enlightenment stands at the root of Buddhist teachings and practice. Enlightenment is itself an unconditioned state, based on noth-ing else, in which the causes and the experience of suffering have been extinguished. The Buddha found the path to this reality, which required seeing through the vast web of illusion that constitutes our normal un-derstanding of the world. He followed that path to its realization and left the knowledge that allowed others to do so, as well. The core elements of that knowledge are shared across Buddhist traditions, expounded in the

Pāli canon of Buddhist texts, and are familiar even to many non-Buddhists under the headings of the four noble truths and the eightfold path. The Buddha comprehended the nature of suffering, the causes of the arising of suffering, the reality of a solution for suffering, and the way to attain liberation from it.

Theravāda Buddhism, the "way of the elders," understands itself to hold to the purity of this root tradition.[21] *Mahāyāna* Buddhism in no way rejects that shared core. But it diverges in lifting up many additional texts as sources of the Buddha's highest teaching, the "perfection of wisdom." It organizes existing Buddhist teaching into a hierarchy of "many vehicles," all of which can be regarded as valid through the perspective of two truths, conventional and ultimate.[22] In its traditions, the term "bodhisattva," which had been a rather simple descriptive term referring to the Buddha in his pre-enlightenment lives, took on a whole new importance.[23] Substantively, *Mahāyāna* came to represent a different aspiration for the practitioner, a new understanding of *nirvāṇa*, and an alternative vision of what it means to be a Buddha. Instead of designating a preparatory stage on the way to Buddhahood, the term "bodhisattva" came to name the outer reaches of attainment described under that title.

In principle, the unconditioned state of enlightenment might seem to be a binary reality. It is either attained or not, and is foreign to increments or degree. But there was some recognized variety among Buddhists in regard to *how* this end is achieved, and in *Mahāyāna* such differences over the path to enlightenment shaded off into a true difference in the *kind* of enlightenment. The title *arhat* ("perfected one") had been a common term to designate those who attained liberation by following the path taught by the Buddha. The historical Buddha achieved awakening, compassionately taught others the way to achieve it, and then entered final *nirvāṇa*. A devotee practices the path that is taught and seeks *nirvāṇa* himself. Typically, we take conventions founded in ignorance (e.g., belief in existent selves and objects) as the way that things actually are, and this misperception leads to suffering. With Buddhist practice, enlightened minds perceive the true ontological character of phenomena as empty and illusory, making possible release from *saṃsāra*, the cycle of birth and rebirth.[24] This release is an ineffable *nirvāṇa*, the end of rebirth, and the end of all entanglement with the conventional products of mind that produce suffering. All this follows the karmic integrity of causes, with results driven entirely by one's own practice: the *arhat's nirvāṇa* is the *arhat's* alone. The *arhat's* practice depends upon the three jewels: the Buddha's own attainment, the *dharma* that the Buddha discovered/taught, and the *saṅgha*, which is the community the Buddha founded. On this last score, it is traditionally assumed that one must be reborn a monk in the final stages of this process.

Mahāyāna regards this kind of attainment as real but insufficient. It distinguishes at least two other types of enlightenment beings: *pratyekabuddhas* and bodhisattvas. *Pratyekabuddhas* are more advanced than *arhats* in several respects. According to some sources, they are capable of attaining awakening even in ages when there is no Buddha, discovering the way afresh for themselves, as Gautama Buddha did.[25] They are thought to achieve a deeper insight into the true nature of things. Although *arhats* have realized the emptiness of the self, which is sufficient for liberation from suffering, they have not realized fully the emptiness of all phenomena. *Pratyekabuddhas* have progressed further on this score, though not to the point of totality. The difference is sometimes expressed in terms of the time reckoned to be required to fulfill this process. It could be expected that *arhat*-hood would take thousands of years and associated births, while a different magnitude of measure, *kalpas*, would be necessary to figure the time for attaining *pratyekabuddha* status.[26] Bodhisattvas represented the fullest extent of liberation and knowledge, the most extraordinary attainment. Accordingly, the bodhisattva path was said to stretch over an inconceivable time.[27]

Before saying more about the dimensions of the bodhisattva attainment, let us take a moment to appreciate the qualities of even, so to speak, garden-variety enlightenment. The state of *nirvāṇa* is totally contrary to that of *saṃsāric* suffering and ignorance. It is an end of all that and an entry into another condition. One cannot really speak of one state in terms of the other. Everything that makes the world as we know it is un-known in awakening from our projections, which means that *nirvāṇa* must be something other than this world.

The specific mechanism of therapeutic analysis is to search things, phenomena, and self for actual existents, for something that remains identical over time, continues apart from our attention, and is not a dependent function of something else. The contention is that the result of this sophisticated analysis is universally the same: no such existents are found. This includes the self-existent "I," which our normal consciousness takes to be the bedrock of life in the world. Such is the *anattā*, or "no-self," teaching.

The miraculous nature of awakening is evident in the tensions it overcomes. We have already noted that Buddhism does not take the teaching of the *dharma* for granted, precisely because of the gap it must bridge. The Buddha's enlightenment under the bodhi tree and the subsequent preaching of his first sermon are two distinct events that were separated by a time of great hesitation on the Buddha's part and fervent entreaties from various gods and humans. We will later consider this hesitation in terms of the importance and specific meaning of compassion for Buddhahood.[28] But for now we can relate the hesitation simply to the physics of the situation, as it were—to the intrinsic difficulty in translating the Buddha's realization effectively to others. How can conditioned terms, themselves the product of illusion, be the means of enlightenment? And even more particularly, how can a practice that can only be carried out by an individual mind unravel the very mind it practices with? Is not any teaching simply destined to evaporate into the world of mental objects, to be assimilated to the meanings it intends to deconstruct? Something like this seems to be behind the widespread traditional assumption that Buddhist teaching degenerates over time. There is a kind of entropy by which any given age becomes increasingly less favorable to practice, and cosmic ages decay to the point even of ignorance of the Buddha's basic truths.[29]

The Buddha's awakening was his achievement alone. Would it not have to be the same for anyone else? In other words, should not *pratyekabuddhas* be the only kind of Buddhas? The Buddha, whose karmic chain is extinguished and whose births are ended, dies. He enters *nirvāṇa* and is gone from this world. The iconographic conventions of early Buddhism make this absence clear, representing the Buddha only with footprints or with the wheel of the teaching, which is what actually remains. The teaching is what binds the two incommensurate worlds together, containing truth and convention at the same time. It does change the environment, since it becomes possible to attain enlightenment by reliance on this resource, which the Buddha himself had not had.[30]

This tension is replicated in the devotee, for instance in the modes of meditation conducive to liberation. The Pāli canon includes instruction in two kinds of meditation, each associated with enlightenment. Samādhi, or concentration meditation, aims to calm the mind, ridding it by stages of emotional and intellectual content until it is empty of thought or sensation, the very nature of *nirvāṇa*. This stills the craving that drives karma and rebirth. *Vipassanā*, or insight meditation, aims to see the true nature of things, bringing perception and understanding in line with wisdom. It is not enough to know how Buddhism teaches the world to be. It is necessary to actually see the world that way and know it to be so. This dispels the ignorance that turns all achievements, even meditative ones, into reinforcements of our attachments. Both practices can be said to lead to release from *samsāra* and to *nirvāṇa*. Yet they seem to point to two quite different events: the end of mind as we know it (i.e., entry into a realm other than the cognitive altogether) and an ecstatic act of knowing that takes place in an illuminated mind.[31] If these are two ways of talking about the same thing, then that thing is itself a marvelous resolution of what seems necessarily distinct for us, a kind of direct, self-executing awareness of the nature of things that takes place with no particular perspective from which the awareness flows. This tension appears in Buddhist texts and to some extent in Buddhist practice, but my point is only to say that awakening is thought to overcome that tension. This is one of the most extraordinary things about awakening. Stilling the mind allows it to see things as they are, or seeing things as they are has a kind of self-canceling effect on the "I" consciousness itself.

There is also a certain separation between compassion and enlightenment. Compassion as a virtue is a necessary component of the right path, and the growth of wisdom encourages it. But it is transient. Compassion is exercised in the realm of *samsāra*. It is a phenomenon tied to the plane of ignorance. Enlightenment contains no ignorance and is absolute release from *samsāra*. Strictly speaking, it seems that where one exists the other cannot. Compassion but no enlightenment; enlightenment but no compassion.

The *Mahāyāna* traditions embraced the foundations of *dharma* that they inherited and filled them with an additional teaching. The simple initiatory act in which one "takes refuge in the Buddha" assumes a whole new character when that Buddha is understood not only as the one who first turned the wheel of *dharma* and left the teaching of the way of release from suffering, but as that one and numberless others who, while completely freed from the illusions and sufferings of this world, continue to be "limitlessly active within it to the end of time" to assist others.[32] This is the place of the bodhisattva.

Mahāyāna regarded the aim of the prior teaching as insufficient, a restriction to practice in the sphere of one mind and one liberation. Instead it commended the ideal of the bodhisattva, whose aim is not the end of their individual rebirth but the liberation of all sentient beings. The bodhisattva path stands at an intersection point in the web of Buddhist assumptions we have been reviewing. It takes up those tensions into an even more extraordinary resolution. In particular, it takes up the tension between the "beyond" of *nirvāṇa* and the delusion of the conventional world and addresses it with two dramatic moves.

The first of these moves is to deny the separation directly. It identifies *nirvāṇa* with *saṃsāra*. Enlightenment is not viewed as another state in the sense that one goes ontologically "beyond" the contingent world of *saṃsāra*. It is simply the same place, so to speak, grasped with full understanding of its nature. *Nirvāṇa* does not exchange the phenomenal world for another plane but realizes the empty nature of that world from within it. Enlightenment is realization of what is the case, and it is the case precisely of the phenomenal world around us.[33] Lessening the distance between *nirvāṇa* and *saṃsāra* allows greater interaction between those who have realized enlightenment and those still entangled in suffering and rebirth. They inhabit, so to speak, the same space but in a radically different way. In fact, this became a distinctive view of the nature of awakening itself, a "nonabiding *nirvāṇa*" or an enlightenment not clung to, contrasted with a *nirvāṇa* into which one disappeared from the struggling world.[34] It might be argued that the historically earlier view of the Buddha's death, his *parinirvāṇa*, was just that kind of disappearance. He had been enlightened, with the residue of a body and (only good) actions, and this residue had finally been burned off. But nonabiding *nirvāṇa* was no such separation. It was the highest form of engagement.[35]

The second move prescribes a new approach to *saṃsāric* misperceptions. Conventional views of the world are not only the source of suffering and the antithesis of wisdom. In the right hands, such conventional views can become instruments of liberation, used to spread wisdom and help people advance toward release. The teaching of the two truths does not simply refer to lower and higher levels of insight but also points to the way in which a wise teacher can make use of that distinction. Skillful means, *upāya*, is the technique by which the right kind of conventional truth can be prescribed or taught to move a person beyond her present understanding and into a higher, but not ultimate, perspective. Conventional terms that imprison the deluded can be used as liberating medicine by enlightened ones. Already in the Lotus Sutra, around the first century CE, this perspective on skillful means appears. It comes to be particularly associated with the bodhisattva as the hallmark of a capacity to aid suffering beings from a location far removed from theirs in terms of understanding.

Together, these two elements—nonabiding *nirvāṇa* and skillful means—constitute the bodhisattva path. Bodhisattvas are those who seek and realize this distinctive form of no-separate-place *nirvāṇa*, which allows them to act continually for the liberation of other beings. They are preeminent in the application of skillful means. Bodhisattvas realize enlightenment within *saṃsāra* and perfect an ability to calibrate their teaching and action to the weaker understanding of their hearers.

The bodhisattva ideal enriches or deepens the relation between enlightenment and compassion by essentially making enlightenment itself an event of compassion. *Mahāyāna*, the "great vehicle," focuses on the release of all sentient beings and defines the supreme liberation itself not in terms of the end of suffering and its causes in the practitioner but in terms of the capacity to end suffering in others. Extinguishing one's own suffering is a necessary condition for helping others, but it is not the primary end. Through the eyes of wisdom, it cannot actually be distinguished from the relief of all beings.

Bodhisattvas stand at an intersection of the tensions we have been discussing, those between wisdom and compassion, ultimate and conventional, a separate *nirvāṇa* and a nonabiding one. These are not just theoretical tensions. They directly affect the practice and ideal in Buddhist life (for instance, does one aim for individual realization or strive for the good of all beings, or does one who progresses in wisdom care about communicating in conventional terms?). The bodhisattva ideal goes to the very heart of this tension, affirming that compassion is the essence of wisdom, when wisdom is understood to encompass not only the true nature of things, but also the most skillful means of sharing the benefits of that knowledge. The path of the Buddha takes on a closer connection with (even dependence upon) that of others, and the path of the seeker benefits from a more complex and intimate connection with a Buddha. The bodhisattva path now points in two directions at once. Its teaching describes the "ascending" path of the bodhisattva (i.e., the way of the aspirant) and it also describes a "descending" path of the bodhisattva (i.e., the fully realized one that distributes benefit for other beings).[36]

The bodhisattva ideal expands the scope of the activity of a Buddha or an enlightened teacher beyond that of a discoverer and protector of the *dharma* (a refuge to which the wise may repair through their own efforts) toward an agency actively directed at their liberation. All this raises new questions of its own. How can one be enlightened, literally mindless, and still exercise the intentions of skillful means in the conventional world? How can bodhisattvas exercise beneficent power for others without compromising the karmic effects of those others' own acts? If all beings have Buddha nature, and if numberless bodhisattvas already exercise limitless liberative power, then how can suffering be so prevalent? If the destiny of all beings is to be bodhisattvas themselves, is enlightenment, in the sense of a "Buddha nature," already the true nature of each being? Such questions are constituted by the specific terms of the bodhisattva's achievement.

Our point here is to grasp the particular wonder of that achievement. To stand before a graceful statue of the bodhisattva Kuan Yin is to feel the power of our normal human impulses to care and be cared for writ large.[37] She is not only a focus for the meditative realization of an oceanic equanimity. Devotees believe that she hears and responds to the cries even of storm-tossed sailors or hungry children for the relief of their worldly cares. The peculiar wonder here is that this call and response is not the emotional or causal shortest line between two points, with one being concerned for another. It is the fruit of a complex backstory in which the bodhisattva, as an enlightened one, stands far beyond either immediate care or the capacity to mix in such matters.

The line of ordinary human empathy, built as it is around the self as the central reference point, has to be radically remade if not completely effaced so that something truly universal may grow in its place. The first marvel is that there is a way out of suffering at all. That special recipe to overcome suffering requires one to see through both the suffering and the reality of the beings fleeing it. The second marvel is that those who have followed that path to liberation might still be sufficiently connected with and participating in the world of reification and delusion so that they can help those who have not. The Buddhist wisdom that has explained so profoundly how this ought not to be so has explored now even more profoundly how it is. Bodhisattvas such as Kuan Yin perform interventional miracles only because they are able to perform the deeper and uniquely Buddhist miracle of collapsing *nirvāṇa* and *saṃsāra* into one.

The Miracle of the Great Exchange

If the Buddha's enlightenment is the key event for Buddhists, then the meeting of God and humanity in Jesus Christ is the key event for Christians. The Buddha and Christ addressed the problem of suffering differently. The root of suffering according to the Buddha's teaching is that things are not what they seem. Life based on the seemingness rather than on the truth will always cling to "things" that cannot be permanent and so always lead to suffering. Buddhism moves from the appearances of our normal world to its non-obvious insubstantiality and nondual emptiness, and then to a counter-counterintuitive return to the conventional world (through the bodhisattvas' skillful-means commerce with it) and so to a true universality of relief for all beings.

Christianity starts with the same appearances and the conviction that those appearances leave out of account the presence of the creator God and the ultimacy of relational communion. From this counterintuitive belief in a transcendent other and a radically different future, faith moves to the counter-counterintuitive affirmation that a union of God and humanity has already occurred in Christ, one that leads to an exchange of qualities and a reconciliation of humans with God and with others, and so to the unfolding of a universality of mutual love and shared life with all beings.

The root of suffering according to Jesus's teaching is that the connections among us (with God, with each other, with nature) are broken or twisted. These relations are not what they started out to be, or what they can be. Since we are literally constituted by these relations, so long as the relations are broken, we will suffer. We can no more live happily with disordered relationships than walk without suffering on broken legs. The four noble truths lay out an analysis of the conditions of systemic suffering, and the means to reverse those conditions—truths and conditions that are always the case. The biblical tradition and gospels lay out a narrative—original blessedness, subsequent estrangement, ongoing reconciliation—that locates suffering as arising in the interactions among creatures and God, and passing away in that same ongoing, living nexus.

Jesus's ministry, death, and resurrection are aspects of one redemptive event, the incarnation. The basic grammar of that event is a "great exchange" between God and humanity. God became as we are, so that we might become as God is.[38] That grammar presupposes a creator God and a humanity created in the divine image. The incarnation assumes a common human nature, a solidarity among persons that is analogous to the organic unity of human beings (by which a biological immunity can be transferred from one to another, for instance). This is the positive basis for the incarnation. The exchange also presupposes human brokenness, which is constituted by continuing acts, the weight of past evil, and the disorientation of our inner desires. That brokenness estranges humans from God and each other. The grammar likewise assumes a just God whose purposes human action often violates, whose holiness is the antithesis of human guilt, and whose self-giving nature is inconsistent with the narrow horizons of our selfish selves. Broken relations with God, others, and nature manifest as sin, evil, and death. This estrangement becomes the negative basis for the incarnation: the great exchange is not only a unification but a healing. The Christ event has a doubly paradoxical character, a unity of God and human not only in what is different (i.e., creator and creature), but in what is opposed (e.g., sin and love, evil and holiness, death and life).

For those who stand close to the Christian story, simply stating it in the presence of the Buddhist alternative brings some things into sharp relief. The achievement at the center of this story is not mainly a realization but a relation. The human Jesus attains to a unity with God, God condescends to a unity with humanity, and that interaction "infects" all those who relate to either one. If the Buddha's enlightenment happens within (and others' attainment of enlightenment always happens similarly within), the incarnation and its effects happen between or among. Jesus is party to God's words and acts; God is party to Jesus's words and acts. Buddha teaches with the authority of his own direct experience. Jesus teaches with an authority based on direct participation in a relation. Jesus is one life with two identities. This is the basic paradox of the Christian event: what looks to be one is actually two; an obviously disparate two are actually one.[39] The tension is only heightened by the unlikeliness of the two identities in question: the imageless creator God and the Galilean villager. We could call this the identity paradox, Jesus as both divine and human. It is mirrored in the paradox of transformation in Christ followers, who at once become more fully themselves and participate more actively in God and each other.

This paradox does not require a fully Trinitarian Christology. Even if one were thinking in "adoptionist" terms, for instance, such that it was only at certain times and in certain ways that Jesus's words and actions were the same as God's words and actions, we would still have this paradox. In Jesus's context, there was an existing paradigm for a prophet. And the theology of prophets clearly avoided this identity tension: prophets were human beings who carried and communicated a divine word. Both they and their hearers clearly distinguished the two, the human messenger and the message they delivered. In the case of early Christian witness about Jesus and, indeed, in many of Jesus's own words and actions, this line is explicitly blurred. The identity paradox is not avoided, but radically heightened.

There is both an "ascending" and a "descending" take on this paradox, starting either with Jesus as a spirit-filled person who becomes God's dwelling place or with the Word or Wisdom of God that assumes humanity. The paradox is a saving one, because the divine-human relation that is here recapitulated (building on the shared image from creation), rectified (healed of brokenness) and promised (modeled for future fulfillment) also touches root problems in human-human relations and human relations with nature. So Jesus's teachings and interactions with others are a healing prescription for our social lives, and his resurrection overcomes the contradiction between the dissolution of our physical bodies and the hope of continuing life in community.

The identity paradox involves a relation between different parties. The reality of otherness is a central part of its tension. The other tensions associated with it are likewise relational in nature. One of these is the tension between nature and grace. Creatures have various characters and capacities in their own right, and the divine nature and capacities surpass all of them. How do these divine and human qualities interact? Does divine action replace human action? How is the reception of divine grace and assistance compatible with human freedom? These questions can be addressed in Christological terms, exploring how Jesus's full humanity coexists with divine presence in terms of knowledge or moral choice. But they are immediate issues for those who would participate in this new life begun with Jesus. This tension, call it the agency paradox, concerns the role of other agency (especially divine action) and self-agency in the transformed life. The arguments over grace and works and Paul's testimony to the indistinct line between me and "Christ in me" are indicators of this tension.

There is a yet more universal context for otherness, the web of relations among all people and other creatures. Here the tension is between love and justice, a reconciliation paradox. The saving work of Christ embodies God's gracious forbearance and heals by forgiving offenders and loving enemies. Yet it is also aimed at establishing righteousness, lifting up the oppressed, and realizing the reign of God's good purposes in a new world. Do these not run at cross-purposes, passing over on one hand what must be condemned and changed on the other?

These are characteristic Christian tensions, part of the warp and woof of what Christians see as most extraordinary about the incarnation and the transformations that stem from it. They fit together. The conundrum in viewing the same thing as both an act of God and the act of a human being fits with the belief in an actor who is both divine and human. The tension between unrestricted forgiveness and impartial justice is mitigated when it is exercised by one who is at once judge and victim. Reconciliation with God, others, and nature is a broad action, and these tensions are part of its recurring pattern in the echoing participations in the divine life by those who become followers of Christ. Reconciliation of relations is the end. Incarnation is the event that instigates it.

Interestingly, the doctrinal history of Christianity has placed more definitional weight on the nature of the event than upon the way in which it works. The creeds specify an incarnational understanding of Jesus and a Trinitarian understanding of God. These are in one sense two sides of the same coin, affirming the divine-human unity for Jesus and the human-divine unity for God, which only a complex or Trinitarian God can encompass. *How* the unity of the divine and the human saves was not collectively specified with the same insistence, though the saving effect operates across the full range of this exchange, so to speak, whether in Jesus's teaching or actions.

For there to be a heresy about the saving work of Christ, there would have to be an orthodoxy about it. Unlike the case with Nicene specifications of Christological and Trinitarian doctrine, such an orthodoxy is not readily at hand in early Christian tradition or in many Christian traditions since. It is notable that the particular saving character of the cross has not been specified by creedal definitions in the same way as Christ's person or God's Trinitarian nature.[40] A variety of understandings have coexisted, whether in combination or as alternatives.

Broad though the scope of this "how" may be, there is special focus on a particular "where": the passion, death, and resurrection. The church's liturgical calendar and the four gospels all reflect that focus. The week surrounding Jesus's crucifixion in Jerusalem is the place where the tensions we have already noted are heightened and consolidated, most dramatically exhibited and overcome. As the letter to the Philippians exhorts its readers,

Let the same mind be in you that you have in Christ Jesus, who, though he was in the form of God, did not regard equality with God as something to be exploited, but emptied himself, taking the form of a slave, being born in human likeness. And being found in human form, he humbled himself and became obedient to the point of death—even death on a cross. Therefore God also highly exalted him and gave him the name that is above every name, so that at the name of Jesus every knee should bend, in heaven and on earth and under the earth, and every tongue should confess that Jesus Christ is Lord, to the glory of God the Father.

Therefore . . . work out your own salvation with fear and trembling; for it is God who is at work in you, enabling you both to will and to work for his good pleasure.[41]

Here we see the exchange or the identity paradox in broad strokes. Equality with God is given up in exchange for human life and a criminal's death, and the human Jesus is exalted by God to share the divine name.[42] And we see the corollary agency tension expressed in Jesus's followers, in which God's Spirit works in them alongside their own working and willing. This passage underlines an enabling aspect of this exchange, the "emptying," or *kenosis*, of what blocked that unity. God emptied aspects of the divine nature that would seem essential to it, and Jesus was emptied of aspects, primarily limitations, of human nature that might seem essential to it. The moment of death is an extreme point in this exchange. Giving up life and self is the most extreme emptying we can picture for a person within human life. Giving up a deathless life free of suffering to take on life subject to both death and pain is the most extreme sacrifice we can picture for a divinity beyond human life.

In Romans 3:22–26, there is a well-known expression of the love/justice tension:

For there is no distinction, since all have sinned and fall short of the glory of God; they are now justified by his grace as a gift, through the redemption that is in Christ Jesus, whom God put forward as a sacrifice of atonement by his blood, effective through faith. He did this to show his righteousness, because in his divine forbearance he had passed over the sins previously committed; it was to prove at the present time that he himself is righteous and that he justifies the one who has faith in Jesus.

God is just, by virtue of what looks to be the very suspension of justice, in passing over sins and freely giving grace to those who have not earned it. This reconciliation with and among others appears also as a reconciliation within the divine between these paradoxical goods. The effects due to flow to us from our sin fall undeserved on God in Christ's death, and their power over us is thus dispelled. The grace of God falls unearned on us and bears renewed faithfulness. Christ takes on our suffering and we take on God's free benevolence. The gravity of our sin is maintained by the cost that God suffers to overcome it. God's justice is fulfilled through mercy.

What is true of the incarnation as a whole here reaches an extreme pitch. God has changed places not simply with the generic limitations of humanity, but with human death and loss in the worst of the degradation that we visit upon each other and the most extreme forms of punishment. At the same time, humans are brought into identification with God's immortality and holiness, "made righteous" or justified. In the resurrection, the humanity of Jesus takes on the divine qualities that seem most incompatible with humanity as we know it—deathlessness and unrestricted relational availability.

With this basic grammar, the pattern of self-giving exchange between divine and human in Christ, theology has woven many different specifications and applications of the work of Christ. Some of these have come to characterize particular confessional Christian traditions. In the Eastern Orthodox churches, this great exchange has been fundamentally understood in terms of *theosis,* human participation in the divine life. In every stage of the human life that God inhabits, from womb to grave, the divine energy is being infused into our nature to renew it. The poisons that deform us are being drawn out. The resurrection is a pinnacle of this process, in which humans share in the divine power to transcend death. Focus is on the exchange of deathlessness with corruptible mortality. A moral-influence theory of the incarnation and cross stresses a communicative exchange. The humility and love exhibited in God's submission to our condition meets responsive repentance and commitment from creatures. A penal-substitutionary view sees God suffering in our place to overcome guilt so that humans may receive forgiveness and grace in Jesus's place. A Christus-Victor perspective (and related themes of ransom) sees an exchange of sovereignty—the liberation of humanity from bondage to powers beyond any individual or conscious human control to freedom through participation in God's reign.

Within some Christian communities, a particular view of the "how" of Christ's death becomes implicitly or explicitly mandatory. Even in these cases, the contention is that this particular view must be affirmed, not that it must exclude others. The different views are not strict alternatives. Jesus's crucifixion need not be any less a moral influence for being also a victory over death. Recapitulation does not rule out reconciliation; sacrifice does not preclude ransom. Of course, these formulations raise their own questions. If the cross is a ransom, to whom is it offered? How can the cross be both wrong, the product of false accusation, evil, and betrayal, and also saving, the means of redemption and reconciliation?

The cross stands at an intersection of Christian convictions regarding God, human nature, sin, incarnation, and forgiveness. Like the path of the bodhisattva, it both embodies and resolves tensions in a web of religious assumptions. In particular, it encompasses the three paradoxes we have already noted (i.e., identity, agency, and reconciliation). The exchange in which God suffers death with Jesus and Jesus is exalted to eternal life with God stretches our understanding of both the divine and the human. The exchange in which God is punished as a criminal with Jesus and Jesus proclaims the forgiveness of sins with God expresses the tension between love and justice. The exchange in which the cross is at the same time Jesus's act of fidelity to God ("not my will but thine be done") and God's submission to identify with Jesus ("emptied himself . . . even to death on a cross") manifests the tension of nature and grace. Each of these is a constitutive event that is replayed and reflected in the life of Christian disciples and communities, in derivative communions with divine life, love, and action.

To stand before a crucifix with its gracious and anguished body is to feel the power of our normal human impulses for care and compassion expanded. The familiar site is not only a focus for the petitionary prayers of those who seek relief and support in their suffering from one who knows suffering. Devotees come also to seek a meditative peace, a stillness of unity. The peculiar wonder here is that unitive meditation is not the practical or causal shortest line between two points, a direct insight of the intrinsic nature of the one meditating. It is the fruit of a complex backstory in which Christ, God, the meditator, and numberless others interact as distinct, nonidentical creatures, far from nondual unity both in individuality and in variety of natures. They seem far beyond the capacity for such unchanging equanimity.

The straight line of a pure identification with the causal, nonpersonal processes evident in so much of our ordinary world has to be deferred in favor of a complicated and laborious path to a mystical unity. The first marvel is that there are distinctive beings at all with meaning and futures. Their way to fulfilment is through love and relations, the very things that seem limited and finally futile. The second marvel is that the God who is as eternal and good as creatures are finite and now broken participates in their life and they participate in the divine life. The Christian story that explained so profoundly how this mingling of divine and human ought not to be possible then testifies even more profoundly that it is so. Disciples achieve still minds and peaceful communion only because of the deeper Christian miracle of participation and communion, the indwelling of many.

Matchless Wonders

These are brief but I hope evocative summaries of the Buddha/bodhisattva and Christ/disciple complexes, and of the attainment and the path in each one. The bodhisattva miracle starts with the central achievement that Buddhist wisdom makes possible: seeing the emptiness of all, including the emptiness of the mind with which we are seeing. It goes beyond that already-extraordinary expression to something that is doubly remarkable, specifically in the context of that first-order wisdom. The bodhisattva permanently unites the enlightenment that transcends this world with the compassion that can only exist in it, draws on unlimited wisdom to deploy skillfully the concepts constituted by ignorance, all for the sake of relieving the suffering of beings. The incarnational miracle is the basis for Christian experience and hope—God's presence in humanity that makes possible a healing of our broken relationships. And it goes beyond this to something also remarkable in its integration of the tensions inherent in the unity of the divine and the human. Christ's self-giving and God's self-giving break down the borders not only of divine and human but also of self-acts and other-acts, of the demands of justice and the gift of mercy. The cross is an intersection of both forms of self-giving for the benefit of all.

These are two wonderful things. There are similarities in the wonder, as we will have occasion to discuss. But they do not match up. The main tensions addressed in one do not exist in the other. As constituted in Christian tradition, the tensions of divine/human, nature/grace, love/justice do not exist in the Buddhist problematic of our human condition and its relief. The processes of karma and rebirth obviate by their very terms any tension between love and justice. Similarly, the tensions between mindfulness and mindlessness, compassion and wisdom, or *nirvāṇa* and *saṃsāra* do not exist as such in the Christian problematic.

O'Leary notes that elements that are unified in the Christian view of God—absolute reality and universal compassion, justice, mercy, grace, personality, eternity—are in Buddhism broken down and "dispersed in partial form across the field of Buddhist representations."[43] So the allotment of reward and punishment is the province of "automatically working karma," while the "feelings of devotion and reverence which theistic religions concentrate upon God are turned toward the Buddhas."[44] Conversely, elements that are unified in the Buddhist view of the bodhisattva are dispersed across a field of Christian representations. "Bodhisattva" covers at once the path of aspirants and the nature of Buddhahood, but Christians who want to think along comparable paths will need to reference distinctions as well as similarities between Christ on the one hand and disciples on the other. When we speak of a bodhisattva we are at once talking about an ideal attainment and an aspiration that leads to that ideal but starts far from it. The realization that unites these two is repeated, identically, numberless times. In Christian terms, we must speak of plural categories, not one. God is both source and participant. Christ is also event and source. Disciples and saints are distinctive individuals. Their attainments are identical neither to Christ's nor to each other's. There is something unique in each case, even while they all participate in Christ and the divine life. They share the path, but in different ways.

It would be easy enough to make the two models more consistent, to interpret one entirely in terms from the other. We could keep our treatment of Jesus strictly within the bounds of a prophet or teacher, and not enter into the strong paradoxes we have noted. A Buddhist practitioner could commend dropping the ideas of karma, rebirth, or celestial Buddha fields to focus simply on empirical techniques that foster equanimity and peace.[45] This would to some extent relax the tensions around the bodhisattva path. In each case, there would be much of value still in play. But to turn in that direction is to move away from the vast range of literature, testimony, and practice that Buddhists or Christians have developed in relation to these questions. People within each tradition return continually to these formative internal tensions as sources of insight and growth. I believe that the same can be true for the tensions between the traditions. Indeed, without the tensions, we dramatically reduce the scope of the distinctive content in either tradition that is of importance for learning in the other.

The three Christian paradoxes (i.e., identity, agency, and reconciliation) can be solved, so to speak, by nondualism. That is, they disappear because their conditions disappear. So Buddhist nondualism (or a Christian approximation) will always be an available option to bring the two models into full agreement. And the Buddhist paradoxes (i.e., wisdom/compassion and ultimate/conventional) can be solved, as it were, by acknowledging complexity or plurality in reality itself.[46] Christian Trinitarianism or any philosophical ground for pluralism will also always be available options to bring the two models into fuller agreement. Nondualism "works" in Buddhism when the ultimate outcome is itself a nondual state. This state can be understood as unrestricted compassion, unbounded love, though no distinct entities or participants may be enduring parties to it. Diversity works, so to speak, in Christianity when the ultimate condition is relational. Unity and mutual indwelling are integral features of this love, though no oneness can displace the particularities that it relates. This means that nondualism cannot be the definitive nature of the Christian ultimate.

Buddhists and Christians revere their respective crucial events and actors for very particular achievements. The bodhisattva is not just a caring person but a caring person who realizes and teaches a kind of caring that we can hardly imagine without a complete renovation of our minds. A bodhisattva is aware that beings are suffering and has compassion for them while realizing that they are empty. The one view somehow does not cancel out the other. The uniqueness of a bodhisattva combines the very specific wisdom insight of emptiness with skillful operation in the realm of illusion for the elimination of suffering. It is these components that constitute in large part what there is to learn about and from on the Buddhist end. Likewise, neither is Jesus or a holy disciple just a caring person. They constitute a set of transformed relations whose nature we can hardly imagine without an experience of the sharing of life "in Christ" with other creatures. A disciple and Christ come to inhabit each other in unity while remaining distinct in person and identity. The one reality does not cancel out the other. Divine incarnation and human participation with each other and God are forms of oneness flavored and constituted by the uniqueness of those related. These components constitute in large part what there is to learn about and from on the Christian end.

So long as Christ and the bodhisattva remain embedded in their own traditions, their similarity cannot be pressed beyond a certain point without changing one or both. It is therefore not a problem but a blessing that the tensions within each path find an echo in tensions between them. In describing the substantive resemblance in the two, Jesus's care for others through healing and teaching, and his selflessness in going to death are usually front and center as an example of bodhisattva qualities. Yet at the same time, the crucifixion is one of the things that Buddhists find most difficult about Christianity. Even those who most want to claim Jesus as a bodhisattva are ambivalent about it.[47] The application of the bodhisattva ideal to Jesus is a generous imputation that is usually qualified with the recognition that Jesus seems too profoundly agitated and socially entangled to have the aura of pure wisdom.

Christians likewise see bodhisattvas as Christ-like by virtue of their care for the suffering of other beings and their renunciation of self. At the same time, the lives of Christ and many Christian saints differ from the Buddha/bodhisattva profile in ways that Ninian Smart summarizes.

> The one's life is storm, humiliation and triumph; the other's is disturbance, withdrawal, huge insight and active serenity. Both used parables and images, but Jesus' were often shot through with mystery and intimations of the God behind. The Buddha's similes were instructional in purpose and his teachings were built on a highly analytic scaffolding. Moreover, the logic of the salvation wrought by the two central figures differs.[48]

Bodhisattvas ultimately see through those they serve and offer to be seen through in return. Christ dwells in others and invites them to dwell in him. The Buddha attracts us in order to point away from himself. Christ points beyond himself by inviting us to him.[49] The application of the Christ model to bodhisattvas is a generous imputation that is usually qualified with recognition that bodhisattvas seem too socially disembodied or ahistorical and their care too purely universal to have the savor of true love.

Too similar to be contrary, too distinct to be exchanged, the bodhisattva path and the Christ path invite us into concrete reflection that never fully reconciles the differences or exhausts the connections. The two occupy comparable structural positions. They are located at the place where the internal struggle of transformation is resolved most dramatically in the two teachings. The problems they solve are not the same at either the level of human transformation or the specific practices they prioritize. Conversation between them stimulates in the Christian thinker what I would call cross-application. Appreciation of the Buddhist teaching in its context suggests ways that teaching might revise Christian understanding. But to support that effort, we will need to explore the bodhisattva path in a good deal more detail in the next section.

PART II

Perfection of Wisdom and the Bodhisattva Path in Śāntideva

2 The Bodhisattva Path

Just as all the Buddhas of the past
Have brought forth the awakened mind,
And in the precepts of the Bodhisattvas
Step-by-step abode and trained,

Likewise for the benefit of beings,
I will bring to birth the awakened mind,
And in those precepts, step-by-step,
I will abide and train.

—*Bodhicaryāvatāra* 3:23–24

Although the figure of the bodhisattva is particularly identified with the rise of *Mahāyāna* Buddhism, the root concept goes back to the early stages of the tradition.[1] The term was first used in a retrospective way to refer to the historical Buddha, Gautama, in his prior lives. Once one recognized that individual's enlightenment and status as a Buddha, and likewise accepted the reality of an ongoing cycle of birth and rebirth from which his enlightenment had liberated him, an obvious conclusion followed. In the lives before his final birth, he had been a Buddha-to-be. The term "bodhisattva" begins with this reference. It points to an "enlightenment being" in the sense of a Buddha in the making.

This usage was cemented in the *Jataka* tales that grew up in the first centuries after the Buddha. There are 547 in the traditional collection of these enormously popular stories of the Buddha's exploits in earlier births as various kinds of animal and in various human conditions. Those seeking to find and follow the Buddha's path to enlightenment naturally wondered about the background to the story, the parts of the Buddha's path that might be closer to their own condition. In early *Jataka* collections, the word "bodhisattva" appears at least once in each of the stories, so we might call them bodhisattva tales.[2] These stories pointed back to an immensely distant and indeterminate time in the succession of lives that culminated in Gautama Buddha. After hundreds of rebirths and many heavenly intervals, he became the Buddha of this age. Part of the Buddha's attainment is the capacity to recall all of his past lives, and so these stories are reported as told by him. They usually conclude with the Buddha revealing which one of the characters in the story is him and which represent prior lives of other significant figures known to the listeners from the biography of the Buddha.[3] A large collection of these tales, some already illustrated in surviving carvings, was in place by the first century BCE.

The *Jataka* collection is a folkloric treasure house that includes many stories that can be paralleled in prior cultural backgrounds. The inclusion of such material makes good Buddhist sense, given the assumption that in his cycles of births, the bodhisattva would have passed through many different worldly settings. In these stories, the Buddha is victorious in battles, helps the weak, sees that good is rewarded and evil punished. Among the tales are a few with striking notes of self-sacrifice, as when the Buddha as prince Vessantāra gave away his wife and children or when as a wounded warhorse he insisted on leading the charge in a final battle and died as a result.[4] There is a famous tale of a deity who went about in disguise to ask for alms from three animals. The Buddha, who in this case was a rabbit, volunteered to give his own body as food. And to save the beggar from the sin of killing an animal, the rabbit placed himself on the fire, only to have the fire miraculously turn to ice and the deity reveal himself.[5] One that became especially prominent involved the Buddha as a young prince who encountered a starving tigress about to devour her four young cubs. The prince presents his body as flesh for the tigress and her family.[6] As Robert Thurman says, the *Jataka* Buddha is the "first bodhisattva" in Buddhist literature, a being "*consciously* engaged in a moral, physical and spiritual evolution" toward boundless Buddhahood. The only reason this is not already a *Mahāyāna* teaching is that the Buddha "only tells what he did and what came of it; he never implies that *all must also do the same.*"[7]

Life sacrifice is not a central theme in that early Pāli literature.[8] But it becomes prominent in the *Mahāyāna* presentation of the bodhisattva path to the extent that giving up one's life for the benefit of others becomes a shorthand summary of the bodhisattva's character.[9] By Śāntideva's time, such radical self-giving, often signified by the giving of one's body, had become part of the standard description of a bodhisattva.[10] In Śāntideva's *Śikṣāmuccaya*, the story is told of a great bodhisattva who had formed the commitment to sell his body and use the proceeds to honor a prior bodhisattva. Evil powers sought to block this intention, but eventually a buyer was found, someone who needed to perform a sacrifice requiring "the heart of a man, his blood, his bones and his marrow." To this the bodhisattva happily agreed.[11]

In the same early centuries after Gautama, belief had arisen in the coming of a future Buddha. This would lead to the natural conclusion that the chain of existences that would lead to this future Buddha must already be underway. "Bodhisattva" thus could apply not only to a singular sequence of lives in the past leading to Gautama. It could apply also to a sequence ongoing now, belonging to an as-yet-unrealized Buddha. The *Jataka* tales assumed that the earthly births of the proto-Gautama were separated by long periods of residence in various heavens, occasioned by the great merit of his lives. These convictions—belief in Buddhas in the making and their residence in heavenly realms—were raw material that would be more explicitly refigured in *Mahāyāna*, with its visions of beneficent bodhisattvas in their celestial realms and its multiplication of those on the earthly path to Buddhahood.[12] All of these elements are part of the common Buddhist understanding of bodhisattvas.

Undertaking the Way of Enlightenment: Text and Reader

Despite frequent reference to bodhisattvas in Buddhist-Christian conversations, there has been no systematic discussion of the bodhisattva path and its importance for Christian theology. A pioneering conference on "Christ and the Bodhisattva" was held at Middlebury College in 1984.[13] But no extensive theological exploration followed. To give focus to my study, I have concentrated on Śāntideva's eighth-century text, the *Bodhicaryāvatāra*, and its interpretation by Buddhist commentators. Though it is among the most popular Buddhist texts, it has received little attention from Christian interpreters.[14] This is a text with wide influence in the Buddhist tradition. The title is variously translated as, for example, "A Guide to the *Bodhisattva*'s Way of Life" or "Undertaking the Way to Awakening."[15] This text and its commentarial legacy describe the path of bodhisattva practice and provide a highly refined understanding of the bodhisattva reality itself.[16] Since the *Bodhicaryāvatāra* comes from the eighth century CE, we are dealing with a mature stage of *Mahāyāna* thought, which integrates strands of the bodhisattva ideal that go back much earlier.[17] At this point, the tradition had undergone centuries of development in India. Indian Buddhism had yet to fall into the decline and eclipse that would come in the next few hundred years. The disparate forms of *Mahāyāna* tradition that would crystalize in locations such as Tibet, China, Korea, and Japan were not yet in place. The *Bodhicaryāvatāra* represents a particularly "ecumenical" source in the tradition, though it certainly has its own party coloring, in Śāntideva's advocacy of Madhyamaka perspectives.[18]

Tradition tells us Śāntideva was a monk in the great Indian monastery/university complex of Nalanda while it was near the peak of its glory. Within a few centuries, this Indian Buddhism would crack and fade in the face of Muslim invasion. But his text would travel in translation to Buddhist traditions in Tibet and in central and East Asia. It remained a common point of reference among them. Its contemporary influence is no less significant than is its historical prominence.[19] The *Bodhicaryāvatāra* stands at an influential moment in tradition, but it is also a manifest classic by virtue of its beauty and depth. It is at once a stirring guide for the path it describes, and a profound if concise exposition of the wisdom that supports the path. Though individual stages and practices that the text describes can be pursued and explored in their own terms, an important feature for a Christian reader, each part is presumed to be permeated with the wisdom of the whole. The ninth chapter, the "wisdom chapter," is famously regarded as a high and challenging point of insight into ultimate truth. Even the more practical and less intricate features of the earlier chapters are understood to be presented by virtue of the skillful means that only this ultimate wisdom makes possible. While the text can be read in an "ascending" way as a manual to guide someone step by step closer to the bodhisattva goal, it can just as well be read in a "descending" way, wherein a skillfully calibrated range of conventional teachings flow out of a Buddha's boundless enlightened knowledge.[20]

What happened between the appearance of early *Mahāyāna* sources (as in the Lotus Sutra in the first century) and Śāntideva (in the eighth century) had been both an interreligious ferment between emerging *Mahāyāna* and emerging Puranic Hinduism (and also between *Mahāyāna* and Christianity and Manichaeism along the Silk Road, as discussed in the Introduction) and a philosophical enrichment. We have already noted the key space between the Buddha's enlightenment and the separate decision to teach the path. *Mahāyāna* emphasizes the importance of this transition and greatly expands the scope of the teaching offered. For instance, a later Japanese tradition divides the Buddha's life into five periods of teaching, with two high points.[21] The first high point follows immediately upon his enlightenment, when he taught the nature of this attainment but doubted whether any could achieve it. The second peak came just before his death, when he taught the Lotus Sutra, with its emphasis on universal enlightenment and the variety of skillful means. Nagarjuna (in the second and third centuries) and Vasubandhu (not long after) had originated the Madhyamaka and Yogācāra schools. Candrakirti in the seventh century had integrated Madhyamaka philosophy with the bodhisattva path.[22] Śāntideva was thus heir to this rich elaboration of the *Mahāyāna* vision that combined compassion and skillful means with sophisticated intellectual arguments. His work poetically and powerfully expressed the first, while it also addressed fine points of interpretation that divided different schools of Buddhist and non-Buddhist thought regarding the second.

The *Bodhicaryāvatāra* is composed of ten chapters.[23] The first four form a kind of ring, with the first chapter praising the awakening mind and the fourth expressing the firm commitment to pursue it, while the middle two chapters constitute a kind of ritual act of dedication and preparation. Chapters 5 through 8 cover the traditional six bodhisattva attainments: generosity, morals, patience, vigor, meditative concentration, and understanding. If *Mahāyāna* teaching and texts in general go under the heading of the "perfection of wisdom," then that perfection of wisdom is concretely defined and described here as a series of distinct perfections in the development of a bodhisattva. In the *Bodhicaryāvatāra*, these perfections are discussed at increasing length, with the first two condensed in one chapter and last two given as much space as the first four together. Chapter 9 treats understanding or wisdom, an ultimate perfection pervading all the others. The entire text draws deeply but unobtrusively on earlier sources. Chapter 9 stands out for its compressed presentation of conflicting opinions and its explicit reference to the views of specific schools. An uninstructed reader, Buddhist or not, would have difficulty following it without commentary. The final, tenth, chapter of the book dedicates the merit attained in the practice of the described perfections to the benefit of all beings and could likewise be seen as the dedication of the merits of the work by its writer or the dedication by the reader of the completed reading of the text. Even this brief overview gives a flavor of the way in which the book combines description and prescription, explanation, and invitation.

The first four chapters deal with arousing the awakening mind and setting a preparatory "field" for practice of the perfections. Here we immediately encounter a recurring feature of Śāntideva's work. The term "*bodhicitta*" parallels the word "bodhisattva" in the sense that it spans an entire spectrum of attainment. Just as "bodhisattva" can refer to someone who has just embarked on the great way or to someone who has attained the fullest possible Buddhahood and any point in between, so "*bodhicitta*" can indicate the desire for enlightenment that starts the process and also refer to the awakened spirit that is the fruit of the process. Generating *bodhicitta* has to do mainly with motivation. Someone might follow Buddhist teaching from an entirely worldly purpose. We may seek to escape pain and suffering and attain heavenly pleasures and favorable rebirths, doing good in a selfish interest. Or one might follow the same path but in genuine recognition of the insubstantial nature of the self and the unsatisfactory nature even of good births—with a sincere desire to achieve true cessation for one's self. Or—and this would be the threshold of true *bodhicitta*—one could pursue the path with the compassionate intent to free all beings. In Śāntideva's view, *bodhicitta* and the bodhisattva vow are higher Buddhist commitments. Those with the first two types of motivation are Buddhists, but they are not *Mahāyāna* Buddhists or at least not *Mahāyāna* Buddhists who have embarked on the bodhisattva path. By contrast, someone who is following some non–*Mahāyāna* tradition but is doing so with the genuine intent to free all beings is in fact practicing *Mahāyāna*.[24]

This alerts us to the fact that though the *Bodhicaryāvatāra* can be read in a sequential way, as if it describes stages to pass through, it gives us a recursive vision in which each of the steps can be revisited at quite different levels. *Bodhicitta* at the beginning looks like the stirrings of a desire to have the desire to have compassion for all beings. At the end, the same word describes an actual compassion for all beings as expressed in harmony with an absolute insight into their true conditions. Śāntideva's eloquent facility in combining the humanity of the first with an exalted vision of the second sets his book apart. It is true that as we come to the perfections described in the later portions of the work, we pass into more rarified air, and the emphasis tilts much more heavily to ideal realization.

Chapters 2 and 3 seem to be structured around elements of a liturgical ritual that existed before Śāntideva's time.[25] This "seven-branched" ritual includes these elements: homage and offerings to the Buddhas, confession of faults, rejoicing in merits, requesting the teaching, begging the Buddhas not to abandon beings, arousing the awakening mind, and dedication of merits.[26] Indeed, since the *Bodhicaryāvatāra* ends with a chapter dedicating merit and opens with chapters that include all of the other elements, we could say that the text presents itself as functioning within the context of that liturgy. It practices what it describes, embracing the Buddhas and bodhisattvas as a way to be embraced by the enlightened qualities they realize.

Who are the expected readers of this text, and how far along ought they to be? That Śāntideva wrote (or, according to tradition, spoke) to monks is reflected in some features of the text such as its ready references to established Buddhist teachings and rather sophisticated controversies. Fundamentally, the text assumes hearers who are ready for a more advanced stage of practice and understanding. This "more" can be understood to mean commitment to the *Mahāyāna* approach as opposed to other Buddhist paths or, assuming that approach, it can be understood as a willingness to begin the practices associated with the specific bodhisattva vow. As with any Buddhist text, reading and study are not meant simply for learning about the teaching. They are intended as a means of practice.

As we have seen, according to Śāntideva, enlightenment or awakening itself can be sought for at least three different reasons, which amount to three different kinds of awakening. In beginning a commentary on the *Bodhicaryāvatāra*, the Dalai Lama refers to these, writing,

> It is not practicing the *Dharma* properly to listen with the intention of gaining material advantage or reputation . . . or higher rebirth in the next life . . . nor should we be wishing only for our own liberation from *saṃsāra*. These are all attitudes we should reject. Instead let us listen to the teachings with the determined wish to attain the state of omniscience for the sake of all beings, who are infinite in number.[27]

As a reader, I do not meet these expectations. I do not have the "determined wish" that the bodhisattva vow represents. I do have a hope for the future of creation and all it contains and a wish to put into practice what I learn in reading the text as part of my Christian practice to participate in God's work.

The Dalai Lama does not hesitate to teach this text to those who have not taken its vow, which seems to correspond to Śāntideva's own conviction that his text is not only teaching about skillful means but is in fact employing them. The Dalai Lama's comments above are in introduction to a commentary on the *Bodhicaryāvatāra* transcribed from what was literally a liturgical event, in which hearers were invited to take the bodhisattva vows. That text is quite different in character from his own more scholastic commentary on Chapter 9 of the *Bodhicaryāvatāra* or some of the other commentaries he has commended.[28] Śāntideva clearly addresses those with exactly the kinds of motivations that the Dalai Lama says we ideally ought not to have. Precisely because the writing of the text is itself a kind of bodhisattva practice, it invites an adherent of what Śāntideva would regard as a lesser vehicle, such as Christianity, into its circle. By addressing their critiques and arguments in Chapter 9, the book explicitly assumes that its readers might include devotees of various contending Buddhist vehicles as well as of Hindu ones.

I come to the *Bodhicaryāvatāra* as a religious reader more than an academic one, a person with existing Christian practice and faith, less an aspiring bodhisattva than one of the beings whom they graciously vow to aid. I am grateful to walk as I can on the path of the bodhisattva, but I do not seek to follow it to its end. I am aware that from a Buddhist perspective, the lack of that intention, a crucial aspect of *bodhicitta*, must be a fatal limitation in understanding and effect. I believe nonetheless that there is much to be learned, that Buddhist wisdom has gifts to bestow even on those who take but partial refuge in it. Indeed, I picture a friendly intersection of the gracious Buddhist hospitality to the adherent of a lesser vehicle and a Christian humility that seeks to grow deeper into the divine love it values above all.

Cultivating Awakening Mind: Starting Where We Are

Chapter 1 of the *Bodhicaryāvatāra* focuses on the nature of *bodhicitta*, the precondition and underlying basis for everything else in the book, the intention that distinguishes this higher way from all others. Śāntideva almost immediately distinguishes two kinds of awakening mind, the mind that resolves to seek awakening and the one that is actually pursuing it, by practicing the perfections.[29] Though it is not as productive as active practice, the first moment that one forms this intention already generates merit. To make this point, Śāntideva suggests that even reverence for the Buddhas is exceeded by an ordinary altruistic intention.[30] How much more valuable, then, is true *bodhicitta*. He tells us that

> a well-intentioned person who thinks, "I shall eliminate the headaches of sentient beings," bears immeasurable merit. What then of a person who desires to remove the incomparable pain of every single being and endow them with immeasurable good qualities?[31]

This is the nature of final awakening mind, the jewel whose attainment is the best that we can hope for, and the disregard for which is the worst failing that we can exhibit. This thought leads naturally into offering homage to "the bodies of those in whom this precious jewel of the mind has arisen," the first step in the seven-branched service.[32]

Chapter 2 continues this homage with focus on gifts, offerings to the *dharma* and Buddhas. The writer pictures flowers, fruits, jewels, cultivated fields, and beautiful landscapes as offerings. Their beauty and value designate the supreme worth of those to whom they are given. The speaker has no achievements or merit of his own to offer, which is why he asks that the offering of these mental images be accepted out of compassion.[33] This praise goes on for a number of verses, culminating with the speaker "taking refuge." This is the classic Buddhist formula of initiation, in which one commits to take refuge in the Buddha, to take refuge in the *dharma*, and to take refuge in the *saṅgha* (monastic community), though here instead of the monastic community it is the "community of bodhisattvas."[34] Then we move to the primary theme of the chapter, the confession of faults.

The relevant word is "*pāpa*," which most translators avoid rendering as "sin" because this word carries too much Christian baggage and associations with guilt, fear, and divine retribution. Alan and Vesna Wallace use "sin" in their translation because they see some parallel connotations in Śāntideva's "emphasis on confessing and purifying *pāpa* to avoid its dire consequences, such as rebirth in hell."[35] The Buddhas are an audience before which the speaker acknowledges the truth about himself. No specific faults or victims are named (perhaps because the audience is assumed to know the catalog of things that fall under this heading), and the primary theme of the confession is for the speaker to see clearly the condition in which she stands.

At this point, Śāntideva is more than willing to meet his readers with an appeal to the first, selfish type of motivation mentioned above, the desire to avoid pain. He speaks directly in the voice of one mired in *saṃsāric* existence and perspectives. When I wake up to the reality of my condition, he says, it is like being led out to have my limbs amputated.[36] The power of Śāntideva's work is partly in this first person perspective, and partly in the graphic imagery, as when he pictures being overpowered by death, "consumed by the fever of terror and smeared with a mass of excrement."[37] Nothing remains ahead of him but the inexorable consequences of his acts, and he cries out to specific bodhisattvas for their protection, now finally ready to follow them: "After neglecting your counsel, in terror I go to you for refuge. . . . Swiftly remove my fear! Even one frightened by a fleeting illness would not disregard the physician's advice; how much more so one afflicted by the four hundred and four diseases."[38]

The pleas to the bodhisattvas for protection and for the removal of fear raise a large question that we will take up later: in what ways can and do bodhisattvas, who have the intention to benefit all beings, actually help those beings? Another question surrounds the idea of confession. For a Christian reader, the word "confession" evokes elements that are not found here: acknowledgement of acts in the context of relationships, confession *to* injured parties, forgiveness and reconciliation. There is certainly no notion of punishment by an outside power here, though fear is the central tone of the chapter. The one whom the speaker has harmed above all is himself. There is regret in abundance, but as Wallace and Wallace rightly suggest, there is no guilt. Perhaps the closest thing to such guilt or relational offense comes at other points in the book, when Śāntideva expresses chagrin at having repaid the bodhisattva's compassionate concern with indifference. For instance, in Chapter 6, he confesses shame at giving pain to the bodhisattvas by harming the beings that they seek to save.[39] But the central importance of confession in its context here is the value of the true understanding of the human situation it expresses and its practical use in identifying the sources of negative karma in an individual's life—sources that may then to some extent be offset by new efforts to generate meritorious intentions and acts.

Śāntideva paints urgent, selfish reasons to flee from the ordinary world and the pain that awaits an unenlightened mind. In Chapter 3, he turns from the lament over this dire condition to rejoicing in the resources for deliverance above all the awakened minds of the bodhisattvas. In quick succession, he moves to the next elements of the seven-branched service: the appeal to enlightened ones to teach what they know and the appeal to them not to abandon beings for *nirvāṇa*. The speaker supplicates those "who wish to leave for *nirvāṇa* that they may stay for countless eons, and that this world may not remain darkness."[40] We earlier saw that *Mahāyāna* had developed the vision of a "nonabiding" *nirvāṇa*, in which a bodhisattva remained accessible to suffering beings. Thus, although Śāntideva frames the issue for bodhisattvas with a request to *delay* entry into enlightenment (bodhisattvas are sometimes described as foregoing *nirvāṇa* so as to serve beings), commentators tend not to take the idea literally. Bodhisattvas are not lagging behind those followers of lesser vehicles who have actually attained individual cessation. They have realized a higher kind of enlightenment while remaining active in the world of ignorant beings.

Following these requests, the next verse makes a quick and profound turn: "May the virtue that I have acquired by doing all this relieve every suffering of sentient beings."[41] This is the final step in the seven branches, dedication of merit. That is, the performance of the text so far—the homage and offerings, confession of faults, praise for virtue, request to the Buddhas—is now dedicated to the good of others. The speaker has begun to practice awakening mind as well as to desire it.

In the remainder of Chapter 3, Śāntideva reaches one of his poetic heights in expressing the fullness of the bodhisattva aspiration.

> May I be a protector for those who are without protectors, a guide for travelers, and a boat, a bridge, and a ship for those who wish to cross over. May I be a lamp for those who seek light, a bed for those who seek rest, and may I be a servant for all beings who desire a servant.[42]

In fact, these beautiful lines lead to verses 22 and 23, which are themselves used as one form for bodhisattva ordination.[43]

> Just as the Sugatas of old adopted the Spirit of Awakening, and just as they properly conformed to the practice of the Bodhisattvas, so I myself shall generate the Spirit of Awakening for the sake of the world; and so I myself shall properly engage in those practices.

Chapter 4 is a transitional point in the text, looking both back and forward. It is not part of the seven-limbed service of the first three chapters, nor is it part of the exposition of the six perfections that will occupy the next five chapters. The aspirational bodhisattva vow has been made, the first kind of *bodhicitta* generated. The tone now turns sober with what might almost be called second thoughts about the gravity of the undertaking. If I make this great vow and then fail, how much greater my offense must be. The downfall is not only my own, but it "impairs the welfare of all sentient beings," who are deprived of what was promised.[44] If I stay as I am, I will continually be miserable, dwelling in hell for an eon because of only a single moment's failing.[45] In fact, on my current course, I cannot even hope to be reborn as a human.[46] Innumerable Buddhas may have come and gone, all seeking to help, but my own karma has so far put me beyond their reach.[47] In short, a brief, rare window of opportunity is open for me, and if I do not bestir myself, an incalculable time and intensity of suffering await me. This was already described in Chapter 2, but is repeated here under the even greater expectations of the bodhisattva path.

The result is a clear-eyed determination:

> While I have promised to liberate beings throughout space in the ten directions from their mental afflictions, I have not liberated even myself from mental afflictions. Without knowing my own limitations, I spoke at that time as if I were a bit insane. Therefore, I shall never turn back from vanquishing mental afflictions.[48]

To liberate others, I must liberate myself. The rest of the chapter turns to the "enemies" of this liberation, the mental afflictions or negative emotions such as craving and hatred. Śāntideva deploys the ironic cost/benefit images of which he is a master. Even my worst enemies could not do me greater harm than do these that dwell in my own heart. Fishermen and farmers bear adversities of work and weather for the sake merely of a livelihood, when I will not bear as much for the wellbeing of the whole world. A proud man enraged by a mere insult will not sleep until he kills the offender. Yet I ignore "my natural enemies, which are the perpetual cause of all miseries."[49] Śāntideva says that he will be "fixed on revenge" against these enemies. And, responding to the unstated objection that obsession with vengeance is itself a negative emotion, he says, "that kind of mental affliction is the exception, for it destroys mental afflictions."[50] Using defilement to halt defilement in this manner is the special province of a bodhisattva's skillful means, and we will see Śāntideva develop the use of skillful means in a much more extensive way in later meditative practices such as "exchanging self and others."

Chapter 4 ends with a reflection on the ultimate weakness of these enemies: They literally have no reason to exist. They arise only from false assumptions. We are introduced explicitly for the first time to the philosophy of emptiness, which is the wisdom perspective that the bodhisattvas have to teach us and from which they operate.

> Mental afflictions do not exist in sense objects, nor in the sense faculties, nor in the space between, nor anywhere else. Then where do they exist and agitate the whole world? This is an illusion only. Liberate your fearing heart and cultivate perseverance for the sake of wisdom. Why would you torture yourself in hells with no reason?[51]

This leads us to Chapter 5, which takes up cultivation of the first two perfections, generosity and morality. These two perfections seem like variations on an overarching common theme in the chapter, the importance of cultivating an attentive mind. Without control of my mind, what good are the vows and intentions that I have generated?

Śāntideva sums up this connection for both generosity and morality.

> The perfection of generosity is interpreted simply as a state of mind due to the intention of giving away everything, together with the fruits of that, to all people.
>
> Where can fish and the like be taken where I could not kill them? When the mind of renunciation is obtained, that is considered the perfection of ethical discipline.[52]

Our bodily acts and speech are simply accompaniments to states of mind, which are where enlightenment actually takes place. It is no good hiding the animals to prevent me from killing and eating them if I have the intention of doing so. And if my intention is sound, then there is no need for such precautions.

The control of the mind has two sides. The first is attentiveness, awareness of what is actually taking place in our consciousness. Mindfulness of what is going on enables control in the second sense of knowing how to diagnose and shape one's own thoughts and, so, one's behavior: "Just as a person smitten by disease is unfit for any work, so the mind lacking those two is not fit for any work."[53] We can pause here to note that Śāntideva has already been illustrating this approach. He says that mindfulness should never be lost, and if it is gone, then it should be "reinstated while recalling the anguish of hell."[54] Aware that I have lost the practice of mindfulness—perhaps distracted by concern with immediate pleasures or pains—I should have the introspective wisdom to diagnose that fact and the further wisdom to know that I can fight this distraction with a concern at the same level. I can combat one defilement by means of another, the selfish terror at the prospect of roasting in hell.

This version of the conviction that "the unexamined life is not worth living" has in view an examination not of how I should act in the world but of what is transpiring in my mind. This awareness can then guide me to guard the relation between my body and my mind. Śāntideva spends several verses advising that when one becomes mindful of certain kinds of contents in one's mind, one should simply shut down external activity completely: "When one sees one's mind to be attached or repulsed, then one should neither act nor speak, but remain still like a block of wood."[55] He follows this with an extended discussion of reasons why the mind should not be seduced into identifying with the body. We do not object when vultures tear apart a corpse, so why care so much to protect our bodies, which are in essence no different from that corpse or a wooden statue?

The body is a vehicle: "Consider the body as a ship because it is the basis of coming and going. Set the body in motion at your will in order to accomplish the welfare of sentient beings."[56] As much as possible, one is to redirect one's mind to *bodhicitta*: "One should always look straight at sentient beings as if drinking them in with the eyes, thinking, 'relying on them alone, I shall attain Buddhahood.'"[57] Morality, which ostensibly has to do with behavior, in fact must be traced back to our perceptions and intensions. At the end of the chapter, Śāntideva recommends some classic Buddhist texts (including his own compendium of teachings drawn from these sources, the *Śikṣā Samuccaya*) for direct instruction on good conduct. But he does not provide such specifics here.[58]

The perfections of generosity have a hierarchy, and one "should not forsake a better one for the sake of a lesser."[59] The text goes on to specify some of the ways in which one should maintain this proportion in generosity. For instance, though the body is simply a servant, one should not harm the body for some insignificant benefit, since this would impair its ability to do greater good. In his commentary on this section, Geshe Yeshe Tobden notes that bodhisattvas are known to give away parts of their bodies or even their entire bodies. But this is only possible at a very high level of attainment, where there is a purity of intention and an ability to transcend suffering.[60] One must first ask if the sacrifice would have a commensurate benefit, and even if it would, it can only be undertaken if one is capable of the right intention.

Śāntideva introduces a major qualification to this hierarchy of generosity: "Even that which is prohibited has been permitted for the compassionate one who foresees benefit."[61] In other words, ordinary morality can be overridden in the interests of the greatest benefit to beings, as bodhisattvas in their wisdom can perceive it. Tobden says that those who pursue lesser forms of enlightenment regard certain kinds of behavior as always forbidden. Such proscribed activities are summarized in the ten paths of non-virtue. But bodhisattvas are allowed to engage in the three of these behaviors that involve the body (i.e., killing, stealing, and sexual misconduct) and the four that involve speech (i.e., lying, divisive speech, harsh speech, and idle speech) for the benefit of others.[62] The three that involve the mind (i.e., coveting, malice, and wrong views) are presumably impossible for the realized bodhisattva.[63] In extremity, a bodhisattva might murder someone who intends to massacre a hundred people, committing the murder in order both to save the hundred and to prevent the murderer from acquiring such terrible karma.[64] This unusual conclusion is justified on the grounds that the bodhisattva has the ability to know the ultimate effects of the actions (those that would have taken place and those that actually do) and has the ability to act without any negative karmic entailment.

Chapter 6 takes up the perfection of patience or forbearance. Chapter 4 deals with the awareness and therapeutic introspection that are necessary methods for all progress, and Chapter 5 deals with generosity and morality as generic perfections whose outward, behavioral manifestations are grounded in the mind itself. Chapter 6 becomes much more concrete. It deals with a specific pairing: anger and the antidotes to anger. From Chapter 2 on, Śāntideva has dealt with negative and positive emotions, with negative karma and ways to overcome it. This is a topic of central importance, even if we are only interested in lessening suffering in this life and attaining happier rebirths, but it is a central part of all higher paths as well. In this realm, there is no more destructive power than anger, as it can negate all the positive merit gained by altruistic action and intent in the normal world.[65] In this sense, "there is no evil equal to hatred, and no spiritual practice equal to forbearance."[66] And anger seems to be most characteristically evoked by our relations with other people. We see others as the source of our problems, and destruction or restraint of our enemies as the solution. To progress farther on this path, we have to overcome that misperception.

This requires three different applications or uses of patience. First, we need to be patient enough to see the nature of our own suffering. We take it as caused by our enemies, and our suffering distracts us from recognizing and attacking its real sources, which lie in our own negative emotions and their causes. Śāntideva says that our attacks on our enemies are wasted effort, like stabbing dead bodies and ignoring the true assailant who causes our pain. So we need endurance and patience to see the true significance of suffering: it is a signal to wake us up.

> The virtue of suffering has no rival, since, from the shock it causes, intoxication falls away and there arises compassion for those in cyclic existence, fear of evil and a longing for the Conqueror.[67]

Second, we can cultivate forbearance through understanding of Buddhist teaching. Here, the point is simply that our anger at our enemies as the cause of our pains is self-contradictory. We feel no anger toward the bile in our bodies that may cause intense pain, so why should we be angry with others, whose actions are just as much a confluence of conditioned causes?[68] We are chasing ghosts.

> Thus, everything is dependent on something else, and even that on which something is dependent is not autonomous. Hence, why would one get angry at things that are inactive, like apparitions?[69]

In accordance with the basic Buddhist teaching of no-self, there is no one there, so to speak, to be angry at, no decision-making agent who has intended to harm me. Both the actions that offend me and the anger I feel about them arise from antecedent conditions without anyone or anything responsible for them.[70] This section ends with Śāntideva considering the objection that his argument may have been too successful. If I or those whom I am angry at or the anger itself are nothing but a mirage, isn't the whole discussion about the importance of resisting anger pointless?

> If it is argued that to resist anger is inappropriate, for "who is it that resists what?," our view is that it is appropriate: since there is dependent origination there can be cessation of suffering.[71]

Precisely because there is no inherent reality behind these things, there is a way out. Illusory antidotes "are used to get rid of illusory sufferings."[72]

In fact, the third form of forbearance is to apply this insight in our own experiences of injury from others. People cause themselves torment as karmic return on their harm to us, even though that is not what they seek. So we can hardly see their injuries to us as born of special malice. If it were just part of human nature to cause others pain, then we could not blame someone any more than we would blame fire for burning us.[73] And if in fact "sentient beings are good by nature, then anger toward them is inappropriate as it would be toward pungent smoke in the sky."[74] It is just as misguided to be angry with a person who attacks me as to be angry at the knife they use. If we are angry at the person who drives the knife, then it is better to hate the anger that drives them to do so.[75]

I am myself also part of the conditions of this event.

> Both his weapon and my body are causes of suffering. He has obtained a weapon and I have obtained a body. With what should I be angry?[76]

My identification with the body and its pain as mine are as much causes of suffering as the attacker and the weapon. Pain cannot be avoided in *saṃsāric* existence. The question is whether it serves any purpose. So there are two very different kinds of suffering. Anger has sent me to hell and its pains thousands of times, with no gain. But suffering endured with patience gives me great merit and allows me to benefit others. This suffering is different.

> If one who is to be executed has a hand amputated and is released, is this unfortunate? If a person is freed from hell by human suffering, is this unfortunate?[77]

If I fall into hatred in response to persecution from others, I end in hell, whose sufferings do no good for me or others. The suffering that comes of forbearance is quite different.

> But this suffering is not of that kind, and it will produce great benefit. Delight is the only appropriate response to suffering which takes away the suffering of the universe.[78]

This requires a reassessment of enemies, or those who act to hinder or hurt us, for they in fact help us immeasurably. Forbearance is a very powerful practice, but we can practice it only when opposed or harmed. The suffering inflicted by my enemy is an instrument for my greater good. In short, Buddhist teaching allows us to see that things are quite the reverse of what we suppose. In the first place, the wrongs that others do to us "are the direct result of our past actions."[79] So we have summoned those who attack us, and yet they are the ones harmed with bad karma and suffering because of their actions, while we are given the priceless opportunity to generate great merit through patience. I cannot practice generosity without someone in need, or patience without someone who does me wrong. Even someone who blocks me from helping others should not occasion anger, for they have only given me a more powerful opportunity to gain merit and help others.[80] In fact, the better my own behavior, the harder it may be to find those who will harm me.[81] A lack of enemies would weaken my ability to practice and advance. Therefore, "since my adversary assists me in my Bodhisattva way of life, I should long for him like a treasure discovered in the house and acquired without effort."[82]

Śāntideva takes this line of thought one more dramatic step. My enemy is the cause and condition of my forbearance, with all its benefits to me. For this reason, I should respect him "just like the sublime *Dharma*."[83] One may object that the enemy did not intend to do me good, but then neither does the *dharma*, which has no intention to cause my achievement.[84] The transmission of Buddha qualities comes from ordinary beings, even malicious ones, as well as Buddhas, and we should pay them the same respect.[85] In our striving on the path, enemies in fact serve as Buddhas to us.

Chapter 6 closes with an extensive passage taken from the *Tathā-gataguhya* sutra, which puts our relations with other beings in the context of our relations with accomplished bodhisattvas and Buddhas. To hinder or harm Buddhas is the worst possible thing one can do in terms of its outcomes for us. But the only thing that will pain them is to harm other beings, and the only thing that will please them is to help other beings. If I am intent on honoring the bodhisattvas, I will deal kindly with those for whom the bodhisattvas made their vows.

> One should render only service to those for whose sake they [the bodhisattvas] cut apart their bodies and enter the Avīci hell. Therefore, one should treat people kindly even though they inflict great harm.[86]

The writer then confesses to giving pain to these great Buddhas by harming the sentient beings whom they have taken under their protection, and asks forgiveness from the Buddhas for displeasing them.[87] Here we have something along the lines of a relational confession, such as was only hinted in Chapter 2. These great compassionate beings "regard all beings as themselves."[88] In order to please them, "I place myself in service to the world. Let streams of people step on my head and strike me down. May the Protector of the World be pleased."[89]

This exalted view of Buddhahood and recommitment to the path includes two final verses that bring us back to less advanced motivations. No king could give any gift that would equal Buddhahood. But leaving that aside, "do you not see that in this life fortune, fame, and happiness ensue from pleasing sentient beings? While transmigrating, a patient person attains beauty, health, charisma, long life, and the abundant joy of a Cakravartī."[90] If the service of all beings is still a stretch, Śāntideva reminds his reader, then there are many proximate reasons to begin on the way.

Throughout the book, we see a repeated dynamic. There are clearly different levels of analysis at work here, some more conventional and others more exalted. At each step, Śāntideva wrings every possible good for motivation and practice that can be gathered from one perspective before adding yet others, which are sometimes rather contradictory to the first. For instance, he can lead us through an antidote to anger at others based on realizing that there is no "one" there to be angry with. And he can also lead us through another kind of antidote that invites us to revere our antagonists as benefactors and even Buddhas. He does not hesitate to appeal to people's most base self-interest, their desire to gain pleasure and escape pain. He makes a passionate case for the bodhisattva path on that ground. He does not disdain what we might call conventional forms of altruism. Concern for other people's headaches is a meritorious attitude, for which we have a kind of intuitive respect. Imagine, he suggests, how much more valuable it would be to stop all the suffering of all beings.

To be instructed not to be angry is one thing. But in his chapter on patience, Śāntideva comes at us with a variety of different but converging arguments and means to achieve that end. He begins with simple self-interest. Anger sends us to hell, where we suffer and then return to repeat the process again, whereas the same amount of suffering invested in patience will release us forever. He then adds a basic Buddhist analysis of the insubstantiality of our categories: the self we think is harmed, the enemy we think harms us, the suffering we think we hate. Analyzed into its component causes or subjects, anger dissipates. And finally, he leads us into a radically counterintuitive perspective in which our antagonists are our benefactors and the daunting challenge of serving all beings is turned around to maintain that they are so many Buddhas serving *our* liberation. There is something here to meet each reader where she is, and to draw her further.

Chapter 7 takes up the fourth perfection, diligence. Chapter 6 took us a good deal deeper in and higher up in understanding the bodhisattva

path. It concentrated on how to deal with suffering generally and especially how we are to process the negative emotions that arise in us in connection with other people. Śāntideva now takes a pause before the even
greater intensity of Chapters 8 and 9, which will push to the final extremity of practice and understanding of the path. But Chapter 7 returns to
the question of how to maintain our commitment and avoid turning
back, dealing both with the faults that derail us and the positive support
that can draw us forward.

Three kinds of laziness are described here: a lack of concern for the
path, distraction by negative emotions, and underestimation of our own
capacities.[91] Śāntideva goes at the first issue, our indifference, with an immediate return to an image of deathbed terror:

> "This I have not done, and this I'm only starting, and this—I'm only half-
> way through."
>> *Then* is the sudden coming of the Lord of Death, and oh, the thought
>> "Alas, I'm finished!"[92]

What will you do when you are so terrified, "hearing the sounds of hell
and befouling your body with excrement?"[93] Vividly revisiting his
earlier, more extensive explorations of our sad condition, he adminis-
ters a sharp slap in the face: "The time that you have now, you fool, is
not for sleep!"[94] A strong dose of negative emotion is used to wake us
up. Śāntideva deploys these passions in the service of spiritual advancement. He exhorts us to marshal our powers and specifically to practice
the equality of self and other and the exchange of self and other (which
will be spelled out in Chapter 8), practices which themselves involve a
daring transmutation of our typical emotions of envy and superiority.

The writer is acutely aware also that such emotions can become both
distraction and discouragement. We may need terror to shake us to attention, but we may easily overcorrect to the point of despair. Śāntideva
deftly pivots to parry the excuse that says "Oh, but how could *I* become
enlightened?"[95] Many Buddhist texts emphasize that it will require many
ages of time and infinite merit to attain a Buddha state, which is hardly
encouraging.[96] Commentators point out the question can be framed differently. The Dalai Lama notes that the goal of *bodhicitta* is to lead infinite beings to the infinite good qualities of Buddhahood by exercising the
capacities of a bodhisattva for an infinite period of time: "With a single
instant of such intention, having these four infinite characteristics,

we can accumulate merit very easily."[97] It is less a matter of time than of purity and boundlessness of intention.

Śāntideva offers a quote from the Buddha to the effect that even insects and worms have gained enlightenment, so why not us?[98] We may be alarmed by the bodhisattva ideal of giving away life and limb, thinking we can never attain it. But this is ironic, because for ages our bodies have already been involuntarily cut and burned and will continue to be for ages more *unless* we take up the path. The pain associated with vigorous practice is limited and healing, like taking out a splinter. Moreover, one need only progress slowly, bit by bit.

> At the beginning, the Guide prescribes giving vegetables and the like. One does it gradually so that later one can give away even one's own flesh. When insight arises that one's own flesh is like a vegetable, then what difficulty is there in giving away one's flesh and bone?[99]

About halfway through the chapter, the emphasis swings from removing the obstacles to diligence to building favorable conditions for it in the "four supports": aspiration, self-confidence, delight, and letting go. We have generated an aspiration for enlightenment out of a fear of suffering, but the weight falls now on generating aspiration based on the benefits of liberation and its good for other beings. Verse 40 declares that aspiration is the root of all virtues, and the root of aspiration is meditation on the infallible process of karma. Every positive step, however small, will have its effect. Yet another vivid sketch, a description of being flayed alive in hell as a result of negative actions, is balanced now with an equally vivid image of a land of bliss, the product of virtue.[100] Karma shows its positive face, encouraging us with certainty about the result of our efforts.

This ironclad connection between causes and effects can be a source of self-confidence. A number of commentators choose this chapter as the occasion for a discussion of karma and rebirth.[101] The sobering distance between my current condition and the extraordinary qualities of a bodhisattva, not to mention the difference between my abilities and the cosmic scope of the bodhisattva's task, would seem to make the proposed path incredible. It is the background of a vast tapestry of time and the continuing rebirths flawlessly calibrated to cause and effect that make the impossible conceivable. It is the prospect of eons of suffering that can energize me against current difficulties, and the prospect of long cycles of incremental improvement that can give me hope to become a hero of great compassion and wisdom.

And if the prospect of becoming a bodhisattva, who will also remain within the cycles of *saṃsāra*, seems less like liberation than a prescription for more suffering, then it is worth noting that commentators maintain that this involvement does not include suffering. Long before pure Buddhahood, the bodhisattva will have escaped all pain.

> By releasing his grip on the "I" and the other mental afflictions, he no longer accumulates negative karma, which is the cause of suffering, and thus no longer experiences suffering itself. Consequently, it does not matter if it takes him a long time to attain enlightenment, since he no longer experiences any difficulties in cyclic existence.[102]

The more that one grasps these dynamics, the more convinced and confident one can become. The confidence that supports diligence is not a self-important pride. That is a conflictive emotion that must be defeated. The zeal that Śāntideva pictures is a growing certainty about the task (i.e., its necessity and beauty), the means available, and my own capacities. This conviction can lead me to truly claim the bodhisattva vocation as my own. It is signified by speaking in the voice of the bodhisattva—"I alone should do it"—and thinking from the bodhisattva's perspective: "This world overwhelmed by metal afflictions is incapable of accomplishing its own self-interest. Therefore, I must do it for them. I am not as incapable as the world is."[103] At some point, the *bodhicitta* generated on the way becomes irreversible: the bodhisattva is not yet fully realized and yet he knows unshakably the nature of the end and the path.

Diligence thus is rooted in confidence. At several points, we have seen Śāntideva hinting at an even more radical basis for this confidence. In Chapter 6, he had suggested that human nature was itself good—that mental afflictions were like acrid smoke in a clear sky. In this chapter, he quotes the Buddha as saying that even insects and worms will attain enlightenment. And he goes even further, attributing bodhisattva-like qualities to our enemies and antagonists, who advance our way toward liberation even at the cost of going to hell themselves. The scope of this confidence is not itself explained, but it appears to rest on a conviction that there is a certain inevitability to the path to Buddhahood, since it is founded on the way that things already are and always have been. It is the natural state of things when various interferences and misperceptions fall away. To put it in terms that Śāntideva has not, the firmest ground possible for this optimism about the path would be to maintain that every being already has a Buddha nature—undiscovered but real.

Within *Mahāyāna* this matter, the question of an underlying germ or basis for enlightenment in all being, was an ongoing concern. If the Buddha's teaching in the Pāli canon was the agreed "first turning of the *dharma* wheel," and the later perfection-of-wisdom sutras constituted a second turning, offering the higher or perfected truth, then the process did not stop. According to their mode of analysis, some Buddhist groups see yet a third or even a fourth turning of the wheel that is marked by higher refinements or perfections. Different Buddhist schools of thought arise regarding such questions, specifying nuanced differences in the understanding of ultimate wisdom. Each of these casts its distinctive, pervasive light back over the common elements in the path as we have followed it so far. These questions come increasingly to the fore as Śāntideva takes us into the last stages of his work.

3 Extreme Wisdom, Groundless Compassion

If the suffering of the many disappears because of the suffering of one,
then a compassionate person should induce that suffering for his own sake
and for the sake of others.

—ŚĀNTIDEVA, *A Guide to the Bodhisattva's Way of Life* 8:105

Expanding and Dispelling the Self

Chapter 8 in the *Bodhicaryāvatāra* takes us to another level, focusing on the eighth bodhisattva perfection, meditation. The word for this perfection, *dhyāna*, covers both the practices of meditation and the ascending states of consciousness they attain. As described above, in Chapter 1, in Buddhist tradition there are two broad types of meditation: calming meditation and insight meditation. Perhaps these could be better pictured as two trees with shared roots, since both rest upon some common practices and build upon the same initial attainments. The first meditative attainment of calming practice is a clarity of mind and a purifying of positive emotions, still operating in the realm of discursive thought. Beyond this, there is meditative concentration, in which conceptual thoughts disappear, and two further levels in which even sensation or awareness of pain or pleasure are dissipated.[1] Insight practice, however, seeks a perfection that utilizes and depends upon the mental activity that subsides in the higher levels of calming meditation. If calming meditation perfects the equanimity of mind, then insight meditation perfects its wisdom. The precise and fullest account of the way that things really are, of the nature of the *dharma*, requires a mind able to know that this is the truth of things, and then, through further training, able to experience the world directly as what it is. To practice insight meditation is to find a sweet spot where the mind is calmed to achieve the greatest clarity of discursive thought, but held back from ascent (or descent) into the bare awareness where thought itself ceases.[2]

Just as one might practice for a long time before being forced to a fork in the road between these two approaches, one might progress on the bodhisattva path without having to choose sides among competing versions of insight wisdom. But, of course, one would not be consciously on the bodhisattva path at all if one had not already chosen the *Mahāyāna* reading of the Buddha's teaching. To be a bodhisattva in the aspirational sense is to have formed this specific intention. Just as, on the ultimate side, enlightenment is the meeting of supreme wisdom and the experience that coincides with it, the bodhisattva beginning point is the intentional *bodhicitta* and the aspirational experience that coincides with it.

At this point in the *Bodhicaryāvatāra,* the discussion of meditation moves us closer to consideration of the nature of enlightenment itself. This will eventually require Śāntideva to pay increasing attention to the subtle differences between contending *Mahāyāna* forms of wisdom.[3] But the first long section in the chapter, verses 5 through 88, stakes out common ground in perfecting calming meditation:

> Realizing that one who is well endowed with insight through quiescence [defined as samādhi] eradicates mental afflictions, one should first seek quiescence. Quiescence is due to detachment toward the world and due to joy.[4]

What follows is a kind of hymn to solitude as the setting for spiritual development. It is attachment to impermanent things, especially to loved ones, that bars us from progress on this front. Even if we are trying to perceive reality and the pointlessness of the cycle of existence, living among other ignorant people makes it too easy for us to be caught up in love, creative striving, grief, rivalry, and anger. We cannot possibly please such people and still stay on the path.[5] As Śāntideva concisely puts it, because of "association with someone else, one encounters adversity."[6] He draws a practical conclusion from this.

> I shall happily live alone with a non-afflicted mind. One should flee far from a fool.[7]

In this environment, it is very difficult to give up identification with one's body, which is only an animated corpse.

A person is born alone and also dies alone. No one else has a share in one's agony. What is the use of loved ones who create hindrances?[8]

This line of thought leads to a pithy conclusion: "Until one is hoisted by four men and mourned by the world, one should retire to the forest."[9] There, free from other concerns and "having a single-pointed mind, I shall apply myself to meditative concentration and to the subjugation of the mind."[10]

The rest of this section, another forty or so verses, is devoted to an extended meditation (some might say rant) on a specific instance of entanglement: sexual attraction to women. The theme is the repugnance of physical bodies and the insistence that there is nothing actually there to serve as the object of lust or devotion except an illusion of our own. Śāntideva spares none of his poetic power here, taunting the listener with the contrast between a beautiful woman's face, tantalizingly hidden by a veil, of which his hearer is avid to see more, and the same woman's dead face being eaten by vultures, from which one turns away in revulsion. Why be aflame with desire for the one and repelled by the other? They are the same. Saliva and excrement both arise from the same food: "Why then do you dislike excrement and like sucking saliva?"[11]

You have plenty of filth yourself. Be satisfied with that alone. Voracious for feces! Forget another sack of muck![12]

Though the body we desire is nothing but filth, for that little enjoyment, "easily attainable even for an animal," a high price is paid with anguish in hell and lost opportunity.[13]

Śāntideva has not invented this theme. Meditation on the impermanence of our bodies, on death as a reality that punctures our illusions of selfhood, is a well-developed practice in Buddhist monastic traditions, including a "cultivation of the horrible" that closely meditates on various stages of decomposition in the human corpse.[14] It is deployed in connection to the body as such, male as well as female. For his monastic audience, he has taken this specific emphasis to bring home his point: "Fearing sensual desires in this way, one should generate delight in solitude and in deserted woodlands devoid of strife and annoyance."[15]

Florid though it is, this presentation is presumably familiar fare for Buddhists of all opinions. And parts of it may have the stylized character of tradition. For one thing, Śāntideva's monastery itself was a far cry from a forest dwelling: it was a cosmopolitan, urban educational center.

It is not even clear how central the kind of meditation he describes was for the monks there.[16] Second, it seems a bit ironic that the bodhisattva path, animated by concern for all beings, should involve this radical exhortation to flee from those beings because of their foolishness and interference. The advice given here is the basic, first-stage counsel provided by all Buddhist traditions for someone who is serious about practice. It is a place to begin, but not a place to stop.

Discussion now moves to practices that bear a more distinctive *Mahāyāna* imprint: "After meditating on the advantages of solitude in this and other ways, having one's discursive thoughts calmed, one should cultivate the Spirit of Awakening."[17] The instruction on meditation so far teaches us to break down our identification with our body and our entanglement with others, especially our positive attractions to them. That teaching could be deployed entirely in pursuit of our personal enlightenment and liberation from suffering. The Spirit of Awakening, however, is the spirit of *bodhicitta*, the concern for the liberation of others. The instruction in the chapter so far seems to be running in the opposite direction: flee from the company of others who are distracting, the better to achieve spiritual progress. As the Dalai Lama says in commenting on this section, a first stage on the path is to assure our own good rebirth, for without that, any future attainments for the sake of others will be impossible.[18] It is necessary to go through stages in the right order. Śāntideva assumes that we cannot help other beings from a position of weakness and ignorance.

But the rest of the chapter turns to practices explicitly intended to ground *bodhicitta*, the desire for the good of other beings, by breaking down the distinction of self and others. Just as it is key to overcoming my own suffering to realize the error of identifying myself with my body, so it is also key to overcome the distinction between my suffering and that of others. The two practices for this purpose are "equalizing self and others" and "exchanging self and others." These are practices of "relative bodhicitta," since they employ our perceptions of existent selves to break them down.[19]

In Chapter 8, Śāntideva shifts his mode of argumentation somewhat. In the previous chapters, there has been a great deal of cost-benefit analysis and poetic irony. The analysis comes with many variations on the argument that ordinary existence promises suffering without end while the bodhisattva path invests a limited amount of suffering for the sake of an enormous payoff. The irony comes in the repeated contrasts between the extremes that we will go to in pursuit of ephemeral goods and the feeble interest that we show in the wisdom that will actually liberate us. In this chapter, Śāntideva strings together some more-direct logical arguments.

Verse 91 states a thesis: just as we protect our body as a whole, though it is made up of many parts, so should we protect the entire world with its many parts. The argument is that there is no way to rationally distinguish these two cases, though we in fact treat them in entirely opposite ways. I will automatically sacrifice a hand or arm to protect "my" eyes, but I am totally indifferent to damage to another person. Śāntideva makes a series of arguments backing up this point in verses 92 through 96. I suffer from pain in my body because of my attachment to my body. It is exactly the same for others who are likewise attached to their bodies. We are perfect duplicates of each other: happiness is dear to each of us, and each of us flees pain: "What is so special about me that I protect myself but not others?"[20] If I don't help others because their pain does not hurt me, why do I protect myself from a future pain, when "the assumption that 'it is the same me even then' is false?"[21]

We can pause for a moment here to recognize that this argument appears to undercut many of Śāntideva's eloquent warnings earlier in the work, where for instance he very explicitly appealed to the hearer's desire to avoid pains to come in hell or in "our" future lives. He straightforwardly used our selfish fear about what would happen at the hour of our death or in our future lives as a spur to move in the right direction. But now he says there is no more reason to care about the future "me" than about other people and their fate.[22] If enlightened self-interest in ending my own suffering led me in the right direction, then the next step is to realize that I cannot actually draw a boundary around a limited amount of suffering as "mine."

> All sufferings are without an owner, because they are not different. They should be warded off simply because they are suffering. Why is any restriction made in this case?[23]

Compassion is a centerpiece of *Mahāyāna*, and we are now seeing how Śāntideva lays the foundation for this compassion. He raises the issue as an objection: "Much suffering comes from compassion, so why should one force it to arise?"[24] To "equalize self and others" in this first respect—taking ownership of all suffering, not just "mine"—appears simply to add to the total volume of suffering in the world. Mine just grew greater, and no one else's diminished. Compassion actually expands the scope of suffering from that limited in the circle of the "I" to that of many or all others, and so increases felt suffering.

But Śāntideva sees a systematic difference between this suffering and the mass of ignorance-induced pain. This is suffering based on wisdom (the unreality of selves) and knowingly induced for a liberating effect. It is helpful suffering as opposed to brute suffering.

> After seeing the suffering of the world, how can this suffering from com-
> passion be considered great? If the suffering of the many disappears
> because of the suffering of one, then a compassionate person should in-
> duce that suffering for his own sake and for the sake of others.[25]

His argument implicitly grants the point that, without wisdom, compassion does simply add to the suffering in the world, and that such suffering would be pointless. This, we might say, is the untenable mid-point of compassion for *some* beings.

But the compassion of *bodhicitta* is wise by definition. To arrive at an experience of unrestricted ownership of suffering is to grasp the task of the bodhisattva. To deliver all beings from suffering is really the only way that the problem can be posed once one has realized the nondistinction between their experiences and ours. There can be no single solution without a comprehensive one. Śāntideva gives an example from the *Jataka* tales. Supuṣpacanda, the Buddha, was a monk who foresaw that if he went and preached in a nearby kingdom, many would attain enlightenment, but he himself would die. He happily went and taught, caring only for the reduction in the total volume of suffering and with no regard to his own. He was brutally executed by an evil king and his body cut into pieces. The king then repented and joined the Buddhist community.[26] Such bodhisattvas will "dive into the Avīci hell like swans into a pool of lotuses."[27] Compared to this, "what is the use of sterile liberation?"[28] Here is a direct repudiation of other views of enlightenment, in which the focus is restricted to releasing only one mind-stream through an individual's practice.

The equalization of self with others is thus the foundation for the bodhisattva's attack on all suffering at once. That equalization can be cultivated with different meditative practices. One family of these practices works with our positive emotions. We can reflect on other beings from the perspective that, over a near infinite number of births, all of them must at some time have been our parents, our children, or other loved

ones: those for whose wellbeing we would be naturally disposed to sacrifice.[29] But Śāntideva now adds something distinctive, the exchange of
self and others. This is a practice that is explicitly built on the use of negative emotions. It is a meditation that seems to play with fire.

For that reason, one commentator stresses that it should not be ap-
proached without prior perfection of the equalizing meditations.[30] One
practices mentally changing places with people after one has largely dis-
lodged the assumption that they are truly "other." To put it another way,
the line that separates one mind from another is entirely arbitrary. The
equalizing insight erases the line and so paves the way to the exchanging one. Why shouldn't I be thinking "her" thoughts as well as "mine"?
"Bodhisattvas can use their vast powers to manipulate reality because
reality is inherently malleable" and "empty of intrinsic existence."[31] More
than an imaginative "as if," these constructions are reflective of the
true character of things.

If the first meditation takes others as also "I," taking their experiences
as continuous with mine, then a second meditation is somewhat the reverse: in it, I put myself in the place of the other to look back at myself as
"you." This looking is done in three modes: from the perspective of someone in much worse condition than I am in, from the perspective of
someone in a condition similar to mine, and from the perspective of someone in a condition much preferable to mine, all defined in terms of wealth,
health, reputation, power, and so on. The meditator is to emphasize the
negative potential in each of these connections. Śāntideva encourages
the reader to inhabit the envy, rivalry, and pride of these positions so
that one's empathy for those in all of these positions increases, and it becomes possible to include them in the scope of one's goodwill.

Śāntideva commends to the meditator the cultivation of the very negative emotions that are aroused in such unequal life circumstances, in
the belief that they can be turned to positive use.[32] His exposition focuses
on the valid complaints that others may have about us from their perspectives, fostering humility and self-criticism. But it also illustrates the
destructive effects that flow to others as the effect of their negative attitudes toward us, fostering sympathy rather than resentment toward them.
And since the position of the "I" in these cases is reversed, as we imagine
changing places, we benefit from effects on both ends, as it were. But
this depends on already loosening our connection to our "own" identity.
Unless the nonduality of experience has been realized, the practice of exchanging self and others may only reinforce the projection of distinct

individuals as real and leave us captive to the destructive power of the negative emotions it evokes.

Buddhism teaches that the self is only a nominal term, used to refer to a collection of conditioned causes and effects under the misapprehension that this collection has an existence of its own. One can deconstruct that self into its components. But Śāntideva here emphasizes another practical conclusion. Since "self" is an entirely constructed idea with no corresponding reality, there is no reason it cannot be completely reconstructed in a different way at the level of conventional truth. We can use other projected selves to fight our entrenched projected self. An egoistic "I" is just a habit, and one can train to replace it with a wandering "I" that breaks down the distinctions. This is just what he does in this chapter, first by "equalizing" or expanding what is included in the "I" and then by "exchanging" selves so that by "I" I mean someone else, and by "you" I mean my normal "self."[33] Many of the supernatural feats of bodhisattvas are the result of their ability to manipulate what looks like reality but is simply the interaction of mental objects. When the barriers between such supposed objects do not need to be observed, any number of phenomena is possible.

Śāntideva now reprises yet again the reasons we should not be attached to our conventional self. A reified self arouses fear and craving in us, and so becomes in fact a terrifying enemy, inflicting suffering.[34] Yet the same conceptual "thing," even when its impermanent character is not fully grasped, can pragmatically point us in the right direction, offering a selfish rationale for selflessness.

> The desire for self-aggrandizement leads to a miserable state of existence, low status, and stupidity. By transferring that same desire to someone else, one obtains a fortunate state of existence, respect and wisdom.[35]

Attachment to my self dictates that I should act with nonattachment.

> All those who are unhappy in this world are so as a result of their desire for their own happiness. All those who are happy in this world are so as a result of their desire for the happiness of others.[36]

There is, we may say, an especially beneficial heuristic role for other beings in the bodhisattva path. In "equalizing self and others," they are instrumental in leading toward realization of the nondifferentiated nature of suffering. "Exchanging self and others" can lead to the very practical help noted above, but it is also a kind of jujitsu in which conventional truth can be turned against itself. Though still at the level of conventional truth, the very same kind of desire directed to the wellbeing of others produces much better results than when directed to one's own wellbeing. The desire to aid the other's self is in one respect as deluded as the desire to aid my own self, but in another it is much closer to wisdom.

Now comes a very compressed verse:

> Take others—lower, higher, equal—as yourself, identify yourself as "other."
> Then without another thought, immerse yourself in envy, pride and rivalry.[37]

Another translation renders the last half of the verse "imagine envy and pride with a mind free from false notions!"[38] This looks on the face of it like an invitation to drink deeply of the poisons of negative emotion, which is why there is the qualification "free from false notions." These emotions can be put to good use when they are exercised from the counterintuitive standpoint of another "I." If there is no justifiable reason to regard the world from the perspective of a single person among all others (the equalizing conclusion), then I may as well regard what I call my "self" from the perspective of others rather than that of the normal "me" who identifies with this body among all others. Paradoxically, experiencing these negative emotions from the standpoint of others serves as an antidote that can extinguish those same emotions in my ordinary self.

In the verses that follow, there is a dramatic change in voice. First, Śāntideva imagines exchanging places with someone in a much lower station and speaks in that person's voice, while looking back at the "he" who is Śāntideva.

> He's the center of attention. I am nothing,
> And, unlike him, I'm poor, without possessions.
> Everyone looks up to him, despising me,
> All goes well for him; for me there's only bitterness.

> All I have is sweat and drudgery,
> While he's there, sitting at his ease.
> He's great, respected in the world,
> While I'm the underdog, a well-known nobody.[39]

Resentment and envy of the advantages of the better-off one then pass into complaint about living in helpless bondage to afflictions and the

heartlessness of the advantaged person who will not even stir to help another's need: "indifferent to the plight of living beings."[40]

Then, swiftly, in verse 147, the context changes. We are now dealing
with people on the same relative footing, striving for an advantage in the
realm of rivalry.

> That I might excel, outstripping him—
> Him, regarded as my peer and equal!
>
> By every means I'll advertise
> My gifts to all the world,
> Ensuring that his qualities
> Remain unknown, ignored by everyone.[41]

Śāntideva expresses the passion of competition, the desire to push all our
best gifts forward and conceal our faults, all the while trying to hide another's virtues and revel in their failings: "I will render him despicable,
the butt and laughingstock of everyone."[42]

And finally, in verse 151, Śāntideva has traded places with someone in
a dominant role. He now speaks from that position of power in the most
brutal way, looking down at his previous self as this "pitiful nonentity
[who] is trying to compete with me!"[43]

> Even if he does have something,
> I'm the one he's working for!
> He can keep enough just to survive,
> but with my strength I'll steal the rest away.
>
> I will wear his happiness away;
> I will always hurt and injure him.
> He's the one who in saṃsāra
> did me mischiefs by the hundred![44]

The meditation of positive emotions encourages us to think of all beings
as having been our mothers many times in the past. But here, that is
turned around—this one must have often harmed me over past births.
All the more reason for me to enjoy my power over him.

It is possible to read these as illustrations for three distinct exercises.
But it is also possible to read these passages as a dizzying itinerary in
which the same speaker explores the range of relations that they experience with others. These relations range from bitter resentment toward
those better off to fiery no-holds-barred competition with those on equal

footing, to the smug self-satisfaction of a supremely powerful figure. In all of these cases, the exchange reveals legitimate faults that others can find in us, regardless of our relative positions. And it also highlights the negative emotions that they may feel toward us, emotions that are profoundly destructive to their future wellbeing. These bring their own consequences and can make us feel pity for them rather than anger.[45]

Commentators prescribe these meditations as antidotes to be applied to specific negative emotions in ourselves.[46] The negative emotions that imagined others have toward us, such as jealousy, become effective means of self-critique: "Putting ourselves in the place of others is very helpful for seeing the faults of the egotistic 'I,' and we become deeply disgusted with it."[47] So when one is feeling pride in relation to others, imagine identifying with their resentment and see how very unappealing one appears. Pride dissipates, and only devotion to others' benefit seems likely to salvage any respect. When one feels intense rivalry, she must put herself in the place of her competitor and see the distortions and selfishness that are fostered by this process in the other person, so that she feels both repelled by her own behavior and aware of the bad fate that awaits her rival because of these emotions. If she feels bitter resentment to any who are better off, then she should imagine herself in the other person's place and give free rein to her worst suspicions about that person's motives. If the better-off person is as mean-spirited as she imagines, then he will not escape the terrible results.

This imaginative exercise leads to a whole new poetic vision of the bodhisattva's life. Starting at verse 155, Śāntideva addresses himself with exhortations on the full scope of this path. Commitment to the good of others is no abstract altruistic principle. It is animated by the same lively emotions as our misguided devotion to our own bodies, but is now distributed in a more universal way.

> Therefore, just as you formed a sense of self-identity with regard to the drops of blood and semen of others, contemplate others in the same way.[48]

As Śāntideva asks, "Why am I not jealous of myself?"[49] For the bodhisattva to be happy while others are not seems just as outrageous to the bodhisattva as to any resentful observer, for the bodhisattva identifies just as much with the observer's situation as with his own.

> Now for others you should spy on everything your body seems to have. Steal it, take it all away, and use it for the benefit of others.[50]

When others reproach the bodhisattva, even without grounds, the bodhisattva cannot help but agree with them, knowing that if she "had carried out this task earlier, this state deprived of the perfection and bliss of the Buddha would not have occurred."[51] One commentator says that when advanced bodhisattvas use this practice, when they picture changing places with someone "better off," they picture a more realized bodhisattva, who reproaches them with failings that they readily take to heart.[52]

This leads to the powerful vows expressed in the following passage:

> When others are at fault, I'll take
> and turn the blame upon myself,
> and all my sins, however slight,
> declare, and make them known to many.

> The fame of others I will magnify
> that it might thus outshine my own.
> Among them I will be as one who serves,
> my lowly labor for their benefit. . . .

> All the harm, in short that ego does
> to its advantage and to others' cost,
> may all of it descend upon itself,
> to its own hurt—to others' benefit.[53]

The bodhisattva intentionally takes a secondary place so that others may be regarded more highly. Śāntideva uses a telling example for his male audience when he commends as a model the behavior of a young bride— "modest, meek and restrained"—who must make her way as a subservient member of her new in-laws' family.[54]

This passage is the first time the bodhisattva is spoken of as taking the blame of others upon himself. As one commentator says, "Now, he will act like the Bodhisattvas of the past (who would take the place of guilty criminals about to be executed). When others are at fault, whether their crimes are great or small, he will take the blame upon himself."[55] Some translations limit the reference of this passage to the bodhisattva's own history: "In brief, whatever offense you have committed toward others for your own benefit, let it descend on yourself for the benefit of sentient beings."[56] The sense would be that one would take the emphasis off others' faults by focusing entirely on one's own. But another commentator notes that in this verse, Śāntideva repeats material found in the *Guru Puja,* in which the writer says, "May all the evil karma and obscuration of every being ripen on me, and bless me so that I might be capable of offering my virtues and happiness to them."[57] And this same idea is explicitly stated at the climax of the final chapter of the *Bodhicaryāvatāra*: "Whatever suffering there is for the world, may it all ripen upon me."[58]

The ambiguity over whether the bodhisattva actually takes on the failings of others must be understood in terms of the instruction and meditation described so far in this chapter. The separate ownership of suffering has just been deconstructed. If all suffering is equally the bodhisattva's, and alleviation of all suffering is the single task, then it follows that all of the depredations of "ego" in any form are likewise the bodhisattva's to rectify. And when a bodhisattva speaks of all the offenses he has committed, the "he" actually means all beings. An awakened one does not take up others' faults vicariously, in place of them, but through wisdom recognizes there was never any line that set them apart. They belong to no "one," or they belong to all beings. The bodhisattva has just trained in identifying with all beings. That identification includes their suffering, and so also in some way it means identifying with their karmic activities, the faults, that occasioned that suffering. If there is no line between beings, then it would seem that there is no way to keep karmic acts and consequences in separate lanes corresponding to different people.

Both Śāntideva and the commentators approach this question of karma rather gingerly. They otherwise insist that karma is an inviolable cause-and-effect process. Selves are insubstantial, more insubstantial than this cause-and-effect process. How karmic effects are distributed to the "one" who set them in motion is already something of a mystery, when the next life in which those effects are experienced belongs to a different "one." But this allocation question is in principle no different from the distribution of the results of my action a moment ago to the new "me" of this moment. It is an even deeper mystery how a bodhisattva could ask all karma to ripen on himself. This tension, exquisitely heightened at this point, will be addressed in a new way at the beginning of Chapter 9, with the teaching of the two truths.

In the final part of Chapter 8, Śāntideva returns to the kind of exhortations that opened the chapter. From verse 167 to 173, he addresses his own mind—the egoistic "I" that has been steadily undermined in the meditations for equalizing and exchanging self—with an ultimatum.

Now give up this hope: "Still, I have my own self-interest!" Unconcerned as you are with much distress, I have sold you to others.[59]

The self should exist now only as a servant of others. Śāntideva presents this internal colloquy vividly, raising the question of the relation between his own mind, which he addresses as "you" here, and the "I" that is doing the speaking: "I shall destroy you, the servant of your own self-interest."[60] His consciousness seems to be inhabited both by a self constructed in ignorant attachment and by another "I" who can speak from a wider wisdom.

Śāntideva returns also to the question of the body, which was so extensively addressed at the start of the chapter. Verse 174 through verse 183 reviews again the futility of identification with the body: "Of what use is this contrivance to me, whether it is dead or alive?"[61] He ends, however, with a newly balanced conclusion:

> Therefore, with indifference I have given up my body for the benefit of the world. Hence, although it has many faults, I keep it as an instrument for that task.[62]

Since the body is no longer simply the tool of self-interest and a deluded mind, it has an instrumental value, and the contempt expressed for it earlier is significantly qualified.

Perfection of Wisdom

Chapter 9 stands out in the *Bodhicaryāvatāra* for several reasons. Although Śāntideva's style is compressed throughout, in this chapter the compression has less to do with poetic, first-person expression and more to do with shorthand for complex intellectual arguments. The content becomes more explicitly sectarian, presenting alternative views and refuting them. This compression has invited much editorial comment, and significant portions of that comment may have been assimilated in the canonical text over time.[63] Among Buddhist readers and commentators, the earlier chapters of the *Bodhicaryāvatāra* are famous for their eloquence and style, but not for the novelty of their ideas, with the exception of the practice of exchanging self and others, which is specially identified with Śāntideva, though it does not originate with him. But Chapter 9 plunges us into disagreements, particularly disagreements among Buddhists, and for that reason it has been a focus of interpretation. The chapter stands out above all because it is presented as the key to all that has come before, both its basis and its goal.

The chapter opens with this:

> The Sage taught this entire system for the sake of wisdom. Therefore, with the desire to ward off suffering, one should develop wisdom. This truth is recognized as being of two kinds: conventional and ultimate. Ultimate reality is beyond the scope of the intellect. The intellect is called conventional reality. In the light of this, people are seen to be of two types: the contemplative and the ordinary person. The ordinary folks are superseded by the contemplatives.[64]

The *Bodhicaryāvatāra* has vividly attacked assumptions that underlie our conventional outlook on the world, with the standard *Mahāyāna* appeal to the "perfection of wisdom." But in contrast to the incoherent and unsatisfactory perspectives that have been punctured, the exact nature of the truth about the actual state of things has been left undefined. There is wisdom that may allow us to attain better rebirth, and even further Buddhist wisdom that may allow us to escape rebirth and suffering entirely. But the bodhisattva seeks a perfect wisdom that is adequate for the liberation of all beings and aims to act in every instance in accordance with that wisdom.

The general term for this perfect wisdom or ultimate truth in *Mahāyāna* is "emptiness." The basic Buddhist teaching is that the world is not as it appears to us, and specifically that there is no self as it appears to us. The no-self doctrine deconstructs the central features of what appears. It is less clear about what, if anything, remains when we take away the false appearance. Among Buddhists, historically, there have been realist schools of thought that held that there are in fact truly existing "things" or *dharmas*, which in various conditioned relations give rise to the appearance of other, illusory things such as a self.[65] Selves can be analyzed away into nothing but momentary conjunctions of these things, meaning that the self does not exist in reality but only in appearance. Over time, this mode of analysis—the search for the really existent—was carried out with wider scope and rigor.[66] Śāntideva belongs to the Madhyamaka school, which took this analysis to what is arguably its maximal point, arguing that all apparent realities were empty, and that its understanding of emptiness trumped all others. So Chapter 9 is an exposition of true wisdom, the true wisdom being *Mahāyāna* emptiness,

and the true form of *Mahāyāna* emptiness being the Madhyamaka interpretation of it.

If we have come to this point in the book (and presumably in the practices that it has presented), then we now learn a new way to look at what
we have seen so far. There are two kinds of truth. Conventional truth
applies to the world projected through our fundamental misapprehensions: selves and minds and objects. So far in the *Bodhicaryāvatāra*,
Śāntideva has been openly and heavily trading in this truth with his
readers. In each of the many times he has appealed to us to recognize
that our indifference to wisdom is sending us to endless rounds of suffering in hell, he has been appealing to our selfish identification with
our bodies and our egoistic desire to avoid pain. His logic makes good
conventional sense to someone who sees the world in a conventional way.
The normal world is what is perceived "by the conceptual, dualistic
intelligence."[67] Ultimate truth is insight into the actual condition of the
world. When Śāntideva says that ultimate truth is beyond the scope of
intellect, he means that it is not something that can be known by mind as
we conventionally understand it.[68]

In Chapter 8, Śāntideva instructed us in a form of contemplation intended to help us project a sense of self that extended no less to other
people than to our own body and mind. In one sense, this was an enormous step beyond dualistic perceptions. In another sense, it only recon-
figured the same elements of ignorance. Instead of one puny body, my
"I" now looks out from the perspective of millions of them. The equalizing of self and other is a true insight into the nature of things, framed
in the terms of the conventional world. It is a higher truth than the belief in my individual self, and it was presented in Chapter 8 as if it were
the ultimate truth. But now we are being told explicitly that it is not.

Chapter 8 was a pinnacle of the work so far, but from the standpoint
of perfect wisdom, we now see it in a different perspective. Exchanging
self and other and equalizing self and other were presented by Śāntideva
as straightforward teaching of the truth of things. But in the light of
Chapter 9, we see that both still make unwarranted assumptions.
Śāntideva likens the relation of our individual self and the parts of our
body to a more adequate projection in which all beings are parts of one
body, with the consciousness of an "I" belonging no more to any one than
another. We care about the pain of a finger or a toe because we identify
these parts as components in a constructed concept, our "body," that we
further identify with another projection, that of my "self." Śāntideva

argues that it is illogical to care for ourselves and not for others, since there is no way to distinguish this circle of a small body and a small self from a large circle with a much larger body (of which all individuals are parts) and a kind of universal self. The power of his image was the incongruity of treating the two similar cases in such contrary ways: our solicitude for our own body and our indifference to the pains of others. But there was an obvious trailing thread in this picture, the fact that *both* perspectives are constructions, resting on impermanent and conditioned elements, whose ultimate status is questionable. This is what Chapter 9 takes up.

The idea of two truths appears as early as the Lotus Sutra. On the one hand, it answers the question of how the newly propagated perfection of wisdom teachings relate to the prior formulations of the Buddha's message. On the other hand, it prescribes an ongoing mode of intellectual practice. If the Buddha's enlightened knowledge allowed him to tailor his teaching to the needs of his hearers, then this explained why his highest wisdom teaching had been given only to some. And it also provided a way to understand all the varying Buddhist and non-Buddhist schools of thought and practice as aspects of one vehicle that was fitted to serve and manifest the same *dharma* in terms accessible to people in different stages of knowledge. There are ways to teach and practice wisdom within the unawakened assumptions of hearers. There are ways that assume higher levels of attainment. And there are those that are only possible for an omniscient enlightened one. Realized bodhisattvas can and do utilize all of these as needed. Those are the skillful means that are the hallmark of the bodhisattva's ability to assist other beings where they find them.

So, though the two-truths idea is both a basis for Buddhist ecumenicity and a ground for flexibility in practice, it is ironically also a primary point of conflict. The line between conventional and ultimate truth is drawn differently as groups define the distinctive ultimate truth differently. After opening Chapter 9 with the statement about the two truths, Śāntideva notes that there are two kinds of people: ordinary people who take the world that they perceive as real, and those with higher insight. Buddhists, and some others, recognize that the world is not as it appears, and so are not ordinary in that respect. But they differ among themselves about the nature of the higher insight. So Śāntideva immediately proceeds to refute alternative views and to defend his own.

Despite the radical and therapeutic analysis of the insubstantiality of things that Śāntideva has carried out in earlier chapters, deconstructing the way in which things seem, he is acutely aware that at the final moment the meaning and purpose of the entire process can go in dramatically different directions. Is the moral of this story that underneath all the unreal and impermanent beings, there is actually one eternal and self-existent being, a creator being or an all-encompassing Brahman? Or underneath all the falsely constructed objects, is there some primordially existing stuff or material? These are options advanced by Hindus and others in Śāntideva's Indian context. He refutes them all in Chapter 9, including, as we will see, the idea of a creator God.

He spends a few verses (5–15) dealing with the objection of Buddhist realists.[69] The general thrust of the realist arguments is that without some underlying reality, there would be no basis for causality, karma, and enlightenment itself. All of the Buddhist teachings would be on the same level as any other illusion: there is nothing that they could be right *about*. For example, no negative karma could come from harming another being, since those beings have nothing real about them. Śāntideva responds that no karma attaches to slaying a fictional character, a kind of second-order illusion, because that is not a sentient being. But it does attach to actions with beings, who are first-order illusions, as it were, and who experience suffering. Cause and effect operate on the same plane, so "slaying an illusion-like sentient being will definitely accrue illusion-like negative karma,"[70] which will lead to illusion-like hells or heavens. Until the very root of the perception of intrinsic existence is cut, the functional reality of this world cannot be denied. Another realist objection is that if there is no objective basis for our normal world, then *nirvāṇa* and *saṃsāra* would be literally the same thing, when in fact *nirvāṇa* is a different state, one which is outside the world that supports rebirth. Śāntideva responds that this is a mistake. The realist Buddhists only know a lower form of *nirvāṇa* which is the cessation of suffering (this is the reason they see *nirvāṇa* as some other place than *saṃsāra*). But the higher *nirvāṇa* is simply the emptiness that is always the case.

While Madhyamaka in one sense advocates a radical reading of emptiness, it self-describes as a middle way between the extremes of absolutism and nihilism. Absolutism asserts the existence of some permanent reality, an eternal being or primal substance. Nihilism completely rejects the reality of the conventional world. As commentator Kunzang Pelden puts it, "to deny the existence of past and future lives and the karmic law of cause and effect is what we refer to as nihilism."[71] The Dalai Lama, who belongs to the same Madhyamaka tradition as Śāntideva, observes that one of the most difficult points in its philosophy is "maintaining the reality of the world of conventional truth following the negation of the intrinsic existence of all phenomena."[72]

The Dalai Lama continues: "Relative truth is what is perceived by the conceptual, dualistic intelligence."[73] In fact, we might say that the intellect is itself a relative truth, not only because it is perceived in these terms but also because it does all its perceiving in these terms. Ultimate truth, then, is either not perceivable and knowable at all, or knowable only by some other kind of intelligence.[74] The two truths are liable to this same examination. Do they belong to relative truth or ultimate truth? The system of two truths is taught "solely for didactic purposes, as an entry to the path. On the ultimate level the division into two truths has no place."[75] The distinction between conventional and ultimate truth is not itself ultimate.[76]

Śāntideva then turns to a competing Buddhist school—Yogācāra—that will be his primary foil in expounding the wisdom of emptiness through the rest of Chapter 9.[77] Starting at verse 15, Śāntideva first summarizes and critiques the Yogācāra view (15–39) and outlines the contrasting Madhyamaka view of emptiness (44–59), and then he further specifies the distinction by considering the emptiness of the self (60–77) and the emptiness of phenomena (78–105) as well as by responding to some objections (106–15). Finally, he offers a summary statement on emptiness (116–50) and a poetic meditation on the benefits of meditating on emptiness (151–67).

Madhyamaka and Yogācāra agree that ultimate wisdom is emptiness. And the arguments that Śāntideva made against the realists are ones that the two schools agree on. However, the two do not agree in their explanations of emptiness. The Yogācāra view is that all beings and objects can be analyzed to show that there is no self-subsistent or objective reality there. They are all empty of such being, and their nature is described by the terms of dependent origination, one conditioned phenomenon dependent on another, with no ontological stopping point. However, the momentary and impermanent character of these appearances is all directly experienced by us. That experience is a flow of momentary perceptions and sense data. This flow is called the dependent nature of things. These phenomena actually exist and are the reference point for both misperception and true understanding. This flow is what is happening in our mind, or, more precisely, we could say that this *is* our mind, insofar as there is any phenomenal reality to it.[78]

Upon this one dependent nature or aspect, two other views may be superimposed. These are not separate or additional realities, but ways of apprehending the dependent nature. One is the constructed or conceptualized aspect, in which through ignorance we project onto this flux of phenomena the existence of actual objects and selves. This is the world as we conventionally see it. The other aspect is the perfected nature. This is the same underlying dependent nature seen as it is in its suchness, the raw flow and flux of impermanent arising, without any of the falsely projected borders dividing it into things or beings. It is seen and experienced simply *as* flux, empty of any assumptions.

We can see the way in which Yogācāra upholds the basic *Mahāyāna* conviction that *saṃsāra* is no different from *nirvāṇa*. The underlying given, the constant flow of impermanent phenomena, is the basis both for the world that is construed in ignorance, which produces suffering and rebirth, and the insight that realizes enlightenment. Awakening is seeing this flow as it actually is. When our minds do that, they experience the nonduality of that flow itself, and so the "I" of a self that is projected onto that phenomena disappears. The Yogācāra view is also called "mind only," since to the question of the way that things actually are, its answer is that all that truly is has the nature of mind or appears in our minds. But neither *my* mind nor any individual mind is real. That is projection, part of the conceptualized aspect of things. The Dalai Lama speaks of an "appearing object" and a "referent object," the first being what we experience phenomenally and the second what we project to be "behind" that experience.[79] Yogācāra holds that for all appearing objects, there is only one, actual referent—the dependent nature or immediate flow of experience. All things are empty of any reference point but this dependent nature. However, true perception of the dependent nature is not empty in that same sense, since it sees this conditioned flow for exactly what it actually is.[80]

To return to the practices of equalizing and exchanging selves for a moment, the Yogācāra view would say that this way of breaking down the distinctions between beings trades in constructed images of distinct selves and, to that extent, accepts conventional views. Yet it is based on something that is objectively true: the stream of experience out of which individual "I"s are constructed is in fact one, undivided flow of phenomena. That is the underlying truth to which the equalizing of selves corresponds. But to Śāntideva and his school, this does not go far enough, for something has been exempted from the universal emptiness insight.

That critique must be applied consistently to the Yogācāra dependent-nature mind, as to all else.[81] What Śāntideva is affirming is not just the emptiness of beings but the emptiness of phenomena.

We have mentioned already the somewhat telegraphic form in which Śāntideva presents the arguments. This often leaves room for a range of variant specifications of a particular point by translators and commenters. Interpreters may not always agree which side of the argument a verse or part of a verse belongs to.[82] So it is worthwhile to sample the nature of the argument. Śāntideva considers a series of Yogācāra contentions and responds to them. Yogācāra holds that everything other than the flow of consciousness in the mind is merely a projected illusion that is occasioned by that flow but empty of any actual existence. The mind, the flow itself, however, is not an illusion in the same way. Our "selves" are mistaken projections on this flow, but the flow is actually there.

Śāntideva counters that for Madhyamaka, the mind is an illusion in exactly the same way that all other phenomena are. His opponents then object that if the mind and its objects are all similar illusions, then what is doing the thinking that reaches this conclusion?

> If the mind itself is illusion, then what is perceived by what?
> The Protector of the World stated that the mind does not perceive the mind.
> Just as a sword cannot cut itself, so it is with the mind.[83]

Yogācāra can argue that it is the dependent nature of the mind itself that lies behind these illusions. But this gives rise to Śāntideva's response in the second half of the verse, objecting that this would mean the (illusory) object known by the mind is in the mind itself. But he claims that this is impossible: the mind cannot know itself any more than a knife can cut itself.

The Yogācāra view is that our cognition of conceptual objects is intrinsically dualistic because it attributes to them an illusory existence. But our cognition of mind itself is less illusory in that there is actually dependent nature as a referent, and in principle a nondual realization of that dependent nature is possible. This in fact gives us a concrete picture of enlightenment. It is the nondual consciousness that accurately perceives the nondual flow that is the nature of things. Yogācāra can argue that if the mind cannot know itself, then we cannot explain memory: we could not recall an experience of our mind if it did not take place in the mind to begin with.[84]

If self-cognizing awareness does not exist, how is consciousness recalled? Recollection comes from its relation to something else that was experienced, like a rat's poison.[85]

The first line states the Yogācāra argument, and the second line gives Śāntideva's response. He contends that memory is not the mind's knowledge of its own contents but essentially an inference about the past, "like a rat's poison." The reference is to an analogy in which a sleeping animal is bitten by a rat. When the animal wakes up, the inflamed site makes it aware that something had happened that it did not record at the time. One infers the past from its present effects, rather than by looking through files of stored experiences. Yogācāra contends that conditioned existence must have something real as the basis of its deceptive appearance—"that is, i.e., a nondual, truly existent consciousness."[86] Śāntideva objects that something that does not exist does not need to depend on something that does, and if the nondual mind already exists, then "all beings would be *Tathāgatas* [Buddhas]" already.[87]

Emptiness necessarily includes a negation, but Madhyamaka and Yogācāra disagree on the kind of negation. Buddhist philosophy recognizes two types, simple and complex.[88] Madhyamaka opts for the first, which states the absence—in this case, the absence of intrinsic existence. Yogācāra opts for the second, which states the absence (also the absence of intrinsic existence) by means of the implied reality of something else. So "a treeless plain" rules out trees at the same time that it recognizes something else. To refer to "an elderly fat man who never eats at night" strongly implies by its negation a complementary affirmation: he must eat during the day.[89] For Madhyamaka, there is no "something else." When one is enlightened, one grasps the mode of existence of all supposed entities, the mode of emptiness. The ultimate state is a "state of awareness that explores the fundamental mode of existence of entities."[90] That awareness is simply the awareness of emptiness in all possible objects of analysis, including the mind that has this awareness. The whole point is to resist any implication that there is something that this awareness rests upon. But for Yogācāra, this negation must rest upon the assumed presence of something that is wrongly thought to have intrinsic being but rightly thought to be impermanent, nondual, and beginningless.

Śāntideva now embarks on a defense of the Madhyamaka view of emptiness, not simply as the final logical step in a progression that might lead through other schools of thought and practice, but as a necessary framework all along the way. Other paths will lead to dead ends and false ultimates, types of *nirvāṇa* mistakenly taken as final. This is true of Yogācāra, even though it claims to be strongly defending the truth of "emptiness." For Yogācāra, true mind, as opposed to illusory mind and its "self," is empty of all dualistic perception, of all reification of its contents. It simply reflects like a mirror the reality of an ongoing flux of experience that itself has no fixed, intrinsic nature. But from Śāntideva's perspective, this makes emptiness too much like a thing itself, an absolute reality or underlying reference point. It runs the danger of "reifying emptiness itself,"[91] whereas the hope is that "by training in the view that all lacks entity, this view itself will also disappear."[92]

Even the teaching of emptiness is empty. Having grasped the very counterintuitive nonexistence of things, one must realize that nonexistence is itself a constructed and projected idea. We need to let go of it as a true description, without doubling back to non-nonexistence as a simple binary return to the existence of things (two negatives making a positive). As Śāntideva puts it, "When neither an entity nor a nonentity remains before the mind, then since there is no other possibility, having no objects, it becomes calm."[93]

He anticipates the clear objection that this stilling of all conceptual activity must mean that the intention of working for the benefit of other beings likewise cannot be formulated. This seems to blow up the entire bodhisattva enterprise. Śāntideva then gives the example of a charmer against poisons who dies after consecrating a shrine, and the shrine continues healing peoples' poisons. Just so, worship offered to Buddhas brings merit whether or not the Buddha is present or has passed into *nirvāṇa*. Although all the bodhisattva's "labors and dualistic mental activity now completely subside, they nevertheless effect the temporary and ultimate welfare of other beings."[94]

At this point, Śāntideva recognizes a blunt challenge to this whole line of approach: "Liberation comes from understanding the [Four Noble] Truths, so what is the point of perceiving emptiness?"[95] Here is the whole weight of agreed Buddhist tradition, complaining that a new view is being substituted for its basic truths. Śāntideva does not equivocate: perceiving emptiness is essential "because a scripture states that there is no Awakening without this path."[96] This appeal to scripture leads into a digression to argue over the authority of *Mahāyāna* texts, texts which not all Buddhists would accept as definitive.

According to our commentators, Śāntideva is making a dramatic claim. He is saying not just that the bodhisattva path is a higher form of enlightenment because it serves the benefit of other beings. He is saying that "the realization of impermanence and the other aspects of the four truths are not in fact the most important aspects of the path."[97] No form of enlightenment as true delivery from rebirth and suffering is possible without the right understanding of emptiness: "Without the view of emptiness as it is revealed in the *Mahāyāna* sutras, it is impossible to obtain any of the three states of awakening."[98] People may attain profound non-conceptual states in meditation, but those will eventually pass.[99]

> The mind that has not realized voidness,
> May be halted, but will once again arise,
> Just as from a non-perceptual absorption.
> Therefore, one must train in emptiness.[100]

We are not just talking about temporary states in meditation. People might attain release from gross forms of suffering and rebirth, might seem to have attained enlightenment, but still remain subject to more subtle defilements. They could remain in a kind of *saṃsāra* in which a "continuum of subtle aggregates is not severed," because they have not meditated, to the point of "perfect realization, on the No-Self of phenomena; and therefore they have not eradicated the extremely subtle defilements that are to be abandoned."[101] They "come to rest for a time in the expanse of cessation—only to manifest and take birth again later on."[102] It seems that even these great attainers may not be aware of their own bondage to this subtle form of grasping at the wisp of true existence.[103] This means they are still subject to "subtle mental afflictions" that produce suffering, though this suffering is of such an exquisitely refined nature that it registers only for the supremely wise.[104]

The supreme wisdom of emptiness shines brighter and brighter as the one necessary truth, without which even the most classic Buddhist teachings are inadequate to truly free us from the realm of *saṃsāra*. Śāntideva now turns to expound this supreme Madhyamaka view of emptiness. What sets it apart is that it expounds both the selflessness of persons, which other schools of Buddhism do as well, and the full selflessness of phenomena.[105] There are subtle kinds of grasping at some sort of actual reality that must be rooted out. We have seen already how for Śāntideva, the Yogācāra *arhat*s fail to recognize the full emptiness of phenomena.

They hold that there is a stream of consciousness continuum underlying our false sense of self and objects—an awareness of phenomena as phenomena which can be purified into an enlightened nondual awareness. From the Yogācāra perspective, the self's existence has been thoroughly negated. But for Śāntideva their teaching still affirms, at some remove, a referent for the self. Its phenomena are not completely empty. And that is a serious taint.

Back to the Bodhisattva

We have for some time lost explicit sight of the bodhisattva, and now Śāntideva reconnects this discussion of emptiness with that role.

> To linger and abide within *samsāra*,
> Freed from every craving and from every fear,
> In order to achieve the good of those who ignorantly suffer:
> Such is the fruit that emptiness will bear.[106]

A bodhisattva will remain free from both "the extreme of cyclic existence and the extreme of the solitary peace of *nirvāna*."[107] So long as there is some basis in reality for distinguishing these two, this paradoxical condition seems impossible. That is why this apparently abstruse philosophical point is important: it is the wisdom basis for the bodhisattva realization.

Having appraised the Yogācāra view of emptiness and explored the contrasting Madhyamaka position, in verses 60 through 77 Śāntideva amplifies the identityless nature of the self, arguing that this is simply an effective "unfindablity." Selflessness is not the case of something being taken for something else. "Self" is an empty category. Seeking the self is like deconstructing the trunk of a banana tree, which proves to be made of onion-like peels all the way down to nothing. This argument leads to two extraordinary verses that express the encompassing paradox in the *Bodhicaryāvatāra*.

> [Question] If no sentient being exists, for whom is there compassion?
> [Answer] For one who is imagined through delusion, which is accepted for the sake of the task.
> [Question] If there is no sentient being, whose is the task?
> [Answer] True. The effort, too, is due to delusion. Nevertheless, in order to alleviate suffering, delusion with regard to one's task is not averted.[108]

The entire bodhisattva path is built around a dynamic—compassion for others—that realization of the path deconstructs. If selflessness is the radical truth that Śāntideva says it is, then it follows that the "other beings" whom the bodhisattva vows to liberate are illusions. And the bodhisattva who makes the vow, insofar as she is a "self" that does so, is also an illusion. Kunzang Pelden says that not only are these reference-point selves without existence, but "neither, on the ultimate level, is there any difference between going beyond suffering and not doing so."[109]

But Śāntideva tells us that these delusions are to be accepted, for the sake of the task of alleviating suffering. This is certainly intelligible from the perspective of the departure point of aspirational *bodhicitta*: we are unable to avoid seeing the world in false terms, and these particular false terms are the most useful on which to build practice. But the paradox is more extreme in the case of realized bodhisattvas, and gives rise to extensive questioning about the extent to which such bodhisattvas accommodate themselves to a world of ignorance with which it would seem that they could have no part. Rebirth is a simple example. Bodhisattvas take rebirth, though in principle they have eliminated all of the causal basis for it.

Wisdom is the sixth and highest of the bodhisattva perfections. And wisdom casts a new light on the bodhisattva vow with which the *Bodhicaryāvatāra* began, which led to a "strange inversion by which compassion no longer exists for the sake of beings, but beings are regarded as existing for the sake of the compassion that the Bodhisattva needs to perfect."[110] Compassion is based on a confusion, as is our idea of a self, and it might seem that both should be equally rejected. But one should cultivate the confusion of compassion because it pacifies suffering, and one should dispel the confusion of a self because it multiplies the causes of suffering.[111] Or perhaps we might say that compassion and other beings are two sides of the same illusion, the compassion felt by an illusory self in regard to illusory others.

We are now beginning to grasp the true wonder of the bodhisattva's achievement. It is not an incremental cultivation of virtues but a simultaneous habitation of the worlds of wisdom and appearance, fully realizing the first and fully present in the second: "In this way, due to wisdom one does not abide in the cycle of existence, and due to compassion one does not abide in tranquility [i.e., *nirvāṇa*]."[112] Even a hint of how this might be possible requires a profound understanding of the way things are, one that is not just counterintuitive to non-Buddhists but accessible only to the highest reaches of Buddhist insight. At the very least, we can grasp now why the idea of a bodhisattva who postpones her own attainment of *nirvāṇa* for the sake of helping others may be conventionally apt but is a far-from-adequate description.

To specify this understanding of emptiness further, Śāntideva will turn from the emptiness of selves to the emptiness of phenomena. But before we follow him, we should pause to recognize that part of the intelligibility of the paradox that we have just described is a return to the conventional world, the realm of the lower of the two truths. In the section of Chapter 9 following verse 77, Śāntideva devotes significant space to objections that the deconstruction of conventional truth leads to an untenable situation in which one cannot make the normal discriminations between reality and illusion that we need for ordinary life. He counters these objections by arguing that it is possible and necessary to distinguish between dreams, illusion, and error on one hand and valid, if conditioned, truth on the other. A major part of Śāntideva's exposition of true emptiness is, ironically, a retrieval of conventional existence. We saw earlier that the Dalai Lama stressed that this was one of the most difficult balances in the Madhyamaka perspective. At the end of the path of analyzing the emptiness of every phenomena, and of resisting the reification of emptiness itself, and of turning aside from a simple nondualistic meditative absorption, where does one arrive?

The conventional world around us has not disappeared. To the contrary, one now sees with a clarity impossible before that it is no less or more empty than any other kind of phenomena. There is nothing to contrast it with. Emptiness might be thought to be an ultimate truth, but "when we take emptiness itself as the object of an ultimate analysis, emptiness becomes a conventional truth."[113] We see that it "shifts its position" from being the indicator of a lack of intrinsic being in other objects, to being an idea that is itself devoid of intrinsic being. The maxim "Let the antidote liberate itself" reflects the wisdom that deconstructs the very path that it follows.[114]

"Intrinsic existence," that which emptiness opposes, is a peculiar thing. The Dalai Lama says that mental obscurations and suffering actually do exist at the level of conventional truth. But intrinsic existence is "not something that existed in the past that, through practice and meditation, can be removed. It never existed to begin with."[115] It is a kind of double negative, a projection on a projection. We think that an object, the "self," is there amid various conditioned elements, when there is nothing that corresponds to that supposed object. But we additionally think that the self has a mode of existence, an intrinsic mode, such that it would be there independent of the conditions. This is an additional mistake. It is an erroneous belief about a fiction. To negate intrinsic existence is not to reject the appearances before us, but to reject a mode that we attribute to that appearance, a mode of being. So the Dalai Lama says that what we negate about our "I" is not the focal consciousness that we are in fact using as we speak about it, but the "object we grasp as intrinsically existent."[116]

A large section of Chapter 9, verses 116 through 150, is devoted to a series of complicated arguments that refute inherent existence. The first one, the so-called "diamond splinters" argument, is of interest to us because it directly addresses the case of God, or Ishvara.[117] This argument refutes intrinsic existence via a critique of causation. If there were any actual existents, then they would have to originate in one of four ways: "from themselves, from another, from both or from no cause at all."[118] Each of these is shown to be impossible, and thus there are no such existents. In what way can God be without cause, but an actual cause of other effects? In what way can a single, permanent existence be the cause of multiple, impermanent effects? In both instances, Śāntideva argues, there is an unbridgeable logical divide. A causal connection between God and the many parts of the world would simply mean that God is multiple and changeable, not divine. A truly permanent God would by definition not be the cause of anything. In any event, all the components of the conditioned world already have causes in other conditioned phenomena. There is nothing left for God to make.

The conditioned and material aggregates (*skandas*) are beginningless. At the purely physical level, this causal succession proceeds without any karmic impetus, each moment the necessary product of its preceding moment. Pure consciousness, "as far as its basic nature of luminosity and awareness is concerned, is beginningless," as well.[119] The actions of sentient beings and karma are superimposed on this basic changeless landscape, resulting in the historical emergence of experiences of joy and pain and what we regard as "normal" human consciousness.[120]

The discussion of the emptiness of phenomena is important, the Dalai Lama says, because Madhyamaka thought does not rest only on the critical deconstruction of inherent existence (which has been stressed in the discussion of selflessness). That is the truth of the nondiscoverability of true existence. It rests also on an active account of the way things *do* exist: dependent origination. Here we might find a clarification of the point above in which we identified Madhyamaka with simple negation. Things are said to be devoid of intrinsic existence not only because the search for such existence comes up empty, but also because the actual mode of their existence is discovered: "Things and events are said to be absent of inherent or intrinsic existence because *they exist only in dependence on other factors. This is the real premise.*"[121]

Dependent origination, like no-self, is a classic Buddhist teaching. Śāntideva is out to show that its wisdom also needs perfecting with the fullness of the understanding of emptiness. All phenomena or things are fabricated, composed of other phenomena or things that are likewise fabricated, leaning against each other like a house of cards. This dependence comes in three types: dependence on causes and conditions, dependence on parts, and dependence on conceptual designation. Trees exist because of other trees, seeds, water, sun, and so on. And each of these depends likewise on other sets of causes and conditions. In a second sense, we could say trees depend on the parts that make them up—leaves, sap, bark, trunk, roots. There is no tree separate from the collection of these things: it is no additional thing or being distinct from that collection. And, in a third sense, we can say that "tree" is dependent on the conceptualizing mind that applies this label to phenomena. The way that things don't exist (i.e., by possessing their own intrinsic being) and the way that they do (i.e., by arising from dependent origination) both point in the same negative direction. In every case, we find the same emptiness that is characteristic of all phenomena, including the mind and self. It is Śāntideva's contention that no other Buddhist approach threads the needle between nihilism and absolutism while evenhandedly maintaining the universal nature of emptiness. In his view, Buddhist realists or members of the Yogācāra school make exceptions.

The peak of the analysis of phenomena is to turn that analysis on emptiness itself. Śāntideva uses an analogy.

> Thus, when in a dream, a child has died,
> The state of mind that thinks he is no more
> Will overwhelm the thought that he was living.
> And yet, both thoughts are equally deceptive.[122]

Similarly, emptiness is the truth of phenomena, but "when we take emptiness itself as the object of an ultimate analysis, emptiness becomes a conventional truth."[123] The end point of this reflection is this conclusion:

Thus there is no being,
Likewise no cessation.
Therefore beings, each and every one,
Are unborn and are never ceasing.[124]

Thus, "the mind, having emptiness as its ultimate nature, abides in the state of natural *nirvāna*."[125] This natural *nirvāna* or "Buddha nature" is the ground of great hope, since beings "abide in natural *nirvāna* and are therefore beyond true suffering."[126] We can see now where Śāntideva can ground the passing reference in Chapter 7 to insects and worms as bound for liberation. Since emptiness is the character of all phenomena and is also the nature of enlightenment, all beings can become Buddhas. Hence, the bodhisattva path is not the special task of a few heroes but is the destiny of every being.

At every step, Śāntideva has pressed the bodhisattva tension to a new depth. The bodhisattva path, which is set off from other Buddhist readings of the *dharma* by its compassion for all beings, regards both the compassion and the beings as conceptual fabrications. The bodhisattva accepts these illusions for the sake of relieving the suffering of beings. So it is even more striking that we have just seen that beings are already, in an ultimate sense, "beyond true suffering." True suffering, presumably, would be based on some truly existent cause. But there is no such thing, so all actual suffering is empty, as all phenomena are. Furthermore, enlightenment and *samsāra* are the same "with regard to the fact that both are devoid of intrinsic existence."[127] We can understand why one scholar summarized his treatment of this argument under the heading "How Śāntideva destroyed the bodhisattva path."[128] It would seem that we are being taught that bodhisattvas (who aren't actually there) have compassion on illusory beings, for the relief of pains (that have no owners) in order that all may attain a *nirvāna* that is no different from non-*nirvāna*.

One of the striking features of the *Bodhicaryāvatāra* is that a reader rarely formulates an objection to the seeming incoherence here before Śāntideva has stated it in pithy form himself. And he makes an impressive case that these problems cannot be met with half measures. Only a strong reading of emptiness will do to meet these objections. If to be enlightened meant to inhabit a different level of reality, as with an "abiding *nirvāna*," then the bodhisattva would be caught shuttling between there and the world of suffering beings. But with the strong reading of emptiness, we can see that the world of convention and the world of wisdom, both of which the bodhisattva "inhabits," are not so different. That is, the difference between them is not based in anything that is ultimately real. The kind of existence that the ordinary world lacks is also lacking in the enlightenment world, even Buddhas are empty.[129] This truth is only accessible to those with the most profound wisdom who, unimpeded by false views, are therefore able to function in both realms in a way that would otherwise be inconceivable.

The bodhisattva has become a Buddha. That is the culmination of the path. But true Buddhahood maintains the bodhisattva commitment. The question remains as to how something can be "entirely free from the conditions out of which the phenomenal world is generated, and yet be pervasively operative in that world."[130] As we have seen above, this would seem to flatly contradict the third noble truth: deliverance from *saṃsāra* means removal from everything that is impermanent and of the nature of suffering, as opposed to being unceasingly engaged with the impermanent. How can the Buddha even be aware of the unreal conventional world or be active in it?

The Dalai Lama points out that if we were to accept the view of some Buddhist traditions that at the historical Buddha's death or *parinirvāṇa*, the continuity of his consciousness disappeared into nothingnesss, then "we would have to accept that after accumulating merit and wisdom for three innumerable eons, the fulfillment was working for other sentient beings for a mere forty-five years!"[131] This would be a gross violation of the proportion in the working of cause and effect. There simply must be a way for the enormous energy generated by the Buddha in the causal stream of the conventional world to be expended in that world as well. It is the scope of this power that marks the effective difference between the release from *saṃsāra* that may be achieved by Buddhists without the *Mahāyāna* bodhisattva path and the liberation achieved via this full Buddhahood. The first generates no ongoing effect on the liberation of other beings, while the second profoundly does. We are still struggling with the question of how the realized bodhisattva can exercise that effect among the beings that are, in a sense, separated from him by his enlightenment.

Before we follow up that question, we should complete our path through the *Bodhicaryāvatāra* by considering its final chapter, which is a litany of dedications. Śāntideva began the book by distinguishing two kinds of *bodhicitta* or awakening mind, each with its own merit. The first was the resolve to pursue *bodhicitta*. In Chapter 3, Śāntideva offered dedications of the merit that flowed from that initial form of awakening mind. His altruistic vows there (e.g., to give away his body for the sake of others) were extreme, but they seemed to move very much within the realm of what we might call "historical" *saṃsāra*. Through the rest of the text, he has explored the second type *of bodhicitta*, which is involved in an actual enactment of the six perfections. This generates its own greater merit, which is now brought into play by reference to the author and the readers themselves. The vows and dedications here have an even wider scope, encompassing a cosmic scale and beings that are outside the human realm. In this way, Śāntideva's entire exposition and the work of the reader who has followed it are made into explicit exercises of the practices that are described.

Chapter 10 is an overflowing stream of compassionate aspirations, beginning in the following way:

> May all sentient beings be graced with the Bodhisattva way of life by
> the virtue I have obtained while reflecting on *A Guide to the Bodhisattva
> Way of Life*. Through my merit, may all those in all directions who
> are afflicted
> by bodily and mental sufferings obtain oceans of joy and contentment.[132]

These wishes reference unrestricted hopes for unrestricted goods: may the ill be healed, may rain and harvests abound, may no being be unhappy, may life spans be immeasurable, may lost travelers find assistance, may monasteries be well provisioned, may the inhabitants of hells be released.[133]

My particular interest has to do with verses like the following:

> By the power of my virtue, may those whose flesh has completely fallen
> off . . .
> and who are immersed in the river Vaitaraṇi whose water is like
> fire, attain celestial bodies and dwell with goddesses by the river
> Mandākini.[134]

> Without experiencing the suffering of the miserable states of existence
> and without arduous practice, may the world attain Buddhahood in a
> single divine body.[135]

And finally, some of the most famous lines in the book:

> For as long as space endures and for as long as the world lasts,
> may I live dispelling the miseries of the world.

> Whatever suffering there is for the world, may it all ripen upon me.
> May the world find happiness through all the virtues of the
> Bodhisattvas.[136]

These make explicit the dramatic power of the bodhisattva to help other beings, to shorten the path to enlightenment that would otherwise be theirs. The bodhisattva's merits and virtues not only lead to the bodhisattva's enlightenment, but are also active for the benefit of those far removed from the bodhisattva's time and place. The exalted aspirations in this final chapter are in fact fulfilled. This is the glorious conclusion of the bodhisattva path.

Powerful as this summation is, it does not really address the paradox that Chapter 9 brought to such a fine point. How can this bodhisattva power be exercised, straddling the conditioned, conventional world and the world of wisdom and *nirvāṇa*? At this point, we need to move beyond the text of the *Bodhicaryāvatāra* to issues that it addresses tangentially but which become very important in later interpretation. Only by filling out this picture will we finally be ready to begin some Christian reflection on the bodhisattva path.

Being Buddha

This question of how full Buddhas can continue to behave as bodhisattvas involves a whole complex of topics, including Buddha nature (*tathāgatagarbha*), Buddha fields or pure lands, famous individual bodhisattvas such as Avalokiteśvara or Amitābha, and the "bodies" of a Buddha. We require at least some grasp of these elements if we are to deal with the bodhisattva path in the terms that contemporary Buddhists find implied in Śāntideva's treatment.

It may be understandable that ignorant beings in the realm of conventional truth, and even aspirant bodhisattvas, should not understand these paradoxes. But we are talking about the different question of how realized beings whose wisdom dispels the very grounds of these distinctions between beings, karmas, and conditions can yet function on the basis of those terms. The issue is what it is like to be a Buddha. It seems clear that the answer to this question revolves around the *Mahāyāna* identification of *nirvāṇa* with *saṃsāra*. We have seen that the distinctive idea of a nonabiding *nirvāṇa* removes the distance that would separate a Buddha/bodhisattva from the conventional world, or compel her to "postpone" enlightenment to remain with suffering beings.[137] The question becomes a more subtle one: how can the bodhisattva be present in this same reality in two or more very different ways, functioning in apparently inconsistent modes at the same time?

The answers to these questions are significant enough that in the eyes of some Buddhists, they represent yet another turning of the wheel of *dharma*, analogous to that which differentiates *Mahāyāna* from the earlier Buddhist teaching: "Rather than simply depicting the ultimate truth *via negatia*, the third wheel reveals the ultimate as an immanent reality; it depicts the pure mind as constitutive of the ultimate."[138] In the Tibetan tradition, those in the Madhyamaka school, such as Śāntideva, can be further divided into those who hold to emptiness as a methodological universal, applied even to the notion of emptiness itself, and those who see practice as simply clearing the mist from something underlying, a more "positive" emptiness, the vast expanse of Buddha nature. One mode of emptiness is self-emptiness, which "refers to a phenomenon's lack of its own essence." But by another interpretation, the ultimate is better described as other-emptiness, which "refers to what exists within reality; it points to the nature of reality that is empty of all aspects of distortion that are extrinsic to it."[139] Self-emptiness avoids the extreme of existence by rejecting all projections. But other-emptiness avoids the extreme of nonexistence by insisting that reality is only empty of all projections and is not actually a bare nihilism.[140]

Buddha nature is pure, nonconceptual, and infinite. It underlies all attributed (and so illusory) essences. Enlightenment is the uncovering of this purity. It is like a sky purified of smoke. If nonabiding *nirvāṇa* interprets the identity of *saṃsāra* with *nirvāṇa* by bringing *nirvāṇa* "down" into the conventional world, then Buddha nature interprets that identity by raising "up" the nature of beings as already being that of the Buddha. Here is a basis for the conviction that all beings will become bodhisattvas and Buddhas. The basis is not a probabilistic claim about future achievements, but an insight about the way that things are currently and permanently. This is, not incidentally, also key to the hope that the way to *nirvāṇa* may not be the unimaginably long round of future births that traditional Buddhism generally assumes it to be. Since

Buddha nature is the true current nature of all beings, beings are never far in principle from its realization. The tantric traditions of Tibet are meant to capitalize on this fact through distinctive practices, sometimes ones that appear at odds with traditional Buddhist teachings.[141]

Full Buddhahood is a state in which the Buddha is connected to the world in unlimited ways. The only way that the bodhisattva vow to assist all beings makes sense at the outset is if the realized bodhisattva is actually involved in helping all beings in the end. How does that helping take place? We will follow the Tibetan tradition one last step in its reflection on this point. The answer to the question involves the belief in Buddha nature as characteristic of all beings and the conviction that the Buddha is manifest in various ways, so as to be present and effective for those in all conditions. These manifestations can be classified broadly under the three bodies of the Buddha.[142]

The supreme body of the Buddha is the *dharma* body (*dharmakāya*), which is the unconditioned and nonconceptual reality of enlightenment. It is what enlightenment is for the enlightened, true emptiness of all essence, totally without impermanence or any physical form or anything else associated with *saṃsāra*. The enjoyment body of the Buddha (*sambhogakāya)* does in fact have some of those conventional qualities. It is impermanent and even subtly physical, but in the most exalted manner imaginable. This is the glorified body of the Buddha, images of which are familiar to us from much Buddhist iconography. This is what attained Buddhahood looks like, insofar as it can be pictured: an outward form that corresponds most directly to the perfection of wisdom within. It represents both what the enjoyment of enlightenment is for the Buddha who attained it, and the magnitude of the power of that Buddha that can flow out through this vehicle to those who respond with devotion. Enormous reclining or standing Buddhas are examples of the Buddha in this body, as the early Buddhist resistance to any image of the Buddha represented the inconceivable nature of the *dharmakāya*. Such expansive figures point to the Buddha of Buddhist devotion—the Buddha manifesting as a powerful presence in the world of conventional truth, accessible to those who can understand. The stylized perfections of this body or its vast dimensions signify a reality greater than can be manifested.

There are other, less subtle manifestations in more conventional physical forms, forms of the *nirmāṇakāya*. The historical person of the Buddha was one of these transformation bodies. The transformation body of the Buddha is the least refined manifestation, one through which the

Buddha's skillful means can reach those who are furthest from enlightenment, even through the vehicle of non-Buddhist teaching.[143] In one sense, then, the historical Buddha's attainment under the bodhi tree and the few subsequent years of teaching are much less final and significant than the post-*parinirvāṇa* career, whose scope is enormously wider. One can look at the historical Buddha as part of the causal chain that leads to this more cosmic effect, an "ascent" perspective. Or one can look at the historical Buddha as an emanation from an existing Buddha realm, a "descent" perspective. The historical Gautama Buddha was a transformation body. So, too, were his previous lives, as described in the *Jataka* tales. It is common for Buddhists to put great figures from non-Buddhist traditions in this category. To equate Jesus and Buddha at this level is to imply significant limitations as well as honor, given the relative standing of the transformation body.

The historical Buddha's attainment of enlightenment was a discovery in the sense that it tapped in to a reality that already existed, the *dharmakāya* or body of perfect emanation. We could think of this as a preexisting causal stream that is responsible for the historical Buddha's manifestation, a stream that has been fed by countless earlier Buddhas. But we could also think of it as the continuing body of that historical Buddha, constituted or energized by that Buddha's attainments, since the historical Buddha's great merits flowed into this continuum like additional energy into a battery. In any event, this is the basis from which the Buddha's continuum can continue to exercise effects indefinitely. These effects could include manifestation as *sambhogakāya*, what we might call "supernatural" embodiments of the Buddha. These are physical and impermanent, though on a level far above that of our ordinary world.[144]

If we think of the *dharmakāya* as realization of the dimension of true emptiness in all phenomena, the identity of the Buddha with the truth about how things are, then the enjoyment body is what that realization looks like when manifested in the best possible way within the constraints of a world that lacks that realization, like a sphere's presence as a circle in a two-dimensional world. The transformation body represents that realization stepped down into crude and less-than-ideal terms, ones accessible to those who are far from the heights of even conventional understanding.

We may follow this discussion one further step. If the way in which the Buddha continues to exercise influence for beings who are caught up in the conventional world is through these bodies (primarily the *nirmānakāya* and the *sambhogakāya)*, then what does this imply about the condition of Buddhahood, specifically about the knowledge of the Buddha? Buddhas are commonly thought to have two kinds of knowledge: knowledge of all phenomena (i.e., subsequent knowledge) and knowledge of the empty nature of all phenomena (i.e., nonconceptual knowledge).[145] The first we might call omniscience of the conventional world (i.e., a complete knowledge of all phenomena and their causal relations) and the second we could call the knowledge of emptiness itself, which qualifies all of the other omniscience as knowledge of phenomena solely in terms of their true insubstantiality. This can be further specified as four kinds of knowing, or four capacities of a single awareness.[146] The first is the nonconceptual or "mirror" knowledge. The other three kinds of knowledge are applications in connection to phenomena: knowledge of the sameness of all phenomena in terms of their ultimate nature, knowledge of all conditions of phenomena that are relevant to teaching about them, and knowledge of phenomena that works to illuminate their nature and relieve suffering. The term "knowing" suggests a subject-object distinction and cognitive activity, but the Buddha's knowledge could equally well be thought of as spontaneous manifestation in terms of the various Buddha bodies. Given this very special character of the Buddha's awareness, and the qualified ways in which it can be regarded as an awareness *of* something, how does the Buddha act to aid beings?

Two very sophisticated and alternative answers are given.[147] Both accept the root Buddhist conviction that conditioned effects can only have conditioned causes. One answer maintains, then, that as unconditioned, Buddhahood is *not* a cause of assistance to beings or anything else in the conventional realm. The second maintains that Buddhahood must be of assistance to conventional beings, and so there must be a conventional or conditioned aspect of Buddhahood itself to convey the benefits.

We will begin with the first, and more common, view. Buddhahood, as such, has no causal connections to the ordinary world. Beneficial effects for other beings cannot come directly from the *dharmakāya*. Instead, we see the Buddha's activity in the world as a spontaneous outflow of the after effects of the Buddha's merits and virtues.[148] Perhaps we might think of this as a kind of transmuted karma, carrying on through the conventional world as a great wave left in the wake of the bodhisattva's attainment: "Because conditioned things only derive from other conditioned things, the conditioned activities of nonabiding *nirvāna* had to be derived from conditions extrinsic to the core realization of Buddhahood."[149] There are two such extrinsic sets of conditions. One is the prior vows and merit of the aspirant's performance on the way to becoming a fully realized bodhisattva. The other is the state of mind of current beings, who are the receptors of those earlier acts. Help for beings comes when these coincide, in the conditioned realm to which both causes belong.

This intersection of bodhisattva effects and aspirant openness is the way in which the bodhisattva vow is actually fulfilled. Such an understanding explains Śāntideva's enormous emphasis on generating the intention of *bodhicitta*, on the intrinsic strength in the bodhisattva vow, and on the practice of the dedication of merit. These are not simply aids to empower the practitioner more speedily to reach the end point, Buddhahood, from which she can exercise maximal beneficial compassion. They *are* the exercise of compassion: the steady intensification of merit and intention establishes the causal stream that constitutes the bodhisattva's effect. The bodies of the Buddha spontaneously manifest in appropriate ways, without any activity on the part of the Buddha. Just as conditioned effects must have conditioned causes, the unconditioned state of *nirvāṇa* must have an unconditioned cause, which is the Buddha nature. So enlightenment is obtained by way of the path, but it is not created or caused by the path, since the path is entirely composed of conventional elements.

We could say that Buddhas are conditionally present by means of the past actions and intentions whose momentum continues in our conditioned world, while in their *dharmakāya* they are immediately present to all of the world in its unconditioned Buddha nature. So a distinction is made between the Buddha Amitābha, and the bodhisattva Dharmākara, whose career preceded Amitābha's full Buddhahood. Here is a different perspective on the postponement question: the bodhisattva need not hesitate to enter Buddhahood, because the bodhisattva's activity continues even in his absence. The bodhisattva's effective compassion continues in the world for the benefit of beings, but the Buddha is not being compassionate in any current engagement with those beings, even though devotion and gratitude are directed to the Buddha. An interesting illustration of this comes from the *Tathāgataguhya* sutra, which teaches that from the night in which he attained Buddhahood until the time decades later when he "attained *parinirvāṇa* without remainder," the Buddha did not speak a word.

But all beings,

according to their various dispositions and interests and according to their aspirations, think that the Tathāgata is teaching in different ways. And each of them thinks, "The Lord is teaching the *Dharma* to us. . . ." But on this point the Tathāgata has no concept and makes no distinction. This is because the Tathāgata, O Śāntamati, is free from all the conceptual diversity that consists of the traces of the network of concepts and distinctions.[150]

The teachings that are actually heard from the Buddha come about "through the actions and promises of the Bodhisattva who became a Buddha at that place and time, combined with the needs, expectations, and awareness of the disciples themselves."[151] The superlatives about the bodhisattva being the supreme refuge and rescuer of all beings do not apply, properly speaking, to Buddhahood itself, but to its prior correlatives and preparation. From Buddhahood itself, it is "too late" to exercise compassion directly. There is no way to generate compassion from the ultimate state. It must be created ahead of time. Here is a crucial reason that the *Mahāyāna* path views itself as superior to other Buddhist paths. If one has not cultivated the bodhisattva path prior to enlightenment, then even the achievement of enlightenment can be of no benefit to others.[152]

The second answer to the question of the Buddha's actions in the world, already noted above, takes a reverse tack. It affirms that Buddhahood *can* exercise causality in the conditioned world and therefore is not itself entirely unconditioned. It is subject in a refined way to the first two noble truths. Therefore, Buddhahood is also in part an effect of conditioned causes: it is constructed by the path that leads to it. Having real conventional causes, enlightenment itself cannot be entirely lacking a conventional character. The Madhyamaka insistence that emptiness is also empty, analyzable into dependent conditionality like anything else, is expounded to the point of using the same mental analysis on the mind of a Buddha as on that of an ordinary person. Rather than being entirely spontaneous and free of any mental conditions, the actions of a realized Buddha require "a set of primary consciousnesses and mental factors (*citta-caitta*) to carry out activity in the conditioned world."[153]

In other words, there is some phenomenal consciousness *of* the world involved in the Buddha's continuing activity *in* the world. The skillful means of the realized bodhisattva actually involve mental processes which mediate wisdom to conventional circumstances. For nonabiding *nirvāṇa* to be a Buddhahood "linked to the world, it must be qualified by the impermanence and conditionality that the first two Noble Truths lend to the world."[154] Many *Mahāyāna* thinkers would flatly reject this proposition. But others supported it, even to the extent of positing a fourth body of the Buddha as the repository for these mental faculties.[155] This bodhisattva/Buddha with conditioned capacities is more straightforwardly consistent with devotional Buddhism that pictures an active responsiveness to the plight of suffering beings. From this perspective, the first view we described errs by falling back into an ontological distinction between the ultimate and the conventional, which flies in the face of the fundamental *Mahāyāna* insistence that *nirvāṇa* and *saṃsāra* belong together.[156] On this second reading, the compassionate engagement of Buddhas is never in doubt, while their realized condition seems less transcendent.

The last aspect of this picture is the Buddha field or the pure land that is constituted by a Buddha. Such a field is the sphere across which a Buddha exerts a spiritual influence. During "his career as a Bodhisattva the Buddha-to-be is said to 'purify' his Buddha field, and the Buddha field is in some sense the result of his great compassion. In other words, the very existence of a Buddha field depends upon the Buddha's wonderful career as a bodhisattva."[157] For instance, many ages ago the monk Dharmākara made the bodhisattva vow, with the additional provision that he would purify the most marvelous Buddha field of all, one whose inhabitants could remember all their past lives, live as long as they chose, and have many other miraculous powers. In addition, those who sincerely desired to enter this land would only have to call on the name of Amitābha, the Buddha that Dharmākara became, to do so, regardless of their condition, so long as they had not committed any of the worst offenses.[158] This is the pure land of Sukhāvatī, where the Buddha Amitābha may be experienced in his enjoyment body, the basis for the Pure Land form of Buddhism.

Buddhist cosmology is an expanse of infinite universes, and Buddha fields are conventionally located, so to speak, within that setting, having a geographical relation to the site of the relevant prior lives of a bodhisattva. According to Buddhist cosmology, many worlds are without a Buddha or a Buddha field, and generally one Buddha is sufficient for any universe and there would be no need for a second.[159] A land that has been truly purified is one where there would be no bad behavior, no seriously suffering beings, no non-Buddhists, no lesser vehicles, and no rebirth into lower realms. There is a "purgatorial" quality to Buddha fields in the sense that there is no sliding back from their level, only varied speeds "forward."[160] Such a field is still an impermanent and conditioned reality, but one that is incredibly well suited for completion of the bodhisattva perfections. It is different from Buddhist heavens, which are pleasant parking places between births where the rewards of good karma are experienced but where it is not possible to advance or fall on the path, as it is in human life.

In the pure land, every good opportunity of human life is intensified so as to make the passage to *nirvāṇa* immeasurably less difficult. Bodhisattvas will by virtue of their progress necessarily spend time in such lands, accelerating their practice toward the point that they will have constituted a land of their own. In fact, it is within these settings that many Buddhist scriptures have their putative origins, since it is here that the most advanced teaching of the Buddhas can be received. The purification of the Buddha field can be seen as a kind of collective, exponential endeavor. A land populated by more and more advanced bodhisattvas who are attending fully to the legacy teachings and merits of its founding Buddha becomes ever more pure and ever more liberating for its inhabitants. Beings have earned rebirth in such a land by merit, and once there, they find merit ever easier to acquire.

We have traced what it means for a bodhisattva to follow through on the bodhisattva vow. This is what it looks like to attain enlightenment for the sake of all sentient beings. It is an extraordinary picture. According to some commentators, the path of the bodhisattva that early sources described was presumed to belong to only a few, or even to one, as the *Jataka* tales were the summary of the lives of the one Buddha of this age.[161] The astonishing feats of self-sacrifice described there enhanced the sense of wonder at Gautama's exceptionalism. As the bodhisattva path became an accepted aspiration for all, its rigorous achievements seemed conceivable only when projected into a distant future, after the three unimaginable eons that were classically allotted to fulfill the perfections. It was unrealistic, practically speaking, to think of being a bodhisattva.

Pure lands help explain how the bodhisattva vow is carried out by those who fulfill it. Pure lands also offer the hope of a realistically shorter path to that end. They take on the quality of an emergency measure. The most common framework for this is the conviction that we live in the opposite of a pure land. We live in a world where the practice and the transmission of the *dharma* have both degenerated. In such a world, in the latter days of the *dharma*, even the incremental, ages-long bodhisattva career looks hopeless. In this connection, the idea surfaces that instead of earning my rebirth in the pure land where I can benefit from the merit and vows of the bodhisattva, I may need the merit and power of the bodhisattva to get me to the pure land in the first place. Only in those more favorable conditions can I begin to make progress. Such dependence on other power is represented by the conviction that, for instance, chanting the name of Amitābha will win one entry to his pure land, despite our failure to achieve even the rudimentary levels of mental clarity or *bodhicitta*.[162] Rather than the mental exercises to still the mind and purify it to the point of wisdom, all that is necessary is to focus one's mind completely with confidence on Amitābha's power. Once in the pure land, one can complete the path by one's own actions.

In these ways, *Mahāyāna* tradition has filled out the basic tension of a nonabiding *nirvāṇa*, an enlightenment that is neither some other "place" nor disconnected with the world of unenlightened beings. In this rich complex of ideas, we begin to glimpse the full texture of the tension that is the glory of the bodhisattva path. In the treatment of Buddhahood, the question is pressed to the extreme: in what way can beings and their suffering (both premised on ignorance) be present to the awareness and intentions of an enlightened one? Skillful means makes intuitive sense, in that someone with omniscient knowledge can tell how to apply which teachings to which persons and situations in order to achieve the greatest benefit for those persons. But if that omniscient knowledge dispels any basis for distinguishing persons or situations, how can it be applied in this way without being compromised at the very same moment? As we have seen, the work of the realized bodhisattva involves the projection of versions of himself, which are likewise impermanent and premised on ignorance such that it is not clear how they can be the immediate products of an enlightened mind. The miracle of the bodhisattva-Buddha is to be embodied in the conventional world and to act effectively in its terms even while dwelling in a wisdom that transcends that world.

The refinement in these dimensions of Buddhist thought is reflected in the subtlety with which Buddhist art expresses the bodhisattva's character, combining tensions within a single image. As a viewer moves toward the feet of some tall Buddha figures, the perspective alters the Buddha's perceived facial expression. The mouth changes from a somber line into a smile. The compelling quality of some Chinese Buddha heads "comes from their combining things that seem incompatible, especially a complete repose or detachment with an active power to help the worshipper."[163] William Empson suggests that one way this was achieved was through a careful asymmetry: "the two qualities were largely separated onto the two sides of the face."[164] The result is a single expression of profound peace composed of an inner contrast and asymmetry. The left side of the face, Empson believed, expresses the nirvanic attainment. It has a "squint of meditation," a mouth line slightly curved down, and a mood at once "withdrawn, patient, childish and ascetic." On the right, the features are more active, outward. A raised eye "seems to wink," and the mouth line is more sensual, the smile "strained, ironic and smug."[165] One gaze falls upon the world, from one face, evoking enlightenment from within *saṃsāra* or communicating with *saṃsāra* from enlightenment.

We have now sketched the bodhisattva path as Śāntideva and his commentators present it to us. Even in this condensed treatment, I trust that some of its beauty and power come through. What is a Christian theologian to learn from this text, when it is taken not simply as data about others' belief but as a theological source? That is the question we turn to now.

PART III

Christian Reflections

4 The Bodhisattva as Aspirant

CREATURES AND NO-SELF

The bodhisattva selflessly realizes Buddha nature for the sake of all sentient beings. We have followed Śāntideva's exposition of this path and now turn to Christian reflection on it. We have seen that "bodhisattva" is a term that encompasses a ground, an ascending practice, and a final realization. Its bookends are Buddha nature as the basis and Buddhahood as the result. The word can be used to look backward to an insect or a blade of grass, or to look forward to beings of cosmic splendor while referring to the same "one" or causal karmic stream. To cover similar structural ground in Christian terms, we will have to talk about distinctly different things: God as source, Christ as incarnation, humans as disciples and aspirants, and all of them in relation across time. If we seek a single consistent theme across all of these Christian elements, relating equally to ground, process, and attainment, then that theme would be communion or mutual participation.

This chapter will focus on the no-self aspect of the bodhisattva path, the bodhisattva as aspirant, and the Christian as creature. Chapter 5, the following chapter, will focus on the realization aspect of the bodhisattva path, with the bodhisattva as Buddha. Chapter 6 will focus on enlightenment for the sake of all beings, with the bodhisattva as helper. In each case, I will explore how we might be instructed by this wisdom.[1]

When we explore the "ascending" bodhisattva path, we immediately come up against an obvious disagreement over whether there is any one actually on the path. Buddhists appear to deny the existence of selves, and Christians to affirm it. The non-reality of the self is central to the Buddhist teaching, and to the liberative practice associated with that teaching. Śāntideva's text rests on the wisdom of *anattā* or no-self. He lays the ground for a bodhisattva's unrestricted altruism in the argument that it is essentially impossible to distinguish between one person and another because they are all equally insubstantial. If selves have no inherent qualities by which they exist or might be distinguished from each other, then there can be no distinction in how I treat them. Śāntideva explains how important it is to understand this and, equally, to experience and act in the world in light of that understanding.

All sufferings are without an owner, because they are not different.

They should be warded off simply because they are suffering.[2]

This core tenet of Buddhist traditions contrasts with Christian convictions about the created and eschatological reality of human persons. Śāntideva proposes that our failure to pursue the *dharma* and to escape our own suffering is based on the continuing misperception that there is a true "I" to be found in our experience. We saw the repeated hellfire appeals that he makes to his listeners to give up their attachment to the self because it leads only to future agony for the self that they are attached to. Better future conditions (e.g., better rebirths, pleasurable heavens) are but intermediate steps. Real release requires recognizing the utter emptiness of the self. And the sole means to do this are to attend *now* to that emptiness, analytically and experientially. The six bodhisattva perfections are progressive purifications of the defilements that together produce our self-impression. That impression is all that distinguishes us from others who are subject to the same defilements and share the same underlying emptiness. As it falls away, a practitioner is immersed in a unity that transcends subject and object, manifest in universal compassion and peace. This is the path that Śāntideva sets out. Though Christian readers may readily agree with Śāntideva's picture of the futile character of the selfish life, their typical response is to look ahead to a renewed and redeemed self, a transformed proximate and ultimate future. In that movement, Christians do not linger over the idea of the insubstantiality of the self itself.

There are reasons internal to Christian theology to be open to Buddhist instruction on this point. I will review how Buddhism enriches our understanding of the negative expressions of our creaturely character and, even more, of the positive possibilities in that emptiness. I will outline an emerging perspective on the "mimetic self" that may assist Christians in appreciating significant Buddhist teachings, while retaining the necessary grammar of personhood in Christian belief. I will explore some implications of these explorations for Christian practice. And I will reflect on how this understanding of our nature as creatures may affect our view of Christ and the cross.

Creatures and No-Self

Terrence Tilley, a prominent Roman Catholic theologian, has commented after conducting his own study of the *Bodhicaryāvatāra* that the greatest contrast he took away from it was that Christians are creatures and Buddhists are not.[3] At every point, it matters that Buddhists find selves to have no intrinsic nature and Christians find themselves grounded in a divine interpersonal source. This is an enduring difference, giving narrative (history) and relation (plurality) a weight for Christians that appears unwise in Buddhist eyes. For Christians, creaturely nature evokes primarily comparative images, whether an existential gap between those who receive the gift of contingent existence and the giver, or a moral gap between primordial goodness and our failings. Buddhism brings laser-like clarity to a different dimension. It provides an illumination, a profound phenomenology of creatureliness in its permanent, nonpersonal emptiness. This offers insight for the negative aspects of human existence, and, even more notably, for positive aspects too readily lost in Christian perspective. Buddhists have the deepest word on what it is to be a creature, standing alone and rigorously analyzed.[4]

Of course, to summarize the question of selves as "Buddhists, no; Christians, yes" oversimplifies.[5] Buddhist thinkers hedge the ultimate truth of *anattā* with recognition of the significance of a relative, impermanent self. This phenomenal self is addressed and assumed in Śāntideva's every line. When a teacher asks a student whether he has meditated recently, it does no good to appeal to the *anattā* doctrine to maintain that there is no one to whom the question applies. Rather than a substance or a being, the Buddhist self is a perspective. We might say it is the perspective for practice. However mistaken its self-projection may be, the individual is the necessary locus of Buddhist practice until it happily ceases to be so. It is through the mind, which is only a conditioned construction, that we can supervene on the constructions that make it up. The mind is the site of both the problem and its resolution. I attend to the contents of "my" consciousness rather than that of other minds as a matter of practical convenience, not as an ontological commitment.

Buddhism grapples with many questions around the space where a self would seem to go. In what ways do rebirths or the effects of someone's actions come to the same one whose karmic causes determined them? The continuity here cannot be the same self whose reality (i.e., inherent existence) Buddhist wisdom otherwise denies at all points. The sameness at issue is explained differently in different Buddhist texts (for instance, in terms of a store consciousness or simply as a causal succession). The same issues reappear with particular relevance in the bodhisattva path. If the subject self is eliminated through this analysis, then there is no self to make the bodhisattva vow. The vow would in any case be meaningless, because the person who made it would not be the same one who carried it out. And there are no "other beings" to be the referent for the bodhisattva's compassion. We saw how Śāntideva stipulated that both the "other beings" who are objects of the bodhisattva's compassion and the bodhisattva herself are not real to the eye of wisdom. They are necessary concessions to the realm of ignorance for the instrumental sake of combatting suffering based on those same illusions.

Under the umbrella of a general "yes" to selves, Christian tradition has its own complexities. Theology starts with a conviction of the enduring significance of created beings. That conviction crystalized at two formative moments in early Christian history. The first was the argument with Gnosticism over the goodness of created human persons, particularly in their embodied nature. The second was the development of the Trinitarian doctrine of God. Yet there are central Christian beliefs—the Trinity itself, the incarnational union of the divine and the human in Jesus, the union of Christ and the believer, the *koinonia* of Christians with each other—that seem to contradict common notions of the self, whether those common in the ancient world or in our own.

Christians reject essentialist views of the self, as Buddhists do. But they do so from the other end of the equation so to speak, desiring to preserve the reality of selves even when they are found in unities and relations that seem to blur crisp boundaries between them. These convictions require at the least a porousness to persons, such that three of them in God are also one, such that Christ is one person with two natures, and such that the one that is me can also encompass Christ in me. Just as the bodhisattva path presents questions about the self at each stage, so does the Christian narrative of creation in God's image, incarnation, and membership in the body of Christ. Though we do not usually think about it that way, Christian theology has an internal need to deconstruct the apparent self if it is to make sense of its central teachings. Buddhist no-self insights are particularly relevant in this regard.

Selflessness is a Christian value, though this selflessness seems to trade in the loss and gain of something real: "For those who want to save their life will lose it, and those who lose their life for my sake will save it."[6] Christian reflection on these questions sometimes pictures selves, even human selves and God's self, contending with each other in a zero-sum game. As Reinhold Niebuhr summarizes the matter, pride is the sin in which we give our individual selves priority over all others; its opposite is the sin in which we deny and denigrate the value of those same individual selves.[7] Many Christian commentators have seen the problem of pride as the place to make common cause with the Buddhist deconstruction of the "I," to deflate an overweening selfishness. They are likely to see Buddhists as falling into the second type of error, since Buddhists question the self's very existence. Christians tend to see the primary question, both interpersonally and mentally, framed by competing claims. If we are to "love our neighbors as ourselves," then we must find the narrow ridge between Niebuhr's two types of sin: abusive self-regard that tramples on others and destructive self-abnegation that denies our intrinsic worth as children of God.

Buddhist no-self alerts us to another aspect of this picture. This is illustrated in the different Buddhist and Christian takes on the problem of the mistaken self. Christians see our vision of the world as unsatisfactory not because there is an "I" that is doing the looking, but because selfishness or feelings of inferiority distort how we see, yielding projections of ourselves and others that are twisted rather than accurate. Buddhists see the problem in the location of the seer *as* an "I" among others, and the projections of self and other as mistaken because they have no objective referents at all. Christians experience many problems with selves, but it does not readily occur to us that the problem is having one. We believe that positive selflessness means curbing the priority of the self as compared to other selves or even giving away the self completely for the sake of others, but not "losing it" in the sense of literally not being able to find it.

Let us take an example of how this Buddhist teaching is applied.[8] Our picture of other persons is usually highly reductive. We take a few fleeting impressions—our knowledge of someone's job, their manner of dress, their name—and spin these into reductive assumptions that become the basis for dismissive behavior: "She's only an old woman." Such highly limiting pictures of others correlate with an equally limited impression of who "I" am, perhaps an "I" who is identified with an inevitably declining body, frightened to see the prospect of that decline reflected back to me in the person of the aged woman. For that reason, I may resist any full or sympathetic interaction with her. This example illustrates how my mental life can become a constant play of phantoms, imaginations about what fabricated versions of other people may think, threaten, or promise for my imagined version of myself. Buddhist teaching would say this is unreality piled on unreality, starting with the unreality of the "I" that is the reference point for the whole exercise.

Christians rarely resist importing into this Buddhist account something that is purposely not there. We think that our limited impressions lead us to have a false image of the other person, as opposed to an appreciation for *who they actually are.* But it is that notion also, the supposition of an authentic self, that the teaching seeks to dispel. We readily picture a contrast between a false me and a real me, an unreal image of my neighbor and one closer to the truth. But to a Buddhist perspective, any notion of a true self or actual neighbor is mistaken in a structural way. Any "true self" is a misleading projection that distracts from the vast potential of Buddha nature that is present under any conceptual projection. Yet it is also true that some conventional projections are better than others, because they are less destructive, less reductive.

There is much to learn from this Buddhist sense of the false self as the unreal self. *Anattā* carefully delineates the manner in which selves do not exist. What selves lack is *svabhāva,* or "self-existence." To have *svabhāva* would mean to be without any external causation and to be permanent. There is no such continuing, unchanged, single-essence entity. Selves may exist in many other ways, but not in this one. The way in which they *do* exist is as mental constructions, as the mutual falling together of causally conditioned, impermanent phenomena. This is true of the mind itself. It is not a "constructor" standing outside this condition but a particular aggregate of constructions.[9]

Impermanence and emptiness are two core Buddhist insights, negative and positive sides of the same thing. The way things are is that they have no essence, no substantial reality. The negative side of this is impermanence, the profoundly unsatisfactory quality that results in suffering whenever we lean against these phenomena under the illusory expectation that they will stay put or hold us up. But the same lack of essence is also emptiness, a positive, even luminous quality of the way that things are that gives no ground for pain or conflict and yields equanimity when we take it as it is. These objects, in their true emptiness, are all that there is and so all that we could need. This way things are is at once the cause of suffering and the basis for enlightenment.

If to be impermanent necessarily means to be destined to disappear entirely as a participant in relation or a distinguishable subject, then Christians do not believe that all of creation is impermanent. If it means to be always subject to change, lacking control of one's own existence, subject to dissolution, including ruptures such as death, resurrection, or recreation, then Christians agree that creation is impermanent. According to Christian teachings, human selves lack the same kind of reality that Buddhism says they lack: autonomous self-existence. Any self-understanding constructed on that basis is as mistaken and unsatisfactory as Buddhist analysis concludes. That Buddhist analysis discovers no self-existent, eternal entities in the entire phenomenal world comes as no surprise in this respect.[10]

What Buddhists find nowhere, Christians likewise find nowhere, except perhaps in God, which we will leave for discussion in the next chapter.[11] In what sense would Christians wish to deny the impermanence of creaturely existents? What would we expect to find in an instant of pure meditative awareness that is focused entirely on our mental contents? Śāntideva tells us that we will find sensation, succession, distraction, emotion, intention . . . but no permanent thing that is doing the experiencing. I see no Christian reason that a creature contemplating itself as a creature would find anything else as the content of immediate awareness.[12]

To be a creature is, by definition, to lack *svabhāva*. Athanasius wrote that God granted humanity a share of the divine image, "seeing that by the principle of its [humanity's] own coming into being it would not be able to endure eternally."[13] Creatures are precisely those that do not have existence from their own power or will, those whose continued existence is not in their control. What is more than impermanent in them is loaned from God, not an intrinsic possession. Human life is conditioned on a set of proximate causes and materials that are themselves, likewise, impermanent and not-self existent. This looks like chapter and verse from the Buddhist teaching of dependent co-origination. Karl Barth states it no less emphatically. Humans are not to be regarded as "self-grounded, self-based, self-constituted and self-maintained."[14] Humanity "without God is not [and] has neither being nor existence." Humanity without God "is not an object of knowledge."[15]

Barth, famously, has his own vision of nothingness as that whose only existence was that it was what God had not chosen. This was in part an approach to the paradoxical nature of evil, which results from an effort to actualize what is not "there" in God's will. Nothingness is "the comprehensive negation of the creature and its nature."[16] But Barth was equally clear that the creature's true nature is, on its own terms, already empty. So the negation of that nature lay precisely in acting as though it were something, specifically something it is not. There is that which God did not choose, an untaken fork in the road, and the attempt to make this nothingness actual only leads to pain and suffering. But there is also the positive emptiness that God did choose, the emptiness of own-existence, that is part and parcel of what it means to be a creature, even in the creature's obedience and fulfilment.

It is the positive face of this nothingness that Thomas Merton took up on his path into dialogue with Buddhism.[17] Interestingly, he found a charter for this exploration in his reading of Barth. Merton summarizes what he found there that resonated so powerfully with his Buddhist exploration: "The great joke is this: having a self that is to be taken seriously, that is to be proved, free, right, logical, consistent, beautiful, successful and in a word 'not absurd.'"[18] Merton is deeply moved by Barth's recognition that "the self before God is not serious, it is groundless. It is not something that exists in its own density and solidity: the self before God is poised on the divine word, the divine communication over an unfathomable abyss."[19] Barth's profound sense of divine freedom and gratuitous election in Christ fosters a frank acceptance of the emptiness and insubstantiality of any projected self. It is not only human religion that Barth readily dispels, but also the presumed selves that pose the problems that our constructed religions are to solve. In fact, the two go together.

The Christian, creaturely no-self just described is unavoidably comparative. There is much in scripture and devotion to the simple effect that God is very big and I am very small. We are passing, and God is eternal: "All are from the dust, and all turn to dust again."[20] On Ash Wednesday, we carry the mark of the grave on our foreheads. Buddhist "corpse" meditations have their parallels in Christian tradition. To know our nature as creatures is to know that we are, from a nonrelational perspective, nothing. The creature's lack of any autonomous existence is contrasted with the nature of God's existence. But the God we are contrasted with is also not a simple self-existent being, but one whose eternal nature is mutuality and self-giving.

For Christians, this lack of essential autonomous being is easily and rapidly conflated with something quite distinct, the breaking off from what *is* possible and hoped for the creature: sharing in the divine life, by virtue of relation. Broken relation and lost communion have the nature of a problem or a fall, something to be remedied. Creatures have come to lack what God continuously has, communion in love. The connection that allows humans to share God's life is broken on the human end. But pure creatureliness itself has no negative moral connotation. As part of the very constitution of creation, it is fundamentally good. Sin and emptiness are not the same thing, but they can quickly run together.

This framework can block Christians from understanding the positive value of emptiness in Buddhism, and from recognizing the benefits that derive from realization of no-self. Christians may reflexively suspect that a view that excludes relation with God (i.e., that pursues analytical investigation of the self within individual consciousness) can only lead to a narrow outlook in which human perspectives alone define reality. To talk about the creature taken alone distorts, since it leaves aside the other end of the relation that makes us creatures. Thus, there are long-standing theological arguments over whether there is any sense at all in talking of a nature distinct from grace. To view creatures by themselves threatens either to inflate selves to the status of jealous deities or reduce them to a cosmic meaninglessness.

There is irony here, because Buddhists and Christians agree about our captivity in this creaturely perspective. Christians hope to rectify it by filling in the perspectives of others, supremely of God, while Buddhists hope to rectify it by seeing through the supposed source of that perspective. Buddhism is a particularly inapt target for the standard Christian critique, since its own therapeutic regime seeks to meet this concern head on. Our commentators recognize that the bodhisattva aim is so grandiose that if it were associated with an individual self, it would be dangerous. It would inevitably either inflate that self to untenable pretensions or plunge it into desperate despair. It is only plausible or safe insofar as the supposed self attached to it progressively dissolves along the way. In this respect, no spiritual path could be more attuned to the dangers of idolatry and nihilism that Christians raise. The perspective of the individual, taken alone, that could imperialistically impose itself on all is what Buddhism is out to remove, root and branch. Buddhism deconstructs the human ego that is thought to be the beneficiary of leaving God out of the picture. Taken alone, the self must be no-self.

In this sense, we can revisit the two faces of sin, abusive assertion and destructive abnegation, and recognize that they both rest on something more basic and structural. This is the condition in which I simply take my eyes' view of the world as the true world. In one case, that view may exalt my self, while in another, it may denigrate it. In both cases, it is the verdict rendered by my own perspective that I take to be unconditioned and objective, whether it is telling me how great I am or how pathetic. There is nothing wrong with looking at the world from my perspective. What is wrong is presuming an autonomous existence behind that perspective, which validates its objectivity.[21] That assumed self literally does not exist, and that is the problem.

This condition of captivity to a world of our own making, which we then further assume is the one true world, is a generative disposition the theological tradition calls original sin. Buddhism holds that ordinary people are born with "mental obscurations carried over from previous lives" and then compound these with "speculative obscurations" that are acquired in the course of their lives.[22] What Christians call sinners are creatures who have forgotten they are no-thing (in the *svabhāva* sense), whose desires are distorted because their relations are broken. Buddhism calls this state ignorance, a condition that will never allow us to flourish until it is corrected. Since Augustine, it has been common to hold that evil has nothing substantial to work with.[23] It is literally nothingness or disordered good. The sinful is an offshoot of the unreal. We could put it another way and say that the condition of original sin that we just described is the disposition of taking nothing for something. And the prime example of that nothing taken for something is exactly what Buddhism is speaking of, the no-self.

The task of adjudicating what is due to our self and other selves is hopeless if our starting point is a mistaken self.[24] Installing a substantial self where there is creaturely no-self is a mistake that Christians view as a turning away from personhood and relationship, and a lapse in moral freedom, with destructive results following in its train. The responsibility for this mistake is shared among humans, and its negative effects spread among them without necessary proportion to their individual actions. It is a condition of dislocated desire, redeemed by renewed relation. Buddhists treat the mistake as a fact found in a circular chain of conditioned causes. It is a splinter that causes a festering wound, producing suffering, to be removed without need to care for its origin. Its results in any particular life are infallibly allotted by cause and effect. Individual humans are the only vehicles of practice that can rectify the mistake. Liberation appears where the remedy of right understanding is applied.

Christianity and Buddhism are in marked agreement on the negative implications of this evasion of no-self. Our failure to accept our own impermanence is a cause of much suffering and evil. Both agree that there is value in practices that disrupt the presumed objectivity of the unreal selves that we project, whether the disruption comes through confession and repentance or mental analysis. Christians have traditionally extended a moral framework over this entire process, focusing on the effect our participation in the mistake has on others. Buddhists have typically not regarded the moral framework as the most profound perspective for the reversal of this mistake.

The Blessings of Emptiness

A Buddhist would say that while Christians effectively grasp many of the negative implications of creaturely emptiness, their understanding of its benefits is severely limited. What Christian understanding lacks most is the luminous, positive tone that should also characterize no-self. For Buddhists, the conventional sense in which selves *are* real is crucial, but it must always be secondary to the no-self truth. For Christians, it is somewhat the reverse. The unreality of our projected selves always seems secondary to the gift received in their relational existence. Creaturely selflessness is an irreducible reality, a structural reality prior to becoming a moral one. So the area of greatest Christian learning is to unlock the goodness of this dimension.

One familiar positive aspect of no-self that is readily recognized is humility. Christian theology has mainly considered humility in epistemological terms, specifically as the incapacity of our minds to grasp fully either God's creation itself or the supreme divine reality. There is literally nothing in a human being with the independent basis for such knowledge. In this sense, no-self is about the relative nature of all supposed truths that lie at the end of a process conducted by that self.[25] The Madhyamaka tradition to which Śāntideva belongs is noted for drawing this methodological conclusion from the no-self principle. No-self equates to Nagarjuna's famous no-view perspective.[26] Emptiness as the truth of things becomes a kind of positional critique. It is not a view of the way things are that stands above all other views, but an attitude to be taken in regard to any view, including this one, when it claims to be absolute. The teachings of two truths and skillful means are cousins of this conviction, since the appropriateness of teachings must be judged by some standard other than their supposed direct correspondence with reality. Emptiness as the truth of things is also empty.

Both traditions hold that there is an ultimate truth but that humans in their own right cannot have it. All persons may be on their way to Buddhahood, and Buddhas themselves may be omniscient. But the Buddha's omniscient knowledge cannot impinge on the conditioned world in forms that can be regarded as absolute in that world. For Christians, this limitation is part of what it means to be a creature. Even eschatologically, persons are not divine, nor do they possess divine knowledge and power except by partial participation. Thus, though the mechanisms are different, for both traditions creaturely emptiness implies a spirituality of intellectual humility.

For Buddhists, the positive realization and practice of no-self goes much further than this. No-self is not just an analysis of the problem. A supreme, nondual experience of that reality is itself the solution, identified with all manner of benefits. These benefits refer to final or transcendent liberation. But they are also the only effective antidote to much concrete suffering within the world of *saṃsāra*. Meditative no-self practice figures in both contexts: the realization of Buddhahood and the immediate response to the difficulties of conventional existence.

When Christians perceive the ontological insubstantiality of human selves, and so the disastrous outcome of trying to build any permanent happiness on their powers, they tend to move immediately to the alternative ground for this task, in God. That is the move that Buddhism directly rejects, thereby suggesting that the answer is to be found instead by remaining with the no-self. Here we are not speaking of an analytical truth that all things are empty but of a concrete experience of the emptiness of all things, most of all the self. Direct, positive reflection on emptiness in this sense is less central to Christianity as we know it. This is especially true as regards making the creaturely emptiness of selves an object of reflection in its own right.

The field of creaturely emptiness is simply an area of truth and practice where Buddhists arrived first and have gone deepest. Christian contemplatives have recognized and explored this territory. But we have nothing like the texture of Buddhist traditions, and they offer a profound advance in our understanding of the creaturely no-self. From the Bible onward, there is ample material about the emptiness of creatures as creatures. They are made from nothing and have no intrinsic essence of their own, dust to dust. And this describes their nature as God's good creation, quite apart from sin. There is a gift in being no-self. But this positive aspect often passes us by. It is an area where Christians frequently stand in their own light. This shows up in the transition (sometimes slippage) from the word creature to sinner. Christian writers have much to say to disparage the egocentric self, but these strong terms (e.g., "worm," "wretch") are applied to selves not because they are empty but because they are taken not to be, because of their supposed sufficiency. We saw that Śāntideva himself had no shortage of hellfire disparagement of the supposed self along these same lines.

To practice basic forms of calming and insight meditation is to know ourselves at an unusual depth as creatures. This is no small attainment. For one thing, it has power to dispel the unreal worlds we constantly fabricate. It is a kind of "time-out" from living in the world we construct and a "time-in" dwelling in momentary awareness. Christians incline to view the spiritual function of our inner mind space as primarily a space of encounter, a realm for communicative sending and receiving. Our activity in this sphere may involve clearing the noise of our normal mental life, as we might hospitably make ready a room for a particular meeting or conversation. From this perspective, time out from filling our minds with our own limited projections is time in to receive balancing input from others, and particularly from God.

Buddhist meditation instruction makes clear that although the practice may occasion or be accompanied by insights for worldly affairs, or even by the exercise of supernormal powers, these things are secondary phenomena, not the purpose of the practice.[27] In a Christian context, such elements as guidance and healing are legitimate primary aims for prayer or meditation. But emphasis on this communicative dimension can crowd out other considerations, so that even in repose we expect the gaps in our mind space to be filled with messages that we are sending ourselves, in memories or plans. Our minds are not solely send-and-receive space. It is not necessary that every time we are present to our minds, God has a discursive message for us, we have one for God, or we have mental mail for ourselves. Christian practitioners of prayer and meditation testify to great stretches of spiritual practice that do not fit those forms. One can simply practice the presence of God.[28] And, I would say, one can practice an awareness of one's self as a creature through the emptiness awareness that Buddhism superlatively teaches and realizes.

The Buddhist genius is to shift inner focus away from the messages that pass through this mind space toward the medium that carries them, the consciousness that reads them. It is here that no-self applies. Of course, there is a self that figures in our inner mental chatter, like a little avatar moving around a screen or a checker on a checkerboard relative to other pieces. And there are selves that figure in our social interactions, like the flickering images of fictional characters projected in light on a movie screen. But it is at the source—the consciousness-experiencing where there is supposed to be an actual referent for those images—that nothing is to be found. This is a somewhat vertiginous picture, as though our normal mental operations were those of a cartoon character happily walking back and forth across a chasm until she looks down, sees the emptiness, and falls into the abyss. But the depth of the abyss is constructed on the measure of a self that does the falling, and we could equally well say that the character looks inside and sees that there is no one walking. At that point, the supposed chasm loses its threat.

Many forms of Buddhist meditation focus our attention directly on our own minds. They lead to the implicit conclusion that the more closely and quietly we look, the more we will realize that there is no solid self to be found. We find thoughts, crossing like clouds in the sky, and we find the empty space between thoughts, but no ongoing one who is having the thoughts. Much of contemporary mindfulness meditation, particularly in non-Buddhist settings, is severed from its explicit no-self context. It cultivates close attention to the contents of our mind with a number of proximate benefits in view: relaxation, focus, clarity. It does not actively contest the conviction of an "I" to the extent that Śāntideva does. It is not hard for Christians to adopt practice of this sort, and it does help us focus more directly on our creaturely emptiness. Simply to note the successive variation of our sensations and fleeting thoughts is to loosen the grasp on the assumption that there is a substantial self, projecting and then suffering those sensations, for instance. But I want to push considerably further.

The body plays a central role in Buddhist meditation. The first step in such practice is virtually always awareness of the body, as in focus on one's breath. Christian theology emphasizes our creaturely nature as an intrinsically bodily reality and defines humans as body-spirit unities.

Many Christian forms of practice make our bodies the landscape of spiritual reflection, through fasting, postures for prayer, ritual, pilgrimage, and sacrament. And there are spiritual exercises, such as those of Saint Ignatius, that use our bodily senses and emotions to enter into biblical scenes and so to come more deeply in touch with our own experience and more deeply into relation with Jesus.[29] What Buddhist practice offers is an unsurpassed practical knowledge of the interrelations of our bodily states and mental processes themselves.

Though the mind is the central locus of Buddhist practice, the very emphasis upon the insubstantiality of the mind breaks down one barrier between mind and body. Both are impermanent. Physical sensations take on a certain equivalence with thoughts and ideas, the higher-level functions we associate more with a ruling self. Meditators notice physical sensations—the rise of an emotion, the appearance of ideas—all as detached phenomena, like the weather. These are to be observed rather than treated as invitations to action or sources of meaning. Particularly, meditators learn to treat mental contents with some distancing and labeling (e.g., these are planning thoughts, those are replaying the past, these are mind-reading others' supposed intentions).

Meditative practices that lead to an experience of this emptiness can have a profound and freeing effect.[30] In getting to know people in my meditation group, I have been impressed with the extent to which many of them found the no-self teaching immediately good news. This was so even prior to any physiological or psychological effects from specific practices that they learned. It is clear that "self" had been a burden to them, whether a frustrating struggle to perfect the self according to some standard, a debilitating sense of guilt and inadequacy about the self, or an obsessive felt obligation to deny self in favor of others.

A common denominator in these cases was the liberating effect of this simple analytical approach to no-self. To see directly that the "I" whose dominance over others I have been laboriously asserting, or whose end I have been fearing in death, or whose inadequacies I am so ashamed of, is literally an episodic phenomenon is a relief. To let go of the search for a solid self, whose reality I have honestly come to doubt, is likewise freeing.[31] Buddhism is not just therapeutically helpful but analytically correct in a fundamental sense. Sometimes the shortest path to overcoming our mental and social ills is not sorting out what is bad or good but the realization of what is not real. This is meditation as the interruption of a reality built on a self of sand.

Śāntideva tells us there is a tremendous leveling power in the no-self insight, which blurs not only the lines between people but the entire ownership of experience. Taking selves out of our stories allows a great sense of identification: all minds are the same. It also fosters great clarification about what is happening phenomenally with us. We think "That is anger talking," "This is the effect of a former trauma," or "That is the expression of a false assumption," as opposed to obsessing over substantial agents orchestrating events. Giving up an obsession with blaming or changing other selves shifts energy to concrete management of emotions and direct control over the suffering experienced as mine.[32]

Meditative experience of this simple emptiness has great restorative and constructive value, since it cuts through so much that causes inner and outer distress. There are manifest goods that come from the capacity to accept the momentary emptiness of phenomena. This is particularly true, I believe, in dealing with physical pain. From the point of view of the sufferer, Christian responses tend to focus on alleviating the causes of pain, whenever possible, and on building a framework of meaning and interpersonal support when it is not, particularly support in relation with God and Christ. From the perspective of surrounding individuals and communities the response is similar: practical care, love, and support, and an emphasis on the suffering person's connections with others to pull them away from isolation and despair.

No-self meditation offers an additional way in which to address moment-by-moment bodily suffering. First, practice of immediate attention to inner mental processes helps diminish what we might call "superadded pain." To whatever physical pain is experienced, the focus on selves can gratuitously project even more, adding fear and anxiety about the suffering that I imagine I will experience in the future to that which I experience now. Second, it offers concrete bodily relaxation and feedback practices that mitigate the generation of physical pain. These practices today are increasingly detached from Buddhist settings and presented in a purely medical setting. They are also those for which it may be easiest to find direct Christian correlatives in forms of repetitive prayer. Third, for more extensive practice, this meditation further diminishes the felt or received pain, both by weakening our identification with the self that registers the pain and by disaggregating that pain into its smallest, momentary sensory phenomena.

One place that Christian tradition has historically operationalized the creaturely no-self is in relation to death. The tradition of the *ars moriendi*, or "art of dying," does not directly use the language of emptiness of self-existence.[33] But it lifts the reality into much higher profile than it receives in the usual Christian theological complex, as the wisdom literature in the Bible also does in relation to the wider canon. Here the insubstantiality of the self becomes a consolation. Its pretenses and efforts at sufficiency cannot be maintained. This is a blessing, since our reliance on the body that supports our person must necessarily be released. Our hope must come from another source. The no-self practices noted above are of particular relevance not so much to the meaning of death as to the process of dying.

Buddhists sometimes say that practice generally is a preparation for dying and in fact is continuous with it. Death is no different than every instant. Nothing substantial survives from one moment to the next, whether in the middle of life or at the end. And the quasi-survival of transmigration is not something to be actively sought. Death, a death untroubled with rebirth, is the capstone of the path to enlightenment. The central Christian divergence here is the conviction that something of crucial value does continue, moment to moment and from death to new life.

But the connecting point is that resurrection is no achievement of the self in resisting death. It is a relational gift. The person constituted by relation with others, and so in fact distributed by communion and love among those others, passes over into death, which the self does not survive. It is raised up, recreated, by God through the power of relation. In a mirror image of the way in which a person is originally constituted, she is raised up again out of all of her that is distributed among others. Resurrection is a recovery by communion. This is not some pallid idea of living on in the truncated memories of a few surviving others. It is a picture of the communion of saints, earthly and risen, with God chief in the communion, who bear the content of each person over the bridge of death when that person is himself mindless and selfless. Dying or raised, we are creatures. Dying or raised, we share the creaturely no-self.

The moral of this story is that there is great value in realization of the creaturely no-self. If Christians see no-self as mainly a preliminary insight, paving the way to deeper relations and more authentic personhood, then they are taught by Buddhists to appreciate the blessings of this insight itself and the way that it can eliminate at the source projections that cause suffering to us and to others. There is peace and insight that come from meditating on, resting in, this creaturely emptiness.

Nondual emptiness is not just a theoretical category used to expand the understanding of Christian theology. It has promise and effect in the practical Christian life, as well. Its grounding goes all the way down in the very nature of our created existence, even into the divine life. But how seriously can we take this creaturely no-self and its positive possibilities, given that Christians are also committed to the reality of persons and relations as much more than useful projections? Are we not talking either of what can only be a superficial adjunct to Christian belief or of a repudiation of foundational convictions? What kind of human person would have as little self as Buddhism suggests and as much significance as Christians claim?

Mimetic Self: Too Little or Too Much?

I mentioned at the start of this chapter that Christian thought in its own way requires us to reconsider both philosophical and common-sense notions of the apparent self. Our exploration of the ways in which Christian understanding may recognize the no-self wisdom in Buddhism may seem to stretch this reconsideration too far. Is it really feasible to articulate an understanding of human selves that allows for less self than we might traditionally assume, but still recognizes real persons in the crucial respects that Christian theology seeks? I believe that there is an emerging perspective in cognitive and social science that illustrates how this works. It is for Buddhist thinkers to say whether and to what extent it might correspond to their notion of no-self, but I think it expresses the nature of humans as creatures in a manner consistent with theological views of persons and with the insight of creaturely emptiness.

A number of thinkers in research areas ranging from animal intelligence to cognitive neurology have converged on a vision of a mimetic self. Recent work "argues that imitation is a rare ability that is fundamentally linked to characteristically human forms of intelligence, in particular to language, culture and the ability to understand other minds."[34] There is much evidence that "interpersonal relations are made possible, in the first place, by resonance mechanisms that provide the common ground upon which the I-Thou relation can be established."[35] Of particular interest in this connection has been the discovery of mirror neurons and subsequent research into their functions.[36]

We are speaking of more than representational imitation, the ability to recognize and reproduce actions. Significant as that capacity is, there is an even deeper mimetic transition in early protohuman history that produced the foundation for a theory of mind, for seeing likeness with others not only in outward terms but also in internal mental states. Other mammals are social but almost entirely "locked each in their own consciousness."[37] Body language and, above all, facial expressions have become the means by which we read each other's emotions and intentions, something that can be done with surprising facility across cultures.[38] It is very likely that the extraordinary effectiveness with which facial expressions facilitate communication among humans is based on some variation of the mirror phenomenon, in which seeing facial muscles move in a certain way on another face activates a pattern for the same movement on our faces, a pattern that we recognize as associated with a certain mental state or emotion.[39] In short, there appears to be a mimetic program in our cognitive equipment, oriented particularly toward living as a self among others.[40]

Mimetic theory has both a scientific and a cultural dimension.[41] The scientific aspect has to do with the neurological processes through which our sense of self is primed by the awareness of other minds. In comparison with our close biological relatives, humans are born with a relatively thin instinctual repertoire and a famously long period of plastic development. We fix on key human models in our environment and update our software, so to speak, by imitating them. We not only learn language and behavior. We also are aware that others have an inner life like our own. Based on that awareness, we build a subjective world of attraction and intention that is in large part caught by inference from the perceived inner lives of others.

In the cultural sense, mimetic theory concerns the shaping of human desires. We have biological instincts that we don't learn (e.g., hunger, thirst, sexual attraction), but even these are heavily constituted in type by the process we just described. For otherwise healthy people to lack the desire to eat or to continue living comes close to violating the biological foundation on which we rest. But these are not unknown cases. It is entirely possible to have a whole range of specific, powerful desires that are wildly overdetermined in any biological or even utilitarian sense. A sex drive may be a given, but the passion for one certain and perhaps unattainable person over all others is not explicable in the same way. A motive that seeks social status and abundant resources may be understandable in evolutionary terms, but the resolute longing to succeed at one particular calling and to pass by other plausible or more lucrative rewards is something of a mystery.

Mimetic theory focuses on the nature of desire. "Desire" is a helpfully intermediate word, located between "craving," the familiar Buddhist term for the source of suffering, and "love," the familiar Christian term denoting the optimal relation among humans and between humans and God. The first is negative, designating the human problem. The second is positive, pointing to a solution. However, Buddhists have a keen appreciation for the positive role of wanting, in the sense of intention and choice, as Christians have for the negative (i.e., idolatrous) side of love. Desire is a helpful term to designate commonality at the crossroad of these different realities.

From a Buddhist perspective, we may say that craving is desire driven by ignorance, a bondage to conventional truth that always produces karmic effects. However, desire illuminated by wisdom (as is the case in skillful means or, preeminently, in the compassion of the bodhisattva vow) conduces to enlightenment. On the Christian side, desire deformed by sin (or what the tradition calls concupiscence) is very much like craving. It is desire for what does not exist in the sense in which it is desired, whether this takes the form of idolatry (i.e., desiring something as if it were God, when it is not) or pride (i.e., desiring one's own good before others when one's own good does not and cannot exist in distinction from others') or some other form. The things desired may be real and good enough in their own right. But they do not have the kind of reality they would need to bear the weight put upon them in the manner in which they are desired. They are thus unsatisfactory, in the Buddhist sense: incapable of giving permanent happiness, and eventually productive of suffering. Desire born of love, by contrast, in a Christian view leads to salvation, enduring communion. The primary good that is produced by such attraction is not possession but sharing.

Mimesis is a positive and creative feature of human nature, supercharging learning and opening the way for a cultural evolution that can parallel the biological. But it also readily generates conflict and rivalry, even in the absence of objective scarcity. The very fact that one designates something by expressed attraction to it may lead others to pursue it as well and, hence, lead to conflict. Taking someone as a model grows similar desires in the disciple. At some point, this can lead to competition with the model. That mimetic dynamic is headlined in the romantic or sexual triangles at the heart of so much literature.[42]

Mimesis is a simple program that generates extraordinary complexity, particularly when it bears not simply on actions or objects, but on others' perceived desires. It is as familiar to us the toddler who will accept no toy but the one that another child has chosen to play with, or the middle-school student who must dress or speak in the fashion of popular others. The intrinsic qualities in the objects we desire and the private authenticity of those desires themselves are secondary to their mediation through those who serve as our models and/or rivals. The legion of our desires, and even the tuning of our biological desires, are specified by contagion. They are caught from persons who designate by their desires what is to be desired. This is a distinctly human and social characteristic. We are neither autonomous selves, nor are we empty vessels driven by society or our genes along mechanically predestined paths. We are "interviduals," who form desires of our own only through models who mediate such desire.[43]

Clearly, this mimetic perspective undercuts a substantial self. Our attractions and intentions cannot be traced exclusively to the intrinsic motives of an autonomous agent. There is no essentialist explanation for desire. However, the mimetic self is emergent and free. It constitutes what is most distinctive of humans, the particular way that individuals take part in programming themselves. In Chapter 3, we discussed Śāntideva's exercise in exchanging self and others. The import of this practice was first to serve as an antidote to specific mental states (for states of pride, for instance, one could prescribe some imaginative change of places with someone who resents your arrogance). More fundamentally, it is intended to disrupt the solidity in our sense of self so as to realize its emptiness.

The mental flexibility that allows this practice is in fact deeply rooted in our mimetic nature. Exchanging self and other is our normal state, and this practice only makes it explicit in a purposeful way. In association with our usual mentality, this capacity for reading each other's minds can fan the flames of defensiveness and sharpen the boundaries we draw between ourselves and others. But Śāntideva sees it can be deployed to soften and then completely wash away those boundaries. In seeking to overcome the negative effects of our false selves, Christians tend to lean heavily on care for the other and an obedient constraint on our desires. What Buddhist perspectives highlight is the power of relaxing and loosening the grip of this self on our experience.

Buddhists and Christians differ over the significance of the self more than its nature. *Svabhāva* is a kind of being that the self would have to have in Buddhist understanding in order to warrant the attention we give it or to escape suffering. Since it does not have this, we must look elsewhere. The self's failure to measure up on this count is evaluative as much as analytical. No amount of circumstantial joy for a self, over any imaginable time, could count as satisfactory, so long as that self is not independently secure against any change in the situation. Buddhist wisdom sees in the mimetic process ample confirmation of that conclusion. Since Christians see the self as constituted by other-relation, they are inclined to see this not as an objection to investing in selves (requiring that we look elsewhere for what is valuable) but as the avenue to their fulfillment. The mimetic self describes an impermanence consistent with both Buddhist and Christian understandings. Buddhists and Christians might differ more over their evaluation than the description. From a Buddhist perspective, the mimetic character of the self confirms its unreliability as a locus of religious satisfaction. From a Christian view, the mimetic character of the self is an encouragement in the hope for personal communion as the very stuff of salvation.

I believe that such a mimetic self is consonant with Christian theological commitments and helpful in integrating much of the particular Buddhist truth we have been discussing.[44] Buddhists try to avoid substantialist language in speaking of the self, and Christians tend to employ it readily. We see how Christians may recognize the Buddhist wisdom of the unreality of the substantial self while affirming the relational person as both real and significant. A mimetic person is real in the respects that Christian faith requires but may not directly violate the *anattā* teaching. There is nothing in selves that has not been caught, borrowed or mirrored from other selves, of whom the same is true, though each is a unique and unrepeatable combination.

This is an image that is very consistent with the Buddhist analysis of dependent origination. The person is not some intrinsically substantial being, but a distinctive locus or point of view that constitutes itself in the very process of apprehending others. A person is a unique intersectional awareness. This proves to be a more hospitable framework than Greek metaphysics is for affirming some fundamental theological convictions such as belief in Christ's divine and human natures. As Joseph O'Leary says, a Buddhist-influenced approach offers additional strategies to overcome a flat opposition to incarnation. These include "showing that the opposition of humanity and divinity is based on a false ascription of substantial existence, or . . . refusing to adhere to the kind of thinking that produces the opposition, or . . . seeing that the humanity and divinity share the same empty nature."[45]

The self, sought within a mind in essentialist terms, is empty in the Buddhist sense. The person, found among others in relational terms, is real in the Christian sense. The self denied in *anattā* is above all an individual self, and the place that self is not found is within individual consciousness. The self or person that Christians affirm as real is above all a social self, and the place it is found is among as well as within. The perspectives largely agree descriptively about the substrate—the mental events and conditioned factors—that lies beneath no-self and person.[46] A self that is constituted by relation is impermanent. In this way, the Buddhist pattern of emptiness coheres with a mimetic view. This is a recognition of what kind of persons we are, not a denial of personhood. Some of the strongest pathologies of selflessness in the sphere of Christianity trade in a very essentialist view of the self in which something substantial in us must be denied or eradicated. A more mimetic view can be helpful in this regard.

John Keenan, who has explored these issues deeply, offers the following distinction between the self that Buddhism finds unreal and the person that a Christian theologian wishes to affirm. Where Keenan says "dependently arisen" one could read "creaturely" in terms of our discussion above. Keenan says that we can take self to mean a center of consciousness that is

> experienced as subject and regarded as our core inner identity, separate from but related to objects that are deemed to stand alone in the outer world. The instinctual urge of such a self is to nourish, protect, and prosper itself, bringing itself into the most advantageous relationship with other selves. By contrast, we may understand "person" to mean a subjective center of dependently arisen consciousness, which is aware of being transient and empty *because* dependently arisen; and with this awareness, it is enabled to focus upon a life course of benefiting and gladdening others.[47]

If we must lose ourselves to find ourselves, then we may say that what we lose is the projected self, the one that insistently denied the creaturely no-self. What we find is the mimetic person, the sufficient vehicle for the good of Christian hope.

The mimetic self can be read in both Buddhist and Christian terms, as we have just described them. The two traditions can agree that we have emergent selves. This emergence process is, from a Buddhist view, the product of ignorance on the one hand and instrumental utility on the other. The mimetic person can be seen simply as a description of the conventional self. That craving should arise from our perception of other's desires is entirely consistent with the nature of ignorance. Mistakenly believing that there are others and objects that they seek, we replicate the same mistake. From a Christian view, the emergence process is a divine creation, and the selves that result are of enduring value. Mimesis has a primordially positive side as well as a negative one. Human creatureliness is made in the image of God, and that means to be constituted by relation.[48] As creatures taken alone, out of relation, we are unconstituted and empty. This is the kenotic dimension of human beings, who can "be" only by making space for others. Being open for others is, when compared with an essential, self-supported self, to have no such self. The mimetic picture of the self illustrates the emptiness dimension of creatures, the apophatic space in our nature that allows for the meditative realizations of no-self. The mimetic picture also illustrates the porous or communion character of the self upon which Christian thought puts such great weight.

We have sketched an initial connection between the bodhisattva way and the Christian way, an overlap in the understanding of no-self and what it means to be creatures. It does not mean that we have independent existence. The good news of biblical creation is that our selves are outward-facing, interwoven phenomena, most real when most connected. This is different from, but not contrary to, the good news in the trajectory of Buddhist teaching that holds selves are empty and never emptier than when sought in an immutable mental refuge. When we take a cross-section of our creaturely status, we see something that Buddhism accurately describes and that Christianity quickly passes over—the lack of any essential self.

In the Buddhist perspective, the faulty nature of our projections of the world goes hand in hand with the insubstantiality of the self doing the projecting. Both point to the same unsatisfactoriness. And the solution is to cut off the projections at their source, stilling the individual mind. In the Christian perspective, the mimetic process in which humans are formed as persons is also the means for healing. The distortions that arise from a false substantiality of the self are mended by the mimetic network that draws us into personal unity with each other and God.

No-Self and the Cross

I have suggested that no-self is an authentic dimension of our creaturely nature. There is a positive blessing in relaxing into or cultivating this dimension. It can be a release from distorting projections, a way of avoiding sin, and an active antidote to many kinds of suffering. I want to consider this creaturely nature now with particular reference to Christ, the cross, and the Christian life.

When Kosuke Koyama wrote of his experience communicating the Christian gospel in the Buddhist culture of Thailand, he noted that a central strand in Jesus's teaching seemed familiar to his Buddhist hearers.[49] The Sermon on the Mount counseled hearers to take no thought for tomorrow and to lay up no treasure on earth, where moth and rust consume and thieves break in and steal. This invitation to detachment from greed and craving sounded the authentic note of no-self wisdom, the cooling of craving. It did so even as it stood alongside hot and passionate words about loving one's neighbors and enemies, hungering and thirsting for righteousness, and the quickening of attachments and desires. Jesus does not defend a false intrinsic self, because his true personhood exists in relation. When Jesus says "Why do you call me good? No one is good but God alone," he expresses this sense of no-self.[50] Once we approach scripture with a perspective on our creaturely emptiness in mind, we can see that many familiar teachings and actions have a no-self side.

In incarnational terms, for God to assume the nature of a creature is to share the fundamental character of creatures we have been discussing, their lack of any essential self. For Christ to be truly a human being is to be empty of such existence, as all creatures are. If the incarnation is creaturehood done right, so to speak, then Jesus does not cancel this fundamental fact but realizes its great positive potential in the selfless way in which he lives his life and in the way in which he gives it up. The temptations of Christ can be seen in this light.[51] Jesus is tempted to turn stones to bread to satisfy his hunger, tempted to throw himself from the pinnacle of the temple to demonstrate his standing with God, and tempted to worship Satan in return for dominion over the whole earth. In each case, Jesus deflects the temptation with reference to God: his true nourishment is the word of God, we are not to test God, God alone is to be worshipped.

Love of God and others is central in Christ's life and teaching. But it is married at the same time to this free recognition of the insubstantiality of the self that one might try to oppose to God or neighbor. The appeal to God is, we might say, a very skillful means to turn aside all these enticements to proceed as though things should revolve around Jesus's self, whether that be Jesus's bodily self, Jesus's spiritual self, or Jesus's social self. At root, the temptation is to act as though Jesus has a self whose substance deserves such assertion. There is no more appropriate sign of the no-self than the erasure of all that our misunderstandings construe as essential to the self. Jesus's acceptance of death is simply the literal expression of what has been true all along. At the cross, Jesus gives up his bodily existence, his social world and even his religious connections altogether. He apparently loses everything that pertains to a self-sustaining creature.

The hymn in Philippians 2:6–11 is a key marker in early Christianity, a reference point for the rapid development of Christology. It is also a prominent text in Buddhist-Christian dialogue because of its explicit language about Christ "emptying himself" to take the form of a slave and suffer humiliation and death. It invites readers to have the same, emptying mind.[52] The passage begins by saying, "Let the same mind be in you that was in Christ Jesus, who, though he was in the form of God, did not regard equality with God as something to be exploited, but emptied himself, taking the form of a slave, being born in human likeness, . . . and became obedient to the point of death—even death on a cross." One traditional reading of this text sees it referring to Christ's putting aside divine prerogatives and powers (i.e., the form of God) to become human.[53] Then, within the human condition, Christ goes further to give up even what humans properly have (i.e., life and self), and doing so in a particularly horrible over-and-above manner that most people do not have to bear (e.g., dying young, tortured, condemned, and abandoned).

There are some interpretations of this passage that would give it a stronger exemplary flavor. Those who see an Adam Christology in this passage contend that the form of God here is the created image of God in all human beings.[54] The starting point is not Christ as divine, but Christ as human. Whereas Eve and Adam had taken their likeness in the image of God as the basis for a selfish attempt to claim literal equality with divine knowledge and power, Jesus does the reverse. He humbles himself to experience even the most difficult aspects of human life. In this sense, the cross has a generally exemplary meaning about the proper humility toward the gifts of human consciousness. Jesus realizes that as a creature, he is no-self. Both his life and his death recapitulate what it is to live in the emptiness that belongs to that human nature. In other words, there was no way in which Jesus could be fully human other than to realize our creaturely no-self character. Since there is also a dimension of self-emptying within God's own Trinitarian life, this realization of the emptiness of intrinsic human being, at the same time, mirrors an emptiness that is proper to God's own character. It is a manifestation of the divine kenosis to take on the creaturely no-self, two overlapping emptinesses.

We can see this aspect in Christ and disciples because it is truly there. But it is not the whole story. In the Introduction, we discussed the three kinds of nonduality in Christianity (i.e., the apophatic, immanent, and communion forms). Christ reflects all of these and so is by no means a pure vehicle for no-self. In scripture or tradition, few images or events of positive emptiness are not at the same time presented as instances of relational trust/communion with God. Typically the no-self/relation complex is presented to us with the relation end first, so to speak. It is because of our openness and oneness with the other that we have no need to project or cling to an essential self.

Buddhist interpreters who take a positive attitude toward Christ emphasize a permanent inner insight into the kind of emptiness just described. Thich Nhat Hanh, for instance, views the cross as representative of an inner, spiritual attitude that realizes no-self.[55] Since each of the things that are not grasped by Jesus—equality with God, biological life, political status, an independent self—are empty, the focus should be on Jesus's insight in seeing through them and letting them go. A sympathetic Buddhist reading of the cross does not treat it as an event in an historical or personal plotline. It sees it as emblematic of wisdom, a meditative achievement. Jesus's sacrifice is an outward sign of an inward disposition, the realization of emptiness. Jesus does not cling to individual existence because Jesus has none, and he knows it.

Death on a cross stands for the realization of something that is always true.[56] Crucifixion marks the death of externally imposed identities and, even more profoundly, of the falsely projected substantial self, an important stage in every spiritual journey. Zhang Chunyi, a Chinese scholar who first became a Christian and then later a Buddhist, adopted a program of "Buddhicizing Christianity." He summarizes the meaning of the cross under three headings.[57] In the first, more superficial sense, he suggested, it illustrated the kind of altruistic act that bodhisattvas perform. In a second, more profound sense, it illustrated the physical body as a source of suffering. At the highest level, it represented elimination of the defilements that are attached to an imagined self.[58] The main point is that the sacrifice is only apparent. Jesus is neither giving up anything as a human being nor setting aside anything as divine. In the same way, Masao Abe reads the kenosis of Jesus as denoting something that is always and everywhere the case, a "single or *nondual function* of self-emptying or self-negation."[59]

The cross can also readily serve as an instructor in impermanence. Hanh emphasizes the crucifixion as an expression of the teaching value in suffering. Contemplating pain can be a wakeup call, a salutary shock to the system, along the lines of Śāntideva's vivid evocations of hell. It is by contemplating suffering that we can find the way out of it. Even more, if one encounters suffering with wisdom and not with anger or hatred, then one can overcome it. In that sense, one can contemplate Jesus on the cross as an instance of the bodhisattva perfection of forbearance. These thoughts came from Hanh's own intensive experience of meditating on Christ on the cross.[60] Just as the young prince Gautama emerged from his sheltered palace and encountered instances of sickness, age, and death that fired his determination to find a solution to suffering, so contemplation of the cross can stimulate our passion for wisdom.

Another Buddhist insight, viewing the cross in the context of advancing spiritual practice, treats it in terms of the *dukkha nanas*. Buddhist texts acknowledge, as Śāntideva did, that undertaking the bodhisattva path initially increases suffering. It does so by making us acutely aware of the truly unsatisfactory nature of things and by encouraging us to adopt others' suffering as our own. Both steps result in difficult stages or experiences, a "dark night" on the way toward enlightenment. These *dukkha nanas,* whether times of bodily pain or psychological anguish during meditation, are mapped out to help meditators anticipate and overcome them.[61] Christ's passion can be seen in this light, emblematic of a heightened suffering that is brought about by heightened insight. It is a necessary way station on the path to the truth.

These readings of Christ and the cross pick out an authentic, if weakly grasped, strand in the gospel and in the life of disciples, as well. Buddhist teaching unfolds this depth of positive no-self, as we discussed in the second section of this chapter. Buddhist efforts to articulate a permanent realization which the cross may illustrate has a parallel in that Christians have often endeavored to make the cross a universal template for life and for inner spiritual practice. That attempt to make the cross relevant to every moment and phase of our life can be distorting. It can, for instance, make an ideal of self-denial an all-purpose prescription in a harmful way. This is similar in part to the caution that Buddhist commentators raise against taking no-self as nihilism. The Buddhist text helps us to specify much more crisply an area in which we can indeed take the cross to stand for a constant pattern, the recognition of creaturely no-self. Here there is a concrete, unchanging ideal that can be actualized identically in the model and the disciples. That realization sees through false selves created or imputed by projection and liberates from the labor of defending an autonomous identity. In this vein, the Buddhist teaching adds dramatic depth and offers significant gifts for Christian understanding and life.

This enrichment does not dispel a consistent, remaining tension. Even the generous Buddhist readings of Christ that we have noted preserve a lingering and fully intelligible reservation. Is the form of the gospel about Christ, and most especially his passion, really adequate to the truth that Buddhists would hope to find in it? The cross is simply a questionable sign for spiritual ultimacy in the no-self mode. Hanh gently puts it this way:

> The image of Jesus that is presented to us is usually of Jesus on the cross. This is a very painful image for me. It does not convey joy or peace, and this does not do justice to Jesus. I hope that our Christian friends will also portray Jesus in other ways, like sitting in the lotus position or doing walking meditation. Doing so will allow us to feel peace and joy penetrating into our hearts when we contemplate Jesus. That is my suggestion.[62]

In one sense, the suggestion is well taken. The writer would like an image whose contemplation evokes the state of attainment that the event in the image makes possible. In Buddhism, this is an experiential nondualism in which the disciple follows the model into one unalloyed condition of peace. The meditating bodhisattva is such an image, a picture of the path and the end at the same time. Contemplation is the necessary gateway for all to reach attainment, and the outward equanimity of the meditator can also be the face of the attainment once it is achieved. For Christianity, the path and the end are integral to each other, but in a way that fits less easily with an image of equanimity and timelessness.

Christians are not rich in central images that express the positive aspect of creaturely no-self, at least not ones that are commonly deployed in that manner. Buddhists have many images of peace and calm detachment.

The rooted, unwavering serenity of Buddha statues comes in rich variations on a familiar pattern of realized emptiness of own-being. There are Christian images that evoke serenity and univocal fulfilment more readily than the cross does: images of a glorified and risen Christ, of the transfiguration, of Jesus with his friends at table, and of the infant Jesus and his mother. Among Orthodox Christians, the classic cycle of icons includes all of these images and more, with the cross standing as one among them. We could mention particularly the icon of holy silence, prominent in the Russian tradition. This icon pictures no gospel event or interaction but represents Christ as Holy Wisdom, an angelic form of great peace and direct meditative appeal. Some images of Mary perhaps have more of this creaturely no-self quality. And there are Asian Christian images of Jesus that take obvious facts of his life—the itinerant path of one who took no thought for food or clothing—and represent him in the bliss and equanimity of a wandering ascetic.[63] Some of these may point in the direction that Hanh desires, allowing a focus on our creaturely no-self through instances of its realization in Christ and others.

Most Buddhist commentators have stated their distaste for the cross less diplomatically. To them, Jesus's life and, above all, his death plainly lack the marks of the highest levels of spiritual attainment. The story suffers from an elemental flaw, which is Christ's disjunctive relationship with God (a nondual identity of divine and human would be no problem, as we have seen). Jesus's belief in God suggests a severe limit to his insight, unless he manifests such belief purely as condescension to the state of his hearers. One author who has reviewed Buddhist comment on Christianity over the last four hundred years, notes that writers often summarized Christian teaching on the cross with little comment or criticism, as though its absurdity were self-evident to anyone: "The message is heard and summarized as a strange story of an angry and unpredictable God who is swayed by his emotions and who is not able to love without seeing blood and suffering."[64] D. T. Suzuki expresses this bluntly: "The crucified Christ is a terrible sight and I cannot help associating it with the sadistic impulse of a physically affected brain. . . . As there is no self, no crucifixion is needed."[65]

The fact that simple narration of the Christian story was often taken as sufficient refutation seems to indicate that Buddhist observers found no compelling similarity between Jesus and bodhisattvas. This may be because the passion was so entangled with belief in God, or conveyed so thoroughly in terms of the substitutionary atonement theory. It may be that the self-sacrificial acts of the Buddha in the *Jataka* tales or of legendary bodhisattvas were understood by Buddhists under categories so different from Christian ones that these muted empirical parallels.

If the Buddha in a prior life gave up his body for the physical wellbeing of others, then this was more a manifestation of nonattachment and moral cultivation than a relational substitution. If advanced bodhisattvas sold their bodies or gave them as offerings to the Buddhas, then this likewise demonstrated their indifference to pleasure and pain and their wisdom in valuing the *dharma* above all. This set an example whose powerful light aided others to do the same. These motives appear to be distant from a Christian story that is marked by the emotional interactions among its protagonists and, even more, by a purported overturning of the very structure that linked karmic cause and effect. The characters of Jesus and the disciples do not suggest bodhisattva-like wisdom. And Christ's act itself (i.e., substituting one's suffering for another's) is so contrary to Buddhist teaching that it seems no one with wisdom would undertake it. So Buddhist tradition generally has not seen much to recommend Christian preaching of the cross.

The most likely comparison parallels the cross not with enlightenment but with penultimate or preliminary stages of bodhisattva practice. The *Mahāyāna* textual tradition explicitly describes acts of extreme generosity as necessary steps on the bodhisattva way, and a gift of the body was at the top of this list: "The bodhisattva has to surrender dispassionately his own body and even his loved ones long before he reaches awakening."[66] We saw an example earlier, in the past life story of the Buddha who underwent torture and execution in order to preach the *dharma* in the realm of a hostile king.

This giving away of the body or its parts is a signature act of Buddhas-to-be in the "ascent" or aspirant mode. It is an advanced stage but not the highest. The examples from the *Jataka* tales come from lives of the historical Buddha long prior to his enlightenment. We learned that the transformation body of an historical teacher such as Gautama is the least subtle manifestation of the Buddha that is accessible to those with the least wisdom or merit. It is a lowly manifestation, though its source is unimaginably exalted. This fits both with Christian understanding of Jesus as having come for the very least and last, and with the Buddhist view that this is the kind of Buddha manifestation that would be accessible to those most distant from wisdom, such as non-Buddhists.[67]

In this light, it is natural to understand Christ in terms not of attainment but of preliminary practice. Jesus's death could be seen as the action of an aspirant bodhisattva or the scaled-down manifestation of Buddha nature that was generated for those of limited wisdom. Both Buddhists and Christians think in terms of an accommodation or condescension of this sort. So when they view transformation bodies (in the Buddhist case) or the coming down of incarnation (in the Christian case), the empirical similarities in the concrete cases may be swamped in significance by the differences in the ultimates they are taken to manifest.

There is an interesting specific case in Buddhist tradition in which such preliminary perfection comes close to identification with enlightenment. This is the self-immolation of bodhisattvas. The Lotus Sutra contains a famous account of the Medicine King bodhisattva, who immolates himself as a public display of devotion to the Buddhas. That example was followed in literal practice by small numbers of devoted monks in the *Mahāyāna* tradition down to modern times. Cults sprang up around some of these self-immolators, and lesser practices, such as burning off a finger, occurred as well on a larger scale.[68] These events were accompanied by ongoing debate among Buddhist thinkers about their legitimacy and value.[69] To liken Jesus's death to such events brings it into an area that is already controversial within Buddhism.

Such immolations take place in deep meditation. Indeed, though in many accounts monks set the fire themselves or had it set, in some the burning was said to be a kind of spontaneous combustion, occasioned by the meditation.[70] The act was understood under the category of *dāna*, meaning "donation" or "charity."[71] Daoshi, a learned Chinese monk who lived in the century before Śāntideva, wrote an extensive defense of self-immolation, drawing on the Lotus Sutra's story of the Medicine King and on the story of the Buddha who gave his body to feed the hungry tigress. He argues that "offering the body—for the benefit of a tigress, for other beings, or in homage to buddhas—was guaranteed to result in enlightenment, often expressed in the form of a new permanent body replete with wisdom, virtue and the ability to save other beings."[72] Among the texts that Daoshi cites is one in which the Buddha tells his disciple, "After my death, if there is a monk who is able to burn his body as a torch or to set fire to a finger joint before an image of the Tathāgata or even to burn a stick of incense on his body, then in a single instant he will have repaid the debts of his previous existences since the beginningless past."[73] Such views indicate that there is some precedent in

Buddhist tradition for the liberating value of bodily self-offering, at least within one karmic stream.

Śāntideva's way to the realization of no-self includes the extreme of giving away one's life and body. This can take the form of a gift for the sake of others, but its basis is insight into the emptiness of self. The fulfilment of this path lies beyond such acts, in the realization of the emptiness of both self and other. A Christian way to the realization of love of others includes the extreme of giving away life or body. Such practices necessarily involve a tacit or explicit acceptance of our creaturely no-self, but its basis is relation with others. The fulfilment of this path lies beyond such acts, in the realization of communion.

We see why the cross is a problematic image for no-self attainment, or even for wise pursuit of that path. This brings us to a basic and important point. The bodhisattva is an exemplary figure, both an every-person seeker and an every-Buddha realization. The image of the Buddha under the bodhi tree is a picture of everyone's future, both proximate and final. It directly represents the path to take toward enlightenment and enlightenment itself. But Christ is both exemplary and not exemplary. There are ways in which Jesus is what every Christian wants to be or should be, and ways in which Jesus is not. There are certain aspirations to be just like Jesus that Christians will treat as systematically misguided, signs of mental illness, or spiritual deformation. But to be part of the body of Christ, or to be a little Christ, or to be one with Christ is part of the normal aspiration of disciples.

This distinction has to do both with Christ being made differently than others are and with the fact that perfectly symmetrical identities cannot exist even between two creatures. Such interchangeable oneness applies only in the nondual dimensions, and these do not exhaustively define either God or humans. The dramatic exchange in Christ between divine humility and human exaltation is not exactly reproduced in the disciples. That is not their vocation. Such disciples nevertheless can have the same mind, as it were, toward their own identity and advantages.

Buddhists may expect finally to have nothing but the nondual consciousness of a Buddha, to realize the absolute in immediate knowledge. Christians do not expect to approach the absolute to that extent, for participation in it will always be mediated primarily by relations, and not exclusively by identity. There will always be more than can be comprehended by and in creatures, even as they share in that "more" by their participation in the divine life and the life of other creatures.

This tension is particularly evident in the cross, but not isolated there, as though it were an anomalous outcropping. The issues that it brings into focus are present across the doctrinal and narrative spectrum. The image of the crucifixion is in one sense a picture of everyone's proximate future: death. And it may represent a necessary part of the disciple's path, a death to self. But there is a nonexemplary specificity about the image. The image of Jesus on the cross is not a picture of everyone's future. This is Jesus's death. It is factually different from most others and far from ideal.

There is an unavoidable element of *wrong* in this event: injustice, cruelty, pain, and abandonment. The Buddhist focus is on what is always and everywhere the case, while the Christian focus is on the relational, historical, and social. The bodhisattva's way is thus emblematic and fixed in a sense that the event of the cross is not, hence, the onceness of the cross and the manyness of bodhisattvas. It would be a nightmare, not a redemption, if every one's nature were an identical Christ nature and if the cross were a necessary part of that nature's realization, as the bodhisattva path is part of the realization of every Buddha nature. Replication of Jesus's way would mean replication of the injustice associated with it. Something crucial is lost if we miss the wrongness of the cross, its force for dismantling what it illustrates. The cross is an extreme and decisive event, not the final condition that it makes possible. Only the love that animates it is the desired constant.

There are three specific ways in which the failures of the cross in a bodhisattva sense are in fact key to its saving significance for Christians. The first of these has already been noted. Suffering is not an ideal. It is unbecoming or inconsistent to attribute it to a bodhisattva, in that immunity to suffering is the heart of the bodhisattva's realization. From a Buddhist view, Jesus's spirit and role are less than exemplary, even apart from his belief in God. For the cross to be experienced by Jesus with pain or fear is to diminish his spiritual achievement. One who has truly seen to the bottom of no-self has cut the cord of ignorance, and suffering has no purchase. The fact that Jesus undergoes brute physical pain, personal anguish, and anxiety suggests that he lacks this attainment. Buddhists who wish to elevate Jesus's stature are reluctant to credit his suffering as real. From a Buddhist perspective, the defining image of Jesus ought to reflect the state of one who is beyond suffering. His passion cannot be something done for others unless it represents a universal perfection that is achieved first by Jesus. Its relevance for others is as an example to do the same.

This same concern is reflected by attributing the true meaning of Jesus's death to his own karmic burden. In polemical and appreciative writings alike, many Buddhist commentators point to the massacre of the innocents at the time of Jesus's birth as the sin that he needed to redeem in his death.[74] This is a telling example, since to Christians these deaths appear as sins of others, similar to the acts of Jesus's own killers. To Buddhist interpreters, the massacre of the innocents, though done by others to others, is part of the train of events caused by Jesus's birth. It happens because of him and so is part of his karmic responsibility. From this perspective, Jesus purified acts for which he had been the conditioned cause, though Christians would see him as assuming the consequences of acts for which he was not responsible.[75]

It is not just that Jesus fails to have the specific qualities necessary to represent the universal final state of all. The second failing is that the plan of redemption lacks that grammar in principle. The risen Lord is a less agitated figure than the crucified one is, the first fruits of the life to come, and in that sense a vision of what is in store for others. But even this state is not identical for all who participate in it. There is no single path for the Christian aspirant. We cannot say, for instance, that the contemplative approach to God is the final and the necessary path for all, in preference to that of action, or of community or of devotion. A variety of vehicles exist even within salvation as well as on the path toward it. The distinctiveness of Jesus's life and person may go beyond that of others, but it reflects the distinctiveness that belongs to each person. Our lives are not identical to any others, as Jesus's life is not identical to ours.[76] It is important that there are some ways in which we are fully, interchangeably one with each other. Creaturely no-self is one such way, whose significance we have been exploring. But that is not the whole story.

The cross is nonexemplary in a third way: It is a social event and not a consciousness event alone. It is cautionary. It illustrates something that is wrong, and yet it expresses love and hope. The wrong that it points to is a problem not only with bodies and minds but also with relations. It represents something among us as much as or more than it represents something inside us. This is but one more reason for sympathetic Buddhists to conclude reluctantly that the cross is essentially a penultimate image. It represents a negative experience, and it is focused on a social world. Because it is so intimately bound to the conventional world, it cannot be an appropriate sign of spiritual ultimacy. For Christians, the interpersonal brokenness and the restored relations that the cross-resurrection addresses are themselves the stuff of communion and heaven. Healing the social world is integral to salvation no less than contemplation is.

Crucifixion exposes not only the open wound of the suffering self but also the open wound of the broken community. It is important in Buddhist teaching that the Buddha shared the disease that he overcame, extinguishing ignorance and suffering in his own mind.[77] There can be no remedy that is not administered within the deluded perception that must be healed. This is sound from the perspective that the root problem is to be found in mind. But the determinative biblical assumption is that the root problem is found at the social location where our selves intersect, where interpersonal sin is expressed and unevenly borne, as much as in the depths of consciousness. And the crucial position in that nexus is the place of the victim. The key point of the cross has to do with what can be seen, and done, only from that location.

When we look upon the crucifix, we are seeing another meaning of no-self entirely: the one who is made into no-self by the activities of others, by humiliation, abuse, and abandonment. The objects of such persecution are typically quite literally invisible, forgotten, unregistered. Jesus on the cross may exemplify the universal truth of creaturely no-self, and its inner realization. But at the same time, he enacts solidarity with those who are crushed and cast out. The image of the suffering Jesus activates all our wiring for empathy, for exchanging self and other most particularly with those in similar situation to his. Bodhisattvas are single ones who have compassion on the crowd of all beings. Jesus stands in the place where all the crowd focuses its hatred on one being. The cross is a disruptive image, disruptive to the essentialist individual self, and disruptive to the social structures in which victims stay invisible nonentities.

Wonhee Anne Joh, a Korean feminist theologian, expresses this perspective:

I find the notion of the "annihilation of the self" a meaningful part of my spirituality of resistance and transformation—individual and social— when I understand it as a call to practice emptying out of self so that I might better let a multiplicity of selves into my being in the world. Such emptying out and letting in gives birth to a "co-arising" of many selves in relation with, to and for one another. The annihilation of self then is a call to practice a kind of way of being in the world whose arch is bent toward the other.[78]

No-self is described by Śāntideva as a path of spiritual realization, but it must also be faced in the guise of social imposition, as an inflicted evil. In this sense, Jesus's death is about change in what Buddhism regards as a world of projection and convention, but what Christians regard as part and parcel of the kingdom of God. It is an unfinished story, lifting up the visibility of victims and signaling God's disruption of the way the world practices political reconciliation. The significance of the cross is diluted, not clarified, by making its suffering generic.

The modern movement for engaged Buddhism mirrors this tension between suffering as universal and suffering in particular.[79] Hanh expresses it in the letter to Martin Luther King Jr., in which he gives a rationale for the immolation of Buddhist monks during the war in Vietnam. He writes that the monks acted as the Buddha did in giving his body to the tigress to feed her cubs. They practiced compassion by sacrificing themselves "in order to call the attention of, and seek help from, the people of the world." Their aim was to "suffer and die for the sake of one's people."[80] Hanh significantly alters the traditional view of this practice. He directs it as an explicit intervention in the relational, conventional world, whose "good fruition" will be to change that world by communicating about specific peoples' suffering and aiming at their conventional relief.[81] The pain suffered has a positive communicative meaning. Making this intervention in the world while "experiencing this kind of pain, they will express all the seriousness of one's heart and mind, and carry much greater weight."[82] Engaged Buddhism aims not to encourage the unusual act of self-immolation but to elevate concern for conventional world acts of justice in response to social suffering into central importance in the path of enlightenment.[83] Christians may give equally thoughtful consideration of a disengaged Christianity, one that can elevate the practice and benefits of positive no-self.

An immolating bodhisattva for social change may be as far as we can come in a thought experiment, a kind of reversal of images. It is a picture of a meditative reconciliation that strains Buddhist categories as much as the attempt to picture Christ's death as a timeless perfection-of-wisdom realization strains Christian categories. Hanh's reading of the immolated monk pulls the realization of pure emptiness in the direction of a purposeful intervention in history for the sake of particular others. Our exploration of the cross as an expression of no-self pulls an engaged participation in history in the direction of including an existential emptiness. A burning bodhisattva and a mindful crucifixion run against the grain in their own traditions. Neither one looks like what normally counts as action in the world any more than the normal images of the bodhisattva and Christ do. But they help us appreciate what is significant in each.

In this chapter, we have focused on what may be the most alien-sounding aspect of Buddhist selflessness for Christians: the reality of never having had a self to begin with. We have been instructed by Buddhist no-self teaching to consider an emptiness of essential being that permeates the life of creatures, going to the very bottom of their nature, and even to the image of God in them. We have touched upon the ways that this can benefit Christian practice and enrich our theological thought.

The aspirant on the bodhisattva path seeks to increasingly dispel the assumption that there is anyone on the path. If we stop at this point, the core no-self teaching and practice, then we have a point of contact with Christianity that extends across all Buddhist traditions. We will see in the next chapter that at least for the particular *Mahāyāna* branch of Buddhism we are studying, this is not the whole story, since it is not clear that there is any path to be on. It is not only no-self that is a constant truth, but Buddhahood, as well.

5 The Bodhisattva as Buddha

IMMANENCE AND EMPTINESS

Chapter 4 focused on aspirant bodhisattvas and no-self teaching, the paradoxical recognition that there is no one on the path to Buddhahood. Buddhist wisdom stimulated reflection on the insubstantiality of creaturely existence and the spiritual benefits of that truth. In Christology, we explored creaturely no-self as a dimension of the incarnation that corresponds to a dimension of emptiness in the divine life itself. Our discussion also considered the extent to which the self that Buddhism rejects and the person that Christianity affirms are different and the extent to which they are similar.

This chapter turns to the other end of the path, to the qualities of a fully realized bodhisattva. We explore commonality and tension regarding the unitive reality that is already the case: Buddha nature and divine immanence. Our comparison deals with the bodhisattva as Buddha, with Christ as God, and with creatures sharing in the divine nature. Our point of departure is the paradox that the one on the path is already Buddha and always has been. This is the teaching of *tathāgatagarbha* ("womb of the enlightened one"), a germ or inner reality that characterizes every sentient being. Buddhist meditative practice is not only a disruption of our normal mental patterns and their attachment to an unreal self. It is also an opening to the truth within those appearances. As our commentators understand Śāntideva, this underlying reality is Buddha nature.[1]

Buddha Nature

When our sources describe the full qualities of Buddhas, they refer to something that is close at hand even though apparently so far away. Buddhahood is not in the distant future or on another plane of being any more than *nirvāṇa* is. Buddhahood is a present reality. The nature of everything in the conventional world is impermanent. But everything that is impermanent is truly empty. And the nature of the emptiness in all impermanence is Buddha nature. If no-self teaches that the conditions of suffering are actually not present, then Buddha nature teaches that enlightenment is an actual abiding condition that awaits recognition. Christians live with the tension of an already/not-yet dynamic in history regarding events, promises, and relations whose fullest meanings have yet to be worked out. Buddhists live in the tension of two contrasting perceptions that are simultaneously true at every instant.

Buddhahood is described with superlatives that seem to imply transcendence. It is cosmic in scope. Buddhas are supreme in wisdom. Since they "perceive phenomena both in their nature and in their multiplicity, they have a knowledge of everything that is knowable."[2] And they are supreme in compassion: "With a great compassion that loves unconditionally and beyond reference, they teach the path and have the power to dispel all suffering and afflictive emotion."[3] Even exalted celestial Buddhas are only the enjoyment bodies of a Buddha, and their still-slightly-conditioned qualities are far short of the Buddha's actual *dharmakāya*. All this suggests distance.

But Buddhas become and remain such in association with two fields: the field of beings and the field of other Buddhas. Bodhisattvas can practice the perfections that cultivate compassion because of the appearance of other beings whose ignorance makes this possible. They are able to cultivate wisdom by taking refuge in the teaching and example of prior Buddhas. These two fields are totally different in their phenomenal qualities, yet without any intrinsic difference in nature. As Kunzang Pelden puts it, the Buddhas are "without defect and are endowed with every excellence, whereas beings are a mass of faults."[4] But they are equally essential to *Mahāyāna* Buddhahood. This is because "there is not the slightest difference between what is called 'Buddha' and what is called 'beings' in that all are endowed with the Buddha-nature."[5]

Looking back from the perspective of attainment, one can see stages in a bodhisattva's realization of *bodhicitta* that reflect growth in wisdom.[6] At first, one regards all other beings with the same respect as one's mother or father. Then one regards beings with the same care as one's own self (the practices of equalizing and exchanging others are used at this point). Next, one realizes the sense in which self and other are the same. Finally, one achieves Buddhahood, in which all is mingled "like water with water into a single taste free from all duality . . . , Buddha and buddhafield . . . apprehended as a single whole."[7]

No-self has to do, in the first instance, with release from suffering, with removing its conditions and causes. It is through cultivating no-self that one realizes one's Buddha nature. Buddhist understanding sees enlightenment as one coin with two sides, the emptied conventional mind and the unconditioned consciousness of Buddha nature. The same emptiness that causes suffering, when ignorantly fabricated into the form of selves and essences, becomes the cause of enlightenment when it is grasped with wisdom. Buddhahood is nothing other than emptiness. Everything that is conditioned is empty, but emptiness itself is unconditioned. No-self practice is a process of removing defilements, dispelling what we falsely think is there. Buddha nature is the pure space that remains after those obscurations are gone.[8]

Emptiness has a ravishing, positive face, one that that goes beyond the compassion that wishes to end all suffering, to a changeless equanimity that emanates bliss. This is *bodhicitta* or the source of *bodhicitta*. This positive character of Buddha nature is not to be reduced to self-associated pleasures, even the sort that can arise as the result of Buddhist practice. It is not to be identified with relative *bodhicitta*, for instance, such as aspirant bodhisattvas generate. The positive quality of Buddha nature is equanimity without an owner, compassion without any substantial subject-object framework. The sources insist that there is no relational or personalist connotation at all to this description. This must be so if that description is to remain consistent with the no-self teaching it complements.

Buddhist meditative practice leads toward positive realization of the nature of mind. Buddhist meditators speak of a "falling open" of the mind into a mental state that is not experienced as "my" consciousness because it does not distinguish observer and thoughts being observed. In between the activities of the mind, there is space, not inert space that is bare absence of anything, but a "luminous," "expansive," "warm" space. The normal contents of our mind are what we identify with our selves. But there is a genuine or pure awareness under that content. Glimpses into this "fallen open" mind are the phenomena that are identified with Buddha nature or Buddha mind. One of the key features of such experience is the nonparticularity of its viewpoint. It is a view from nowhere, an awareness without a subject, location, or identity. It is, in short, a consciousness feasible only when self is dispelled.[9]

To experience this consciousness is to *be* this awareness, since there is no question of mental content in, so to speak, a mind that is distinct from that content.[10] This is what is meant by referring to it as a nondual experience. The apophatic nondual experience that we discussed in the previous chapter was notable for what falls away. The nondual experience that we are speaking of here is marked by positive qualities, unrestricted compassion, and objectless benevolence. The bare awareness of emptiness is also a bliss awareness.

To attain Buddhahood is to tap into an existing way in which things are that is unchanging, peaceful, conducive to compassion. To anticipate or return from this experience is immediately to fall into the realm of thought, speech, or action, where it cannot be expressed. No view or idea about it can be claimed as absolute, because any such view is on a different plane from the experience.[11] Buddha nature manifests an unrestricted perspective denoted by qualities such as omniscience. Yet omniscience might be regarded as a function of the way that Buddhahood is perceived from within its intersection with the conventional world more than as an intrinsic attribute of Buddhas. We saw Śāntideva and his commentators struggle to explain how bodhisattvas inhabit this experience of the realization of Buddha nature and yet act in the realm of thought and selves. In conventional terms, it seems that love and compassion are not features of fullest enlightenment. And yet significant Buddhist traditions explicitly use this language, especially language having to do with compassion, holding that of all types of compassion or love, the deepest are those of nonconceptual awareness.[12] We will take up this question more directly in the next chapter. For now, I want to focus further on the nature of attainment itself.

To speak of Buddhahood is to speak of what at other times is referred to as *nirvāṇa*. We reviewed the special *Mahāyāna* understanding of a nonabiding *nirvāṇa* as integral to the distinctive bodhisattva path. Bodhisattva Buddhahood is *nirvāṇa* for others. A very early text says,

> Monks, there is a not-born, a not-become, a not-made, a not-compounded. If that unborn, not-become, not-made, not-compounded were not, there would be apparent no escape from this here that is born, become, made, compounded.[13]

In one sense, this nature is the opposite of the character of human selves. What selves prove not to be, Buddha nature is. It is unconditioned and permanent, whereas they are not. It is proof against suffering, but they are necessary causes of it. If we were to continue the logic of this list, it would seem that we would say that Buddha nature has the *svabhāva* existence that human selves lack. But the reversal does not extend that far. Buddha nature also is empty of such existence. This is an important point. It seemed that the lack of an essential self is what made human experience intrinsically unsatisfactory. But this is not true. Buddhahood also lacks such existence, yet it is bliss and peace.

Individual attainment on the bodhisattva path is realization of this not-made and unborn. The very language of individuality undergoes a change. The vast scope of the bodhisattva's vow refers its attainments not to the individual person who makes the vow but to Buddha nature. When Śāntideva says, in the great concluding statement of the Bodhicaryāvatāra, "For as long as space endures and for as long as the world lasts, may I live, dispelling the miseries of the world," the "I" refers not to some persisting personal entity but to this underlying reality.[14] As Jesus speaks or acts in the place of God as a human voice, bodhisattvas grow to speak in the voice of Buddha nature.

We might think of Buddha nature as similar to an attractor. An attractor is a condition or set of values toward which variables in a mathematical system tend to converge. "Converge" suggests a time element, which is misleading. Buddha nature is the way that things really are. Its character becomes more and more evident through the field of Buddhist practice, but it is not coming into being. It is like photographic film that already bears an image, but the image is developing into visibility. The attractor is a helpful image because it has a nonpersonal suchness that parallels the way in which Buddha nature is typically described.

Alternatively, think of the frequency activated by striking a tuning fork. If we imagine Buddha nature as a vibration on a particular frequency, then that same preexisting vibration could be picked up or discovered in many media, the same vibration manifest in them all. This is the Buddhahood that exists as germ or potential in all sentient beings. When realized, it is nothing other than it has always been. We could say that the question of whether there is anything there, so to speak, in the self that is subject to the vibration is what Buddhists address when they debate the reality of mind phenomena. "Nature of mind" is a phrase that can be taken in two ways. The nature of an individual mind is that it is impermanent, empty, a conditional conjunction of conditioned elements. The nature of mind *per se* is the unconditioned spaciousness of Buddha nature, the universal vibration.

How might we understand this pure mind in Christian terms? I suggested in Chapter 1 that there is a nondual modality within the Trinitarian life and, hence, in the divine relation with the world. The kenotic withdrawal, so to speak, of God in the act of creation allows human creatures to have their own nature, one empty of any *svabhāva* essence. In the previous chapter, we explored this apophatic nondualism in terms of creaturely no-self. Buddhist teaching expounds the nondual experience of this creaturely emptiness with wisdom that surpasses Christian resources. In Chapter 1, I also suggested that there is an immanent nondualism, a nonpersonal and active presence of the divine life in creation. This is the dimension that we take up in this chapter, the one that corresponds most closely with Buddha nature. While our Buddhist sources contend that these experiences, no-self and Buddha nature, are at root the same reality (i.e., emptiness), they are clearly distinguished at least for the purposes of instruction.

At this point, we look to Christian theology's description of a divine immanence in, with, and under all that is, an immanence pictured in relational terms. "Image of God" names this immanence in human beings, the presence of the pattern in our "own" natures that is imprinted by the positive connection with God. We can also think of this as a constant, causal presence of God. That presence upholds the order among conditioned factors that allows and maintains our existence, the matrix of the material world, its laws and emergent qualities. Such immanence can be understood from the creature's side as an ongoing participation in the divine life itself, a foretaste of the fuller participation that is salvation. There is a flow of divine life from creator to creature, a oneness indivisibly shared among those within whom it circulates.

This is the Christian theological framework through which to approach the teaching that those on the bodhisattva path are already primordially Buddha, or that their true nature has always been true Mind. Such an underlying state only needs uncovering and purification. Christians may say a similar thing of the original shared goodness of the divine presence that sustains life within humanity. To put it somewhat oddly to Christian ears, God's relations to us include a relation of emptiness and a relation of identity. The apophatic and immanent dimensions each have a nondual experiential character that is rooted in divine self-giving. The apophatic dimension is grounded in the divine self-restraint that gifts the creature with the space to have its own relative existence, space that is empty in the *svabhāva* sense. The immanent dimension is grounded in that sharing of the divine life or power that sustains creatures that have no intrinsic life of their own. There is a one-ness in which we are immediately and qualitatively what God is.

I said earlier that Christians need not object to the Buddhist conten-tion that no being exists in the *svabhāva* sense, save perhaps for the case of God. This of course is an enormous exception. We delayed consider-ing it until this chapter on attainment and Buddha nature. In Buddha nature, we encounter something of the character that Christians ascribe to God: an unconditioned ground. Buddhists readily acknowledge the existence of gods that do not violate the *anattā* doctrine. These gods, like humans, lack inherent existence and are subject to ignorance and in need of liberation. According to Christians, God does not conform to this description. It seems clear that God does not neatly conform to the definition of the god of classical theism either, since an undifferenti-ated philosophical absolute of that sort gives little purchase to the bib-lical, relational qualities of God. Should the god of classical theism exist, it would be a clear violation of the Buddhist teaching on inherent existence.

But the Trinitarian God is neither kind of god, and so does not evi-dently violate that teaching. Eternally coinherent, its divine persons share or constitute the divine nature. The Trinity is codependent, ever arising, in the sense that what each has from or shares with the others is a con-tinual gift, not an independent possession. Trinity has an external con-sistency of effect but is internally dynamic. None of the persons can be God without the others. They are mutually dependent and nourished by each other. God's existence is from persons or from the communion of persons. Each of the persons pours out its life into the others, and by that emptying makes way for their indwelling. It is precisely the kenotic di-mension of the Trinitarian life itself that prompts theologians to see con-nections between emptiness and Trinity.[15]

As there is no *svabhāva*, no essential human self, we can also say that there is no essential divine self. If Buddhists maintain that God is a suc-cession of mutually conditioned phenomena, Christians need not nec-essarily object. God is not impermanent as creatures are. But it is true that within the Trinitarian life of God, there is no substantive single di-vine self, some giant version on the cosmic scale of what is presumed but lacking in human persons. Instead, the nature of God is a communion of persons in relation, each mutually conditioning the others. As Chris-tian theology traditionally rejects the idea that God is *a* being, so we can say that God is not *a* self. Person and relation are co-arising divine realities. The Trinity reflects a mimetic view of God, a life of mutual indwelling signified by the term *perichoresis*.[16] The mimetic nature of humanity reflects the image of the Trinitarian creator. Being empty and constituted by relation is in fact part of what it means to be made in the image of God, since God too is empty of an isolated, monadic existence and is constituted by relation. The difference is that the divine relations are mutually coeternal and ceaselessly cosustaining.

This understanding of God as Trinity implies a relational ontology in which relations are as much realities as the things that they relate, and one does not have priority over the other.[17] Selves and relations are mutually arising, constituting each other. The created world reflects this same quality. The mimetic self that we discussed in Chapter 4 is the human face of this relational ontology. Such a person is empty of any stand-alone ontological self at the same that time she is a fully actual relational self. The Buddhist view of dependent co-origination looks at projected entities, such as the self, as floating on a nexus of conditioned causes, each of which is likewise empty. This dependently originated world has its own internal coherence within the frame of two-truths teaching. But none of it adds up to anything that can prevail against suffering or participate in any final satisfaction.

When Christians talk of the relation between the divine and the human in the incarnation, they contend with different sets of supposed properties of the divine and the human. If we assume that God is eternal, omniscient, and omnipotent while humans are contingent, fallible, and limited, then any unity of the two requires rethinking of these two sets. Is God really God without possession or exercise of some of these divine qualities? Are humans really human if they are able to exercise or participate in some of those same qualities? Such reflection at the least unsettles the idea of any essential, static nature on either side. If divine or human persons/selves are substantial, bounded essences, then the unity posited in the incarnation is incoherent. Only some kind of no-self clears away that obstacle to communion. Only some kind of mimetic, real self, constituted by relation, indwells such a unity.

Keith Ward points to this when he notes that there is a divine kenosis in creation itself.[18] In adding free, rational creatures to the universe God places limits on the divine life as well as limits on control, knowledge, and experience. But these chosen constraints are not a zero-sum subtraction from divine properties. They are the condition of novelty, an addition of new forms of divine realization through cooperative, suffering love. God makes possible a new kind of fulfilment, one that contingent creatures and God participate in together.

Theosis, Divine Energies, and Bare Awareness

The kenosis of creation is a divine constraint that enables new kinds of good, including the sharing of the divine life. That sharing takes place across the various dimensions of divine relation with creation. Eastern Orthodox theological traditions explicitly develop one aspect of this divine immanence, the sharing of the divine energies. There is an incommunicable dimension to the divine life in which God remains unknowable even while in relation. Creatures cannot become the same one as God. They have distinct identities. This incommunicable dimension is signified by darkness, and the apophatic ideal is to relate with God precisely as unknowable mystery. Only in such cognitive ignorance and relational reverence may the full nature of God be approached. Creaturely no-self is a natural part of this spiritual path.

The mind of Christ that the hymn in Philippians 2:6–11 says is in Jesus and should be in us is a no-self mind, manifested in the succession and depth of what it gives up. But there is another side of that mind, a oneness with the divine in identity-awareness. We noted in Chapter 1 that Christ's unity with God is represented in the Philippians passage by a kind of exchange, in which Jesus takes on the "name that is above every name." That proper name for God, revealed in the third chapter of the book of Exodus, is not to be spoken. Its unsayability corresponds with the divine nature that cannot be fully thought. The name is avoided as an act of reverence, with a stand-in term such as "Lord" used instead to express both personal commitment and humble awe. Christ is one with God not only in the personal and communion ways that can be spoken, but also in this way that cannot. This is the "name" that all three persons of the Trinity share. Gregory of Nyssa says that it signifies the "uncreated Nature alone," which is in the Father and the Son and the Holy Spirit and "surpasses all significance of names."[19]

For this particular dimension of Christ's oneness with God, there is no language. There is only silence, and the space where language would be. This is a dimension of unity that can only be addressed obliquely in the conventional or created world. Yet even this dimension is shared in a proportionate way with humans. What Orthodox theology calls the divine energies are communicable aspects of the divine life, distributed with creatures in the act of creation. Such uncreated energies are biblically illustrated in the transfiguration of Christ, the burning bush, and other manifestations.[20] These energies are particularly signified by light.[21] Eastern Orthodox theology understands the divine energies to permeate all things, particularly all animate things: "All things are permeated and maintained in being by the uncreated energies of God, and so all things are a theophany that mediates his presence. At the heart of each thing is its inner principle or *logos,* implanted within it by the Creator Logos; and so through the *logoi* we enter into communion with the Logos."[22] This vision of the divine energies is simply a realization of what is always present, a removal of obstacles in our sight. As a blade of grass may be thought to have Buddha nature, so it may be thought to be alive with the glory of God.[23]

We can go a step further and say that the power of the divine energies is love. The love generated in the relations of the Trinitarian life is shared with nature. That love is intersubjective at its source, flowing from the Trinitarian interbeing. The uncreated energies are a universal immanence of God in all nature, a universal participation of all nature in God. As such, they constitute a nondual identity. The representation of these energies usually takes nonpersonal form, as in the fire of the burning bush or tongues of fire at Pentecost. All creation, sentient or not, carries this charge of the divine presence. When shared with creatures that lack subjectivity, such presence might be called energy or creativity.[24] For creatures with deeper subjectivity the divine energies undergird persons and relations of love, in line with those in the Trinitarian life. They enhance and deepen the relational qualities of persons. So the light of the nondual energies may be represented in an icon or painting as a halo or mandorla around Christ or other figures. Humans who enter into I-Thou communion with God retain their finite nature as creatures, but they become part of the mutual love in the divine life.[25] Thus the sharing of the divine life is an unrestricted reality for all creation, but it takes on a distinctive communion dimension for those who are themselves persons.

The created energies of God figure within the theology and practice of Eastern Orthodox Christianity, as Buddha nature figures within the Tibetan Buddhist scheme that we have studied. *Theosis* or "divinization" is the overarching understanding of salvation in the Orthodox perspective. We become "by grace (that is to say, in the divine energies), all that God is by nature, save only identity of nature."[26] The saved are "enlightened ones" who have realized the fullness of the divine image that is the watermark of their own being. This may be the closest parallel to Buddha nature that we can frame: an underlying presence that is of a piece with our own existence. Yet it is a participation, not an exclusive identity.[27]

This is why, in Orthodox spirituality, mysticism of the divine energies is associated with high levels of spiritual attainment. The more fully one becomes a person and the more deeply one relates with God and others, the more that one is filled with this energy, as the space for it expands. The deepening of participation in the divine life has to do with the discipline of human receptivity, not any episodic quality to the divine presence. As spiritual sight is purified, the divine energies that suffuse the created substrate of our lives shine forth more brightly. Orthodox theology directly refers unusual realizations of this reality to mystical experience, a wordless and nonconceptual unity with the divine life: "One must be raised above created being, and abandon all contact with creatures in order to attain to union with the 'rays of the Godhead.'"[28] So creaturely no-self is part of what makes this participation possible.

I believe that no-self meditative attainments are rooted in the true emptiness of the creature. Similarly, Buddha nature meditative attainments point us to the energies of the divine immanence. Creaturely emptiness and the immanence of the divine energies are two dimensions that Christian theology affirms always underlie existence. In less sentient parts of creation, these dimensions have the quality of an impersonal glory, which manifests in vitality and creativity.[29] In more sentient creatures, the presence of divine energies constitutes a shared divine bare awareness. This awareness could be likened to the kinds of sensitivity that exist in mental or physical processes below the plane of conscious thought, such as the implicit sense of location in space or an unconscious registering of internal bodily conditions.

I wrote in Chapter 4 of the Christian tendency to see our mind space almost exclusively as a site for encounter and communication. But by analogy to human preconscious awareness, we can imagine the divine mind as having an immediate apprehension of the universe from within. At this level, God's perception would be a view from everywhere, reflecting God's implicit presence in all of creation, a consciousness with no active separated subject (just as our nonconscious modes of awareness need have no explicit subject), but one that is permeated with beneficence and peace. This is a mode of God's presence in and to the world. A receptive sentient mind can commune with this awareness, which is always available underneath the business of communicative consciousness. One can tune in to the carrier wave of divine presence on the frequency of mind, a form of immanent divine energy. We become aware of divine awareness as it genuinely exists, as a dimension inside all that is.

We are well aware of types of experience that are not communicative, that involve profound self-forgetfulness through unity with a wider process. Play, sexual ecstasy, athletic absorption, becoming lost in nature, attentive perception in making or contemplating art—these are all instances of intense awareness without either contrasting identity or the communication of information. These are in fact glimpses of a divine bare awareness, a wider, luminous mind. We are talking about experience of this character, with the difference that its occasion is not, say, the flow of athletic absorption, but attentiveness to our own mental phenomena. We experience consciousness as one with this luminous and open presence.

The nondual dimension of relation with God, an experiential identity, comes in the creaturely no-self form. We discussed this in connection with Buddhist no-self teaching in the previous chapter. It comes also in the form of identity with the divine immanence, participation in the divine energies. That is what we have taken up in this chapter in connection with Buddha-nature teaching. These are two threads of timeless oneness in which Christians can be tutored by Buddhist wisdom. We can hope that under their different terms, Buddhists and Christians are referring to the same things in these cases, even while they organize and value those things differently. And just as Buddhists would contend that no-self and Buddha nature can be distinguished but not actually separated in experience, Christians may say a similar thing about creaturely emptiness and the bare awareness of divine immanence.

However, there is a certain mismatch in Buddhist and Christian visions of ultimacy. The purity and coherence in the character of *nirvāṇa* stand in contrast to a pluralism and composite character of Christian salvation. Buddha nature, *nirvāṇa*, and no-self are three distinct terms. Buddhist analysis powerfully explains how these point to one consistent reality under different names. Christian thought approaches the question of attainment on at least three distinct tracks. One is the human creature, with that creature's historical transformation and eschatological fulfillment. A second track relates to Christ, as the realization of a constitutive event of reconciliation. The third references God, in whose fulfillment both of the first two participate. Realization means something distinct in each of these cases, but each is internally a case of participation and relation (i.e., creatures with other creatures and God, human and divine in Christ, and the Trinitarian persons in God). The Christian nondual dimensions as we have described them (i.e., apophatic and immanent) belong to one of three complementary aspects of Christian salvation. Personal encounter and personal communion (i.e., with God and others) are the other two. These three are equally ultimate or coexistent though not identical.

When Buddhists speak of Buddha nature as unconditioned and unborn, that which has always been, they are speaking in a key that Christians identify with God. When Buddhists speak of no-self, that which has no inherent existence, they are speaking in a key that Christians most readily identify with creatures. When Buddhists speak of bodhisattvas who overcome suffering and realize their Buddha nature while extending compassion to struggling beings, they are speaking in a key that Christians associate with Christ and those who follow the Christ-path toward God and neighbor.

In the Buddhist telling, it is good news that the differences between these three are apparent and not real. They are three faces of the same emptiness, which can be seen either as Buddha nature or as *saṃsāra*. According to the two-truths teaching, this insight does not prevent transitory distinctions from retaining their appropriate usefulness in the conventional realm, including their usefulness to assist people at various stages on the path to realization of their identity with Buddha nature. All the variety that exists in the conventional world exists either as the outworking of karmic causes or, in the mode of skillful means, as a pedagogical accommodation to ignorance. The richness of Buddhist distinctions (e.g., the two truths, three jewels, four noble truths, and eightfold path) belong to that world. Buddhism commends nonduality as the final unification of the conventional realm and the ideal realm. The nonduality of emptiness can characterize both without contradiction and still be ultimate.

The richness of Christian distinctions (e.g., one body/many members, two natures in Christ, three persons in God, and even four gospels) is constitutive. It is Christian good news that the distinctions themselves participate in the fulfillment. Variety belongs both to creation and to salvation, participation in greatest good. Just as the not-oneness of God's Trinitarian communion is the highest realization of love, so the multiplicity of persons is the condition of the greatest intensification and sharing of experience. Love shared is multiplied. A communion relation is the signature pattern of attainment in the Christian vision, a recursive mutual participation of creatures in each other and God, modeled on the mutual participation that is the divine life. Communion is itself a distinct type of nonduality, not identical with those that we have been discussing.

These two patterns are in a complex tension, not a flat contradiction. For Christians, attainment is in some respects a realization that is identical for all and in other regards unique for each. Since relations and persons subsist in salvation, changes in them are an important part of what salvation means. For Buddhists, attainment is realizing what is and has always been the case for all. Since persons and relations are not substantially real to begin with, enlightenment need not involve them or any particular pattern for them. Realization of Buddha nature is described as an unrestricted positive attainment without any remnant of a self. But persons, human and divine, figure centrally in Christian attainment and hope.

Attainment and History

Rather than simply comparing descriptions of Buddhist and Christian attainment, I propose approaching the question from another angle: Buddhist views of arising and Christian views of creation. Ultimate religious fulfilment lies beyond the horizon of direct observation. But when considering the final role or nonrole of selves, we can ask how the two traditions understand the appearance of selves/persons in history or consciousness, and how such perspectives relate to salvation and Buddhahood. We can look back, so to speak, at perspectives on the emergence of self-consciousness in a historical, evolutionary setting. And we can look in, as well, to consider the self in terms of brain function and cognitive science. The first, the study of history, is a characteristically Christian impulse. The second, the study of the mind, is a characteristically Buddhist impulse.

Attainment suggests a change, but the extent of change involved in attainment is very much at issue between the two traditions. This is just as true when we look to beginnings as to ends. To explore one topic is to illuminate the other. Buddhists are as averse to speaking of a beginning of Buddha nature as Christians are to speaking of a beginning for God.

But while Christians readily see the emergence of nature, the appearance of sin, the activity of Christ, and the transformations of redemption all as changes, Buddhists hold consistently to two kinds of permanence: the unchanging flux of *saṃsāra* and the unconditioned stability of enlightenment. This is particularly relevant to our discussion of Buddha nature and divine immanence, identities that are always the case. "Creation" is a problematic term for Buddhists, who see Buddha nature as beginningless and view change as applying to the waxing and waning of obscurations of it. Creation for Christians is the origin of the divine immanence in creatures, the ubiquitous good that can be accessed in bare awareness.

I say that the turn to history is a typical Christian move, since history itself is a subject for fulfillment in the Christian understanding of salvation. History produces what participates in and is constitutive of salvation. This includes the human person, a created reality or, in phenomenological terms, an emergent one. The "I" of human introspection arises at some point in biological and cultural development. From a Buddhist perspective, this is prime evidence of its insubstantiality. Buddhism classically catalogs five components or *skandas* of the human being: matter, sensation, perception, mental states, and consciousness. The "I" arises within the aggregate of these conditions, both as a false projected identity and as a circumscribed but legitimate functional instrument. We could say that in common, unenlightened experience, the "I" is always arising out of this aggregation. It is an insubstantial projection, which Buddhist teaching has the means to unwind. In the presence of the perfection of wisdom, it could never arise. Since the self has no moment-to-moment enduring reality, there is little interest in asking at what time or in what way it first began arising. That question can be addressed equally well in each present instant. Christian theology, by contrast, takes a great interest in this kind of origin question.

Whenever the "I" first appeared, it and all subsequent selves must have done so for the same reasons that Buddhism believes it arises now, through some combination of delusion and temporary utility. A self may serve conventional purposes. In fact, in implementing Buddhist practice, it can serve supreme ends. But it is not part of primordial Buddha mind or of enlightenment. Its reification and the desires based on that reification cause all suffering. This condition, the universally ignorant inclination to mental poisons that lies alongside the universally incipient Buddha nature, is simply the empirical situation that Buddhist analysis discovers. It has no past and no future. Enlightenment takes place completely within this unchanged condition. From a Christian perspective, there is a directional arrow attached to emergence of self-consciousness. It is a positive and irreversible step, not only for humans but for the wider world. Personhood, awakening to otherness, is a gift. Persons are new, additional vehicles of value in creation and they bring into play new kinds of meaning and fulfillment, even for God.

To frame this discussion in terms of what we might call big history, we can use Robert Bellah's magisterial work on religion in human evolution.[30] Bellah synthesizes enormous swaths of scholarship, painting history as a cumulative succession of cultural epochs he titles the episodic, the mimetic, the mythic and the theoretic.[31] The earliest stage of human or protohuman culture he calls episodic. Our primate ancestors lived immersed in an immediate perceptual awareness of the current moment, leavened by an episodic implicit recall of past events that might have some confirming or cautionary relevance to practical needs in the current setting. Sometime after two million years ago, a transition took place that supplemented this with the rise of a mimetic culture, marked by music, dance and ritual, but not yet language.[32] By gesture and expression, humans were able to communicate events, actions, and emotions from one consciousness to another, information in nonlinguistic form. This correlates with a rudimentary emergent self. It involved a nascent theory of mind, a perception of what is happening in another's subjectivity and replicated in one's own. Around 250,000 years ago, mythic culture arose, with the formation of language. With it came the communication of information in linguistic form from one mind to another, and also an expanded theory of mind in which one perceives or imagines what others are thinking.

Then, at the turn of the so-called axial age, around 500 BCE, theoretic culture emerged, roughly parallel to the transition to literacy. This culture was marked by a second-order critical use of mind to reflect on its own products. In this, Buddhism took a unique pioneering role, applying critical reflection not only to the mind's products but also to its processes. The Buddhist notion of awareness without self-consciousness seems to have a firm historical ground in the earliest stages of this story. There was a time, the period of episodic culture, when all the experience there was came without a conscious mind attached to it. It still does for all but a small sliver of our biological relatives. This deep insight is paired with the sophisticated self-reflective tools of theoretic culture, applied to painstaking analysis of the mental software, so to speak, that runs the elements that are inherited from other cultural eras.

One of Bellah's key assertions is that the core process, as it were, of each of these cultural epochs is conserved in later human culture, the way in which biological systems like the single cell or protein synthesis are conserved and repurposed in later emergent species. For instance, the oceanic awareness of episodic culture, with its absence of any conscious self, does not disappear from the human repertoire with the rise of mimetic self-consciousness any more than ritual or mythic narrative disappears with the rise of theoretic culture. From this perspective, the human person is an emergent reality, composite because its causes and substrates are various and conditioned. Bare awareness and various kinds of self-consciousness are sequential stages in the history of human subjectivity. These are layered dimensions of possibility in contemporary human consciousness, built upon the historical layering of components in the biological brain. Bellah does not view this sequence as a simple progression from lower to higher. Instead he sees these cultural core processes as the full register on which our human reality is played out.

Buddhists are convinced that the self that arises in this process cannot itself be part of the true nature of things or put us in rapport with the true nature of things. Only its getting out of the way can do that. That this emergent consciousness, after long and tortuous process, has allowed humans to solve many functional issues in an extraordinary way (e.g., finding truths about the natural world, improving the physical conditions of human life, and elaborating Buddhist teachings) does not change that fundamental judgement. Self-consciousness and attainment belong to different planes.

Śāntideva, like most Buddhist writers, emphasizes the extraordinary felicity of a human birth, since the world of human selves is the only one where an individual's practice can change karma and advance toward enlightenment. All of those born into the world carry the burden of a karmically reified self or at the least the residue effects of one; otherwise, they would have escaped rebirth altogether. It remains a mystery how there came to be selves in the first place. They would seem to be the only medium through which one could get into the bad karmic straits that require liberation, while they are also the only vehicle that can pursue that liberation, requiring a world of other selves to do so. Given ignorance and projected selves, it is easy to grasp the remedial value of our entire conventional world, the theater of karma and practice, and its associated realms, its hells and heavens. But it is less easy to see what positive reason there would be to be born into it and constituted a self, absent some prior deficit. Bodhisattvas maintain their activity in the world precisely because that deficit persists in suffering beings.

Many Buddhist writers see an evolutionary perspective as supplying a practical and scientific answer to the source of this deficit. It is an explanation that melds readily with a view of self-consciousness as a conventional phenomenon. The struggle for survival in the biological world looks much like *saṃsāra*, once we add the mechanism of rebirth to carry the struggle continuously from one life to another. Larger brains and self-consciousness developed to allow social mammals to cope tactically with the relational costs and benefits of life in larger groups. The self arises to deal with penultimate, functional issues. It is for that very reason that it causes suffering and obstructs understanding.

Self-consciousness arises at a late stage in a mental arms race, when human competitors in natural selection developed a theory of mind to war-game the strategies of enemies and allies and to develop their own. We could apply to selves Rousseau's quip about the arts and sciences: they "owe their birth to our vices; we would be less doubtful of their advantages if they owed it to our virtues."[33] The self is a fabricated product of the very cycle of birth and rebirth from which insight can liberate us. From this perspective, selfhood is an epiphenomenon of *saṃsāric* process, and the satisfactions derived from selfhood cannot participate in the ultimate. Christians see the selves-making of the evolutionary process itself as good, believing its products may participate in the ultimate.

Buddhists and Christians have at least one common interest in evaluating this evolutionary story. Both go against the grain by affirming a kind of altruism that a strict application of natural selection appears to rule out. Both stress evidence for the capacities for cooperation and empathy that are found in this evolutionary history.[34] And both see the problem with an evolutionary justification for intrinsic selfishness as resting in a mistaken view of the "self" whose interest is to be propagated. Buddhists see the notion of self itself as systematically deluded, and Christians see it as insufficiently expansive. They converge in opposing the characterization of a narrow, autonomous self as the actor whose survival interests must drive all behavior.[35]

One recent appreciative exposition of Buddhism in connection to modern psychology lays out three evolutionary strategies that were essential to biological and human survival, and notes the way that Buddhist wisdom reverses them.[36] The first strategy is creating separation between "self" and world and, eventually, between one mental state and another. Separate units and their reproduction are the very basis of natural history, the premise of evolution. The second strategy is maintaining stability: physiological and, eventually, mental homeostasis. The third strategy involves discriminating action, seeking out positive resources, and avoiding danger. The last two activities presume the effectively bounded unit-self that was established in the first strategy.

All three together drive biological survival. But, the writer notes, nature "does not care how they *feel*."[37] We are wired to experience pain as a warning signal in the face of compromised boundaries, disruption to our stability, and lost opportunities or looming threats. The classic Buddhist teaching about *dukkha* tells us that these signals will be endless because the three evolutionary strategies run up against three implacable realities: everything is connected, everything changes, and many threats such as aging and death inevitably defeat us.[38] Whatever short-term successes there may be, there is no long-term solution.

Three Buddhist counterstrategies confront this dilemma. They address the separation into discrete units and its attendant discontents with the recipe of pure nondualism. They address the illusion of stability with the teaching of impermanence and address the futility of desire with instruction in indifference to pain or pleasure. In some ways, Buddhist virtue, mindfulness, and wisdom are unnatural: "Virtue restrains emotional reactions that worked well on the Serengeti, mindfulness decreases external vigilance, and wisdom cuts through beliefs that once helped us survive. It goes against the evolutionary template to undo the causes of suffering, to feel one with all things, to flow with the changing moment, and to remain unmoved by pleasant and unpleasant alike."[39]

This account provides what most Buddhist teaching regards as unnecessary, an account of where the ignorance and delusion come from to begin with.[40] They originate and thrive as the success formula of our biological evolution. If we extend the evolutionary process over many lives, through birth and rebirth, then we have an effective picture of karma, the infallible engine of the conventional world. The structure of that world is out of synch with the true nature of things. Suffering serves the life interests of the biological self, but those life interests will never put an end to suffering. Only the *dharma* teaching can do that. This is a compelling way to fill out the idea of conventional truth. Evolutionary strategies that keep us and our species alive are just that: functional practicalities. The evolutionary process is "natural" only in terms of a reified world of objects projected by ignorance.

Buddha nature is natural in a different sense. It is what is unconditioned, always the case. So we can glimpse something of the character of attainment from this discussion. In regard to the separation/connection dichotomy, attainment is nondual. In regard to the stability/change dichotomy, attainment is unshakably stable, needing no defense against impermanence, though amenable to representation under numberless changing forms for those in *saṃsāra*. In regard to the agency/futility dichotomy, Buddhahood is endlessly effective but exercises no agency. In all three respects, attainment is completely unconditioned. The three survival strategies are about avoiding pain and postponing biological death. They win temporary victories at best. Endless rebirth, the greatest imaginable success in the evolutionary game, is total failure, a constant defeat in Buddhist terms. The Buddhist strategy is about ending suffering comprehensively, not just the gross suffering of death and pain, but the more-subtle forms of suffering that attach to any conditioned causes or self and to any scheme of meaning for the world.

Christian teaching has objections to the sufficiency of the separate, immutable, and self-actualizing agent that parallel Buddhist criticism. But its notion of attainment is different. Here we see that the difference between Buddhists and Christians does not involve a single question of origin, but rather an attitude toward the continual appearance of novelty and beings. While the common denominator in Buddha nature is its unconditioned character, the common denominator in Christian salvation is its relational character. Creatures, Christ, and God are all distinct but knit together in a recursive relational pattern. If we take the same three strategies as a frame for comparison, then we can say that theology meets the discontents of separation with the prescription of communion, a mutual participation. It responds to the challenge of stability with the hope for a dynamic fulfilment: persons-in-relation endure through change as foci of value precisely because they are not substantial selves. And in regard to the futility of agency, theology holds out hope that the community of God and creatures can maximize the values of experience and that conditioned good need not be intrinsically unsatisfactory.

In all three respects, attainment is conditioned by relation and mutual participation. Interconnection is a mark not just of the conventional or conditioned world, but of a future salvation as well. "*Saṃsāric*" process produces creatures and relations that did not exist before and those creatures participate in religious attainment, enriching it for all others who also participate. The process of history itself has a significance insofar as it produces emergent persons and resulting relations. These are plural, not nondual; contingent and not unconditioned. Having arisen (i.e., come into being) is an index of unsatisfactoriness for Buddhism, one that prompts the search for the unarisen. Coming into relation is a gift for Christianity that prompts the search for communion with the other. To say that Jesus is God in this connection means that this historical, contingent person participates in the ultimate attainment and that others do so also.

By virtue of our study to this point, we can highlight the areas in which Buddhist and Christian attainments may coincide. We have seen two aspects of Christian salvation that we can relate to the unconditioned, two aspects that are constant and whose realization is the same in all. One is the creaturely no-self, and the other is the bare awareness of divine immanence, the play of divine energies. The divine immanence has been constant throughout the process that Bellah describes, the divine energies steadily shared with creatures in the mode of their capacities. The developments over biological and cultural history throw up new forms in which these same unconditioned states are experienced. But the character of those states remains constant.

Attainment and Self-Consciousness

In addition to this look back into evolutionary history, we can look in, too—into our neurological function. We can ask not so much where our minds come from but how they work. Cognitive science is an area of prime interest today in relation to Buddhism. This is particularly true of Buddhist analyses of mind and the practice of meditation. The relevant research focuses particularly on the brain's self-referential activity, its internal perceptions.

Just as Buddhists and Christians have a common interest in altruism in the context of evolution, so they have a common interest in free will in the context of cognitive science. Buddhism presumes that the conventional self has freedom for the chosen practice that makes insight and realization possible. Mind must not be entirely determined by the physical brain. Christianity presumes that the created person has freedom for the actions and desires that lead into relationship and communion. For creatures, person and relation depend on some conditioned basis, as belief in the resurrection of the body suggests, but they cannot be fully reduced to those conditions. Recent research on brain plasticity offers some support for the kind of top-down agency that both traditions presume. Brain plasticity in general has to do with the rewiring, so to speak, of our neurological pathways and inclinations through purposive behavior. There is more scope for this kind of self-transformation than previously thought.[41]

Brain plasticity is key to the plausibility of Buddhist practice or any other religious practice that expects to effect change within a lifetime, let alone a wider future transformation. Perhaps the most basic element of self-consciousness is the capacity for attention, and the most basic element of freedom is the capacity to differentially direct that attention.[42] The ability to focus attention and thus to change the contents of our mind is the central act of Buddhist practice. This cultivation of an attentive mind is the basis for all the bodhisattva perfections Śāntideva discusses.[43] The self that does this cultivating is necessary for enlightenment but is not part of enlightenment. It has no essence but it is functionally essential. Instruction in how to use our attention to remake our brain appeals to a unified self of the conventional sort to serve the realization of the Buddha mind. In Christian perspective, the capacity to direct different qualities of attention to varying aspects of our mimetic models (and to internalize the same kind of attentions from others) is the basis for the transformation of desire and constitution of loving communion. The person who exercises this freedom is remade by it, through, and for love of God and others.

Enlightenment is not something that happens in a brain. If so, it would have conditioned causes in physical, neurological processes. It is a product of the mind. Contemporary Buddhist writers often argue that Buddhism itself confounds the Western categories of science, philosophy, and religion, combining elements of all three.[44] But Buddhism certainly has an empirical focus on the mind that invites interaction with scientific investigation. That exploration can shed some analogical light on the nature of attainment. In recent years, studies have indicated that long-term meditation can produce measurable changes in brain function, and that simple and relatively brief forms of meditation can have positive health effects.[45] Of course, such studies do not begin to measure what Buddhism sees as the final outcomes of these practices.[46] I would like to focus on two areas that relate specifically to the selflessness of enlightenment.

Researchers have identified brain states that correlate with experiences of nonduality. In these states, the functions that normally locate us in relation to our environment are suspended or muted.[47] Our sense of self is closely tied to our bodily nature. The fact that our bodies are located in relation to other bodies is significant in establishing a point of view and identifying ourselves as one among others. The superior parietal lobe is an orientation-association area of the brain whose primary function seems to be to represent the orientation of our body in space.[48] It does this through a constant processing of the sensory inputs that provide data on our relative location. When deprived of this input through meditative practice, the brain cannot establish the normal boundaries of the body and the self that we associate with our bodies, and so the brain perceives no border between self and the outside world. When this information is cut off, the brain has "no choice but to perceive that the self is endless and intimately interwoven with everyone and everything the mind senses."[49]

Whether or not ultimate reality is itself nondual in nature, the research confirms a biological correlate with our perception of it as such, a neurological state that can be evoked by meditation practices that are oriented to just such outcomes or by other means (e.g., sensory deprivation, drugs). Insofar as the self is a neurologically constructed impression, the conditions for this construction can be stilled, leading to a cessation of that self. Cognitive data such as this correlate profoundly with Buddhist insights. They suggest that Buddhist teaching and practice are skillful means that dismantle layers of cognitive function that have grown up over history, over a primordial oceanic awareness, an original consciousness such as Bellah says is a basic conserved core process in human minds. Such data support the idea that a sense of a separate self is a "neural delusion."[50] Self cannot figure in attainment because even at the physiological level, there is nothing there to begin with.

In this case, it is abnormal activity of the brain that is taken to reveal the true nature of things, while typical behavior does not. This leaves open the question of why we should regard the self as unreal because we can lose awareness of it, when we do not regard the world as unreal because we can lose awareness of it. We have blind spots in our vision, points on our retinas that register no light input. By carefully limiting our normal ability to see (e.g., by covering one eye and focusing on the particular blind portion of the field in the other), we can experience the invisibility of a segment of the world. Typically, our brains fill in those spaces in our visual field by extrapolating what we expect should be there based on the large sample of data that we do have, including the way that one eye compensates for the blind spot in the other. We fill in the blanks with what are, in one sense, fabrications. But they are almost always accurate representations of what is actually there and will be perceived when our eyes move so as to allow direct vision by normal parts of our retinas.

The fact that our representation of ourselves to ourselves supervenes on input of various kinds is somewhat similar. There may be a central blind spot, as it were, in our view of ourselves, and our minds may be able to narrow our vision to nothing but the blind spot and so be unable to construct anything at all from that lack of input. Yet that does not invalidate our normal perceptions. From a Buddhist perspective, such induced states are windows on emptiness, not a blind spot. The cognitive circumstances that are described can be seen as correlated with nondual experience of the divine immanence or the creaturely no-self (perhaps, by its qualities, more the first than the second).[51] These cognitive conditions reflect enhanced sensitivity to the nondual dimension of our experience and our relation with God. Buddhists are right to see religious significance here, as opposed to a mental malfunction.

A second area of brain research points to the dissipated or fragmented neurological correlatives of the conscious self. Various parts of the brain are more prominently involved in the experience of different aspects of self: an object self, a reflective self, and an emotional self. Identification of neurological correlatives to these varied aspects of self can undermine the presumption of any unified actor. Thus, one Buddhist scientist writes, "from a neurological standpoint, the everyday feeling of being a unified self is an utter illusion: the apparently coherent and solid 'I' is actually built from many subsystems and sub-subsystems over the course of development, with no fixed center, and the fundamental sense that there is a subject of experience is fabricated from myriad, disparate moments of subjectivity."[52] Therefore, "the self has no inherent, unconditional, absolute existence apart from the network of causes it arises from, in, and as."[53]

In this case, a Buddhist argument is that the normal functioning of the brain reveals the true situation, the lack of a unified self. Such a self is a fiction that the brain manufactures to make sense of its own operations, papering over the more basic reality of the gaps between what are only loosely collected processes.[54] Our awareness works quite well for many purposes without any subject. I do not consciously find my way home from work or reason out whether I have touched something that is dangerously hot. On this view, a fictional self proves to have certain practical, evolutionary value, which is why it has persisted, having utility relative to a conventional world of conditioned factors. The main point is that "the self is like someone running behind a parade that is already well under way, continually calling out: 'See what I created!'"[55] The self is nothing special, just another mental object. We could say that the self is even less real than other mind phenomena, such as immediate awareness, because it falsely projects stability and agency onto itself, a mistake that other mental phenomena do not include. The cognitive circumstances described here (such as the oceanic nondifferentiation discussed above) can be seen as correlative with nondual experience of the divine immanence or the creaturely no-self (perhaps, by its function, more the second than the first).

Some scientists assess the same data referenced above and find the self more central and less anomalous than just suggested. They view the argument from the fragmentation of the self as similar to an observer who takes snapshots of someone reading a recipe, turning on the oven, sifting flour, and mixing ingredients but concludes that there was never anyone baking a cake.[56] Antonio Damasio, for instance, argues that "for all intents and purposes, a conductor is now [with the emergence of consciousness] leading the orchestra, although the performance has created the conductor—the self—not the other way around."[57] To Damasio's mind, it is not reasonable to deny the specialness of the conscious self and the extraordinary leap in freedom and creativity that it makes possible. He views the subroutines or plural "selves" and the sometimes episodic character of self-consciousness as suggestive not of a fictional quality to the self, but of the self's skill at delegation and efficiency in managing the processes that constitute it.

It would be impossible to exercise deliberative control effectively over all of a human organism's activities. Nonconscious processes were in place, running the show, before human consciousness arose. Consciousness effectively acts by selective attention, by intermittently restraining some of the nonconscious "executives" and enlisting them to "carry out pre-planned, predecided actions."[58] The conscious mind can only actually exercise any kind of control if most of the time and for most purposes it is *not* actively involved. Only in this way can there be any time or space for the conscious self to plan or to do science, study religion, or practice meditation. The self is a complex, distributed over many subprocesses. It is no more a fiction than an animal's awareness of its location in space is a fiction (i.e., referring to no physical site) because it is constituted simultaneously by input from multiple neurological, sensory subroutines—visual, tactile, auditory (none of which themselves alone contain that awareness of place). The "I" causes behaviors that those neurological subroutines would never have carried out without it. Even experimental data that seem to show some actions preceding awareness of a conscious intention to act are, to Damasio, completely consistent with this picture. Many decisions are in fact significantly authored by the self through its conditioning and training of the subroutines.[59]

These increasingly elaborate pictures of our brains undermine all or nothing attitudes to the self. They question a naïve assumption of a substantive self, a Berkeleyan or Cartesian self—one that is real, though nothing else may be. They equally question an eliminative attitude to the self—a naturalistic or analytical insistence that there are components but no self. As there is much in the neurological picture to support Buddhist analytical insights, there is much in it to support the relational self that corresponds to Christian theological interests. "Self" as Buddhism analyzes it is a projection that sits on top of many conditioned factors, a mere name attached to them. From another perspective, "self" is a recursive reality that emerges on many levels of life (e.g., molecule, cell, organ). There is a subpersonal kind of self we could identify with a cell or an organism, distinguishing the boundaries around which various processes are organized. The different sides of the boundaries are distinguished by different results (e.g., oxygen brought to the "inside" and carbon dioxide expelled to the "outside"). One set of chromosomes is copied to a particular organism, but the mirror image set is not.

Just as different selves may be said to be operative in our neurological patterning, self can be seen to function in various ways at different levels of life. Terence Deacon points out that "self" in this sense is not some special substance or power, but simply a name for the dynamical reflexive process that expresses the teleology of a life unit. "Teleology" is a loaded word, so we could use another term such as "homeostasis" or "reproduction." But the key thing is that the homeostasis and the reproduction function in regard to some particular set of components. Deacon sees the self as a reality that integrates a whole nested set of earlier, continuing selves that comprise the basic distinctions that constitute a cell, or an organism, or a body.[60] This occurs in cooperative as much as competitive terms that are witnessed by the symbiosis of microbes in larger host organisms (e.g., bacteria in the human intestinal tract) or the capture, so to speak, of bacteria to become permanent parts of a cell.[61] Symbiosis is a kind of mutual indwelling that blurs the separation of selves, as it also presumes and builds on it. The parts interact to the effect that what results is not entropic dissipation to a less differentiated state, but a constrained continuity or reproduction of this composite reality. The "self" in such self-organizing or self-perpetuating organisms is not a conscious agent, but it is a reality nonetheless.

Deacon's argument is that human consciousness is not an anomalous mystery that appears atop the whole of biological history. It is an emergence that is consistent with a recurring dynamic in that history. Consciousness adds new scope and complexity to something that is already there. For instance, an organism has feedback processes that regulate its temperature within an implicit boundary. In addition to that sort of protoself, an enlarged mammalian brain adds feedback processes that regulate a social homeostasis, an optimal management of the set of relationships with other distinctive members of a biological cohort. A social self has been added to a metabolic protoself.

These may all be viewed as conditioned or created causes and results. The point is that if "self" is an empty name projected on collections of factors, it seems to be projected at all levels as an aspect of life itself, even where there is no evident mind to project it. An individual is transient. "Selving," in nonpersonal terms, is everywhere in nature. One might say that this is *saṃsāra* through and through, that the dynamism of nature is driven by ignorance at its most fundamental level. Buddhist wisdom then sees through this flux to the changeless positive emptiness beneath. Or one may see in the constancy of this process and its succession of novelties something worthwhile in itself, which a Christian perspective expresses in the conviction that divine wisdom, *logos*, animates nature and history with a fundamental good.[62]

Damasio takes a tack similar to Deacon's when he argues that the story of human subjective consciousness must begin not in the neocortex but in the brain stem, in continuity with the kind of protoself that Deacon references. To his mind, the existence of varied subroutines in the brain's neural geography does not by any means dispel the reality of our conscious self and its agency.[63] The emergent reality of the self is consistent with the inability to find a substantial self. Self-consciousness is no ghost haunting an otherwise atomized neurological machine. It corresponds to the way in which the body is already organized as a self "of a lower order."

> There is no inner intender as witness to a Cartesian theater because the locus of perspective is a circular dynamic where ends and means, observing and observed, are incessantly transformed from one to the other. Instead, the logic of the mutual reciprocity of constraints creates a relational ontology with respect to which autonomy and agency, and their implicit teleology, can be given a concrete account.[64]

The "circular dynamic" referred to is the dynamic by which the self is constituted.

Sensing the subjectivity of others reinforces and intensifies our own subjectivity. This mimetic process can be grounded in neurological detail about this circular dynamic, some of which we discussed in Chapter 4. Even very young infants already have the capacity to read intentions (e.g., the goal orientation of actions that they have never seen before) from the behavior of what they take to be animate agents.[65] Viewing an unsuccessful attempt by a model to separate two objects, the infant will imitate not what they actually saw happen but what they inwardly simulate to be the aim of the action.[66] Theory of mind involves a strong time component. For instance, one can attribute memory to another person in terms of expecting how she will behave (e.g., will she remember in which closed box the food was previously placed?) or one can infer an intention (e.g., she was seeking to attain this future state, even though I did not see it actually occur). In other words, one is simulating that others are persons across time, as one is one's self in so simulating.

Much recent research bears on the way in which our sense of self is developed in tandem with our sense of others. We recognize others as having a subjectivity like that which we experience. Seeing other persons—distinct from us, interacting with us, multiplied around us—reinforces the sense that we are one among others. They are like me. This means that there are selves that are not me. The dependence of my self-consciousness on the awareness of other minds is simply the most prominent example in our experience that distinct identity and connection go together. This interactive relation supercharged learning and cultural creativity. The capacity to share what is in another's mind is tremendously unifying. Yet it could not exist until we distinguished that there *was* another mind and it was not identical to ours. Insofar as the content of two minds are not the same, we have the basis for encounter and exchange. Insofar as they are discovered to have the same content or one comes to share what is present in another, there is an achieved communion, which is quite different from the apophatic and immanent awareness identities that we discussed earlier in the chapter.

The Buddhist inclination is to stress interconnectedness in the conventional world to illustrate that the self, understood as separate, is an illusion. But we have been illustrating that one can also say that the distinct, conscious self is the most dramatic instance of interconnectedness yet developed in the universe. To phenomenological identities of emptiness or immanence, it adds the multifaceted mindfulness of relationality. We have unique selves by virtue of our connections, and the less self, the less connection. The Christian inclination is to stress that the person, understood as relational, is a precious emergent reality. For Buddhists, it is essential to understand the interconnectedness of everything in order to know that interconnectedness is empty. For Christians, it is essential to understand the interconnectedness of everything in order to appreciate that relation is real.

Neurologist David Galin has attempted to relate the cognitive data to the schemas of Buddhist and Western Christian-influenced philosophies. He concludes that to do justice to the data, notions of self and person, transience, and stability are all needed. His summary definition is that

> a person is a dynamically changing, self-organizing, multilevel, quasi entity without sharp boundaries, and embedded in a causal thicket; self is the current organization of the person; and I is the self's point of view, its set of currently possible discriminations.[67]

More specifically, a "person is extended over time, and self is the current organization of the person. Self is the way in which all subsystems of person are related to each other at the moment."[68] Buddhist *anattā* teaching leans on the insubstantiality of the self in this picture, an insubstantiality that Christians may also recognize. Following that emptiness is the path to enlightenment. Christian views of creation and emergence lean on the significance of the person in this picture, whose dynamic features Buddhists rely upon in their teaching. Deepening the fullness of persons in relation is the path to salvation.

From both our historical and neurological discussions, the picture that emerges is an intensive interconnection among beings and, particularly, minds, what Thich Nhat Hanh calls "interbeing."[69] Hanh is clear that this interconnection is the realm of dependent origination, of *saṃsāra*, of form. But since, as the Heart Sutra teaches, emptiness is form and form is emptiness, this dependent interconnection is also the stuff of enlightenment, the form of which enlightenment is the emptiness. Put another way, "Buddha is made of non-Buddha Elements."[70] The Christian God made the creation and will never be without it, taking it up into the divine life and salvation. Buddha nature makes nothing, but it is never without the conventional world or elsewhere from it. The two belong together, in each case. There is thus tantalizing similarity and dissonance between the Buddhist statement that interbeing is empty and the Christian statement that relation is real.

Like two viable scientific theories, the two religious perspectives account for the same data in different frameworks. Buddhism and Christianity are as distinct from each other and yet as cross-wired together within the field of religion as are the different readings that we reviewed of the same data in human cognition. Whereas one saw the evaporation of the self into its parts, the other saw the emergence of the person with its constituents. Both can be said to overcome the idea of an inherent self. These approaches sometimes yield the same practical effects and other times do not.

We might use the analogy of tuning a radio receiver across a spectrum of signals. As one tunes toward the Buddhist frequencies, one dials up the intensity of emptiness and dials down the reactivity and suffering that flow from projection. What the enlightened or awakened mind brings to the conditioned world is the capacity to see what is equally and always true behind its appearance. This leads one to view all events that pertain to that world with equanimity and to sit lightly to the distinctions made within it. As one tunes to the Christian frequencies, one dials up the significance of persons in relation and the satisfactions that turn on them, and dials down the despair and suffering that flow from isolation or broken connections. Since salvation encompasses life together, this leads one to invest more heavily in the conditioned beings and relations that participate in that realization. Insofar as the Buddhist dial never extinguishes the conventional world of selves as the form of emptiness, and the Christian dial never establishes an ontologically isolated being (even in God), these do not flatly oppose or cancel each other. But there is a tension that seems to set an undefined limit on the extent to which they can be intensified at the same time.

Practicing Bare Immanence

These forays into evolutionary history and neurological complexity throw light on how Buddhists and Christians assess the costs and benefits of the conscious self in reference to religious attainment. If, on the one hand, self is no part of that attainment, then one will see self in the present as more apparent than real and look to its appearance in history or mind mainly in the mode of diagnosis of a root disorder. If, on the other hand, persons figure in attainment, that conviction will cast a glow of significance over their emergence in history and their role in mind, a glow the Buddhist will see as prone to reification. Buddhist wisdom suggests that the problems of beings and their suffering cannot be solved in any framework that includes beings and suffering. The solution comes by looking to a level of analysis or reality in which these things lose their coherence by unwinding their arising in our mental constructs. Christian hope suggests that the reconciliation of persons and relations cannot proceed except in renewal and continuity with the processes that produced them. Those historical and mental networks of emergence are not only sources of delusion but also the stuff of redemption.

Buddhist practice uses the conditioned or momentary self to cancel out that conditioned self and the suffering that it entails by realizing the emptiness of all its constituent elements. Christian practice works its way ever deeper into the web of persons and relation, looking toward mutual indwelling as a mode of love that is sustained beyond suffering. That web of relations is itself an object of redemption. From the Buddhist view, suffering is intrinsic to conditioned existence, while from the Christian view it is a contingent fact of relational existence. What Buddhists call "gross suffering" is incompatible with both enlightenment and salvation. But on the more rarified levels of subtle suffering of the sort that some Buddhists think persists even in what other Buddhists experience as enlightenment, this is not true. Such features may be included in salvation as Christians perceive it. Christians may simply regard such qualities as characteristics of contingent, created nature. That nature is not unsatisfactory in principle, but only when its subjects assume their self-sufficiency and become sinful and estranged. These characteristics of contingent creatures are more part of the good than an intrinsic problem.

In Chapter 4, we explored creaturely no-self, a permanent, apophatic dimension of humanity. Apophatic nondual experience comes through suspension of our false sense of self and direct experience of the contingency of our own mental processes. In this chapter, we have reflected on divine immanence, as a source supporting changeless, positive qualities of meditative experience. The experience of Buddha nature is what divine immanence looks like in the general field of consciousness: a bare nonconceptual awareness. Similarly, we might say that mathematical laws in science are a form that divine immanence takes in the general field of the intellect. Buddha nature is both what is sought and what is always the case. A positive nondual experience suspends our sense of self through an experience of direct identity with divine awareness. It is a participation in the nonpersonal mind of God, one possible only in relinquishing our limited, located perspective in favor of the indwelling of the divine energies whose quality is the same in all beings at this level, a kind of background radiation of the divine presence.

Just as the velocities and trajectories of bodies in space allow us imaginatively to run the tape of the universe backwards, as it were, toward its origin, so this signature immanence has a qualitative vector imparted at its source, an impetus toward creativity and wellbeing. This is reflected in the characteristics (e.g., luminous, vast, and compassion-inducing) attributed to Buddha nature. Nonpersonal images such as the earlier image of an attractor are the most apt expression of this phenomenal reality. And it is this wisdom that Christians have special occasion to study in Buddhism.

It is true that Christians understand this immanence-identity as relational in a wider sense. Our awareness can become divine awareness because that presence has been actively shared with us, and because individual consciousness freely opens up to it. The Buddhist paradox is that the focused attention and actions of an individual mind are necessary conditions for attainment of the global consciousness of Buddha nature. The Christian paradox is that the pure identity of divine awareness is an integral element of the fullness of loving relationship. One must lose one's life to find it. This includes losing one's life in immanent unity as the way to find or realize the person-self that includes this dimension.

Study of Śāntideva's bodhisattva path leads us to focus on the permanent, positive features of God's presence as the Christian context for appreciating his wisdom. The self-sharing of the divine life has a narrative character, but it also has a constancy that is manifest in the conditions of creation. This divine presence extends to all of nature as well as humans. To say that humans are made in the image of God affirms this constancy in a particular way. It points not just to a permanent potential but also to a divine presence that is everywhere and always actual. Śāntideva's commentators explain that everyone will be a bodhisattva because everyone already has Buddha nature. The reason that everyone can have communion with God is that everyone already is made in the divine image and gifted with the divine presence. So, in their own ways, the two traditions frame an underlying universal constancy and a correspondingly constant path.[71]

The no-self and the Buddha nature are each realized experientially as identical in all because they are in fact numerically the same "one." Living with this teaching leads me to recognize two concrete respects in which Christians may say the same thing about what is literally and qualitatively the same in the attainment of Christ and that of all people. The first is the creaturely no-self. Precisely because it is empty, it is the same in all who realize it. Jesus's experience of it is no different from anyone else's. The second aspect is the bare awareness dimension of the divine presence, participation in the divine energies. Such positive awareness, being without concepts or location, is an identity consciousness no different in Jesus than in anyone else. The divine energies indwell us at a level below cognitive mind and personal interaction, as they indwell all of nature. That presence, a bare taste-of-water awareness, deserves the term "primordial," which Buddhists give it. Perhaps Christians can relate it to the oceanic consciousness that Bellah takes as a baseline in the era of episodic culture. Human encounters and communion with God come in numberless flavors and qualities. That variety persists as a constitutive dimension of the Christian vision of salvation. Yet this does not contradict the reality of these two elements, nor should it blind us to their importance.

Nondual identity with no-self or pure mind are rightly facets of Christian spiritual life. They are disciplines of practicing what is already true. In this respect, unitive prayer or meditation is not a means to anything else. Dialogue with Buddhism has inspired many to expand their understanding of prayer beyond episodic conversations with God. Christian monastics, mystics, and indeed many ordinary believers have been acquainted with the spectrum of spiritual practice that runs beyond the encounter or communion modes of prayer. Christians recognize that, at a fundamental level, we cannot enter God's presence, as that presence is permanent. Roberta Bondi writes that our Christian "monastic ancestors were convinced that prayer is natural to us, like breathing, if we only discover it in ourselves."[72] The apophatic and awareness dimensions ground that conviction in a work of recognition, in a prayer too deep for words. This type of prayer is a taking of refuge in an original unity with God and an original selflessness ("original" in the sense of prior to self-consciousness or action).

Christian prayer in its common understanding—thanksgiving, petition, and confession—is but the middle or encounter register of prayer in the wider sense. That mode of prayer, with its own rich variety, is suspended between two others. On one end, there is a communion mode of prayer, such as Christ-mysticism and charismatic prayer by those swept up in the Holy Spirit. These are intensely relational, but the relation between believer and Christ or Spirit is compressed to a thoroughly internal reality as opposed to an external encounter to the extent that the exchange of self and other extends to relation between the person and God. It is not an isolated "I" who prays, but it is the Spirit who prays through me, or I who pray through Christ. This is a distinct meaning of nondualism, an intermingled oneness in which the unity is a shared exchange, one whose nature is too deep for words.[73] On the other end of this spectrum, there is meditative realization of nondual identity in both the apophatic no-self and the immanent awareness forms that we have discussed. These cultivate immediate awareness of what is always the case. In that sense, they can literally be prayer without ceasing, for their requisite conditions are always in place and they are a kind of precognitive awareness. The characteristic form of such prayer is silence. The internal quality of this silence is a more pure emptiness, a more pure nondualism, than that of communion prayer.

These latter prayer-realization practices seek God in the specific senses in which God's presence can be said to be literally changeless.[74] And it is here that we can unreservedly become disciples of Buddhist teaching. God is present in the change of seasons or the birth of a child or the relief of poverty in ways that are narrative and differential. But creaturely emptiness and the bare awareness of divine mind have no different flavor to any experiencer. Insight meditation seems to correspond to the rigorous analytic dissipation of projections in Śāntideva's way toward no-self emptiness. Calming meditation seems to correspond more to the luminous and positive qualities of bare awareness of underlying immanence or Buddha nature. But since the two types of meditation are crosswired in various ways in Buddhist practice, it is hardly necessary to segregate them sharply for Christian practice. The important thing is that both offer a route to the nondual dimension Christians frequently miss. Buddhists do not agree that these teachings should be viewed in the framework that I have described, though they might be content to view that framework under the heading of skillful means. I contend that though Christian practitioners may necessarily fail in generating the final exclusivity of intention that the Buddhist practice seeks, they can pursue these meditative paths with full confidence and trust in specifically Buddhist guidance to these forms of emptiness and immanence.

To give these practices such importance, not only as stimulation to Christian adaptation but as taken at the direct hand of Buddhist administration to us, may seem unwise to many Christians. I have tried to suggest the theological basis for doing so. This suggestion does not downplay the reality of sin and estrangement. It commends these practices because they take human distortion so seriously that they proceed only by unwinding the "I" whose every discriminating act is tainted by those limitations, by stepping back from the entire world that is projected by our actual self.

In the long-running theological battle about what remains intact in humanity after the rupture of our relations with God, neighbor, and nature, I suggest that these two remain: the emptiness of our creaturely selves and the immanence of divine energies. They remain intact because they remain God's work, the continuing activity of creating and sustaining our nature. Our ability to access them is clouded by sin and ignorance. On this score, we could hardly improve on the sobriety of Śāntideva's estimate of the arduous nature of the path from our current condition to their realization.

We might say that within the prayer practice that fulfills Jesus's teaching that we must lose our selves to find ourselves, these are concrete movements that correspond to the losing. Buddhist wisdom uncovers the fact that rather than simply a painful subtraction preliminary to a subsequent gain, this emptiness is itself already full of blessing. States that we view as the threatening outcomes of following Jesus's injunction—lost control of our identity, phenomenological emptiness—are revealed in Buddhist practice to have a liberative effect in their own right. They are not only clearing space in which better relations can grow; they can be themselves already a recovered unity with God.

The holy envy that prompts my gratitude for Buddhist teachings comes with the realization that they, like traditional Christian beliefs, can be developed in less as well as more helpful directions. One might, for instance, follow much of what I have been saying and take the supposed line of thought a step further, to add an argument such as this: Both Buddhist and Christian attainment are ineffable. Buddhist meditative traditions and Christian mystical traditions both include nondual experiences. Therefore, the highest attainment in either tradition is the identical ineffable, nondual experience. That is not my argument, as I have two serious objections to that conclusion.

The first is that nonconceptual experiences need not be identical with each other, any more than electric shock and nausea are. There are profound mystical experiences of relationality (what I have called "communion experiences"), as there are profound mystical experiences of identity, which have been to the fore in our discussion. I have treated apophatic nondualism as distinct from immanence nondualism, since even Buddhist texts distinguish no-self and Buddha nature. But Advaitic Hinduism and Buddhism have long debated whether the unitive experiences in the two traditions are identical. Close attention to the claims and practices of nondualism makes it more difficult, not less, to appeal to nondualism to paper over the variety that goes under that name.

The second, related reservation involves the claim that the identical experience is the highest end in both cases. Such a conclusion forces Christians to a definitive hierarchical ranking of elements that otherwise should retain a coequal or integral character. There is a big difference between the recovery of a nondual dimension in Christian practice and thought and the absolutizing of this above all other dimensions.[75] The pure mind that is realized by the bodhisattva, the consciousness without a location or self attached, is the one ultimate mode of religious attainment on that path. For a Christian, the bare awareness of divine mind must be one among the continually available modes of divine presence, alongside personal encounter and communion. It is not destined to replace them. This is a pervasive divergence in the two traditions. The dominance of the personal and communion modes in Christian theological reflection (evident in the mixed reception of Christian nondual mysticism) has long impeded deeper learning from Buddhism. But this learning cannot displace the coinherence of all these dimensions, whether understood as layered and interacting simultaneously within a person or understood more narratively, as realized differentially in different persons but shared fully in a wider communion.

Christ and the Bodhisattva

We are coming closer to some of our central questions. To what extent is Jesus similar to a bodhisattva? Can a Christian follow the bodhisattva path? In what ways is the Christian's relation to Christ and to their salvation in Christ similar to a Buddhist's relation to bodhisattvas and their own future Buddhahood? Our discussions in this chapter and the previous one cover two central facets of the bodhisattva path, no-self realization and the identity-awareness of Buddha nature. I believe that both are intelligible in Christian terms as authentic connections with God. This appreciation does more than foster practices of instrumental use to Christians. It expands our understanding of God and opens up dimensions in our understanding of incarnation and salvation. In this respect, the bodhisattva path points somewhere we want to go, toward acceptance of the emptiness that is part of our character as creatures and toward an identity awareness of divine immanence.

To look at Jesus through these no-self and immanent awareness lenses is to see something fresh. Christian theologians often debate the character of Jesus's oneness with God and the shape of that unity in his own consciousness. If there is merit to our description of the Trinity-based dimensions of God's relation with the world, then Jesus's oneness with God is enacted in each of those dimensions. The overarching Christian conviction that Jesus is God will be specified somewhat differently in each case. What we see freshly in these conversations is the identity oneness that falls in the "everywhere the same" category. Creaturely no-self and divine bare awareness are primordial levels of oneness that have existed from creation: the same for all, a fact of shared nature or image. They can be obscured but not diluted. The Jesus who realizes our creaturely no-self is the fully human figure who drops every projection of a substantial self with the wisdom of insight into its emptiness. The Jesus who realizes the bare awareness of divine mind is in that dimension entirely one with God, whose awareness this is. In these two respects, Jesus is one with God exactly as any creature can be and, in fact, already is.

Viewing Christ through this Buddhist window, we gain new appreciation for some features in our existing theologies. So-called Adam Christologies are particularly appropriate for these elements, since they stress the work of Christ in developing what is already there in our created natures. And wisdom Christologies—those that focus on the divine *Sophia* or *logos* that is the constant expression of God in creation and is incarnate in Jesus—offer a convergent emphasis on some of the same themes that we have discussed. But I believe that Buddhist thought sparks genuinely novel elements for theological reflection on the incarnation and life in the divine image: appreciation for participation in the bare awareness of God or the positive benefits of the immediate experience of our creaturely no-self.

In Chapter 4, we examined Philippians 2:6–11 from the point of view of creaturely no-self. We saw that Buddhist-Christian interpreters could read the images of descent and exaltation in this passage in terms of constancy rather than change. On this view, emptiness (i.e., the absence of substantial being) is the true nature of things, including the divine. Christ realizes that emptiness, both in divine and human forms. Being in the form of God, Christ does not grasp equality with God but embraces emptiness by taking human form. Similarly, as a human, Christ realizes the emptiness of human "being," the reality of no-self. He manifests this by taking the lowliest of human forms and giving up all those things that humans attempt to appropriate to defend their supposed substantial selves: shelter, power, and even life itself. In this respect, the cross is not the midpoint in a journey but the sign of a timeless wisdom, the constant practice of emptiness.

Now we consider this passage from the perspective of Buddha nature. We see Christ's constancy less in apophatic terms and more in terms of positive identity with divine presence. Christ realizes the actual awareness and energies of God as shared with all creation. There is an underlying nonduality of Christ with God. This nonconceptual shared awareness is a feature present in all humanity, not only in Jesus. These are the characteristics of God that Buddhism refers to as the "unborn" and that Christian theology more commonly called "deathless" or "uncreated." Apophatic kenosis is about not grasping what is never truly there. This constancy is expressed outwardly as a movement of renunciation, a move away from self-generated objects of desire. But positive kenosis is about uncovering and exalting what has never been absent. Its outward image is uncovering, a veil lifted from an encompassing awareness.

As Seiichi Yagi says in a classic essay on Buddhist interpretation of Christ, the primary point is "the unconditional given of our existence is that God is with each one of us. . . . This is comparable to the fundamental notion of *Mahāyāna* Buddhism that every living thing has a 'Buddha-nature.'"[76] Or, as John Keenan says, these successive positions of Christ are not about "taking a vacation" from being God, but more a catalog of various dualistic views of God that must be transcended.[77] Because of the identity awareness, there is no exaltation that could be added any more than there is any separate role or status that could be grasped at. To express the nondual identity positively, it would be more apt to look to Jesus's "I" statements, especially in the Gospel of John—statements such as "I and the father are one" (John 10:30) or "I am the way, the truth and the life" (John 14:6).[78] Claims such as "Before Abraham was, I am" (John 8:58) express an assumption of authority and knowledge incongruous with the humility of the no-self. Yagi and many Buddhist interpreters take such statements to belong to the identity relation, which is somewhat analogous to the shift in use of "I" by the bodhisattva from reference to the conditioned self to reference to Buddha nature.

On these readings, the full humanity and the full divinity of Christ are two sides of the same thing. The realization of no-self makes possible the realization of divine mind or energy. This nondual unity with God is preverbal and nonconceptual. Jesus was one with God at these levels by an identity-realization that was and is open to all to achieve in the same way. Others could and should do the same. When Christians think about the "ontological" identity of God and Jesus they do not usually approach it this way, but there is much to recommend such a perspective.[79] In an existential, meditative manner, Jesus realized humanity in the image of God, in both the apophatic (i.e., related to no-self) and positive (i.e., related to Buddha nature) aspects. Any other person who does this does so in the same qualitative manner. Buddhists who attained enlightenment had been doing so already for centuries prior to Jesus.

In these respects, Jesus realized a liberation that was already true (i.e., that this is already our nature, and this is already God's presence with us), a kind of salvation by recognition.[80] This is Christ at the most bodhisattva-like. The greatness of this oneness with God is precisely its nonuniqueness. Jesus is divine in underlying nature in exactly the same sense that all creatures are, and his realization of that identity is qualitatively the same as any other's realization. This dimension of identity with God is not limited to humans. It extends in some proportionate way to all sentient beings and to all of nature. This is a very important point, for it enriches Christians with a fuller vocabulary in which to express God's presence in the natural world. Incarnation is God's participation in humanity and history, but no less in all of nature.

When we consider Christ in light of bodhisattva teaching, we focus on the realization of timeless states: no-self and Buddha nature. We saw that the image of the cross works much more effectively in the first case than the second. In regard to the no-self, Jesus's acceptance of death represents the timeless truth of creaturely emptiness and mirrors the emptiness of the divine life. But it is quite the opposite for a positive identity-awareness with God. Our discussion further illuminates the Buddhist uneasiness about the cross as an image of spiritual attainment. In search for the kind of Jesus image that Hanh desired, an image exuding an attractive serenity, we found more fertile ground in the resurrection appearances. The risen Christ is a first fruit on a path that others will follow, embodying the new life that they will share. In a profound way, this is a revelation of our own nature.

The risen Christ is a human body/person through whom the divine image shines with the power of the uncreated energies. The risen Christ, whose glorified body is a transformation of his earthly body, points to such a future for our own humanity, as do images of the transfiguration and the halos and mandorlas around the saints, and the tongues of fire resting on the disciples. In this way, Jesus's death and resurrection can stand for the existential truths of no-self and divine presence, the realization of permanent spiritual possibilities, an identical path for those who follow. It is not the cross but the resurrection that most obviously corresponds to this continuing, positive divine presence. The risen Christ is plainly a figure who shares in the divine energies and shares them with others, a radiant source. That Christ stands on a plane similar to that of celestial Buddhas, who demonstrate the equanimity that should mark those whose wisdom has taken them beyond suffering. The risen Christ also has more of a manifestation character, appearing in different forms to the woman in the garden, doubting Thomas, and the disciples on the road to Emmaus.

These Buddhist-inspired readings specify a constancy that Christians generically invoke but only partially grasp. Yet as exhaustive accounts they strain out crucial narrative and event characteristics of Christ and redemption. The oneness of Christ and God takes place in the personal and communion dimensions as well as the nondual dimension. These types of oneness exist in the Trinitarian life, where they are continually arising or renewed. And they are manifest in the incarnation. In creation, these are emergent forms of oneness. Our discussions of history and the brain touched upon this emergence.

There is a personal oneness that is an achievement of shared purpose and will, exemplified in the way in which Jesus and God relate to each other in love. There is also communion oneness, in which the two indwell each other. The value of these types of oneness is bound up with their uniqueness. Whereas identity oneness is marked by perfect replication, these kinds of oneness are marked by a rich variety. Jesus is divine in the hypostatic or personal union with the divine nature in a manner that is empirically and vocationally unlike anyone else, a sole savior. Others who realize these same dimensions of oneness with God will do so in manners that are also qualitatively and vocationally distinct from his. They share most deeply in Christ's unity with God in these dimensions through a communion with Christ that includes the specificity of their own persons.

When Christians confess Christ to be fully human and fully divine, they are invoking oneness across all the dimensions that we have just discussed. There is an identity-oneness, as there is a personal unity and a communion oneness. This outlook requires a pluralism in Christian expression, somewhat parallel to skillful means in Buddhism. Here the variety has not so much to do with fitting the teaching to the level of the hearer (that is an important but distinct question) as it does with expressing these coordinate dimensions. For instance, the personal oneness between Jesus and God involves mutuality and agreement. This is not an ontological condition, but a relational achievement (e.g., "not my will but yours be done"). The communion oneness between Jesus and God involves the ability for each to speak or act in the place of the other (e.g., "you have heard it said ... but I say to you"). In these cases, the oneness is relational and not purely nondualist in nature.

It may clarify the distinction to recognize that the most characteristic correlative to identity awareness is not words but silence, the literal silence of stilled voices and quiet minds.[81] Speech can only be a limping sign of such oneness. The communicative speaker-hearer distinction implicitly violates the nondual unity the language may seek to describe. This is less so for personal and communion dimensions of oneness: speech participates to a deeper extent in what it represents, since it is also a medium for establishing and expressing this kind of unity.

Buddhist and Christian interpreters seeking harmony stress identity realization as the central truth of the Jesus story. If these realizations are exhibited most perfectly in silence and their verbal expressions are always fraught with ambiguity, then the Jesus story is problematic. If Jesus exhibits these realizations, then he does not seem mainly concerned to teach them. Such meditative attainments are largely off stage in the gospel accounts. The foreground is taken up with other matters. We might fill in the forty days in the wilderness at the start of Jesus's ministry with explicit practice of these realizations, or the times when Jesus withdraws from the crowds to be alone.[82] Yet if no-self and identity with Buddha nature are the sum of ultimate truth, then surely Christ is an imperfect bodhisattva or, as some Buddhists suggest, a manifestation appropriate to earlier stages of wisdom. Jesus's imperfections as a bodhisattva, from a Buddhist view, are from the Christian view an index of the inadequacy of the bodhisattva role as a description of Jesus.

The Buddhist path that we have followed yields profound illumination. At times, it feels also like a constraint, a barrier as well as an illumination. In routing all our thought about Jesus and the Christian disciple into the channels of permanent conditions and transient representations, we strain out something central. A Christian naturally thinks of cross and resurrection not only as the signs of timeless truths but also as events of transformation, an interaction between the divine and created, pages in a story. Neither the work of Christ nor the destiny of the creature can be fully described as insight into what is always the case. Both involve transformation, change in the persons and relations that also participate in salvation. Plainly, Buddhism appreciates change (impermanence is a root teaching). But all change is at the conventional level. The deeper one's wisdom is, the clearer the line that distinguishes the conventional and the ultimate. Ignorance confuses them and wisdom distinguishes them.

For Christians, creation and incarnation represent a mixing of the ultimate and the contingent that is good in principle and not only apparent but also real. The conventional world has a destiny that goes beyond being seen through. The Buddhist cosmology is vaster than the Christian cosmology, but a hard line between pure mind and convention runs through it all. The enormity of its variety is transient and traceless while the core of emptiness is changeless and still. The Christian cosmos is infected with difference in both dimensions. Sometimes it is said that the difference between Christians and Buddhists is that Christians affirm a truly transcendent reality, God, while Buddhists do not.[83] The difference could be posed the other way around, specifically in the claim that enlightenment and emptiness alone are truly transcendent (i.e., impervious to suffering and change), while nothing in Christianity is so. Whether creatures or God, all beings either fail the test of suffering or, if claimed to meet it, prove nonexistent. Buddhism diligently separates the unchanging from the impermanent, whereas Christianity mixes them.[84]

In the linguistic, conventional world, if we privilege identity aware-ness, we can say that any form of words is only a finger pointing at the moon of nonconceptual experience or inexpressible reality. But it is a dif-ferent question when we treat persons as opposed to words, and particu-larly when we speak not of one representation among others but of the entire conventional world itself as such a representation and the source of representation. Most Buddhist interpreters would say that any sin-gle sign is completely dispensable in regard to the end state, a transient finger pointing to ineffable enlightenment. But if we hold firmly to the *Mahāyāna* coordination of *saṃsāra* with *nirvāṇa*, then it does not seem we can say the same of fingerness itself. Form is a necessary correlate of emptiness and Buddha nature. Distinction between the two can never be the eradication of the entire world of forms except in the immediate nondual experience itself. Christians are constitutionally committed to the notion that the created world, the history, and the emergence we have explored in this chapter are part of what they point to, because the creation is integrally bound up both with God and with ultimate attainment. It is not just that these are two generic sides of the same condition that can-not consistently be separated (the *saṃsāra/nirvāṇa* dynamic). Rather it is the continuing particularity in the divine and the creation that must be included in what counts as perfection, which means that nondual identity cannot be the supreme religious realization.

Sallie King, a notable Buddhist-Christian "dual belonger," expresses this tension concretely in her account of the conflict she experienced be-tween her Buddhist-mind and her mother-mind.[85] Her Buddhist mind held the convictions that all that is impermanent is unsatisfactory, all at-tachment causes suffering, and nothing in the world of birth is ultimate. Her mother-mind became convinced that there is ultimacy in this world in love: "We are born in human form for a reason, I came to think . . . , to seek love and give love."[86] Motherhood induced the greatest form of selflessness that she could conceive, a selflessness inextricable from love of the particular in its impermanence.

Love of her child was indeed attachment. But she concluded that this attachment was not delusion and simply rejected the teaching that it was.[87] King likens the gut-level attachment to her children that keeps her bound to the relational world to the bodhisattva's willingness to turn away from *nirvāṇa* and return to *saṃsāra* for the sake of beings. But it is also fundamentally different. King does not *wish* to be delivered from this attachment. She does not remain in the world of loving relations with the hope of delivering other beings (least of all her children) from it. The ultimate is to be in it with them, and to desire they should be in it with others. This counts even more than the elimination of all suffering. In this sense, it is *saṃsāra* itself that she is unrepentantly attached to.[88]

We have seen ways to interpret the cross and resurrection in harmony with Buddhist wisdom as windows on timeless spiritual truth. There are equally important ways that they are not so understood, ways that they are interactive events and patterns in continuing relational transformation. The cross has an enduring significance for Christians as an intervention in the conventional world, for the purpose of transforming that world as a whole and of leading it into a new stage of realized community. The wrongness of Jesus's death is a key part of its significance, a measure of what is to be changed at the same time it is an event effecting change. To identify with Christ is to identify with those in the victim's place in history and to build a different kind of history. The resurrection of the crucified one has a significance as the perfection of Christ for continuing relation and interaction with creatures. It is a rearising of Christ's person for continued life within the process whose terms (i.e., person-relation) are precisely those within which Buddhism says the problems of suffering cannot be solved. To live in the world while seeing it *this* way (i.e., in ignorance) is to suffer; to live in it while seeing it *that* way (i.e., in wisdom) is to be free. The vision of a new heaven and a new earth is one in which new ways of seeing go hand in hand with changes in the world that is seen. Christ's death and resurrection are not simply about the fate of individuals. Christian theology sees these as cosmic in their scope. Death is not only a biological event but also a pervasive power, and resurrection is not only raised bodies but the instigation of a new heaven and a new earth. To put it in Buddhist terms, it is all of *saṃsāra* that is to be raised. Rather than compassionate ones lingering behind to help us or leaving a legacy to liberate beings, all of creation is drawn forward into new and deeper relation.

We have viewed Buddhahood from the aspirational bodhisattva path and the bodhisattva attainment. This discussion has prepared us to move to a final phase. Both Christ and bodhisattvas live for the good of others. We have explored now how those respective goods are different as well as similar. That equips us to face the question of how aspirants are to be helped, which pertains to the soteriological or liberative activity of Christ and bodhisattvas. We have laid out the framework for that saving or freeing work, but it remains to address it directly

6 How Do Buddhas Help?

BODHISATTVA AS BENEFACTOR AND CHRIST AS SAVIOR

The practical similarity between Christ/disciples and Buddhas/bodhisattvas is their orientation toward others, their unrestricted compassion. To attain enlightenment for the sake of all sentient beings is by definition to be a helper to all beings. Throughout the Buddhist world, suffering beings address their appeals to bodhisattvas and look to them for aid. In this chapter, we turn to these simple questions: How do bodhisattvas help? And how might reflection on that helping inform Christian theology?

Many Faces of Compassion

So far, we have not focused on any particular bodhisattva. The teachings that we have reviewed suggest that there is only one bodhisattva path and that bodhisattva-Buddhas could not differ from one another in their non-dual realization. But the characteristic form of the bodhisattva is precisely as a helper, and such helpers come in different guises. One of the most famous is the bodhisattva Avalokiteśvara, the "Lord who regards the cries of the world." This figure appears in Chapter 25 of the Lotus Sutra, arising as a roughly chronological contemporary to Jesus and the gospels.[1] The Buddha explains this title by saying that if numberless billions of beings in suffering and agony were to call Avalokiteśvara's name, he would "immediately hear their cries and all of them would be freed."[2] This applies to concrete worldly needs, whether they be the attack of robbers or the desire to bear a son. If someone, guilty or not, is imprisoned, then her bonds will be broken if she calls on this name.[3] This bodhisattva is a prime example of the skillful-means/one-vehicle theme of the Lotus Sutra. He appears in more diverse forms than any other bodhisattva, taking whatever status is required—that of a monk, a woman, a child, or a deity.[4]

In the Lotus Sutra, he is one of many bodhisattva figures. But as *Mahāyāna* Buddhism spread from India, his prominence grew. This change came most decisively after the transition to China and East Asia. A key aspect was a shift in gender that took place around 900 CE in the northwest Chinese end of the Silk Road.[5] Avalokiteśvara became Kuan Yin (or, in Japan, Kannon), the preeminent object of appeal and representation of mercy in Buddhist religious life in these cultures. Kuan Yin assumes many forms herself. The most common catalog of these lists thirty-three, each responsive to particular conditions such as childbirth or peril at sea.[6] With the concrete figure of Kuan Yin, we come much closer to the texture of bodhisattvas in ordinary Buddhist life. Her benefits and assistance are sought by virtually all, not only those who in their lifetimes vow to take up the organized pursuit of the bodhisattva perfections.

Just as the *Jataka* tales retrospectively outline Gautama's bodhisattva path, Kuan Yin acquired her backstories, as well. One of the most popular accounts says that Kuan Yin was once a princess named Miao Shan.[7] If Miao Shan belongs to Avalokiteśvara's family tree on the ascending bodhisattva path, then she also has a pedigree on the other, "descending" side, as well. Avalokiteśvara is an emanation of Amitābha Buddha, who became the central figure in the Pure Land Buddhist tradition. Looking at things from a chronological perspective, we could say that Miao Shan became Kuan Yin (Avalokiteśvara), who became Amitābha Buddha in the realization of *dharmakāya* or ultimate Buddha nature. One could equally well say that Buddha nature manifests as Amitābha, an enjoyment body (a *sambhogakāya*), who further manifests as Kuan Yin on another level, while Miao Shan herself is an even less subtle or *nirmānakāya* manifestation of Kuan Yin. In a sense, the first approach adheres to the no-self itinerary, as increasingly subtle selves are cleared away. The second comports with the Buddha-nature itinerary, as this supreme reality is manifested to the relative levels of sentient beings in their ignorance.

According to her legend, Miao Shan was intent on a Buddhist monastic life, but her royal father wished her to marry. He allowed her to go to a nunnery but told the nuns to make it so hard for her that she would quit. Finally, in a rage, he sent troops to burn down the nunnery with all inside. In some versions of the story, the nuns die. In others, the princess-nun magically thwarts this effort. In the end, the king executes Miao

Shan by strangulation, after swords and spears shatter without harming her. She awakens in one of the hell realms, where her prayers for the tortured souls there transform it into a paradise. The devils in charge complain to the king of hell, who sends Miao Shan back to her body, and for many years she cultivates her full bodhisattva nature.

During this time, her father the king becomes ill. His doctors tell him that he can be cured only with a medicine made from an eye and an arm from one without anger. A messenger is sent to a mountain where a great bodhisattva was rumored to live. He finds Miao Shan and makes his request. She tells him that her father disrespected and suppressed Buddhist truth and killed innocent nuns. "This should bring retribution," she says. Then she immediately gouges out both eyes and cuts off both arms to give the messenger. These offerings heal her father. He travels to thank his benefactor, only to recognize his daughter. Embracing her, he says, "I am so evil that I have caused my daughter terrible suffering."[8] But she assures him that she suffered no pain. She tells him that she would now see with diamond eyes and receive golden arms: "If my vow is true, all this will follow."[9] One of the most popular images of Kuan Yin represents her as having a thousand arms and a thousand eyes, all directed toward the relief of those in suffering, the abundant fulfillment of that vow.

Three Ways That Bodhisattvas Help

Although much of the development we just described postdates Śāntideva (Kuan Yin was beginning to emerge just at his time), we saw that the appeal to the bodhisattvas was already a matter of course in his writings. But the fact that bodhisattvas are so central in the popular as well as the learned Buddhist path only presents our first question in a more concrete way. Given all we know of the no-self teaching and Buddha-nature teachings, and the strict link of individual karma to individual actions, how can bodhisattvas effectively aid others?

We can begin with the aspirant bodhisattva who is cultivating the six perfections. Clearly, someone striving along that path will do much good to those they encounter. Śāntideva emphasizes that others, and most particularly enemies or difficult people, are unsurpassed opportunities for the bodhisattva to advance in practice. This has the coordinate effect that those around the bodhisattva will reap the effects of this selfless action. Inner cultivation is expressed in forbearance toward others' misdeeds, zeal for their wellbeing and indifference toward one's own advancement over them. A great deal of the aid that bodhisattvas provide to suffering beings is delivered prospectively by human beings who are themselves on the way to bodhisattva-defined enlightenment. Cultivating perfections such as patience, zeal, and concentration in the practitioner works out as interactive compassion, care, and wisdom for those around her. In this ascending mode, *bodhicitta* is expressed in concrete personal exchange and particularly in the teacher-student bond. Teachers such as Śāntideva guide with skill and deep relationality, and the power of such direction for a student can at times be regarded as supernatural in that it exceeds the effects that conventional wisdom could be expected to have. One can function as a bodhisattva by participating in the qualities of realization before one is a bodhisattva in the fully realized sense.

Bodhisattvas help in their direct ethical activity and, finally, in extraordinary over-and-above acts such as the gift of their own bodies. Even if these gifts are fundamentally offerings to a Buddha, there may be intermediate human beneficiaries, as well. Miao Shan's gift of arms and eyes is a paradigmatic example of this. Dramatic as this is, such selflessness might still be regarded as a byproduct of the search for one's own enlightenment and release from suffering, not a feature of enlightenment itself. That is reflected, for instance, in Śāntideva's injunction to consider how much benefit results from practicing forbearance toward an enemy, while that enemy will suffer horribly as a result of his antagonistic actions.[10] Such counsel could fit well with the path toward the abiding *nirvāṇa* that *Mahāyāna* regards as a lesser way. But this does not fully capture the weight of the meaning of the bodhisattva's enlightenment itself being for the sake of others. How does the bodhisattva's *realization* help others?

The first clear answer to this question relates to merit. Bodhisattvas accumulate enormous stores of merit, from which other sentient beings benefit. In fact, it is a consistent bodhisattva practice to dedicate the merit of any achievement to the good of all beings. This readily evokes in a Christian reader the idea that there is a transfer of merit from the bodhisattva to those who have less. And such language does at times appear in Buddhist texts. But on the whole, this implication is carefully avoided, as there is no valid mechanism for or agent that enables such transfer to take place and it would clash with basic tenets of karma. Sallie King remarks that she has never seen any explanation given for how dedicating merit to others or wishing loving-kindness for them actually works to have any effect on the others.[11]

One way to interpret the value of the accumulated merits is to see them as actually constituting bodhisattvas as objects of devotion. Bodhisattvas are fertile ground for others to acquire merit by expressing reverence towards them. Dedicating the merits of one's efforts to a bodhisattva or, even better, to many of them, elicits the greatest possible value for those efforts. So the bodhisattvas transfer merit to others in the sense that their own perfections or merits make them potent objects of others' reverence. When devotees practice that reverence, the sum of merit generated is multiplied many times over what it could be for any other kind of activity. Buddhas are called "fields of merit" for this reason. As Śāntideva says, "The merit due to faith in the Buddhas is the very greatness of the Buddhas."[12] Acts of devotion toward a bodhisattva are simpler forms of practice than the more demanding cultivation of the perfections themselves is. Yet these acts produce merit in proportion to the level of realization of the object reverenced, not in proportion to the actual virtues of the practitioner. So such reverence can quickly build the practitioner's capacity, enabling her to grow in other virtues. Bows and incense offered before the Buddha's image are simple ways of gaining merit and building resonance with the Buddha's model and are appropriate practices for those at advanced and beginning stages.

This role for Buddhas as merit amplifiers illuminates the emphasis that Śāntideva places on ritual honors that are rendered to bodhisattvas and on acts of dedication as integral parts of the bodhisattva path.[13] At the less-mainstream end of this spectrum stand the self-immolating monks discussed earlier, who offer their entire bodies as gifts to the Buddha. They apply the same principle at an advanced level. The extremity of the act and the elevated status of the one to whom it is offered combine to augment its effect exponentially. The devotee who attains enlightenment can then in turn become the object of such devotion by others. The bodhisattva's attainment in becoming the object of this worship is said to be for others because it energizes or amplifies those others' own practice through the intrinsic value of their reverence for the Buddhas. Become great, so that others can become great by exalting you.

In this respect, bodhisattvas are said to be "perilous beings," because mistreatment of them is "particularly grievous, while good things done to them are very meritorious."[14] Even the offering of a single drop of water in devotion to a Buddha will "turn into inexhaustible virtue tending to liberation."[15] So the great merit that bodhisattvas accumulate is dedicated to attracting the veneration of others, who build their own merit in ways that would not be available if they could not worship the bodhisattvas and their attainment. Buddhas act by being the object of others' devotion. This suggests that at some point, ascending bodhisattvas and descending bodhisattvas pass each other, or their causal effects mingle.[16] Those who are cultivating the bodhisattva perfections throw off much benevolent action to those whom they encounter along the way (e.g., by practicing patience and selflessness), while fully realized Buddhas are the fruitful objects of others' devotion. There is thus an operative cooperation of bodhisattvas past (i.e., now realized) and present (i.e., aspirant). Realized bodhisattvas aid other beings by serving as powerhouses of merit for them.

A second way that bodhisattvas help is through what we might call the legacy of their activities in the conditioned world. At least some actions that accrue merit—such as teaching or copying a Buddhist text or writing one—are themselves of direct assistance to others. Only a heritage of past teaching and practice makes the *dharma* available to people in any time and place. The activities that build the bodhisattva's merit also contribute to building the path for others. These activities continue to have resonance and effects, like blazes on a trail.

Bodhisattvas leave their responses to the cries of others behind them. The unconditioned cause of the unconditioned realization of enlightenment is Buddha nature itself. But all the conditioned actions that help ordinary beings to progress on their worldly path must belong to the career of bodhisattvas prior to their enlightenment, while they were themselves conditioned actors. This is like the "wish-fulfilling gem" that Śāntideva uses as an illustration.[17] The gem continued to grant wishes after the one who had given it those properties was gone: "The main force enabling bodhisattvas to take birth in an existence corresponding to their intention is the power of their former wishing prayers for the benefit of others."[18] The continued manifestation of bodhisattvas in the round of birth and rebirth is impelled no longer by normal karmic forces but by the power of the prior benevolent intentions when the aspirant bodhisattva acted in the conditioned world.

This conviction that vows and intentions exercise their own causality in the conditioned world helps us appreciate the emphasis on *bodhicitta* and on the bodhisattva vow itself.[19] Great bodhisattvas who are named are often distinguished by having added distinctive elements to the basic vow. Amitābha, for instance, vowed to create the specific pure land of Sukhāvatī. Since the realms of such celestial Buddhas are still, however subtly, conditioned realms, such a vow and its corresponding fulfillment do not violate the nonduality of enlightenment and Buddha nature themselves. The difficulty that we ordinary beings may have in crediting this kind of causality (in which a bodhisattva vow effects results after the bodhisattva is beyond any action in the conditioned world) rests in the inability to recognize that all conditioned causality operates at a level of mind-construction. The products of mind-construction can be altered in ways that would be impossible in a world composed of actual entities. The omniscience attributed to Buddhas encompasses precise knowledge of all conditioned causes, and such knowledge would allow control over the causation that obtains in that conditioned world, the mental production of mental results.[20]

We saw that Śāntideva directly acknowledged that for the sake of alleviating suffering, the bodhisattva accepts the delusory assumption that there are other suffering beings and that the aspirant bodhisattva has a self to make vows with. This paradox actually makes more sense now that we grasp that these illusions are accepted for the sake of laying down a pattern in the conditioned world of which they are a part. Bodhisattvas go beyond suffering, since they have annihilated its causes. Their firm commitment to remain engaged in the conditioned conventional world where suffering arises is itself what remains active in that world. This is consistent with the fundamental no-self teaching, as there is no self to be located in either the conditioned or enlightenment realms. The conditioned momentum of bodhisattva vows and actions carries on in the world of *saṃsāra*, while the realized bodhisattva is finally one with Buddha nature and not an agent of such conditioned relations. The tension according to which the bodhisattva is both conditioned and unconditioned at the same time is resolved by indicating that the bodhisattva leaves a trail in the conditioned world that continues to exercise its effects. The conditioned practices undertaken by devotees allow them greater access to those effects, which are experienced by them as manifestations of the unconditioned Buddha nature. Bodhisattvas are like extinguished stars whose ancient light still travels far through conditioned space in order to fall today on those who have turned in the right direction, at the right moment. Meanwhile, Buddha nature or the realized bodhisattva is mindless of all this.

This leads us to the third, closely related way that bodhisattvas help: by manifesting in the various forms that are most conducive to liberation for other beings. This accounts for the various bodies of the Buddha. As one commentator puts it, "By the power of prayers prior to Buddha-hood and by the power of virtue enacted by sentient beings who are to be trained, manifold appearances, which are totally illusory, are dem-onstrated. They issue from *dharmakāya* in such a way that they do not involve any deliberate effort."[21] Though changeless, the Buddhas "show themselves to the vision of others as if they were actually changing."[22]

Fully realized Buddhas cannot actually act or intend in the usual meaning of those words. Their appearances to others are free from any deliberate effort or thought such as "I must bring about the benefit of sen-tient beings in such and such a way."[23] This is an impersonal process. Buddha nature, free of all thought or intention, bestows good by means of its qualities, not discriminating action. As one root text puts it,

> When releasing a deluge of heavy drops or hurling down hailstones and thunderbolts, a cloud does not heed any tiny beings or those who have sought shelter in the hills. Likewise, the cloud of knowledge and love does not heed whether its vast and subtle drops will purify the afflictions or [increase] dormant tendencies towards holding the view of a self.[24]

According to a commentator on this text, Buddha nature or *dharma* does not discriminate benefit or harm, does not attend to the fact that its manifestations will "purify the afflictions of those who have devotion towards the Great Vehicle, whereas they may increase the dormant ten-dencies towards holding the view of an [existing] self in those who are hostile to it."[25] In this respect, the cloud of compassion and karma work in seamless unity. The skillful means by which teaching is tailored to re-cipients is not any conscious activity of the realized bodhisattva. Just as soft sounds can be heard only by those with acute hearing, the Buddha's teaching reaches only "the ears of someone who has great karmic fortune, having become a supreme disciple whose mind is rid of mental poisons."[26] The *dharma*, like water, is all of one kind when it falls on various grounds, but because of "the ground, which is the mind stream and make-up of beings to be trained [and] their different aspirations, it acquires many kinds of tastes."[27]

The realized bodhisattva-Buddhas do not actually go to hell to rescue souls or take birth again and again to assist suffering beings. It is the bo-dhisattva's past intentions and vow to do such things that, intersecting with current beings' readiness for spiritual insight, generate the appear-ances of such events. These appearances are not inferior in any way to other entities in the conventional world. Bodhisattvas "themselves" are entirely empty. So in truth, all bodhisattvas, viewed in the descending frame, are manifestation bodies.

Realized bodhisattvas help by being available at levels of conditioned existence that are inconsistent with Buddhahood itself, and by being available as objects of devotion and sources of instruction, according to peoples' readiness and need. The oddity of enlightened bodhisattvas' continuing to take rebirth can be seen in this light. The continuation of bodhisattvas in the *saṃsāric* realm is a type of manifestation, a posthumous effect of their prior vow and intentions. Those causes exert a kind of karmic force that makes these bodies appear. Even celestial Buddhas in pure Buddha fields are such manifestations. In principle, *dharmakāya* is the body of the Buddha that is fully nondual, the actionless and purposeless source of the manifestations.

As to the very-worldly miracles that are popularly associated with Kuan Yin and other bodhisattvas, we might say that these are relatively coarse manifestations, appropriate for people at early stages of practice or who live in a degenerate age when the *dharma* is not well taught.[28] The cries of suffering people represent a basic, unpretentious spiritual openness that allows the always-there rain of *dharma* to manifest for them in the form of concrete, conventional goods. This is somewhat similar to the way that Jesus commended the simple faith of those who turned to him for physical healing, which was emblematic of a more profound transformation.

As aspiring bodhisattvas cultivate the perfections, they throw off evermore-impressive benefits of this kind. Realized bodhisattvas manifest through such acts because they once vowed to be active in these forms. This is the weight of the specific vows that are such striking features of Śāntideva's text, committing the bodhisattva to the most humble and utilitarian kinds of assistance: providing a boat for a river crossing, a bed for the weary.[29] Some kind of omnibus well-wishing will not suffice; a causal intention needs to be attached to specific needs. Particular manifestations of Buddha nature come only to those who are at the right level of readiness, but there is a vehicle of manifestation at every level. This is the nature of the grace-and-works dynamic in this strand of Buddhism. Meditative and ethical practices of an individual aspirant evoke the conditioned bodhisattva manifestations that those advanced bodhisattvas intended for the benefit of suffering beings.

Full bodhisattvas are themselves beyond participation in or discriminating response to these specific practices. But it would be contradictory to suppose that true Buddhas are less helpful than aspirant bodhisatt-vas are. They help on a larger, cosmic scale in the three ways that we have outlined: by being the object of others' merit-producing devotion, by leaving a causal wake in the conditioned world, and by manifesting according to the levels of need among aspirants. As objects of devotion, bodhisattvas are the most easily accessible path of merit. Any who sim-ply calls upon them or respects them gains merit (i.e., self-executing good karma) by that very act.[30] They transfer merit in the very specific sense that they have acquired so much themselves that they have become low-hanging fruit available for the practice of others who accrue benefit simply by recognizing their greatness. Bodhisattvas help because all the activities they undertake in the conditioned world as they walk the way of the six perfections leave behind a momentum in that world. Their vow, for instance, continues to exercise a causal effect in bringing about what it intended. And bodhisattvas-Buddhas manifest in the form of celestial beings, deity images, or historical teachers, often according to intentions established by prior vows (the second way of helping). In this manner, they become appropriate objects of devotion (the first way of helping) and sources of instruction for people at whatever level of aspi-ration they achieve.

This discussion gives us some grasp of the rich repertoire of aid for beings that flows from the bodhisattva path. We can imagine a Buddhist statement of how bodhisattvas help that is parallel with our Philippians passage: "Though knowing himself to be empty of all form, in his wis-dom he realized emptiness was not something to be grasped. For the sake of the relief of suffering beings, he vowed the continuing appearance of an 'I' among other beings, manifest as real in the projections of those in deepest ignorance. For this reason, he is worthy of supreme reverence as the object of others' devotion. Even the slightest honor toward his name earns boundless merit, so that he may lead to the realization of the emptiness of all." Put in this way, this description can only express the ascending perspective of a bodhisattva, his vow in the conditioned world, since a realized being can have no such intentions or actions. A bodhisattva does not wait for all other beings before entering enlighten-ment, but leaves behind manifesting versions of self to assist them.

In all these ways, the bodhisattva helps by virtue of a presence in the conditioned world. This is true even though, in nondual oneness with *dharmakāya*, the bodhisattva is no longer part of that conditioned world. Indeed, an enlightened one does not experience herself as a bodhisattva, having no awareness of beings in a self-other framework. Buddha nature is the source of these benefits and the realized bodhisattva is nothing other than Buddha nature. The bodhisattva path runs through the conditioned world in order to help connect others to this same underlying nature. The diversity in the variety of bodhisattvas and the multiple forms of each amounts to a vast, self-executing practice of skillful means that matches beings and their needs with manifestations best suited to liberate them from suffering.

Deity and Benefactor Meditation

This background helps us to appreciate the complexities of Tibetan meditation practice, in which various Buddhas, bodhisattvas, and other images become direct objects of attention. Such practices can be seen in both an "ascending" and a "descending" light. The practices aim at generating *bodhicitta* within the practitioner, through concentration on the images. They can equally be seen as manifestations of celestial bodhisattvas or Buddhas to the trainee who has reached a level to be able to see or engage such a manifestation. Tārā, a female bodhisattva and meditation deity, is an example of such a figure who is prominent in Tibetan meditation.

In the particular practices that I have been following, certain Tibetan deity meditations have been modified for use by Westerners. The root meditations involved extremely detailed visualization of these figures. The particular bodhisattvas are for these purposes often treated as embodiments of particular qualities that the meditator seeks to perfect. Different meditations on these images are intended to evoke *bodhicitta* in the practitioner, specifically through the experience of being the object of *bodhicitta*. Then the practitioner learns to direct that attitude toward others, eventually realizing the unrestricted nondual Buddha nature.

Śāntideva's teaching on exchanging self and others set the pattern for these practices. As Śāntideva expounded them, these exchanges were primarily ways of relativizing our sense of individual identity and realizing no-self. In the forms I am about to describe, the weight shifts more to realizing unconditioned goodness or Buddha nature, and directing that outward. In a further form of meditation called *tonglen,* this exchange is even more directly modulated as a specific work of compassion directed toward particular instances of suffering.

This adapted tradition expounds meditation based on the *tathāgatagarbha* teaching by using an exercise called "benefactor practice."[31]

Rather than focusing upon elaborate and (to a non-Tibetan) alien deity images, the meditator is invited to picture actual persons who have acted as benefactors in her life experience. This involves tuning one's focus entirely to the well-wishing and encouragement experienced from such a person, basking in the awareness of that unrestricted kindness. Another significant modification involves freely interchanging the language of love with that of *bodhicitta*. In focusing on the benefactor, one seeks to be as free as possible from other aspects of that relation or person that might dilute the positive quality. The better to achieve this aim, sometimes one is invited to focus not on a person but on a moment of experiencing such care from someone. One meditates upon this person or moment as one would the deity image, seeking clarity, detail, and immediacy. Over time, one then moves to mediate on extending this same received *bodhicitta* to another person—to someone dear, to a stranger, and eventually to someone distasteful or hostile.

Benefactors, and the positive emotional charge associated with them, are used to get in touch with the power of *bodhicitta* as it flows from them to us and from us to others. It is this flow or awareness that is Buddha nature. One benefit of benefactor practice, the receiving and extending of well-wishing through actual acquaintances and ourselves, is that it emphasizes the conviction that Buddha nature is not some ultimate "other" or the attainment only of great and unfamiliar figures. It is the true underlying reality of all those around us and of ourselves. If there is intrinsic merit in reverencing the Buddhas, then similarly it is an important practice to revere and honor benefactors, who have, however fleetingly, functioned as Buddhas to us. Such devotion can be a source of merit as much as homage to established Buddhas.

At the same time, once in touch with the quality of benevolence, it is important to divorce it from these benefactor persons and from ourselves. It in no way depends on the benefactors, as they are empty. Thus, at the end of such meditation, one is invited to dissolve all consciousness of the persons whose effects on us have been invoked, focusing only on the qualities of mind that have resulted. When people in a meditation retreat expressed concerns about ambivalent feelings that they associated with those they chose as benefactors, the teacher responded by saying, "Love is continuous; the persons are not." Buddha nature is a flow, we might say, and practice is a way of modulating that flow from and through projected selves/persons until we realize that the flow is real and those constructions are not. The persons that were obstacles to this recognition are, by skillful means and practice, made instruments of its realization, sweeping themselves away in the process. The practice does not change anything. It makes us aware of what is always there.

These practices operationalize skillful means. As bodhisattvas accept the delusion of selves for the sake of relieving suffering, these meditations use the conventions of love between persons. Our attachments to persons are placed in service of getting in touch with the way that things really are. Through receiving and giving love, one establishes contact with the qualities of Buddha nature and then retains the qualities, without the selves. We use the very features that distinguish us from Buddhas to become one. To say that we practice as beings, not as Buddhas, means that we practice by means of reified attachments that have not been fully purified, even as the power of the positive qualities evoked in the practice suggest the character of an underlying Buddha nature.

Benefactor meditation includes another variation or adaptation, which extends *bodhicitta* to one's own negative emotions. These emotions are personified, and then, in line with Śāntideva's exhortation that our enemies are Buddhas to us and as such are actually benefactors, received with compassion.[32] Rather than approaching the anger or fear or anxiety as threats, one meditates on them by extending loving-kindness and acceptance. Further meditation focuses on them as expressions of loving-kindness toward us. These angry or anxious parts of ourselves are expressions of concern, intending our wellbeing. Anger expresses concern that we should be protected, and anxiety a compassionate wish that we not lack any good. In this way, we make friends, so to speak, with the emotions that cause us suffering when we struggle against them.

Benefactor practice aims at awakening compassion and benevolence toward all beings, including me. *Tonglen* is a more targeted application of the same techniques. Rather than starting with generating and directing benevolence toward suffering beings, it begins by actively taking in the specific suffering of another. This may be as concrete as breathing in and visualizing the specific pains borne by a friend or even an enemy, then breathing out the loving wish for confidence or health or whatever that person needs.[33] Alternatively, one can take one's own suffering as the entry point for this solidarity, imagining all those who also experience the same difficulty and focusing wishes for well being on this condition as such.

One obstacle to traditional Tibetan meditation for many Westerners is perplexity about what kind of status or reality attaches to the object of meditation. From a Buddhist perspective, it is not problematic to regard the deity images as simply projections, as opposed to actual beings, since all conventional beings are such mental objects. This does not preclude regarding them at the same time as manifestations of Buddha nature or unconditioned consciousness. The adapted practices turn this table by taking as objects of meditation things—persons and emotions—that we consensually regard as real, and then purifying them of reified notions to leave only the qualities and perfections.

In the conventional dimension, aspirant bodhisattvas will and act benevolently, and the legacy of realized bodhisattvas continues to exercise its effects. In the unconditioned dimension, Buddha nature does nothing and intends nothing. As the pure realization of emptiness present in all form, it is the attractor of equanimity and peace. As the Heart Sutra teaches, these are the same: emptiness is form and form is emptiness. But the gulf between recognition and ignorance of this is an abyss, the difference between suffering and enlightenment.

Christian study of these sources trains us in a different modality, like working with one's nondominant hand. Buddhist commentators maintain that from the Buddha side, there is no discriminating action in or personal (as in self-other) awareness of the world of beings.[34] The Buddha's action in the world of appearances is itself an appearance, generated from the conditioned causes produced by the bodhisattva on their way to Buddhahood. By contrast, God's action to create and sustain the world is a relational commitment, with precisely the purposeful, discriminating, and personal dimensions that are carefully ruled out in regard to Buddha nature. God acts and empowers the acts of others. Training in the Buddhist perspective restrains the characteristic Christian impulse to look for help only in God's acts of communication, participation, and initiation, or in purposeful human agencies of an analogous sort. It challenges us to recognize that God also acts in a dimension of nondiscriminating presence and bare awareness, and that we can draw this into explicit Christian reflection.

Christian Reflections

In this chapter, we have filled out what it means to have compassion on all beings by specifying the bodhisattva's role as helper. Bodhisattvas realize an unconditioned state of consciousness, but their benefits extend to those in the conditioned world. How this paradox of manifestation from the unconditioned to the conditioned works, this marriage of wisdom and compassion, has been our question from the beginning. The three categories of helping that we described above are aspects of the answer. After two preliminary comments, I will reflect on each of them from a Christian perspective.

One obvious and profound similarity in these two paths is that the disciple/follower of Jesus is called to practice altruistic acts toward neighbor and enemy in much the same way that an aspirant bodhisattva does. Śāntideva's material on cultivation of the perfections is full of concrete instruction and inspiration that flow easily across traditional boundaries. This is an area for continual mutual encouragement.

Buddhist analytic distinctions between conditioned and unconditioned causes lead to a powerful focus on the kinds of assistance that inhere in changeless conditions. This is a dimension that Christians undervalue or even ignore. God helps in many ways, including through constituting the unvarying states that we have called creaturely no-self, which is associated with Buddhist *anattā*, and bare-awareness immanence, which is associated with Buddha nature.

The first way that the bodhisattva helps is by acquiring such merit and perfections as to become a powerful object of devotion for others. This speeds the acquisition of merits and perfections by the others in turn, even though such devotion is a direct practice not of those perfections, but only of a commitment to them. The availability of a bodhisattva sets up a sort of resonance that supercharges any existing practice. The key here is that such devotion is effective of itself. The action of the bodhisattva in being the object of devotion is self-executing.

Study of the bodhisattva sensitizes us to a resonance aspect of Christ's work, in regard to the changeless dimensions of creaturely emptiness and immanent consciousness. Outward ritual actions of reverence to a Buddha have an intrinsically meditative meaning, which is sometimes highlighted by the use of repetitive chants. Praise of the bodhisattva is the actual means of clearing and emptying the mind so as to attain the states that we discussed in Chapters 4 and 5. Some traditional Christian forms and practices, such as the Jesus prayer, explicitly move in this direction. In fact, much of Christian worship, including modern forms of music, can be helpfully understood in this light. God and Christ work by their intrinsic qualities as objects of devotion in this sense. The absence of explicit cognitive content, or the blending of such content into an emotional and nondiscursive mode with the experience of a certain mindlessness, is a form of worship not clearly thematized or valued in many Christian communities. This may be the most distinctive learning regarding the first bodhisattva benefit. It suggests the devotional link through Christ to both the immanence and emptiness dimensions that Buddhism accesses so powerfully.

Another learning would recognize the automatic benefits that flow from the devotional or intellectual appreciation of the divine qualities. When worship and reverence are directed precisely at the greatness and inexpressibility of God and Christ's capacities and intentions, there is an automatic effect extended to the devotee. Śāntideva sees this as a flow of merit that meets the recognition of the desirability of *bodhicitta,* a recognition expressed by reverence to bodhisattvas. This is actually a fresh perspective on faith as the true apprehension of God's actual nature and meaning for us. Distinct from the changes or actions that may follow upon faith, there is a grace inherent in this kind of insight-devotion. It transforms our orientation and perspective.

In these respects, God affects us by simply being an acknowledged object of worship. Perhaps a more familiar connection for Christians relates to the way in which Christ acts by being the attractive object of our devotion, a devotion that shapes us as able to express love to those to whom we are less easily attracted. In this sense, devotion is not an affirmation of status but an adoption of Jesus as a mimetic model. In discussing Buddhist ideas of merit, we had to resist importing Christian ones. That would include taking merit as a marker for accomplishments, a kind of currency that may be redeemed from God in exchange for some reward. One might by the merit of study acquire knowledge, which is then shared with others who had no means of acquiring it on their own. Christ's obedience or self-giving are often thought of in this key. The bodhisattva path, by contrast, resists the suggestion that some kind of transfer takes place between what are only projected selves.

In Christian perspective, one kind of merit attached to Jesus is that through the course of human life, the divine incarnation emerges as a person like us. A participant in the process of mimetic formation, Christ can likewise be a participant in our formation, bringing to that formation divine qualities, as well. It is Christ's availability in our plane of interpersonal contagion that allows us not simply to imitate external acts of Jesus's life or obey commands, but to form our desires on the model of his. In this sense, the material is already within us, but it is the posture and context of devotion to Christ that aligns it. Christ is a source of transformation by making some quality, such as a loving will, so palpable that it calls forth a like quality in those with open and receptive hearts. We are all possible models for each other in this mode. Unlike the realization of the dimensions of emptiness and immanence, we cannot say that this realization takes place in all in exactly the same way that it does in Christ. As a resonance attractor, as it were, for the formation of desires, Jesus is a unique figure and calls forth uniqueness in others.

Devotional relationship with God and Christ operates in a continuous spectrum with our human relations and formation. What can one do for another that he cannot do for himself? One answer is that we can be open to sharing our life, including our inner life, as a model and participant in the shaping of others'. In this respect, every merit of our own is a benefit to others. This dynamic is no different in kind in relation to Christ, only in the scope and nature of the person involved. This mimetic formation takes place in three interlocking spheres. Christ's external actions and teachings, as well as Christ's inner states and desires as apprehended by followers, are appropriated in their inner lives. The first sphere of that mimetic formation is our purely inner lives, our desires and emotions. The second sphere is relational mimetic formation, in which it is our interactions, outward and inward, with real neighbors that are shaped. The third sphere is the broader social environment, in which it is the relational life in the divine nature and the relational life of Christ with others that is the mimetic pattern for formation of new human communities, such as the church.

Mimetic formation requires living persons as its participants, but it does not turn primarily on a conscious modeling of one to another. Christians think mainly and first of the explicit actions and communication between God and humans, and humans with each other. Bodhisattva benevolence leans strongly away from this mode. This makes us aware that, in fact, much of Christ's saving activity lies in this dimension, as well. In part, it works of itself without being purposefully constructed. Those who practice spiritual and ecclesial formation are well aware of this. As an object of reverence and love, Jesus automatically operates as a blessing to those who "take no offense at him."[35] This is an insight of value for Christians in their internal practice. But it is of great relevance to the interfaith context.

Such formation is a bridge for sharing Jesus (as in simultaneously relating with Jesus alongside others, not only transmitting the Jesus story to them) with those large numbers of people—Hindus, Muslims (particularly Sufis), and Buddhists—who in fact take him as an object of respect and devotion. That devotion sometimes expresses itself in a non-dual dimension. We have seen how Christians can more fully recognize validity in this, even as Christians themselves cannot rest with it as the sole and comprehensive truth. If we are guided by Buddhist insight, then we can reflect on the ways that such devotion has its own intrinsic effect. Christians have historically more often emphasized Jesus as a perilous being. As the smallest slight to a bodhisattva earns boundless bad fortune, Christians have tended to stress the dire consequences of slights to Christ or an absence of full doctrinal confession. This can drown out the field-of-merit quality in Christ, in which Christ's work is accomplished in part by availability for reverence and formation.

In this connection, we can consider the Buddhist custom of the dedi-cation of merit.[36] The performance of practices expressing devotion toward Jesus, or respect toward those who have themselves been formed on the model of Jesus (e.g., practices such as fasts, pilgrimages, or regimes of prayer) are all things Christians at times dedicate to the good of others as well as themselves. This is done on the assumption that benefits natu-rally flowed to those who practiced such devotion, or even to those who simply asked in faith to participate in Christ's merits. This could be ap-proached in a selfish or single-path manner, spiritual goods sought for benefit of the seeker. But these benefits can be shared with others. In fact, intercessory prayer is always an act of this sort: one person's devotion coupled with the request that it be applied or dedicated to the good of another. In this respect, Christians have developed their own ways of see-ing Christ as a field of merit, a face of God whose tenderness and inti-macy with us awakens practices of love and obedience that are themselves a medium of care toward others.

The second way that the bodhisattva helps is through the legacy of actions and commitments that they undertook in the conditioned world. The paradigm examples of this seem to be the bodhisattva vow itself and the variations on it produced by different bodhisattvas. It is not easy to understand the way that this works, though perhaps the key lies in the conviction that all conventional entities are no more or less real than mental contents. Vows, or for that matter routine ritual invocations (e.g., "may all beings be happy") set up ripples in this world that have their own effects in it. The more pure and concentrated the consciousness in which the vow is made, the greater its subsequent effects. Even Buddha-lands and celestial Buddhas are part of the wake of a bodhisattva's actions in the conditioned world. Since they themselves still have a conditioned quality, they can rightly be said to have conditioned causes: the intentions of aspirant bodhisattvas to aid all beings.

Viewed in this perspective, the activity of Christ and God in the world is a train of conditioned historical events in history. If we kept faith with a Buddhist interpretation, we would say these were actually all mental events, meditative intentions. A good candidate might be Jesus's statement in the gospel of John: "The glory that you have given me, I have given them, so that they may be one as you and I are one" (John 17:22). This has a vow-like quality, and it is the force of this intention that would continue to function in the conventional world.

So, we might say, the Jesus story and its memory remain available in history as a source of inspiration and instruction. Christ lives on in the memories and impressions that others carry and the effects of those impressions. But the usual formulations of this idea impute much less power and weight to these elements than the Buddhist model does, which stresses strongly that the bodhisattva practices set up a causal chain, objectively effective of itself, within the conventional world. Buddhist reflection carefully avoids the framework of one existent agent's actions changing another existent agent, since it is such selves that need to be transcended. This leads to a purity of insight on what we might call "phenomenon-to-phenomenon causality." Like a deep groove worn in a snowy hillside that speeds following sleds down the incline, or a strong magnet left among weaker ones, the bodhisattva legacy reproduces itself.

Shubert Ogden draws a helpful distinction between constitutive and derivative representations of God: Jesus is constitutively representative of God; sacraments and scripture are derivatively so. Sacraments represent God by pointing to Jesus; Jesus "represents God love by constituting them."[37] Sacraments, thus, are similar to Śāntideva's wish-fulfilling gem. They continue to manifest grace by virtue of the impetus given to them in history and the web of human relations. Our study helps us appreciate just how much power attaches to them in this vein.

This reinforces, for instance, the perspective that Christians place under the heading of "recapitulation." Christ in the incarnation walks the path that humanity has taken since Eve and Adam, remaking and empowering it anew for the exercise of divine presence. That attractor continues to have its effect from within the historical and social world, and it was instituted in the life of Jesus, particularly in vow-like activities (e.g., sacraments such as the eucharist and teachings such as the beatitudes, which wish blessedness on entire categories of persons) and in the community that is the body formed in his literal wake.

In intra-Christian discussion, views of Christ's work of this sort are sometimes seen as weak notions of divine agency, a mere influence of historical memory that downplays any contemporary activity of the risen Christ. Or they can be seen as akin to superstition, with physical objects or certain gestures being endowed with intrinsic, independent power. But from our Buddhist examples, we can appreciate that this is not necessarily accurate. Buddhists view spiritual causes and effects as operating in the realm of mind, the same realm that can project physical events, and so they see such attractors as a force as realistic as any other. Christians do not have access to the same metaphysical suppositions but do have their own reasons for affirming that the insertion of these new possibilities into the human historical community remains active among us. Indeed, Christians have an added consideration, which is that they see great importance in the ripple effects of such legacies within the historical process itself. These vows and jewels were not left for future spiritual realizations alone, but for effect on the texture and substance of historical life.

The third way that realized bodhisattvas help is by their manifestation in different forms at different spiritual stages. Popular bodhisattvas such as Kuan Yin are popular precisely because they manifest at the level currently accessible to most beings. The variety among bodhisattvas can be viewed in this same light.[38] Buddha lands are notable as places where the center of spiritual gravity in the population is higher than in this world, and so the appropriate common manifestation is a celestial Buddha, not a figure such as Kuan Yin or the historical Buddha. By locating agency on the side of the spiritual aspirant, Buddhism views the manifestations of the Buddha as skillful means, legitimate in their diversity because tuned to the needs of different seekers. There is a kind of reciprocity between the seeker and the source, with Buddha nature accommodating itself to the conditions of aspiration in the seeker.

Christians view and experience such manifestations as living presence as well as legacy. The one who left these things behind is present and active now. Christ is not only an object for relation, established by gracious acts in the past, but also a party to relation. Incarnation dramatically inserts God into the mimetic and interpersonal human network of influence and formation. This heightens and confirms the two-way traffic between the creator and created. Whether the manifestation is a spiritual encounter or illumination, Christians see it not simply as a confluence of conditions in an individual's current mental state with the conditions established by a spiritual adept's earlier vow. They see it as a genuine encounter, a mutual participation with distinct participants.

Causal streams from the wider past and the biographical present do in fact play into such events. But the Holy Spirit, the manifestation of divine presence and intention, and the openness produced by personal human choices meet in real time. As a manifestation in the Buddhist vein, the historical Jesus looks meager and limited. That historical person is only one type of manifestation, and the repertoire of bodhisattvas is literally limitless. But the Christ of Christian faith is the one manifest as risen Lord and indwelling Spirit as well as historical companion. The bodhisattva manifestations that occur in human conditions now were preprescribed through the prior conditioned causes that were left by earlier bodhisattvas. If this is so, then they are not interactive in a two-way manner, nor do they need to be. From the Christian point of view, the living divine presence interacts in real time with human conditions, and it is not the number of the manifestations but the scope of the divine ability to respond to and incorporate particularity that is the wonder. This adds another crucial feature to the encounter, the communication of new information. The divine-human encounter is not only a meditative realization but also an actual exchange. As a result of this exchange, relations and the related parties, including God, are altered.

A great strength of the Buddhist tradition is its recognition of different states and aspirations among people, and the corresponding need to tailor teaching and practice to that variety. This variety belongs to the category of skillful means and has to do with the availability of a vehicle for those at every step on the ladder of enlightenment. The variety belongs to the conditioned world of impermanence. None of it pertains to the unconditioned world of enlightenment itself. Compared to the impersonal adjustment of Buddha nature through different vehicles, the Christian charter for variety is rooted in a pluralism of players, including creatures, who are integral to fulfillment itself. It is the Holy Spirit that tunes divine manifestations to creatures and their providential paths. It is the saints who testify to the various itineraries to God. The Christian convictions that God acts in history and that Jesus is a continuing, personal agent multiply the opportunities for purposeful interaction with God in the context of varying human circumstances. For instance, in the realm of soteriology, Christian theology has felt no need to choose between the helper roles that Christ may play: teacher, healer, prophet, victor over powers, sacrifice. To affirm one of these is not to rule out the others. Christ manifested as each, and more. In this respect, we could say that there are many vehicles of Christ's work.

Christians could extend the category of such vehicles to apply to most of the denominational or confessional differences within Christianity itself. It is true that the conviction that Christ is a concrete, historical figure encourages a Christian expectation that those who encounter the living Christ should be able to conform their accounts of him to each other substantially. Ecumenical advances among the churches on this front have led us to see most of our differences within a shared unity in the body of Christ. One way to view the continuing role and vitality of different Christian traditions would be in this light. When a person's spiritual path requires or is enriched by it, a particular face of the Christian tradition presents itself. There are manifestations of Christ as sacrament, as word, as healing. These may be pursued with a practical exclusivity, a wholehearted commitment, without compromising a sense of unity and spiritual equality. There is no need for a definitive theoretical ranking of these differences, since differences coexist in fulfilment as well as in history. The Buddhist variety of vehicles is ordered in a firm hierarchy that obtains in the conventional world. But that hierarchy is swept away in nondual realization. Christian variety of vehicles or perspectives need not assume a definite rank order, since salvation itself is a relational and complex reality.[39]

Perhaps over time, something such as the Trinitarian framework that we are using in this work, coupled with concrete learning from other religious traditions, will shift Christian theological practice. It will lead to a Trinity-based outlook on religious diversity analogous to the ecumenical outlook that is explicitly Christology-based. Christian ecumenism is rooted in the shared aim and experience of perichoresis-communion among the different dimensions of relation with God and each other. Christian interreligious learning would recognize that this diversity is organized differently in other traditions and that, by virtue of that fact, these traditions can offer their own alternative visions and ends. Study and practice of elements from other religious traditions could be seen as appropriate for those with the need or desire to amplify their realization of specific dimensions of God's relation with us, even while the ways that specific religious traditions organize and prioritize those dimensions remain unique and the source of their particular instructive powers.

Benefactor Practices in Christian Perspective

The benefactor practice described above closely fits the shape of Christian devotion and the community of saints. God and Christ are exactly benefactors who immerse worshippers in love directly and whose love is mediated toward others through us, as it is also mediated to us through others. Prayer is a kind of benefactor practice, particularly contemplative prayer that focuses on God's qualities. For Christians, participation in this kind of meditation practice evokes a strong sense of communion, the living presence of another within us. As we saw in Chapter 4, this mimetic process runs with the grain of the way in which we become persons in the first place. The benefactor practice both remembers (i.e., heightens awareness of what is already the case) and remakes our inner life by purposely selecting others as models and objects for our formation.

Some of my fellow meditation students testified to a special appreciation for this approach. Their experience with other forms of Buddhist meditation instruction had set up practice as a fight with the ego, an effort to stamp out self-consciousness, which only amplified negative emotions. Instead, they characterized this particular benefactor practice as loving away the self. Indeed, one teacher was fond of saying that "until it feels loved, the self won't let go." In this sense, benefactor practice, the transposition of a long-standing Buddhist tradition into a Western context, is particularly accessible in language and structure for those from Christian backgrounds.[40]

Christian love of others readily entangles itself with concerns about how to concretely live out love to any given neighbor, particularly how to negotiate all their difficult or conflictive features (in association with our own). Selective focus on persons who fill us with a sense of worth and wellbeing, rather than those in need of care, can seem like a defection from our calling.[41] That reaction may be evoked all the more by a practice that is initially perceived to treat others as vehicles to elicit positive emotions. But devotion has an important role as spiritual practice that generates and regenerates love's sustaining power and presence. We have ample instruction to this effect, as in the First Letter of John: "If we love one another, then God abides in us and his love is perfected in us."[42]

God, Christ, and sainted models in events or persons beyond our own direct circle of acquaintance play the role of benefactor and can do so even for those who tragically have few examples of such radiant love in immediate experience. It is true that many are blocked from prayerful or spiritual relation with these transtemporal benefactors either because they feel unworthy to receive divine love or because painful human interactions have left them without the means to prime the pump, so to speak, of such relations. Benefactor practice is extremely helpful in its ability to sift out positive qualitative experience and to abstract the good elements from even troubled relationships. For instance, when one is encouraged to remember that all beings at some time have been his mother, this is not meant to evoke problematic aspects of concrete relations with a current parent. It is to focus on the pure, uncomplicated donation of life, the same in all. Likewise, in concentration on a benefactor in one's own life, one can focus on the salient signs of compassion and love.

Precisely because Christians believe in God, there is a tendency to expect perfection in the benefactor. And similarly, classical deity or bodhisattva objects of meditation in Buddhism are taken as near-perfect embodiments of the qualities in question.[43] It is the very distance of the model from us on the moral or ontological scale that gives it power (we saw this in our discussion of the supercharged merit produced by any expression of respect toward exalted Buddhas). But the modality of benefactor practice demonstrates that this process can start much closer to creatures and their mundane interactions. Nothing like perfection is required in our models because we are not limited to one benefactor, and we can gather moments or experiences from many.

Though Buddhists typically see selves as obstacles to the flow of awareness and compassion, benefactor practice leans heavily and skillfully on those selves to open that flow. Christians typically regard persons as recipients and transmitters of love. Benefactor practice is consistent with that conviction, especially when we understand persons as the somewhat loosened, porous, and mimetic selves that are at once receivers, generators, and amplifiers of the life and desires of our models. Persons are real actors in the practice (as lasers act to focus the resonance of many strands of light into one particular beam) and distinct beneficiaries of it (as the recipient of an inoculation has a changed immune system). The examples just given are of a nonpersonal sort in order to stress continuity with Buddhist thought. But Christians will stress that persons are actors and recipients also in the personalizing dimensions that grow positive particularity. Selves are real enough to be the actual sources of the value and intensification added in the process of sharing love.

In this sense, Buddhists and Christians seem very well suited for an exchange of penultimates. That is, Christians can quite easily adopt benefactor practice as part and parcel of Christian practice. The dissolution of the benefactors and the generation of generic forms of loving-kindness can be related to an experience of nondual divine immanence. Christians may take that experience as a blessing, as one dimension of unity with God, but not as an exclusive reality to crowd out other dimensions. The connection with the benefactors and the exchange with them is not something to be definitively dissolved. It is a foretaste of the goal, a participation in salvation. What is instrumental in Buddhist practice has a more ultimate significance.

And at least some Buddhists seem pleased to take actual interpersonal relations as templates for meditative practice. The substantializing of these conventional selves and their attitudes can be understood as a kind of skillful means, not as a capitulation to conditioned categories. Just so, Buddhists might regard these generative relations with actual benefactors as continuous with the Christian heaven after death. This makes sense in Buddhist cosmological terms as analogous with the Buddhist heavens that serve as pleasant way stations between births for those whose merit occasions it. Though the frameworks and aims may differ, the practical commonality is impressive.

We saw earlier that for Buddhists the validity of the meditation practices need not depend on the reality of the benefactor objects. It is of no significance whether the deities actually exist, the benefactors are real people, or, if real, are pictured accurately. If thought to be mental projections, then they are no more so than the one who entertains them. This awakens Christians to the true power of mind-to-mind causality, the real significance that attaches to the pure concentrated experience of benevolence or *bodhicitta*. But there are limits to how far we can take the dissolving of the persons at the end of this meditation practice. It makes sense as a kind of ritual conclusion to the exercise, one that Christians might frame as an appreciation and mental leave-taking. And it is instructive to think of this as a kind of purification of the positive emotions as they flow from us to others. But it does not make Christian sense to view it as an attempt to strain out the patterns of particularity in the sources of our loving-kindness. The powerful presence of those who love and instruct us dissolves only in the sense that it continues as a less conscious quality of our own distinctive selves and as part of the wider web of such communions.

Christians tie their benefactor practice closely to the conventional or created world. The most basic way to put this is that love creates: it is an innovative force as well as an equalizing one. The creative act is relevant not only at a moment of cosmic origin but all along. Meditation is also relation, and relation adds value and novelty to the world. Changes in persons and relations, and in the social patterns of these, are as significant and of as much enduring significance as consciousness-realizations. The identity dimensions of oneness with God, apophatic and immanent, may be in a sense born redeemed. That is, their unities are uncompromised and permanent and so, whenever realized, are the same in all. This is not true of the fuller dimensions of human nature and creation. Each new level of emergence is the material of a fuller redemption, and participates in it like the conserved core processes that Bellah discussed in evolutionary history. Such personal and social types of emergence are subject also to newly emergent forms of distortion and sin.

As Buddhism stresses the constancy of certain conditions (i.e., impermanence in the conventional world, permanence in enlightenment), Christianity recognizes a givenness in our mimetic, communion natures. We indwell each other and each other's consciousness, to one emotional and relational effect or another. Forgiveness, a person-to-person facet of the larger reality of reconciliation, is a good example of this dynamic. It is a topic with particular Christian resonances. It does not necessarily travel well in Buddhist settings, where it may be seen as unneeded or misguided.[44] Its natural habitat is the relational context we have described. Forgiveness does not have to do primarily with phenomena-to-phenomena causation. It has to do with person-to-person relations. It has to do with mutual indwelling. If as persons we are constituted by our relations and by the others who live in us as part of what we might call our second nature, then enemies inhabit us as surely as those we love, if more painfully.

Forgiveness has an element of rectification in the social world. It is part of a wider movement, a complement to confession, repentance, and restitution on the part of those who harm or offend. In this respect, it is part of an active effort to repair damage that has been done, as far as possible.[45] It is an act in wider relation. Ideally it is part of a mutual endeavor though, as is true of confession and repentance also, forgiveness has application even when practically cut off from that mutuality. Forgiveness is not only about reversing past acts. It is about changing the way that people indwell each other. Forgiveness changes the present and future manner in which one who has committed harm exists in the inner life of the one who has been harmed, and vice versa. That presence can be a continual wound, whether one is or is not consciously aware of the wound. Or it can be a source of the melioration of present suffering, an encouragement, and future hope. Forgiveness alters the mode of this mutual participation. The presence of a repentant and reconciled offender in my consciousness and even in preconscious awareness is constitutively different from that of an unreconciled one. In this sense, forgiveness is about removing a kind of suffering that exists in the present, not about dealing with a suffering that happened in the past.

The Buddhist view of identification of offender and victim sees them both alike as Buddha nature. Their apparent separation is a conditioned, passing perception. The terms in which suffering occurs are misapprehensions, and the misapprehensions are the causes of the suffering. Since forgiveness is intrinsically tied to those terms and is meaningless apart from the interpersonal frame, it is at best a stopgap approach to afflictive emotions in the conventional world. Since the boundaries between victim and offender exist only at that level, Buddhist wisdom jars our conventional views. This is powerfully expressed in a series of "I am" lines from a Thich Nhat Hanh poem, when he pictures himself both as a frog and as the snake eating it, as a twelve-year-old refugee girl raped by a pirate and as the pirate who commits the rape.[46] The "I" here is not a personal one but a Buddha-nature reference.

At the extreme, such a deep insistence on unity can seem like indifference to injustice. But many in my practice group treasured the clarity and the control offered in this teaching, with its implication that the causes of all suffering reside in the minds that suffer it. Our mental defilements are all within range of our practice and so then, too, is our suffering. There is literally no thing and no one else responsible for our miseries. That attitude opens the way for unparalleled focus on effective antidotes to the afflictive emotions (e.g., anger, helplessness) in the sole venue under my power, my own consciousness.

Forgiveness appears unrealistic, unjust, or unworkable from many religious perspectives. At the extreme, it appears as indifference to or minimizing of injustice, an indifference of a different flavor than might be threatened in Buddhist nondualism. Forgiveness can be seen as an additional cost placed on the victim by the offender, a revictimization or an unrealistic hope. From a Christian perspective, the boundaries between victim and offender are blurred not so much by their ultimate identity as by their relational coinherence. Most of us know people, religious and nonreligious, for whom forgiveness has figured in profound interpersonal reconciliation or individual transformation. Many in my Christian community find liberation either in the practice of unilateral forgiveness or in a trust in God's forgiveness of others even when they find it impossible themselves.

One part of the practice of forgiveness is an active choice to release one's self from bondage to anger, the continually reprocessed resentment that eats away any space for new life. Christians can learn much from Buddhist practice to address negative emotions directly in the theater of our mental lives.[47] But forgiveness is also part of the larger work of reconciliation. It is a good that makes sense for those with a future, and most of all for those with a future together. Reconciliation that extends to the past, healing of memory, is part of salvation. We see this most clearly in our more intimate relations, in which forgiveness is often a key element that determines whether those relations have a future at all. We are inextricably part of each other, and the question is not whether but how we shall continue to function, each within the other.

A Buddhist teacher I know recounted that earlier in her life, she had practiced intensively for many years and yet found herself only "more screwed up" than she was to begin with. She had earnestly vowed to heal all beings but had yet to comprehend her own suffering and the way that even her Buddhist practice had become complicit in that suffering. An excursion into therapy, which she described as revisiting her life in a narrative form, opened up insights that prior teaching and meditation practice had not. It allowed her to start with the specificity of her experience, as opposed to the universal Buddhist categories for it. A kind of incarnational attention to her individual story deeply affected her.

I connect the beneficial impact of this self-reflection with our discussion of forgiveness not because her case necessarily involved explicit interpersonal reconciliation. I do not know that it did. But it clearly involved a careful narrative exploration of the way that specific persons and experiences had shaped her inner life, a rearrangement of the way these past stories functioned in her own current identity. Infused by these insights, the power of her Buddhist teaching and practice grew dramatically. One index of that is the experience of Christians among her students, who can testify that they found in her meditation teaching a dimension of healing that was missing for them in years of Christian practice.

This mutual indwelling looks different as we move from the intimate world of interpersonal relations to the wider social world. It is no less true that we indwell each other on this level. The rise of mass communication and digital interaction only intensifies that reality. But reconciliation and its components such as forgiveness take on a different character in the social world. Forgiveness is an issue most dramatically presented in close, continuing personal relations; justice is an issue most dramatically presented in the social and structural aspects of our relations. Just as forgiveness belongs to the restorative aspect of the ongoing mutual constitution of persons and relations, there is a restorative or reparative dimension in our mutual constitution on a wider scale that is expressed more structurally than in immediate interpersonal terms.

Person-building and community-making, with their creative and reparative aspects, are on a continuum with an eschatological future, which will include transformed persons, relations, and that social web itself. These realizations, however partial now, are taken up in the common future. Forgiveness and social justice make sense in Buddhist terms as conventional means of countering afflictive emotions, but they are way stations toward fully dissolving the very conditions (i.e., persons, others, relations) in which they operate. Alteration in the *structure* of the conventional world is not an object of the Buddha's activity. Interconnection must be realized as nondualism. From a Christian perspective, interconnection is on the way to becoming fuller communion. This is not a difference that is based on superficial acquaintance but one that remains evident to those with deep familiarity with the two traditions. Its recognition fuels the common observation in dialogue that Christianity has much to learn from Buddhism in contemplative realization and Buddhism has much to learn from Christianity in social engagement.[48]

Bodhisattva and Christ I: Diversity and Person-Making

Bodhisattvas help suffering beings through all of the virtue and wisdom that they share on their ascending path, the bodhisattva way.[49] And through the fulfillment of that path, as realized bodhisattva-Buddhas, they help beings by serving as an object for their devotion by leaving a legacy of conditioned effects in the conventional world, including the intention to be manifest in that world in forms corresponding to the needs of every human state. Through these means, the bodhisattva assists others to the unconditioned and unchanging state of enlightened ones. Though bodhisattvas are objects of reverence and their manifestations radiate compassion, they register neither the devotion they receive nor the suffering of others in any normal sense. They do not intend or feel anything in real time toward us, individually or collectively. This is the very distinction between them and struggling beings that makes them helpers.

Christ also assists disciples by serving as an object of devotion, but the routes of helping extend explicitly into the registers of the personal and the social. The object of this assistance is to bring peace through identity (about which Buddhists might agree) and also to support change and nurture difference. Christians look to Christ for help with life within the conditioned world and for instruction and power to change the very nature of that world. They look to God and God's creatures for grace in the person-making that shapes each of us and for the continuing relations that will carry that process beyond death. Impermanence, as well as being an occasion of suffering, has positive uses that directly contribute to and participate in religious fulfillment. We have seen in our discussion of forgiveness how impermanence can be an openness to reconciliation and healing. But in an even deeper and prior dimension, impermanence is the theater for person and relation building.

God encounters us as a particular other and empowers our encounters with each other as creatures precisely in order to call forth individuals, particularities, and the love that runs across them. God's action is not only a play of multiple forms used to induce the realization of the timeless identities that already obtain. Divine action intends, attracts, and stimulates the quality that Duns Scotus named "haecceity," which refers the unique characteristics not only of types of being but of individuals. Thus God's love calls forth different types of creature and, to an increasing extent in the sentient realm, calls forth individual characters and vocations.[50]

This relational fertility is manifest in person formation, in the interactions through which people develop their distinctive skills and joys, including their relations with particular persons and dimensions of creation. Becoming a parent, an artist, a skilled craftsperson, a friend— all these create actual persons in the specific (e.g., in relation to this child, this craft, or this friend). Such emergent additions to the world are part of the divine intention, elements in the world's current and final goodness. What Buddhists regard as the conventional, karmic world exists in the Christian view as the vehicle for this positive purpose.

The value of these relations is not composed of qualities (whether love, joy, or peace) that are called forth through them and finally distilled to a generic, pure consciousness. That would be the hope in the bodhisattva way. Such universal benevolence or awareness remains when the persons and their specificities are dissolved, whether temporarily in meditation practice or in definitive nondual realization. The Christ/disciple path seeks a universal benevolence whose character is the well-wishing to and for this diversity, a love for things that do not come in the same shape. Here we can remember the previous discussion, in Chapter 5, about Sallie King's refusal to see her love for her child as an afflictive attachment. This is not a flat contradiction but a divergence. One could view that maternal love as a teacher, as many Buddhist students feel deep affection for and delight in the distinctive personalities of their venerated teachers or sect founders. That affection can be seen as a kind of karmic match of vehicle and condition. But the Buddhist hope that these things fade and remain no part of the attainment sought diverges from the Christian hope that they remain and flavor the attainment itself.

Persons are mimetic and episodic in the senses that we discussed in Chapter 5. That is, our selves are distributed within our own brains such that there is no single place where they are located, and such that selves are not in continuous possession of themselves. Persons are also distributed socially. They are constituted by reading others' interiority and consciously and tacitly appropriating desires and purpose in novel configurations. We are "interviduals" (socially) and "interselves" (neurologically). This distribution of the person is consistent with our understanding of creaturely no-self. But it is also consistent with Christian hope for persons, since that hope does not rest on the sustainability of an isolated and self-contained entity. Our persons are to some extent held in trust with others. We can be read back from the patterns of our presence in others whom we participate in and from the aspects of their life that participate in us.

This investment in diversity faces Christians with difficult questions about the nature and plausibility of divine action or about the value through time of the persons and narratives so formed, questions with which Buddhists need not concern themselves. But person-making, relationships, and the transformation of human community seem so empirically central to life that difficult questions also arise about the plausibility of Buddhist accounts of realization that abstract so radically from them.

Buddhists find access to a fully unconditioned state, while for Christians all of transcendence is contaminated with an irreversible participation in the conditioned or created. The marvelous assemblies of the bodhisattvas all exist in the conditioned realm, reflexive manifestations of prior bodhisattva-path causes, while emptiness or Buddha nature is an uncaused reality in, with, and under that *saṃsāric* flux. The Christian communion with God is a mixed community. Its members are at wildly varying levels of "realization," in Buddhist terms. The existence of such variation is not only consistent with the Christian ideal of communion. It is essential to it. Creatures, sinners, saints, Christ, and the Trinity all belong to this body together. Buddhists see that the way to overcome the suffering that comes from impermanence is to realize identity with emptiness that is beyond change. Christians see that the way to joy is through love that is distributed in communion and persists despite change.

Numerical and qualitative diversity is a richness found in both the Buddha/bodhisattva path and the Christ/disciple path. This diversity is driven in the Buddhist way by two things. The nondualism of attainment means that bodhisattvas are numerically beyond counting, equal to the number of beings that start out to complete the path to enlightenment. Second, the two truths or many-vehicles teaching means that the manifestations of bodhisattvas are likewise beyond numbering, since they are evoked by every stage of human suffering. In the Christ/disciple path, diversity takes another character. It is driven first by the variety in creation and creatures, a diversity of players. Though sentient creatures may share the nondual identity dimensions of no-self and immanence, they also have emergent personal and communion dimensions to their lives and, thus, distinctive emergent identities. So diversity is driven secondly by the variety of relationships and the variety of dimensions of relation that exist originally within the divine life itself and are present derivatively with and among creatures. This means that the players themselves relate and interact on several planes at once.

There is great wisdom in the Buddhist understanding of multiple vehicles. Earlier in this chapter, I reflected on some ways in which Christians might learn from it. This does not mute the disagreement over whether difference has a final positive significance as well as a transient instrumental one. Diversity of vehicles appears to be a permanent feature in Buddhism. Through endless eons of time, there will always be new waves of suffering beings finding the way to release, aided by the legacies of innumerable bodhisattvas. The supply of suffering beings never ends, and so the variety of vehicles to serve them will never end, either. That multiplicity exists to refine away the defilement of supposed differences, self from self.

The Christian view of salvation does not see religious fulfilment as the vanishing point of difference. The diversity that Christians embrace never stops. It is a feature of realization as much as aspiration. Multiplicity of perspective is part of fulfillment, constitutive of its richness and fullness. Different selves and the variety of gifts and relations that go with them are as integral to salvation as they are to the path to it. From a Christian outlook, the conditioned/unconditioned distinction seems in this respect too sharp, too dualistic. The presumed veil between the two has been pierced in creation, incarnation, and, by extension, salvation, in which creatures share in the divine life. From a Buddhist outlook, these convictions confine Christian salvation to the realm of the conventional and thoroughly conditioned world, for that salvation includes at least some of what Buddhists mean by the term "suffering." And the Trinitarian God, whose transcendence as creator violates standard Buddhist norms, is at the same time too intrinsically enmeshed in the conditioned world to have the qualities that Buddhists typically regard as truly ultimate.

For Buddhists, everything is interconnected in the web of dependent origination. Interbeing is an aspect of impermanence and of the unsatisfactory or suffering-enabling character of *saṃsāra*. This interconnection can be evoked to break down the illusion of distinct beings and so to liberate innate nondual awareness. For Christians, everything is interconnected. This signifies the promise and power of relation. Interrelation is an aspect of the mutual indwelling that is an intrinsic goodness in creation. The differences that it constitutes and reflects are themselves integral to an ultimate satisfaction, a unity in difference. Interbeing is an original goodness, its texture now broken or corrupted, and also a future, redeemed good.

We can review the work of a Buddha and Christ across a spectrum of three registers of suffering in Buddhist analysis. First, there is gross suffering, the sort of disease or pain that both traditions would readily recognize. Second, there is impermanence itself (as in mortality or finitude), which Buddhism views as pain-entailing whenever it is combined with any element of attachment or enduring particularized identity. Under such conditions of attachment, impermanence necessarily produces experienced loss and suffering. Those aspects of the conventional world that we might normally regard as the opposite of suffering—physical pleasures, intellectual satisfactions, creative accomplishments, rewarding relations, and spiritual experiences—are permutations of such attachment. They are unsatisfactory not in an immediate, phenomenal sense but in a deeper sense of insufficiency and instability. The Christian view of creation resists this categorical judgement. And third, there is subtle suffering. The mind identifies in fleeting, nearly imperceptible ways with conditioned states and conditioned reactions to those states, even if this identification does not rise to the level of reified attachment. Intra-Buddhist disagreements about enlightenment often turn on what it means to purify this element. What we have discussed under the heading of emergence or person-making are realities that Christians view as preconditions for and foretastes of heaven, of actual participation in the divine life. There are aspects of these last two types of suffering—from which bodhisattvas vow to deliver beings—that are integral to Christian salvation. This means the ministrations of bodhisattvas would be needed in heaven no less than in hell.

We can specify this further by breaking suffering into a more detailed set of four categories. The first is simple pain, the neurological concomitant of physical existence. This is the negative end of the phenomenal spectrum at whose other pole lie the sensations of health and vitality. The second kind of suffering we might call the intrapsychic static or painful backwash arising from our mimetic natures and constituting broken or wounded personhood. To this belongs distress experienced because of the false projections and mistaken reification of ourselves, others, and associated subjective intentions or attitudes. Under Buddhist analysis, *all* mental activities ultimately fall under this heading. At the other pole from this suffering lies what Christians regard as the fruitful reality of reconciled and flourishing persons. Buddhists may regard such positive manifestations as stages of liberation through skillful use of the conventional projections involved. Third, there is suffering inflicted from one to another or through groups and structures from some to others, constituting broken or wounded community. This is the result of willful indifference or malice, or of the free choice of lesser goods over higher ones. At the other pole of this suffering is flourishing relation: love, mutuality, creativity. Fourth, there are sufferings that flow from the subtle identification of mind with conditioned states, an investment that makes impermanence an intrinsic engine of loss through age and change. At the other pole to this are the openness and creativity that impermanence makes possible as emergent goods.

The bodhisattva path understands the middle two, the person-oriented modes of suffering, as extensions of a root unsatisfactoriness that are best explained in terms of the first and last modes. Misapprehended conditions underlying sensation and identity are the root of all suffering. The Christ/disciple path tends toward the reverse, centering its concerns in the distortion and fulfillment of relations. In each of the four modes, there are positive phenomena correlative to the suffering described. A characteristic Buddhist virtue in approaching fluctuations on these scales (between neurological pain and pleasure, say, or between social evil and justice) is a clarifying equanimity born of wisdom. A characteristic Christian virtue is to invest in the future possibilities on each spectrum, a transforming attachment born of hope.

There is special insight in the bodhisattva's understanding of suffering as such, in which pain of the first and fourth types becomes the preferred standard for understanding the other two. For instance, the pains that we associate with personal, relational dimensions are conceived fundamentally in the terms of the stimulus and response that we associate with conditioned physical phenomena. We discussed in Chapter 4 some of the ways in which Christians benefit from attending to this perspective. In this connection, it is striking to note that research on the relation of meditative practices to pain indicates that different sorts of meditation can result in different ameliorative effects on pain using different neurological pathways.[51]

Two neurological examples correspond well with the two types of Buddhist meditation that are outlined early in this book. One reduces pain through a dissociative path by reducing mind activity and redirecting concentration to a repeated word or focal point. This follows the line of calming meditation, which at early stages is the kind of relaxation-response mindfulness that is used widely today in medical contexts.[52] At deeper levels, this kind of meditation is associated with an oceanic perspective, and Buddha nature. There is no boundary that distinguishes self and universe; the mind falls open, so to speak, and pain recedes into a wider context. I suggested that Christians correlate this with an immanence awareness that pervades creation.

The second example finds that meditation can reduce pain by intensifying rather than relaxing concentration. Following the line of *vipassanā* meditation, such an approach undertakes direct analysis of the mind processes. In the practice of nonmedically oriented meditation, this corresponds to the counterintuitive technique of going directly at the pain experience. Concentration focuses on the pain sensation as the center of attention, with the result that it is largely dissipated into its less distressing mental components. The pain and the self alike have no center, and so there is both less to experience and less place, as it were, to experience from. This meditation is associated with a more dispersed, episodic self or with no-self teaching. I suggested that Christians understand this kind of deconstruction to be possible because of the no-self reality in our creaturely nature.

The bodhisattva path approaches all types of suffering through this perspective. Christian insight tends to approach the first and fourth types of suffering through focus on the middle two types. Thus, the characteristic Christian response to the pain of gross suffering has been, on the one hand, to act to eliminate its empirical (Buddhists would say secondary) causes and, on the other, to seek a spiritual or relational purpose in it and to hope for its eschatological removal. The concern for practical remediation, reflected in the healing miracles of Jesus, has positive historical effects. Today, it fits well with an interest in the meditative approaches to pain just described, as exactly this kind of practical good. The interest in the use of such practices to relieve pain in the conventional world is in some respects distinct from and even in tension with one of their primary Buddhist uses. An equanimity of indifference to pain or pleasure can be a great blessing for particular application as an antidote. But it makes no sense to Christians as a comprehensive aim. Christian ideas of hating the world, which parallel many of Śāntideva's teachings, have more to do with the power of pain and pleasure to deflect us from loving relation and with a hope for a new creation that structurally supplants this one than with an ideal state of equanimity regarding conditioned events.

For the fourth kind of suffering, the unavoidable losses that are attached to investment in conditioned states or beings, Christian help comes in seeking a frame of meaning and community within which suffering is borne in relation and in hope of resurrection and new creation. Christianity focuses particularly on intersubjective suffering—types two and three above. There is much overlap in the concrete Buddhist and Christian approaches to these. We discussed similarities and differences in our earlier consideration of unreal selves (the Buddhist diagnosis) and false selves (the Christian diagnosis). Much Christian attention is directed at changing the conventional causes of such evil through social and self-transformation and anticipating a more comprehensive eschatological change in the conditioned world itself.

Some of what comes under the heading of impermanence and subtle suffering is an inextricable part of emergence and person-making. The Christian hope for rescue from pain and evil always has in view the flourishing of the sufferer, a restoration to relation. Bodhisattvas that manifest to deliver those in distress do so purely (this is their perfection) because suffering is occurring. They do not manifest with a view to any purpose or destiny for the particular one afflicted, a specific future or vocation that suffering impedes. Christ and Christians care for each other through the losses of aging, death, and finitude because relation gives the care of suffering meaning. They do not act with a view to an equanimity between pain and pleasure.

Theodicy is a Christian, not Buddhist, problem. In the Buddhist cosmos, suffering is mysteriously ever new, ceaseless as the ranks of bodhisattvas who vow to end it are endless. Though suffering as such will never end, there are no ones to be the subjects of that endlessness. That unowned phenomenal distress is both invisible and baseless from the perspective of enlightened mind, of *dharmakāya*. Christianity looks toward a systematic end to the production of suffering. In that state, there would be no more suffering sentient beings coming in on the front end and, depending on the view of hell, either a complete end of it on the back end or the continued suffering of a finite number of the lost.[53] Christian theodicy is the confluence of a question and someone to whom it can be asked. It is a challenge to God to make good on the world, a challenge inextricable from a hope and call to take part in the transformed life that hope anticipates. Evil is a counterfactual offense, one whose existence flies in the face of a good creator and an eschatological hope.

No such framework arises in Buddhist terms. This is often reflected in the radical contribution that Buddhist perspective brings to discussions of social justice. Sallie King describes a Tibetan scholar and monk who participated in a peace council meeting with Israelis and Palestinians. The monk said that he saw no possibility for peace so long as parties clung to their identities as victims and their demands for justice. It would be better, he suggested, to understand the sufferings as a result of karma. Using Chinese treatment of Tibet as an example, he said that this must be attributed to something terrible that Tibetans had done to the Chinese in the past.

With general karma, "if a group in the past together killed an enemy, that group would later be reborn and killed together."[54] The same would apply to German treatment of the Jews. Instead of viewing such things as wrongs that need some future righting, we might view these evils as already the righting of wrongs that exist beyond our time horizon: the closing of a chapter rather than the opening of new wounds that incite new conflict. This plane of affairs will take care of itself. A true end to conflict in the ordinary world can arise only as a complement to liberation from captivity to its terms, through refuge in the unconditioned.

We recall that Śāntideva instructed his readers to treat those who did them harm as benefactors, even Buddhas. Alternatively, as the Tibetan monk suggests, one might regard the mistreatment at the hands of others as the necessary outworking of individual or group karma. These are not contradictions. Karma is an integral mechanism of the conditioned world, while Buddhas and bodhisattvas are understood as the manifestations of *dharmakāya* or Buddha nature. This suggests that the entirely of *saṃsāra* itself can be perceived either in an ascending perspective as the outworking of conditioned karma or in a descending perspective as compassionate opportunities foreseen by Buddhas. Karma is acknowledged in Buddhist teaching to be the most inscrutable of doctrines. Its operations are known only by omniscient Buddhas and, of all teachings, seems to be the one whose application is most to be accepted on faith in authority. It is similar in this sense to Christian belief in God's providence. The vindication of karma looks toward an omniscient understanding of past causes. The vindication of providence looks toward future acts of God.

In this connection, reincarnation and resurrection both are signs of hope that are consistent with their wider systems. The two agree that death is not the end of the story and that what follows comes in continuity with the effects or formation of this life. Without reincarnation, unawakened mind streams would lead straight from death to endless hell or animal realms—karma becoming a final judgement. Rebirth offers the chance to alter the trajectory, extending the continuity of the causal stream into enough lives for selves to be outgrown. Rebirth is an intrinsic necessity, given its antecedents. Nothing that emerges, is experienced, or is accomplished within all of these lives finally sticks to its subjects or the process. Reincarnation, limitlessly repeated, is a process whose entire premise is extinguished in the liberation of enlightenment.

Without resurrection, unregenerated persons would end in their current states—their earthly lives becoming the sole causal determination of the future. Resurrection ensures that the subjects whose emergence is constitutive of salvation will be around to take part in it. It extends relation and person-making into enhanced conditions, a celestial field for perfecting mutual participation. Resurrection is a relational gift whose basis is not in the creaturely no-self of those who are raised. The purgatorial or intensifying life to come cherishes the particularity that enters it. Resurrection, once for all, is a bridge that carries relationship forward, preserving and perfecting it.

Bodhisattva and Christ II: Why Christ Suffers and Bodhisattvas Don't

The basic idea of atonement is illegitimate in Buddhist perspective. As one Chinese monk writes, "For the Son of Heaven as well as for the ordinary man the fundamental thing is moral self-cultivation. If the Lord of Heaven buys back the people from their sins, then they can commit evil acts with impunity, confident that the Lord of Heaven in his compassion will buy them back."[55] The idea that one person would suffer for the sins of others appears not just mistaken but also repugnant, violating the fundamental nature of karma. José Cabezón recalls serving as translator for a Christian who was visiting in a monastery in south India. One of the senior teachers at the monastery invited the visitor to share his views. The ensuing conversation concluded with the teacher's perplexed question "How can the death of one individual act as the direct and substantive cause for the salvation of others?"[56] Here we can hear two large complexes of thought grinding against each other, producing a clear statement of Christ's deficiencies as a bodhisattva.

Our prior review allows us to understand the multiple facets that are summed up in the teacher's question. How can *one* individual play this role when the bodhisattva role is necessarily multiple? How can it be done for *others* when the point is for each one themselves to realize their Buddha nature as bodhisattvas? How can a *death*—a conditioned historical event—be a substantive *cause* of salvation (understood as enlightenment) when enlightenment is an already existing and unconditioned state? That state is uncaused and certainly has no causes in the conventional realm. We might add, though the teacher perhaps was too tactful to specify this, that the suffering character of the death only multiplies the perplexity. It illustrates the problem and offers no recommendation for the spiritual standing of the one who experienced it.

Though the death of a self-immolating bodhisattva might seem a counterexample within the Buddhist tradition, we have seen why it would probably not qualify this teacher's judgement. It is a rare event, not at the root of Buddhist teaching. Its significance is understood strictly in terms of the bodhisattva modes of helping that we have examined, and not in terms that Christians readily apply to the cross. We might say a similar thing of that vein of unitive mysticism in Christian tradition that could focus on Christ's resurrection as a manifestation of nondual identity with the permanent divine immanence latent in us all. Its convergence with Buddhist teaching is qualified by the fact that it is (like self-immolation in Buddhism) a minority emphasis in the tradition. And it is qualified in that it is commonly interpreted within the Christian terms of relation and participation, rather than as their sole ultimate truth, as Buddhists understand enlightenment in relation to the conditioned world.

If we move away from particular focus on death, *tonglen* may seem a Buddhist practice that approximates acting or suffering for others. It is a practical implementation of Śāntideva's bodhisattva vow: "Whatever suffering there is for the world, may it all ripen upon me."[57] At one level, *tonglen* is a method for an individual dealing with her or his own afflictive emotions. One breathes in the negative emotion, realizing that it is the identical phenomenon felt by others, and breathes out the wish for wellbeing and peace to all, including one's self. Its more advanced versions include an intention to take actively into oneself—in addition—the pain of others. Rather than viewing one's own suffering as like all others, one affirmatively claims the other's suffering as one's own. This is the way in which Śāntideva regards compassion as increasing the perceived suffering. As Pema Chödrön says, if we are angry, we might say to ourselves, "Since I'm already suffering from this anger, may this pain ripen in me, so no one else has to feel it."[58] This is a very practical way of focusing *bodhicitta*, the universal benevolent intention, around a particular slice of universal suffering.

I find no way in which such a *tonglen* practice is considered to break with the general bodhisattva pattern of assistance and causation. Such a break would result if one person's practice were actually to remove another's suffering. The varied forms of *tonglen* seem to be run on a spectrum from rudimentary to advanced methods of perceiving the undifferentiated nature of suffering as such. It is about detaching suffering from all its owners, not about redistributing it in any way. Whatever *tonglen* does, it does within the path we have outlined, on which the practitioner attains to enlightenment for the sake of all beings, and the beings benefit from that bodhisattva practice in the ways that we have described. When benefactor practice turns its well-wishing toward difficult people, it still does so as an antidote to the emotions that those people evoke in us. This is a powerful force to allow us to show compassion to them in conventional actions. From a Christian point of view, this would seem to come very close to an instance of taking on another's pain in a way that results in a benefit to them. But it has no effect upon their own practice or enlightenment except in the ways already explored.

Here, where the two traditions seem so close, a crucial distinction remains regarding the views of causality. There is nothing in one's enlightenment that *could* be caused by another, since there is nothing about the event of enlightenment that represents a change in any substantive sense. Jesus's death, or any possible event in the conventional world, could not be a substantive cause of salvation/enlightenment because there is no such thing in principle. This applies to enlightenment as a category and to any individual's attainment of it, for here, likewise, there is no change of status or substantial nature within that one, but only the liberating dissipation of projections. Christian salvation is itself a texture and quality of relations, and some participants in those relations can be causal in relation to others' realization, because their participation is in part what constitutes salvation.

The Buddha/bodhisattva is a satisfying image of attainment and path compressed together in identity. This is so because the fundamental dynamic addressed is that between form and emptiness, the conventional world and the wisdom world: "These two truths are like the two sides of a coin. When you look from one side, you see the dependent arising. . . . When you look from the other side, you see the emptiness of the phenomenon."[59] Both are absolutely constant in their character and relation, equally available at all times. So they are best represented in terms of simultaneous presence.

Christ, crucified or risen (and necessarily *both* crucified and risen), is more manifestation-like than realization-like in Buddhist terms because the Christ event and meaning are embedded in narrative and in the conditioned realities of creatures and relations. The fundamental dynamic in Christian perspective is movement within the world and movement toward a world to come. This dynamic deals with the next world, in the sense of the next temporal *version* of this world (i.e., history, both personal and collective). And it encompasses also the eschatological world to come, recreation in a more comprehensive way. In this sequence, no single image stands perfectly and permanently for path and end at once. This is why the objects of faith (i.e., God, Christ, Spirit) are understood as themselves living agents, actively engaged in the participatory process. Images of the cross or resurrection are paradigmatic representations of that engagement, constant purpose in unceasing relation.

As the monk's question suggested, these different views of causality are particularly relevant when we ask if suffering plays any role in connection to helping. We have seen that in *Mahāyāna* terms, suffering can have a helpful role for the immediate subject involved. It can be beneficial as a kind of wake-up call, a motivator in the early ranges of practice. It also can serve fruitfully as a direct object of meditation at more advanced levels. We have seen it is much more problematic to attribute benefit to someone's suffering on behalf of another.

Christians agree that immediate suffering may stimulate reflection and fruitful change, including a focus on the enduring rather than the ephemeral (however, Buddhists and Christian may disagree in defining those). As Buddhists view misfortune or mistreatment as prime opportunities to practice the bodhisattva perfections, Christians may view their suffering as an opportunity to practice selflessness, to deepen their relations with God, and to discover solidarity with others. They may view it as chastisement and instruction for amending the conduct of their ethical lives.

There are at least three further points we can make on the specific question of whether any one's suffering can be a help to others. The first is that suffering can be an act of solidarity, of deepened and unbroken relation. Sharing in the suffering of others builds empathy and unity with them. It is one of the powerful experiences that foster deep personal identification, freeing up the exchange of love and joy, as well. As an object of devotion and personal interaction, Christ's experience of suffering makes him both more available and more transformative. This factor is inextricable from the causation by participation at the root of the great exchange of the incarnation that we discussed in Chapter 1. Christ's participation in human mortality and loss goes hand in hand with the exchange through which humans participate in divine energies and love.

Exchanging self and other, according to Śāntideva, is above all a meditative exercise in which we imagine human inner life from various perspectives. This is key in Christian practice, as we have seen in our discussion of mimetic relation. It is stressed more as a concrete than a meditative exchange. The pioneering Jesuit missionary to Tibet, Ippolito Desideri, translated the second of the two great Christian commandments into Tibetan as a command to count "all other human beings worthy of being cherished like yourself, as if you exchanged [self and other]."[60] This exchange is not only the way we are constituted as persons. It is also a way of addressing suffering, in that suffering shared is in some measure lessened, shorn of the pain of isolation and rejection. It is also concretely true that suffering can be in part substituted for another's, as when a friend or relative spells a parent in the care of a chronically and seriously ill child. Some of the immediate distress of the situation is taken on by one and lifted from the other. The same is true when an addicted person, struggling with recovery, asks another to temporarily manage her financial affairs. The associated burdens and cares are added to one who did not have them before, who bears them instead of another bearing them. Most of the time, suffering is a concomitant aspect of the task, not the direct aim. But there are situations in which the pain of solidarity is the only concrete act available to us. This is a redemptive capacity in human life, but it is a dangerous one. Suffering with another in a way that has no practical benefit and, to an extent that is destructive of one's own wellbeing and of that of additional others becomes an oppressive weight. Buddhist teaching has made us aware of some of those dangers and also of some direct antidotes to the negative emotions arising from this kind of connection.

There is a second way that suffering can be part of helping. This is when suffering is related to historical activity and relations that transform the very texture of the created world and its social nexus. It is a communication through action. It is important that the suffering in view here is no simple neurological phenomenon or subjective condition. It is attached to decisions and context that make it a kind of witness. In this respect, Christ's suffering in the place of the outcast victim has a powerful historical and social meaning. It is not simply a solidarity in generic contingent suffering, but an identification with and a signification of the particular desolation that social evils impose. It is an integral part of a larger representation and action that includes proclaiming the forgiveness of sins and the coming of the kingdom of God. Its effect is perfected in its bearing on the conditioned historical world, but that effect cannot be segregated to the existing world alone, since it addresses a world itself destined to be changed and taken up, so to speak, into consummated relation.

All conditionally manifesting bodhisattvas are helping others to become conditionally manifesting bodhisattvas of exactly the same sort, and to realize ultimate enlightenment qualities in the same way. It is their place beyond suffering that makes this possible. The suffering God and the loving Jesus are helping others to achieve distinctive individualities. It is their supreme relational qualities that make this possible. Christ on the cross is a definitive sign of love, but only a penultimate sign of salvation. The crucifixion images part of the way, but its suffering is no intrinsic part of the end.

There are forms of suffering that attend events or transitions in history, moments of reconciliation or emergence. Such suffering is, in fact, on behalf of others who will share in the benefits it gains and those beneficiaries will not have to repeat it themselves. Whether in medical and technological discoveries or social transformations, the exchange of some peoples' blood, sweat, and tears makes possible new life for others, removes suffering that they would otherwise undergo or are already experiencing. Buddhists will rightly observe that this is not a one-way street. Gains won can be overturned, and all such developments could be temporary and futile. Christians rest their hope not on the historical irreversibility of any particular development, but upon their sacramental and proleptic quality.

In the special case of Christ's suffering and death, we can say that it works in the pattern of these first two kinds of helping-suffering. That is, the passion is an intervention, a causal force in history. This is particularly so with regard to the awareness of victims and the formation of human communities.[61] It is also an act of solidarity, building empathy, and strengthening the mimetic connection between God and humans for the full range of spiritual formation. But there is another dimension that is unique to the case of Christ.

This third way that suffering figures in helping relates to the unique dynamic of reconciliation between God and humans. Certain theological doctrines, such as substitutionary atonement, frame that reconciliation in a very specific way, an exchange in which Christ vicariously bears the suffering due to sinners while humans receive the rewards due to Christ's obedience and gift. But the broader context within which to place that interpretation is the causal modality of mutual participation.

Theology assumes that human beings indwell each other, and that the incarnation radicalizes a similar indwelling between God and humans. We have taken Buddhist instruction on the constant, nonpersonal identity dimensions of this indwelling, apophatic, and immanent. But if the incarnation signals humans' free acceptance into communion with God *before* we have been completely remade by contemplative practice or transformed through mimetic devotion into more fit companions, *how* do we humans and God then mutually indwell each other? Christ's suffering relates also to this question.

If the self is a purely conventional entity, then this relational concern would not be so central. That is in fact the case in Buddhism. But since Christians look to communion as the nature of salvation, account must be taken of the obstacles to that indwelling. This is not simply a matter of God waiving punishment for sins. The announcement of such clemency is central to Jesus's preaching, and it is not an entirely novel message among the prophets. The question goes to another level. It deals with the depth of intimacy and communion that God seeks.

The contrast of our finite creaturely natures *per se* with the eternal divine is a morally neutral one. Communion across these kinds of difference is experienced in Christian terms as a great good. It is a more complex matter with the persons and relations that emerge in history. The dimensions of difference that they add to the communion are also goods. But as actually constituted, there are ways that these, that we, are actively discordant and do not fit with God. God cannot will our hatreds and indifference along with us. We fail to align ourselves with God's benevolence and love, and the conflicts among us are rife, as well. The divine and the human are interwoven in the constitution of humanity, yet currently these are in painful measure morally and spiritually foreign bodies in each other. The incarnation is an infusion of divine life and personal availability, from God to humanity. It is also a kind of infection in which humanity, with all its problematic potentials, is incorporated into the Trinitarian life.

On the human side, this misalignment means that the process of spiritual growth involves friction and discomfort. The divine energy that is shared with us cracks distorted or destructive attitudes and impulses. Śāntideva's observation that compassion initially increases suffering corresponds to Christian commentary on the "dark night" and the birth pains that shadow new life. The cross testifies that there is a corresponding reality in God's redemptive activity, that communion and re-union with broken creation has a cost on the divine end. The creation-emergence process produces the material for new kinds of communion. With the advent of sin, it also produces the challenge of reconciliation for conflicted relations among persons. And this is itself a new kind of communion.

The cross is a new experience for God. If we frame this newness in purely structural terms, then it has to do with the cost of God's permanent engagement with the created order, the venture that makes divine life captive to the world's redemption. That way of putting it focuses more on what God's providence can make of fractured pieces of creation. But there is also an existential dimension to the prospect that broken and sin-recovering creatures participate in the divine life, as God's spirit participates in them. The existential question is not what justifies this possibility but how it is actually experienced as healing.

Bodhisattvas are able to help because they have a conditioned side. We could say this side is the product or result of ignorance, as the entire conventional world is. Bodhisattvas, who are pure wisdom, become ignorance for us. God is able to help because of taking on communion with the created world, in particular because of becoming incarnate. The incarnation of Christ includes a dimension (manifested in an event, the cross) that is the result of sin: "For our sake he made him to be sin who knew no sin."[62]

Just as bodhisattvas cannot violate karma to help beings, God cannot violate goodness or divine purpose to help beings. If God accepted with equanimity fallen humans and a tortured creation as determining participants in his life, then God would have changed natures. If God acted externally as punisher and enforcer to expel humans from that life, then God would have failed in the intended aim of relation with them. The reconciliation of divine mercy with divine holiness is an unavoidable tension raised by communion with us. The constructive suffering that flows from regeneration and renewal is the unavoidable tension raised by that communion for us. Ours would not be possible without God's.[63]

Christ's suffering belongs to the mode in which God experiences and effects reconciliation. This suffering is not, to my mind, the forensic precondition that allows God to offer that reconciliation to begin with. Among Christian theories of the cross, substitutionary or satisfaction views stand closest to the idea of karma: every magnitude of sin/offense has to be balanced out by an equal magnitude of negative consequence before sinners can be saved. Karma and this approach to justice share a certain intrinsic logic. Yet the difference is sharp, as such views of the cross directly assert that merit can be personally administered by God and directly transferred from one to others. This paid-in-full approach is one way to formulate principles that distinguish Christians and Buddhists. Christian understanding includes the kind of exchange on behalf of others (i.e., substitution or representation) that karma appears to rule out. That exchange is precisely what Buddhist observers have typically dismissed out of hand as incompatible with their core teachings. One person's death or sacrifice or love cannot lead to another's enlightenment. To think so is a category mistake about the nature of enlightenment, associating conventional, relational causes with an unconditioned state that can only be addressed via the specific mind that achieves it. Since Christians understand salvation as a relational reality, they see nothing inconsistent in holding that relational causes constitute it.

Broader and, to my mind, deeper Christian views of atonement (deeper than penal substitutionary ones) diverge no less from Buddhist assumptions. Rather than a lawlike price that God must pay before reconciling with creatures, suffering is the cost that follows on the choice to love sinners and to be in communion with them. It is the birth pang of new life together. This is a relational kind of causality rather than a legal or mechanical one. And the historical particularity of the cross—its role in calling us away from violence and toward recognition of our own victimizing practices—is a concrete force in overcoming suffering and removing estrangement with God.

The Christian path seeks the reconciliation and the flourishing of relations. Love that heals brokenness engages suffering that attends that reconciliation. Love does not seek pain or demand it. The path itself looks forward to an end to suffering. We should add the qualification that this does not apply to some segment of what Buddhist analysis calls "suffering." Christians accept as a constituent aspect of salvation, as a positive good, the most subtle forms of suffering described by our Buddhist commentators. That subtle suffering stems from rarified mental seeds of identity and diversity. It is the elimination of those germs that distinguishes true enlightenment from false facsimiles.

The *Mahāyāna* path seeks the end of suffering for all beings. The compassion that ends suffering uses the relational appearances of the conventional world no further than wisdom dictates is necessary to serve that end. This means that Buddhists of this sort accept as a constituent aspect of enlightenment—as a positive good—the ultimate absence of relational activity and experience. From a Christian perspective, that kind of emptiness registers as diminishment. It is the flourishing, not the stilling of those capacities, that distinguishes salvation from false facsimiles.

The eschatological transformation that belongs to salvation will take place through an escalation and perfection of person-making and community formation. This contrasts with an identity realization such as enlightenment that does not need or include those things. The basic mechanism for those processes, for mimetic formation, will have to be in working order to get us to that future. In other words, this transformation will be driven by the continuing and intensifying communion of God with humans and humans with each other. The question of how to justify God's mercy toward sinners is posed in terms of justice for those harmed by sin. But before or after forgiveness, such justice turns on God's ability to keep faith with those who have been harmed, keeping faith by means of future reconciliation and transformation. Forgiveness is justified, in that sense, if it is central to the capacity to realize that transformation. Causality by participation is the mode for this renewal: it is by our participation in the divine life and in the life of others that wounds will be healed and new life realized. From this perspective, it is crucial to ask what purchase points exist in God and humans for this ever fuller communion.

Absent incarnation and passion, in the communion of humans and God, each would know the other mainly in their incompatibility: the holy in tension with the corrupt, the judge against the sinner, both pairs of mutual irritants. But with incarnation and passion, humans know God not only as judge but also as fellow sufferer of the results of sin. They know God not only as author of the person-making process but as a partner-participant in its poignant glories. God knows all humans as part of the family that succeeded in living up to the fullness of the stature of Christ. This is the healing of memory, the recipe for mutual indwelling that clears the way for the future life together. If this healing were purely forensic, then it would not be enough. It must change how each one is experienced as part of the other.

The incarnation is an exchanging of self and other. Its very premise is that Jesus bears results that he did not cause or deserve, while others receive benefits that they could not cause alone. God becomes a human person, subject to the formation that makes every human person. This means that Jesus is constituted in the same mimetic process. It is by drawing together and sifting the humanity of Mary, Joseph, friends, disciples, and antagonists that Jesus receives humanity and becomes a person. Jesus's deeply human love for these people becomes part of God's love for humanity. At the same time, the human person of Jesus is given over also to the divine formation in the participation that goes on among the Trinitarian persons and is incorporated in the divine life.

God's forgiveness of sins is a simple event. What the incarnation does is to surround it with an entire relational and experiential context in which it can be appropriated by both God and humans in their shared future. In intimate communion, we sense and catch, as it were, each other's inner lives. A close friend might pick up on my nagging disapproval, a hidden unhappiness, and be troubled by that crack or disjunction in our relationship as a distant acquaintance never would. So, too, in the communion between humans and God. What the incarnation has done is to give both God and humans positive mimetic purchase in the inner life of the other. When God looks at humans, God sees not only sinners worthy of condemnation and suffering beings worthy of compassion. God sees also the humanity of Christ, delighting in its fulfilment of the hope in creation. More than that, God sees all others as actual participants in that humanity. Where does Christ's humanity come from but the formational contributions of all those people in his life, back to Eve and Adam?

When humans live close to God, they sense not only a holiness that shames them and a generous judge that forgives them. They feel at the core, as well, one who suffered what they have suffered on account of sin, and one who delights in their humanity for all it has proved to be in Christ and can become in each person's distinctive life. All this prepares the environment for the most intimate life together, for the kind of mutual participation that can actually heal the brokenness that remains, and that can build and inhabit a new creation. God has shaped the inner landscape as well as the outer so that, despite this terrible rupture in relation and the fabric of creation, the resources exist to repair and renew. The most powerful resource of all is the instrument of formation, this inner filament of relation, signified in Jesus's simple words in the Gospel of John, "I do not call you servants any longer, because the servant does not know what the master is doing, but I have called you friends."[64] Human to human, and between humans and God, we experience each other not just as enemies, or pardoned offenders, or compromised rulers. The rupture has been subsumed in a larger story, in which we can see in each other so much more than the opponents that we became, including new kinds of regard for each other born of the reconciliation.

This exchange of places yields at times outright reversals. If the cross is an expression of God's compassion, then it becomes an occasion for us to feel compassion for Christ and for God as well as for our scapegoated neighbor. If God reaches out in the incarnation to a degraded and hostile humanity, then Christ's life becomes an occasion for God's admiration and exaltation of humanity. God and Jesus suffer together in order to open the paths of communion.

We began, in Chapter 1, by describing the bodhisattva complex and the Christ complex in terms of their structural similarities and concrete differences. As we have detailed the bodhisattva path, the tension between the two complexes has become more fractal—the differences and similarities interwoven at finer levels of detail. Each complex encompasses a paradox, but they are not the same paradox. We can illustrate this by considering what is excluded in each case. A suffering bodhisattva is not included within the Buddhist paradox, as a sinful Christ is not included in the Christian one. Suffering is what one overcomes by being a bodhisattva. And the sinfulness of broken and estranged relation is what Christ overcomes, and what Christ-followers overcome also in their measure.

A suffering bodhisattva is not an option in Buddhist grammar because only an enlightened one can help. Whatever enlightenment may be, it is certainly the end of suffering. The true paradox is that of a conditioned Buddha, an enlightened one who yet possesses conditioned qualities and has effects in the conditioned world. This helping paradox involves the continuing legacy of the enlightened one and their wisdom state within saṃsāra. This is achieved by the bodhisattva's manifestations. A sinful bodhisattva is possible insofar as, in line with their skillful manifestations, bodhisattvas may violate at least the precepts that have to do with bodily (as opposed to mental) morals. Only the conditionally manifest bodhisattva can be an aid to liberation.

A sinful Christ is not an option in Christian grammar because only the fully loving, fully relational one can help.[65] Whatever divine love may be, it is certainly the opposite of relational malice and indifference. The true paradox is full indwelling of the divine and the human. This helping paradox involves a divine availability for relation and participation in the historical world and beyond. This is achieved through incarnation and replicated through the communion that perfects indwelling among persons and creature. A suffering Christ is intelligible in these terms, even entailed, as part of the helping. Only the suffering God can save.[66]

Christ and the bodhisattva are healers, but they do not treat precisely the same diseases. The wellbeing that each promises leaves behind some chronic condition that the other regards as an affliction. The cure for ignorance and projected selves, like some powerful chemotherapy, destroys too completely the healthy cells of persons and their communion that are needed for the new life of salvation. The cure for sin and evil, like a powerful symptom-repressing analgesic, leaves the root poison at work and the seeds of suffering unextinguished.

Conclusion: Crucified Wisdom

Chapter 1 sketched the bodhisattva path and the Christ way, the one a miracle of identification and realization, the other a miracle of participation and reconciliation. The depth of our consideration of one leads to a fuller appreciation of the other. We return to that comparison but are now focused on the learnings for a Christian pilgrim. We end with no grand resolution to the tensions that make this study so fruitful. No appeal to combine the oppositions or subsume them all in nondualism will serve that purpose. Each tradition has already gone too deep and deployed all the intellectual tools at our disposal too thoughtfully to be superseded in that manner. Buddhism cannot be taken whole into Christianity or vice versa. Christians can only search in their own way to take account of the wisdom they find there.

Mahāyāna teachings have the capacity to subsume Christian convictions effectively within their terms, as representing only preliminary or crude versions of the truth. The counterintuitive teachings of *Mahāyāna* wisdom extend nonpersonal, causal forces to account for all conventional entities as arising from conditioned causes or as appearances screening the luminous, unconditioned emptiness of all mental products that is both *nirvāṇa* and our original nature. What meaning might the term "incarnation" have in this perspective? We have seen that Buddha nature is a kind of pulsating emptiness, radiant with unconditioned qualities. This emptiness is opposite of or inside every moment of *saṃsāra*. It rains, so to speak, its presence indifferently on all of the conventional world. We might stretch to say even that emptiness is incarnate in form as its shadow. This strains Buddhist categories, but it has some resonance in that conventional forms can be, in their place, authentic signs of emptiness. This is so even though it is also true that every moment of conventional existence is constituted by ignorance.

If we take a step too far and suppose that Buddha nature stands for God, then we have a kind of deistic incarnation. The deist God creates and then leaves the creation to go its own way. Buddha nature of course neither creates nor acts. It simply stands parallel with its shadow, *saṃsāra*. It is the always-available, unconditioned flipside of the dependently arisen coin with its variegated suffering forms.

How far does *Mahāyāna* go in the direction of the Christian counter-intuitive conviction that personal and relational causality far exceeds the power we attribute to it in the conventional world? The ascending bodhisattva path has much to offer in this connection, as we saw in our discussion in Chapter 3. For the fully realized bodhisattva, the closest thing is found in the legacy trail of that bodhisattva's activity in the conventional world. This conditioned wake of action and intention is personal insofar as it is responsive to the particular condition of different beings. It has an interpersonally unitive aspect, insofar as the bodhisattva's path requires making others' experience—primarily their suffering—her own. All of this is left behind by the bodhisattva who, as realized, has no suffering and no relation.

The Trinitarian understanding of God is the Christian template for this study and the matrix for active incorporation of our leaning. A complex God generates different dimensions of relation with creation. Salvation is the fulfillment of relation in all of these dimensions—the nonpersonal, personal, and communion channels. If creation is to be redeemed in each dimension, and in their interrelations, then the channels for exchange must be kept open for all of them. The study of Buddhist sources can fill out this picture. Buddhist sources are famously detailed on the intricacies of meditational states and practice, as they are also on the philosophy corresponding to these. Christians have tended to lavish their detail on relational and community concerns, whether between God and humans or among humans. Studies like this one may extend the breadth of the Christian vision by clarifying the place for the non-differentiated flavors of emptiness and immanence.

Christian recognition of the truth that Buddhists realize stems from the nonpersonal dimension of the Trinitarian life, with its apophatic and immanent aspects. Emptiness and immanence are two sides of the indwelling of the divine persons in God. That indwelling in the personal and communion modes is particular in that each person makes way for the coinherence of the others and each gives itself for coinherence in them *as* a distinctive other. The indwelling in the nonpersonal dimension is formally the same exchange. But what is shared is each one's version of the bare awareness of the unity of the whole. I likened this to the preconscious unity in an organic body. What the first person shares with the second, in this sense, is not the first person *as* the first person, but the first person's bare awareness of the unity. We might say that it is the first person's oceanic consciousness of the divine life that is exchanged with the second person's oceanic consciousness of the same.

This is the correlative in the divine life for that mode of God's relation with the world that has this same nonpersonal character. When Christians speak of God's mystery or ineffability, these apply as much to the mystery of God's personal or hypostatic nature as to this nonpersonal dimension. But the mystery in that case has a concrete form: the incarnation in which the mystery is flesh. It is in Christian apophatic theology that the mystery of the nonpersonal dimension tends to stand out most with the character of emptiness. For here the mystery precisely does not take on "flesh," but remains beyond word or image or any mental product. This is the place for Christians to take up the *Mahāyāna* wisdom, because the unconditioned consciousness that it realizes corresponds to the apophatic mystery. This is the grounding for an identification realization as an authentic part of Christian faith and practice.

From that perspective, I will summarize some of the learning gleaned from our study of Śāntideva and the bodhisattva path. We will consider first learning for practice of the Christian disciple, then some implications for Christology, particularly in relation to the cross.

The nonpersonal or emptiness dimension takes two forms in Buddhist teaching: no-self and Buddha nature. In Christian terms, it takes the forms that I called creaturely no-self and immanence awareness. I specified how an identification with or a realization of this dimension of relation with God is truly a nondual realization, one lacking any mental products. If I have rightly understood *Mahāyāna* teaching, and if this understanding of Trinity in that light is sound, then there is good reason to take instruction from the bodhisattva path. Since for Buddhists, this dimension is the ultimate, with no second and no reservation, they know a depth that Christians rarely do. Bodhisattvas understand and practice this kind of nondualism better. That advantage may apply particularly to the no-self aspect since, of the two, the immanence awareness has received more explicit attention in the Christian tradition than what I have called creaturely no-self.

Argument and sometimes persecution have swirled around Christian unitive mysticism because the idea of total identification with the divine raises all kinds of theological flags about creation, God's transcendence, the unique place of Jesus, and human hubris. In the clarity of Buddhist teaching, all these fears seem to be realized. There is no creation, no God, no special place for Jesus (as we discussed, the hubris charge seems misplaced). Yes, this kind of identification as the sole ultimate and the sole end is an alternative to Christian hope. But most Christian mystics have held this identification in a larger relational framework (for instance, in expressing their experience in terms of unity with Christ and not exclusively as an unconditioned emptiness). Critics of such mysticism are mistaken when they suggest that nondual realization itself is outside legitimate Christian spirituality. The realizations of emptiness and immanence, which have no Christian cognitive markers because they have no markers at all, are valid parts of Christian spiritual practice.

In this sense, there is value in taking instruction on such realization directly from sources in Buddhism. Christians have some of their own modalities for this practice and will no doubt develop more in conversation with Buddhism. But the point is that these are not just techniques to be repurposed in another faith practice. Their end, as sought and practiced in Buddhism, is grounded in God. Christians can affirm both that technique and its end, even while they affirm the coequal ultimacy of the personal and the communion dimensions. What this means practically, given the understanding of salvation as communion, is that such practice and its realizations need not be the activity of all Christians and will not be the sole and exclusive aim of any.

We have seen some of the concrete ways that direct cultivation of the no-self and immanence realizations in their own right can enrich the path of the Christian disciple. Such disciples will not hesitate to value these practices also for the benefits that flow from them into the personal and relational dimensions that have an ultimate significance for Christians. The use of practices as specific antidotes to negative emotions and as correctives to the false substantiality of our projected selves can serve to foster and deepen the relations in which Christianity invests its particular hopes, including the relation with God. We saw that the modified benefactor practice, already including so many elements congenial to Christian perspectives, could be an especially effective way of combining some of these elements. It is an exercise in generating love of neighbor, self, and God that is based in recognition of the fact that one is the recipient of that love.

The special window opened on Christology by our study of the bodhisattva focuses on the way in which Christ, in the incarnation, embodies creaturely no-self and the immanence awareness. This is the nonpersonal dimension of God's relation with the world that comes closest to the Buddhist meaning of nonduality. That consideration led us into aspects of incarnation that are not usual topics for Christian reflection. Both creaturely no-self and immanent awareness are constant and unchanging conditions in all of creation. Christ's embodiment of them is not unique because their nature does not vary in expression. The realization of them is qualitatively the same in all who experience them. This realization predates Jesus, attained by the Buddha and others in the Buddha's path. This is the sense in which all can be one with God as Christ was one with God, because this is the dimension in which all *are* constantly one with God. This is the way in which we can all be Christ, the closest parallel to the sense in which Buddhists understand that we can all be Buddha. This dimension of incarnation is realization.

We saw that positive Buddhist interpretations of Jesus stress exactly this dimension. They emphasize the way that Jesus's giving up his life reflects the no-clinging of no-self or the way that his identification with God reflects realization of a permanently unconditioned dimension on the other side of the conventional world. But these two aspects of nonduality do not exhaust Christ's meaning. Jesus's imperfections as a bodhisattva flow necessarily from the relational aspects of his incarnation and from the particular Christian form of nonduality, communion. These are the things that trouble generous Buddhist interpreters of Jesus, especially in regard to the cross. For Christians, they are no less integral to the saving work and end of the incarnation than is the identity relation.

The tension of similarity and difference between the Christ/disciple and the Buddha/bodhisattva must be addressed finally by each tradition in terms of the categories that it uses for diversity within it. For Śāntideva and *Mahāyāna*, the two-truth teaching is the recursive framework for differences. It applies first to the difference between the conventional world of appearances (in which it is true that beings exist) and the wisdom world of enlightenment (where higher truth understands they do not). This distinction could be applied again to discriminate among different religions and different kinds of Buddhist teachings. Some of these are regarded as skillful means, preliminary or even penultimate rungs on the hierarchy of teaching and practice, and one is regarded as the true perfection of wisdom teaching.

The two-truths perspective is applied yet one more time, at this point, to affirm that even this supreme teaching remains a conventional truth. That teaching is itself empty and so vindicates emptiness as the truth of all phenomena. The Madhyamaka Buddhist rationale for two truths is a no-view one. That is, truth is something about which no view (i.e., human teaching) can be correct, though the teachings can be ordered in an objective hierarchy that can lead toward this no-view realization (Buddhists disagree about how to organize that hierarchy). *Two* truths are needed for a nondual truth, so that there is always one to negate the view that is held to be the truth.

Two truths thus explain the differences between those who see the world through Buddhist teachings and those who do not, the differences among all the various Buddhist (and other) vehicles, and even the difference between truth and Buddhist truth. These are the categories through which sympathetic Buddhist students of Christianity will understand and assimilate what they find of value in it.

Both kinds of truth are available and apply at every moment, and the wonder of bodhisattvas is that they are able to reflect the coincidence of both at once, to beneficial effect. We might picture this as one of the elegant Zen calligraphy images of a not-quite-closed circle. What appears to be the inside of the circle is in unbroken continuity with the outside. Let us suppose that we start on the inside of the near-circular line and imagine an endless ladder running along it toward the opening in the near-circle. This ladder represents a hierarchy of objectively ordered teachings or views from the most ignorant to the most insightful. Every rung on the ladder, every point of line defining an "inside," is at the same time a point open to the limitless expanse of emptiness "outside" the suggested circle. The line of the near-circle gives an irresistible impression that it defines a contained interior space. The conventional world is just this sort of illusory containment. In actuality, that world is in unbroken, nondual unity with the unrestricted and unconditioned. In a profound sense, this vision is grasped all at once or not at all, rather like those optical illusions perceived at any time as one of two alternative images.

For Christians, Trinity is the primordial ground for pluralism and difference, reflected in creation and incarnation. It has served as the basic framework for this study. But at this last stage, it would be well to try to learn from the Buddhist approach to difference, when assessing the difference with Buddhism itself. Is there a place for the two-truths teaching in theology?

The twoness that comes most readily to Christian reflection might be the distinction between God and creation, or the distinction between a broken relational nexus and a healthy or redeemed one. To the simultaneity of the conditioned and unconditioned in Buddhism, Christianity might parallel the fact that we are simultaneously fallen and contingent creatures who are loved and redeemed, both one with God and estranged from God. However, none of these things but God are permanent in the important Buddhist sense of having no beginning and no end. So long as creatures have existed, they have been loved and, in real respects, one with God. There are other ways in which creatures were never one with God (e.g., they were not without beginning). And there are ways that some creatures became estranged from God and each other, ways that await transformation and renewal. All of these are necessary elements in a description of the human situation. They all have a place in the current reality.

When we look at things this way, we can see that the two-truths teaching has a place of direct application in line with our earlier discussion of no-self and immanence. Their dimension is the dimension in which we have always been one with God. And here the core Buddhist two-truth teaching applies: the conventional teaching that this oneness is reality is the truth, in contrast to conventional teaching that rejects oneness. But it is also true that the experiential realization of this reality is an ultimate truth, beside which the correct conventional teaching is itself empty.

Mahāyāna sees a hierarchy of conventional truths, serving to lead to that unconventional insight. Two truths can apply to any number of actual pairs, in which one functions as the higher and one the lower. A Christian application would need to underline that this "higher" and "lower" can rightly refer to the world itself. For instance, we can readily see two truths in the cross in this respect. There is what was done to Jesus by those who saw his death as both a religious and political virtue, the scapegoating sense in which it is good for one man to die for the sake of the people. And there was what God was doing by identifying as the victim of that violence and raising the victim from the dead. Quite apart from any eschatological significance to this event, it has a very concrete meaning within history, instigating an awareness of our own victims and a search for community not based on unity against victims. The cross has a worldly as well as a theological meaning. This relates directly to what we discussed in Chapter 4 as ways in which the cross is not exemplary. What killed Jesus is something that ought not to happen. Jesus's suffering is likewise not ideal but consequent to the overcoming of that evil. To this we can add another pairing, that between the cross as an act of God within history, with effects on history, and the cross as an act of relational reconciliation between God and humans, which we discussed in Chapter 5.

We have used a Zen open-circle image to represent the insight nature of Buddhist truth, its emptiness, and its simultaneity. As we have noted a few times, it seems not in the nature of Christianity to have a similar, synoptic image. To those dimensions in which all persons and creatures simultaneously have the same identity relation, the Christian recipe for pluralism adds the simultaneity of many different creatures having their own distinctive relations with God and each other. Narrative is a form that fits better with this character. The Zen circle seeks to approximate a view that is without perspective, in the sense that it does not conform to our inclination to see a completely closed figure or a completely open one. In a wordless, visual apprehension, we take in a none-of-these impression that stills all contrast or mental content.

That experience or perception of nonduality fits well with the no-self and immanence dimension. The immanence awareness we discussed, for instance, is a view from everywhere that lacks perspective in the sense just described. But that is like a freeze-frame or partial cross section of Christian truth. The Christian image would need to encompass process and relation. Even the eschatological end is not a cessation of relation. It elevates the created order from its pain and evil, the unsatisfactoriness that is intrinsic to it in Buddhist views, for continued exchange.

Christian scripture is narrative and history. Rather than something that cannot be seen at all, it is something that cannot be seen or experienced alone. If we stay with the visual mode, then we could think of a classic icon representing Christ or one of the figures or narrative events of salvation history. Such icons typically employ a kind of reversed perspective in order to suggest that the viewer is being seen as well as seeing. What is apprehended or embodied in such a case is the communion, the mutual participation in a whole that is larger than its personal parts but joins them. Or perhaps we could think of benefactor practice itself, in which it is no image that stands for the truth, but the mutual indwelling of the diverse participants who share it.

We can all become Buddhas. We can all be what the Buddha is: emptiness and Buddha nature. It is true that none of us belongs to the karmic stream that produced the historical Buddha of this age. We cannot be *who* Gautama was, in that sense. But that is actually an empty category in any case, since such identities relate only to the conditioned world and not to the unconditioned one. Our being Buddha is in no way different from any other one's being Buddha. There is profound equality and symmetry in that. This is what we are, and the one relief from the pain of being is to be Buddha. Our nature allows one happy option: we will suffer until we recognize and realize that option. The good news is that numberless bodhisattvas have gone this way already, and their power pulls us after them.

We cannot all become Christ. We cannot be who Christ was, historically, relationally, and vocationally. That means we cannot fully be what Christ is in interpersonal location and effect, or in perfect identity. But we can share in all of these things by participation, in connection with Christ, God, and our neighbors. Being in Christ or having communion in Christ's body does not denote endless replication of a condition that is qualitatively indistinguishable in each instance. It signifies a cumulative complexity of mutuality. But our learning from the bodhisattva path suggests a notable change in this summary statement. There are specific and usually unrecognized ways in which we *can* be fully what Christ is. We can be what Christ is in identity with the creaturely no-self, for this is a dimension that is the same in all. We can be what Christ is in identity with the divine immanence awareness, for this is also a dimension the same in all. In these ways, Christ is what the Buddha is.

This does not displace the conviction that we cannot be the same one that Christ is. We have the gift of being the ones that we are. God, in Christian belief, is already three equally good but not identical ways of being. Creatures can become entirely good and entirely happy while not being either Buddha or the same one(s) that God is. There is more than one way to be ultimate and more than one way to be perfected, because different ones make up the perfection and the good. Our creator shaped us for relations: we suffer until these relations are reconciled, united by communion through the same one, not by being the same one. The good news is that the patterns of perfected relation are as diverse as we are—each creature, each person. The dimensions of relation need not be worked out the same for each of us. Numberless creatures are already part of this communion, and the fullness of salvation depends on that variety, on sharing rather than on identity.

I end with a reflection on the benefactor practice, in which these two traditions have come closest for me. The process of person-making and community forming through mimetic indwelling is the live thread in Christian faith. Whether we are speaking of the manner of God becoming human, the way that Christ works and lives in us, or the ways that we all inhabit each other, we are referring to the same grammar of emergence, reconciliation, and hope. That mimetic path leads both to individuation and to communion. The path is rooted in the Trinitarian dynamic of coinherence, which ultimately points to the coinherence of the dimensions that we have discussed, the coinherence of emptiness and immanence identities with personal and communion relations. God, who is our great benefactor, has not stinted in giving us others, in making us benefactors for each other. The bodhisattvas are such benefactors.

NOTES

Preface and Acknowledgments

1. For one such perspective, see Peter Harvey, *Introduction to Buddhism: Teachings, History and Practices*, 2nd ed. (New York: Cambridge University Press, 2013), 4. By contrast, Paul Williams' exposition of *Mahāyāna* follows the two-vehicle perspective. See Williams, *Mahāyāna Buddhism: The Doctrinal Foundations*, 2nd ed. (London: Routledge, 2009).

2. On the Rimé tradition, see Chapter 27 in Geoffrey Samuel, *Civilized Shamans: Buddhism in Tibetan Societies* (Washington, D.C.: Smithsonian Institution Press, 1993).

3. Perry Schmidt-Leukel, "Finding God in the Bodhicaryāvatāra: An Interim Report on as 'Christian Commentary to the Bodhicaryāvatāra,'" *Journal of Comparative Scripture*, no. 6 (2015): 9–35.

Introduction: The Bodhisattva Path and the Christ Path

1. I have sketched this development in S. Mark Heim, "Shifting Significance of Theologies of Religious Pluralism," in *Understanding Religious Pluralism: Perspectives from Religious Studies and Theology*, ed. Peter C. Phan and Jonathan S. Ray (Eugene, Ore.: Pickwick Publications, 2014). A significant straw in this wind is the recent series of Christian commentaries on non-Christian sacred texts published by Eerdmans. In regard to Buddhism, see John P. Keenan and Linda Klepinger Keenan, *I Am/No Self: A Christian Commentary on the Heart Sutra*, Christian Commentaries on Non-Christian Sacred Texts (Grand Rapids: Eerdmans, 2011); and Leo D. Lefebure and Peter Feldmeier, *Path of Wisdom: A Christian Commentary of the Dhammapada*, Christian Commentaries on Non-Christian Sacred Texts (Grand Rapids: Eerdmans, 2011). Perry Schmidt-Leukel's anticipated commentary on the *Bodhicaryāvatāra*, the primary text considered in this work, will be a major contribution to this field.

2. For a survey of the way in which various Christian writers are approaching this challenge in relation to Buddhism, see Amos Yong, "On Doing Theology and Buddhology: A Spectrum of Christian Proposals," *Buddhist-Christian Studies*, no. 31 (2011): 103–18.

3. Quoted in Loren D. Lybarger, "How Far Is Too Far? Defining Self and Other in Religious Studies and Christian Missiology," *Journal of the American Academy of Religion* 84, no. 1 (2016): 147.

4. Daniel P. Sheridan, *Loving God: Kṛṣṇa and Christ: A Christian Commentary on the Nārada Sūtras*, Christian Commentaries on Non-Christian Sacred Texts (Grand Rapids: Eerdmans, 2007), 8.

5. In the Christian case, such figures include those who were, in their own time or subsequently, viewed as stepping outside the tradition (e.g., Aquinas, whose views were initially resisted, or Origen, who was later deemed a heretic) and those who were explicit adherents of other traditions, such as Maimonides or Averroes. In the modern period, we can think of the influence in Christian theology of Martin Buber or Abraham Heschel.

6. Wendy Farley, "Duality and Non-Duality in Christian Practice Reflections on the Benefits of Buddhist-Christian Dialogue for Constructive Theology," *Buddhist-Christian Studies*, no. 31 (2011): 135–46.

7. The following examples use categories for learning in comparative theology outlined by Catherine Cornille in "Discipleship in Hindu-Christian Comparative Theology," *Theological Studies* 77, no. 4 (2016): 869–85.

8. See for instance Francis X. Clooney, S.J., *Hindu God, Christian God: Faith, Reason, and Argument in a World of Many Religions* (New York: Oxford University Press, 1999).

9. Aloysius Pieris, *Love Meets Wisdom: A Christian Experience of Buddhism*, Faith Meets Faith (Maryknoll, N.Y.: Orbis Books, 1988).

10. See for instance Wendy Farley, *Thirst of God: Contemplating God's Love with Three Women Mystics* (Louisville: Westminster John Knox Press, 2015).

11. John P. Keenan, *The Meaning of Christ: A Mahayana Theology*, Faith Meets Faith (Maryknoll, N.Y.: Orbis Books, 1989).

12. See the notable work of Ruben Habito, as in Ruben L. F. Habito, *Healing Breath: Zen for Christians and Buddhists in a Wounded World*, rev. and updated ed. (Boston: Wisdom Publications, 2006).

13. See Paul F. Knitter's discussion of this in *Without Buddha I Could Not Be a Christian* (Oxford, U.K.: Oneworld, 2009), 194–95.

14. See for instance John B. Cobb and Christopher Ives, eds., *Emptying God: A Buddhist-Jewish-Christian Conversation* (Maryknoll, N.Y.: Orbis Books, 1990); and Roger Corless and Paul F. Knitter, *Buddhist Emptiness and Christian Trinity: Essays and Explorations* (New York: Paulist Press, 1990).

15. This is the focus of Cobb and Ives's *Emptying God*.

16. John P. Keenan, *Gospel of Mark: A Mahayana Reading*, Faith Meets Faith (Maryknoll, N.Y.: Orbis Books, 1995); John P. Keenan, *Emptied Christ of Philippians: Mahayana Meditations* (Eugene, Ore.: Wipf and Stock, 2016).

17. Knitter, *Without Buddha* 12–13.

18. The early Pāli canon of Buddhist teaching and practice may be taken as roughly parallel to the early Christian scriptural canon and attendant texts. We can liken the subsequent rich developments in the Buddhist *abhidharma* traditions to the growth of Christian theological traditions. In *abhidharma* and theology, emphasis falls on

intellectual reflection and exploration, though they are hardly separate either from personal spiritual practice or community life in *saṅgha* and church that accompany them. In both traditions, some of the most notable works would understand themselves as oriented as much to practice as to explanation. Within these streams of ongoing reflection in the two faiths, we can also distinguish broad but distinctive movements, such as *Mahāyāna* in its many forms, characterized by its particular reading of the bodhisattva path, or Latin Christianity and its descendants, marked by particular emphases within Trinitarian thought, Christology, and ecclesiology.

19. See Whalen Lai and Michael von Brück, *Christianity and Buddhism: A Multicultural History of Their Dialogue*, Faith Meets Faith (Maryknoll, N.Y.: Orbis Books, 2001); and Paul Tillich and Tomoaki Fukai, *Paul Tillich—Journey to Japan in 1960* (Boston: De Gruyter, 2013).

20. Of particular interest for our discussion in this book, given the importance of Tibetan commentators on Śāntideva, is the recently published work of the Jesuit missionary to Tibet Ippolito Desideri. See Donald S. Lopez Jr. and Thupten Jinpa, *Dispelling the Darkness: A Jesuit's Quest for the Soul of Tibet* (Cambridge, Mass.: Harvard University Press, 2017); and Trent Pomplun, *Jesuit on the Roof of the World: Ippolito Desideri's Mission to Eighteenth-Century Tibet* (Oxford: Oxford University Press, 2010). Also interesting for our topic are the Kakure Kirisitan, the "hidden Christians" of Japan who maintained their own version of Christianity after the expulsion of Catholic missionaries. The sole surviving text from that oppressed Christian community, whose outlook was shaped by the surrounding culture of Buddhist-Shinto Japan, can be found in Christal Whelan, *Beginning of Heaven and Earth: The Sacred Book of Japan's Hidden Christians* (Honolulu: University of Hawai'i Press, 1996), For a wider survey, see Lai and Brück, *Christianity and Buddhism*.

21. See the Introduction in Paul Williams, *Mahāyāna Buddhism: The Doctrinal Foundations*, 2nd ed. (London: Routledge, 2009).

22. Sally Hovey Wriggins, *Silk Road Journey with Xuanzang* (Boulder, Colo.: Westview Press, 2004).

23. There are two Sanskrit titles. The Tibetan version uses the longer Sanskrit title, *Bodhisattvacaryāvatāra,* or "Entrance to the Way of the Bodhisattva." The shorter Sanskrit title, *Bodhicaryāvatāra*, is more widely used and has the sense of "Entrance to the Path of Awakening." See Śāntideva, *Way of the Bodhisattva: A Translation of the Bodhicaryāvatāra*, trans. the Padmakara Translation Group, 2nd ed. (Boston: Shambhala, 2006), 195.

24. Martin Palmer and Eva Wong, *Jesus Sutras: Rediscovering the Lost Scrolls of Taoist Christianity* (New York: Ballantine, 2001).

25. Interestingly, these finds include three manuscripts of the *Bodhicaryāvatāra,* which preserve a shorter version of the text that may be closer to the original. See the translators' Introduction in Śāntideva, *Bodhicaryāvatāra*, trans. Kate Crosby and Andrew Skilton, Oxford World's Classics (Oxford: Oxford University Press, 1996), xxx–xxxi.

26. Richard Salomon, *Ancient Buddhist Scrolls from Gandhāra: The British Library Kharoṣṭhī Fragments*, Gandhāran Buddhist Texts (Seattle: British Library and University of Washington Press, 1999).

27. See Palmer and Wong, *Jesus Sutras*, 135.

28. The texts are translated in Palmer and Wong, *Jesus Sutras*; and Yoshirō Saeki, *Nestorian Documents and Relics in China* (Tokyo: Toho Bunkwa Gakuin: Academy of Oriental Culture, Tokyo Institute, 1951). Translation of these texts is a particularly challenging task. The translations in Palmer and Wong's book should be regarded with caution. See Max Deeg, "Towards a New Translation of the Chinese Nestorian Documents from the Tang Dynasty," in *Jingjiao: The Church of the East in China and Central Asia*, ed. Roman Malek, Peter Hofrichter, and the Monumenta Serica Institute, Collectanea Serica (Sankt Augustin, Ger.: Institut Monumenta Serica, 2006), 117–18.

29. The Buddhist text is the *Kāraḍavyūha*. See Hans-Joachim Klimkeit, "Apocryphal Gospels in Central and East Asia," in *Studies in Manichaean Literature and Art*, ed. Hans-Joachim Klimkeit and Manfred Heuser (Leiden: Brill, 1998), 191. The *Kāraḍavyūha* was much more profoundly shaped by Hindu influences. See Alexander Studholme, *Origins of Oṃ Manipadme Hūṃ: A Study of Kāraṇḍavyūha Sūtra* (Albany: State University of New York Press, 2002).

30. Har Dayal, *Bodhisattva Doctrine in Buddhist Sanskrit Literature* (Delhi, India: Motilal Banarsidass, 1970), 42.

31. See Donald S. Lopez Jr. and Peggy McCracken, *In Search of the Christian Buddha: How an Asian Sage Became a Medieval Saint*, (New York: W.W. Norton & Company, 2014). 207

32. Most notable in this connection are the "Turfan texts" discovered during German expeditions to central Asia from 1902 to 1914, but only slowly translated. See Hans-Joachim Klimkeit, *Gnosis on the Silk Road: Gnostic Texts from Central Asia* ([San Francisco]: HarperSanFrancisco, 1993).

33. In Hans Jonas, *Gnostic Religion; the Message of the Alien God and the Beginnings of Christianity*, 2nd ed. (Boston: Beacon Press, 1963), 206.

34. Jonas, *Gnostic Religion*, 207.

35. Hans-Joachim Klimkeit, "'Jesus' Entry into Parinirvana: Manichean Identity in Buddhist Central Asia," in *Studies in Manichaean Literature and Art*, ed. Manfred Heuser and Hans-Joachim Klimkeit (Leiden: Brill, 1998), 254–69.

36. Klimkeit, "Jesus' Entry," 267.

37. Hans-Joachim Klimkeit, "Adaptations to Buddhism in East Iranian and Central Asian Manichaeism," in *Studies in Manichaean Literature and Art*, ed. Manfred Heuser and Hans-Joachim Klimkeit (Leiden: Brill, 1998), 240.

38. Klimkeit, "Jesus' Entry," 257.

39. Klimkeit, *Gnosis on the Silk Road*, 125.

40. Klimkeit, "Adaptations to Buddhism," 252. See also Lopez and McCracken, *In Search*, 207–11.

41. Mani's account of this "fall" has interesting properties, set in a scheme of three creations. The first creation is identical with a fall, in which the confusion of the two principles is prompted by an "invasion" or attack from the material side that covets and envies the light. The supreme spirit emanates divinities to fend off this attack, but they are defeated and literally swallowed up to create the mingled state of matter and spirit. The Father of Light issues forth the Mother of the Living, who in turn evokes "the First Man," who goes into battle. Klimkeit says the First Man offered himself up

as a bait for the powers of Darkness in order to satisfy their greed temporarily and then destroy them in the long run. The evil forces tear him apart and devour him. Demons then use light that they had eaten to fashion souls, as the living element in humans. Having tasted light, forces of darkness become addicted and won't give it up. This leads to a second creation, in which the divine calls forth another deity, a great builder, who resuscitates the first man to make him long for his true home and also reconstructs a world as a mechanism for liberation of the captured light. Unlike other Gnostic myths, in which the creator is an evil demiurge, here it is a good deity but one working with the mixed material resulting from the first creation by demons. This then leads to a third creation, in which a Third Messenger is called forth to extract and retrieve the pieces of light and return them to unity. Jesus the Splendor figures in this role. See Klimkeit, *Gnosis on the Silk Road*, 10–17.

42. Klimkeit, *Gnosis on the Silk Road*, 71.
43. Klimkeit, *Gnosis on the Silk Road*, 5.
44. See Klimkeit, *Gnosis on the Silk Road*, 5.
45. Those who agree on the need may frame it somewhat differently. From one perspective, this may be an imperative crisis: without the aid of other traditions, Christian faith is itself unsustainable. This is the view reflected in Knitter's aptly titled book, *Without Buddha I Could Not Be a Christian*. Buddhist additions must supplement or replace fundamental elements of Christian tradition whose incoherence otherwise promise to bring down the entire structure for many persons, if not entire communities. From another perspective, it is less dissatisfaction with one's own faith than admiration for the other that drives the study. This is what Krister Stendhal calls "holy envy." I feel that kind of awe at the depth of Buddhist wisdom, and a desire to share in it as a follower of Christ. And this path of learning unfolds from a natural, internal impetus in Christian faith toward the widening fullness it expects. I believe that such studies will eventually become routine sources of insight and enrichment in our ecclesial communities, reflections of the fact that interfaith openness is simply a way of being Christian.
46. S. Mark Heim, *Depth of the Riches: A Trinitarian Theology of Religious Ends*, Sacra Doctrina (Grand Rapids: Eerdmans, 2001).
47. This is apart from any role that such traditions might play in leading people to the Christian end, salvation. Such cross traffic, so to speak, is also possible, but it neither exhausts the religious significance of the traditions nor denies their capacity to serve their own ends in distinction from Christian ones. S. Mark Heim, *Salvations: Truth and Difference in Religion*, Faith Meets Faith (Maryknoll, N.Y.: Orbis Books, 1995).
48. It is not the "persons" of the Trinity who are separately engaged by various religions; it is dimensions, each of which is characteristic of God as a whole, a feature of the interrelation of the divine elements. No religion relates to just a "part" of God, but to features that belong to the fullness of God.
49. This discussion is developed more fully in Chapter 5 in Heim, *Depth of the Riches*.
50. One can conceive a specific transcendent order without any personal being as its source, a divine will without a God whose will it is, so to speak. The Tao of Taoism, the *logos* in Stoicism, and the Kantian moral law would be examples. At one end of

the range, there is revelation of some transcendent order, and at the other end there is the personal God of monotheism whose expressions of will and purpose take iconic form. The key point that distinguishes both of these from the nonpersonal dimension just discussed is that their transcendence allows for—indeed requires—contrast and tension. The transcendent being or iconic order points to the fact that the divine is not empty, nor is all being already in perfect identity with it. There is a distance between us and the divine, between us and our religious end, which must be traveled. This dimension manifests moral emphasis, a drive toward transformation. Revelation bridges the gap with the transcendent, pointing the way for change. The motto is not "thou art that," as with nonpersonal nondualism, but "become what you are called/ structured to be."

51. One may see analogies here even in the fundamental biological world, for instance where mitochondria are believed to have been separate organisms that became incorporated as organs of larger cells, a process that moved from encounter, to symbiosis, to differentiated life as one body. Lynn Margulis and René Fester, *Symbiosis as a Source of Evolutionary Innovation: Speciation and Morphogenesis* (Cambridge, Mass.: MIT Press, 1991).

52. Salvation is thus not qualitatively identical in any two persons, and this is congruent with the wider point that there can be distinct religious ends.

53. This is why religious ends are not narrowly restricted, one to a tradition. The breadth of elements in any tradition, and even in a single religious text, encompasses subtraditions that can easily allow persons to pursue or rest content with goals distinct from the prevailing aim. Each religion orchestrates a pluralism of tendencies and possibilities. The lively concern in all traditions over right teaching and practice indicates that within the broad sweep of one religious path it is possible to pursue different religious ends. This is precisely the dynamic behind internal reform movements, schism, heresy, and the appearance of new religions. Such phenomena may involve or call forth new religious sources, but they can function very well within a shared canon and lay their claims on those terms.

54. There is an alternative mode of apprehending this impersonal dimension of the triune life, one that stresses the divine sustaining, constant presence in all that is made. The constant flow of the divine life is taken as the substratum of one great self whose body is the world. From this perspective, it is a mistake to take emptiness or flux as the real story. Every individual part may change and pass away, like cells in a body, but the one self goes on. The *Advaita Vedanta* tradition of Hinduism expresses this truth powerfully. Brahman, the one unshakable reality, sustains all things by pervading all things. Either of the apprehensions that we have described are forms of nonduality. The boundaries that mark off any persons or creatures from others are only apparent. All things are empty, or all things are literally one divine being. The convictions that *saṃsāra* is *nirvāṇa*, or that *ātman* is *Brahman* are two distinctive religious conclusions born of such insight. They point to two distinct religious ends and are the subject of a long and sophisticated debate between Buddhists and Advaitans. For the balance of this study, it is the varieties of Buddhist nonduality that will concern us, though the idea of Buddha nature raises some of the same issues within Buddhism proper.

55. David Loy, *Nonduality: A Study in Comparative Philosophy* (New Haven: Yale University Press, 1988), 17.

56. Loy, *Nonduality*, 17.

57. Joseph Stephen O'Leary, *Buddhist Nonduality, Paschal Paradox: A Christian Commentary on the Teaching of Vimalakirti*, ed. Catherine Cornille, Christian Commentaries on Non-Christian Sacred Texts (Grand Rapids: Eerdmans 2017), 276.

58. See Chapter 4 in Leo D. Lefebure, *Buddha and the Christ: Explorations in Buddhist and Christian Dialogue*, Faith Meets Faith (Maryknoll, N.Y.: Orbis Books, 1993).

59. See Chapters 4 and 5 in Keenan, *Meaning of Christ*.

60. I would highlight my appreciation for John Thatamanil's search for a version of nonduality most appropriate for interfaith learning. For his analysis of Śhankara and Tillich and his own positive proposal, see John J. Thatamanil, *Immanent Divine: God, Creation, and the Human Predicament* (Minneapolis: Fortress Press, 2006).

61. In general, I think Buddhists would say that the personal and the communion dimensions are necessarily absent in enlightenment, the immediate condition of realized ones. But the *bodhisattva* discussion pursued later in this book opens some conversation on that point. For Christians, however, the permanent validity of emptiness and immanence coexist with the permanent validity of the relational dimensions.

62. Such would seem to be the view of the Dalai Lama. See His Holiness the Dalai Lama, "Problem of Exclusivism," in *Buddhism and Religious Diversity*, vol. 4, *Religious Pluralism*, ed. Perry Schmidt-Leukel (New York: Routledge, 2013), 241–51.

1. Two Problems, Two Miracles

1. Raimundo Panikkar, *Intrareligious Dialogue*, rev. ed. (New York: Paulist Press, 1999), 34. In this passage of *Intrareligious Dialogue*, his examples are "Brahman" and "Yahweh."

2. Kathryn Tanner, *Economy of Grace* (Minneapolis: Fortress Press, 2005), 20.

3. Tanner, *Economy of Grace*, 23–27.

4. "The wisdom that realizes emptiness and the ignorance that grasps at true existence are in contradiction with each other." Geshe Yeshe Tobden, *Way of Awakening: A Commentary on Shantideva's Bodhicharyavatara*, ed. Fiorella Rizzi, trans. Manu Bazzano and Sarita Doveton (Boston: Wisdom Publications, 2005), 348.

5. So, for instance, the smoothest way to Buddhist-Christian agreement is unlikely to be the same as that toward Muslim-Christian agreement. One may, at this point, default to some version of perennialism—the belief in the identical content and aim of all religions—but in that case there is no substantive need for detailed study of particular religious traditions, save by way of illustration.

6. Rose Drew, *Buddhist and Christian?: An Exploration of Dual Belonging*, Routledge Critical Studies in Buddhism (New York: Routledge, 2011), 11.

7. Drew, *Buddhist and Christian*, 12.

8. I use the word "atonement," aware of the confusion that may attend it. For some, the term is attached to a very specific doctrine of the saving power of Jesus's death as a substitutionary sacrifice. I do not intend any such limitation. I mean the word to

apply to all of the reconciling work, as it were, of Christ, which encompasses the entire life, death, and resurrection of Jesus. But our conversation does give special attention to the self-giving of the passion and to the conviction that Christ "died for us."

9. See S. Mark Heim, *Saved from Sacrifice: A Theology of the Cross* (Grand Rapids: Eerdmans, 2006).

10. For a compendium of different views, see Marit Trelstad, *Cross Examinations: Readings on the Meaning of the Cross* (Minneapolis: Fortress Press, 2006).

11. See K. Schmied, "Jesus in Recent Buddhist Writings Published in the West," in *Buddhist Perceptions of Jesus: Papers of the Third Conference of the European Network of Buddhist-Christian Studies*, ed. Perry Schmidt-Leukel (St. Ottilien, Ger.: EOS-Verlag, 2001).

12. Joseph Stephen O'Leary, *Buddhist Nonduality, Paschal Paradox: A Christian Commentary on the Teaching of Vimalakirti*, ed. Catherine Cornille, Christian Commentaries on Non-Christian Sacred Texts (Grand Rapids: Eerdmans 2017), 17.

13. For a thoughtful expression of the basic conflict from a Christian perspective, see Harold A. Netland and Keith E. Yandell, *Buddhism: A Christian Exploration and Appraisal* (Downers Grove, Ill.: IVP Academic, 2009). For the same from a Buddhist perspective, see Gunapala Dharmasiri, *Buddhist Critique of the Christian Concept of God* (Antioch, Calif.: Golden Leaves, 1988).

14. O'Leary, *Buddhist Nonduality*, 280.

15. This initial move is common to *Theravāda* and *Mahāyāna* traditions, and only in Yogācāra or mind-only traditions might it seem to be revoked in favor of a more primordial "idealism."

16. I'm particularly influenced here by Gadjin Nagao, *Foundational Standpoint of Mahyamika Philosophy*, trans. John P. Keenan, SUNY Series in Buddhist Studies, ed. Kenneth Inada (Albany: State University of New York Press, 1989).

17. O'Leary, *Buddhist Nonduality*, 25.

18. For the purposes of this argument, this could as well be a state of penultimate meditative attainment or a modest mystical religious experience.

19. O'Leary, *Buddhist Nonduality*, 236.

20. O'Leary, *Buddhist Nonduality*, 233.

21. The predominant tradition in Sri Lanka, Myanmar/Burma, Thailand, Cambodia, and Laos. See for instance Walpola Rahula, *What the Buddha Taught*, rev. ed. (New York: Grove Press, 1974).

22. The predominant tradition in East Asia (China, Korea, Japan, Vietnam) and Tibet. *Mahāyāna* comes in many varieties with their own subtraditions (e.g., Zen, Vajrayana [Tibetan], Pure Land).

23. See further discussion in Chapter 2.

24. To phrase it so simply runs the danger of suggesting what Buddhist argument calls nihilism, an insistence on the ontological nonexistence of entities so extreme that it denies that they do in fact arise, dependently and transiently, from causal antecedents and so have a relative reality. This will be addressed more fully in subsequent discussions.

25. Paul Williams, *Mahāyāna Buddhism: The Doctrinal Foundations*, 2nd ed., (London: Routledge, 2009), 153–54.

26. Har Dayal, *Bodhisattva Doctrine in Buddhist Sanskrit Literature* (Delhi, India: Moti-lal Banarsidass, 1970), 76. A *kalpa* is not specifically defined, but is a vast period, sometimes equated to the time between the beginning and the dissolution of one world order.

27. Dayal, *Bodhisattva Doctrine*. Within some branches of *Mahāyāna*, there are teach-ings that hold much quicker, or even immediate enlightenment to be possible.

28. We will pick up this topic at the beginning of Chapter 2.

29. See David Wellington Chappell, "Early Forebodings of the Death of Buddhism," *Nu-men* 27, no. 1 (1980): 122–54.

30. This austere view of the Buddha's attainment can be found in many Buddhist presen-tations, from standard works that lean toward the *Theravāda* tradition to con-temporary ones oriented to a secular audience. In the first case, see Rahula, *What the Buddha*. For the second case, see Stephen Batchelor, *After Buddhism: Rethinking the Dharma for a Secular Age* (New Haven: Yale University Press, 2015). But for many Buddhists, this picture ignores the expanse of the Buddha's prior lives and the rich cosmology within which they were set. In that setting, the Buddha had received teach-ing from other Buddhas and was in fact reintroducing the *dharma* in this age, not discovering it independently.

31. Paul J. Griffiths, "Concentration or Insight: The Problematic of Theravāda Buddhist Meditation-Theory," *Journal of the American Academy of Religion* 49, no. 4 (1981): 605–24.

32. John J. Makransky, *Buddhahood Embodied: Sources of Controversy in India and Ti-bet*, SUNY Series in Buddhist Studies (Albany: State University of New York Press, 1997), 1.

33. On this interpretation, the conventional and the ultimate are two perspectives on the same reality. Viewed in one way we see *saṃsāra*, the "positive" appearances arising from causes and conditions. Viewed in another way, we see the emptiness of those phenomena, the emptiness of inherent existence.

34. On "nonabiding *nirvāṇa*" (*apratiṣṭhita nirvāṇa),* see the helpful discussion in Makransky, *Buddhahood Embodied*, 85–87.

35. My language suggests that "nonabiding *nirvāṇa*" is a subsequent interpretation added to an original Buddhist *dharma*. But *Mahāyāna* traditions, the focus of this book, view the teaching found in their (chronologically later) texts as preserving the original content both of the Buddha's teaching and his nirvanic realization.

36. Gadjin Nagao, "Bodhisattva Returns to This World," in *Bodhisattva Doctrine in Bud-dhism*, ed. Leslie S. Kawamura (Waterloo, ON: Wilfrid Laurier University Press, 1981).

37. Kuan Yin is a form of the bodhisattva Avalokiteśvara, discussed more in Chapter 6.

38. "He, indeed, assumed humanity that we might become God." Athanasius, *On the In-carnation*, trans. John Behr, Popular Patristics Series (Yonkers, N.Y.: St. Vladimir's Seminary Press, 2011), 93.

39. That this same reality can be re-experienced by others who are neither Jesus nor God is the basis for the Christian belief in a third, the Holy Spirit, who in being one with the believer leads them into participation in God's unity with Jesus and Jesus's unity with God.

40. Although parts of the Christian church may regard a penal substitutionary view of the cross as part of the essence of Christianity, that theology was not explicitly formulated in the Western church for a thousand years and never held a prominent place in the Eastern Christian churches.

41. Philippians 2:5–13. If these words were written by Paul, then they come from within thirty years after Jesus's death. If, as many suppose, they come from a hymn that already existed in the community before Paul's time, then they stand even closer to Jesus's death.

42. We can only note here another exchange that is less apparent and which we will take up in later discussion of this passage. What is this name that is bestowed on Jesus? It makes good exegetical sense that it is the unpronounced, undefined proper name for God in Jewish scripture. The tetragrammaton is the "name above every name." When the writer says that "every tongue shall confess that Jesus Christ is Lord," the word "Lord" is the typical stand-in word used to represent exactly that name. It points to the fact that Jesus now bears this ineffable name, as the one who bears that ineffable name has now taken on the name of Jesus. See R. Kendall Soulen, *Divine Name(s) and the Holy Trinity* (Louisville: Westminster John Knox Press, 2011), 11.

43. O'Leary, *Buddhist Nonduality*, 41.

44. Helmuth von Glasenapp, *Von Buddha Zu Gandhi* (Wiesbaden: Harrassowitz, 1962), 157–58, quoted in O'Leary, *Buddhist Nonduality*, 41.

45. See for instance Batchelor, *After Buddhism*.

46. So, for instance, one could reinterpret all of Buddhism through the lens of an early Buddhist school—the *Pudgalavāda*—that insisted on the reality of persons, and thus dispel much of the difference with Christianity. This would be similar to reinterpreting all of Christianity through the lens of the most unitive mystics in its tradition, and to dispelling much of the difference by converging on nondualism.

47. See discussion of this in Chapter 4.

48. Ninian Smart, *Buddhism and Christianity: Rivals and Allies* (Honolulu: University of Hawaii Press, 1993), 12–13.

49. As Bonnie Thurston says, "The Buddha directs me away from himself. The Christ invites me to himself. In the Four Reliances, the Buddha teaches, 'Rely on the teaching, not the teacher.' In Christianity, the teaching is the Teacher." Bonnie Thurston, "Buddha Offered Me a Raft," in *Buddhists Talk about Jesus, Christians Talk about the Buddha*, ed. Rita M. Gross and Terry C. Muck (New York: Continuum, 2000), 124.

2. The Bodhisattva Path

1. The epigraph to this chapter comes from Śāntideva, *Way of the Bodhisattva: A Translation of the Bodhicaryāvatāra*, trans. the Padmakara Translation Group, 2nd ed. (Boston: Shambhala, 2006), 50. This is one form in which the bodhisattva vow is administered. See Geshe Yeshe Tobden, *Way of Awakening: A Commentary on Shantideva's Bodhicharyavatara*, ed. Fiorella Rizzi, trans. Manu Bazzano and Sarita Doveton (Boston: Wisdom Publications, 2005), 71.

2. A. L. Basham, "Evolution of the Concept of the Bodhisattva," in *Bodhisattva Doctrine in Buddhism*, ed. Leslie S. Kawamura (Waterloo, Ont.: Wilfrid Laurier University Press, 1986), 22.

3. I had not appreciated, until a Buddhist friend pointed out to me, that in this sense the tales do not simply trace the single karmic train that led to the Buddha's final life. They are a sort of ecology of progress toward enlightenment, in which various paths of transmigration repeatedly interact with each other.

4. See those numbered 12, 23, 222, 303, 316, 407, and 547 in E. B. Cowell, "Sasa-Jataka," in *Jataka: Or Stories of the Buddha's Former Births*, trans. H. T. Francis and R. A. Neil (Cambridge: Cambridge University Press, 1897).

5. See Cowell, "Sasa-Jataka," 3:34–37.

6. See Robert A. F. Thurman, "Buddhist Messiahs: The Magnificent Deeds of the Bodhisattvas," in *Christ and the Bodhisattva*, ed. Donald S. Lopez and Steven C. Rockefeller (Albany: State University of New York Press, 1987), 67. The five ascetics who were in the audience for the Buddha's first sermon had been the tigress and the four cubs. This *Jataka* tale is not in the original Pāli texts but is found in early Indian versions. In some renditions of the tale, the bodhisattva realizes that the tigress will not kill him and prefers dead meat. He leaps off a precipice to present his body as a meal. See C. B. Varma, "Story of a Tigress from the Illustrated Jataka and Other Stories of the Buddha," *Illustrated Jataka: Other Stories of the Buddha*, Indira Gandhi National Centre for the Arts, accessed June 9, 2018, http://ignca.nic.in/jatako25.htm.

7. Thurman, "Buddhist Messiahs," 67 (original emphasis).

8. It is no more common in the Pāli Jataka tales than instances of the Buddha as a victorious warrior (see those numbered 23, 24, 182, 226, and 283 in the Cowell edition). Indeed, number 23 has been counted in both our lists, since in that story the Buddha is a warhorse who insists on serving in a final attack despite his wounds and dies as a result, sacrificing life for victory.

9. As evidenced by the Chinese pilgrim Xuanzang finding multiple stupas that had been erected to mark the sites of such sacrificial acts from the *Jataka* tales. See Sally Hovey Wriggins, *Silk Road Journey with Xuanzang* (Boulder, Colo.: Westview Press), 51–72.

10. See for instance the extensive discussion in Śāntideva. *Śikṣā Samuccaya: A Compendium of Buddhist Doctrine*, trans. Cecil Bendall and W. H. D. Rouse (Delhi, India: Motilal Banarsidass, 1971), 40–43.

11. Śāntideva, *Śikṣā Samuccaya*, 40–41.

12. Basham. "Evolution of the Concept," 28–29.

13. See the resulting publication, Donald S. Lopez and Steven C. Rockefeller, *Christ and the Bodhisattva*, SUNY Series in Buddhist Studies (Albany: State University of New York Press, 1987).

14. Henri de Lubac and Paul Williams are two scholars who have engaged the text at length. See Schmidt-Leukel, "Finding God in the Bodhicaryāvatāra: An Interim Report on a "Christian Commentary to the Bodhicaryāvatāra," *Journal of Comparative Scripture*, no. 6 (2015): 13–14. De Lubac's major relevant work was Henri de Lubac, *Aspects of Buddhism* (New York: Sheed and Ward, 1954). Williams's case is particularly interesting because much of his study of the text was undertaken prior to his conversion to Christianity, when he was a Buddhist. See his essays in Paul Williams, *Altruism and Reality: Studies in the Philosophy of the Bodhicaryāvatāra* (Surrey, U.K.: Curzon Press, 1998).

15. A number of recent translations are available. When not otherwise noted, my quotations are from Śāntideva, *Guide to the Bodhisattva Way of Life*, trans. Vensa A. Wallace and B. Alan Wallace (Ithaca, N.Y.: Snow Lion Publications, 1997). The other translations that I have used most often are Śāntideva, *Guide to the Bodhisattva's Way of Life*, trans. Stephen Batchelor (Dharamsala: Library of Tibetan Works & Archives, 1979); Śāntideva, *Way of the Bodhisattva: A Translation of the Bodhicaryāvatāra*, 2nd ed. (Boston: Shambhala, 2006); and Śāntideva, *Bodhicaryāvatāra*, trans. Kate Crosby and Andrew Skilton, Oxford World's Classics (Oxford: Oxford University Press, 1996).

16. The commentaries I have considered most extensively are Bstan- 'dzin rgya-mtsho, *For the Benefit of All Beings: A Commentary on the Way of the Bodhisattva*, Shambhala Classics (Boston: Shambhala, 2009); Gyatso Kelsang, *Meaningful to Behold: Becoming a Friend of the World*, 5th ed. (Ulverston: Tharpa, 2008); Kunzang Pelden, *Nectar of Manjushri's Speech: A Detailed Commentary on Shantideva's Way of the Bodhisattva*, trans. the Padmakara Translation Group (Boston: Shambhala, 2007); and Tobden, *Way of Awakening.*

17. The origins and development of *Mahāyāna* are complex issues. See the brief discussion of the history of Buddhist-Christian interaction in the Introduction. Some Indian commentators have entertained the possibility of Christian influence on Śāntideva himself in elevating the relative importance of mercy to wisdom. See Har Dayal. *Bodhisattva Doctrine in Buddhist Sanskrit Literature* (Delhi, India: Motilal Banarsidass, 1970), 43.

18. We will explore the nature of the Madhyamaka school in Chapter 3.

19. This contemporary influence is manifest in the focus given to the text in the oral teachings and publications of the Dalai Lama. See the commentary by the Dalai Lama, in Bstan- 'dzin rgya-mtsho, *For the Benefit.*

20. An analogy of sorts in a Christian classic might be Augustine's *Confessions*, in which every stage of his biography is read simultaneously in terms of his own motives and understanding at the time and of the divine purposes and wisdom that he has later come to appreciate as part of a divine plan.

21. Notto R. Thelle, "What Do I as a Christian Expect Buddhists to Discover in Jesus?," in *Buddhist Perceptions of Jesus*, ed. Perry Schmidt-Leukel (St. Ottilien, Ger.: EOS-Verlag St. Ottilien, 2001), 149–50.

22. See Paul Williams, *Mahāyāna Buddhism: The Doctrinal Foundations*, 2nd ed. (London: Routledge, 2009), 61–66.

23. The division into ten chapters does not appear to have been original (the current Chapters 2 and 3 were combined), but the Dunhuang discoveries confirm that the content in all ten chapters in the current text goes back to an early stage. There had been some question as to whether Chapter 9 was part of Śāntideva's work. It seems that it was, though significant portions of the canonical Chapter 9 are missing in the Dunhuang texts and this may reflect amplification by commentators. See the Translators' Introduction and also the introduction to Chapter 9 in Śāntideva, *Bodhicaryāvatāra*, 110–11.

24. See Williams, *Mahāyāna Buddhism*, 195. See also Francis Brassard, *Concept of Bodhicitta in Śāntideva's Bodhicaryāvatāra*, McGill Studies in the History of Religions (Albany: State University of New York Press, 2000).

25. See the introductions to Chapters 2 and 3 in Śāntideva, *Bodhicaryāvatāra*.

26. See for instance Bstan- 'dzin rgya-mtsho, *For the Benefit*, 21–22.

27. Bstan- 'dzin rgya-mtsho, *For the Benefit*, 8.

28. Compare Bstan- 'dzin rgya-mtsho, *For the Benefit of All Beings* with the commentary on Chapter 9 in Bstan- 'dzin rgya-mtsho, *Transcendent Wisdom*, ed. and trans. B. Alan Wallace, 2nd ed. (Ithaca, N.Y.: Snow Lion Publications, 1994); or with Tobden, *Way of Awakening*.

29. Śāntideva, *Bodhicaryāvatāra*, 1:15–17.

30. Śāntideva, *Bodhicaryāvatāra*, 1:27.

31. Śāntideva, *Bodhicaryāvatāra*, 1:21–22; Śāntideva, *Guide to the Bodhisattva Way of Life*, 21.

32. Śāntideva, *Bodhicaryāvatāra*, 1:36. That the homage is rendered to the bodies of the Buddhas reflects not only the distinctions of different Buddha bodies (e.g., *dharma* bodies, enjoyment bodies, transformation bodies) that will be discussed later, but also the awareness that the homage is a conventional action, taking place on the level of the Buddha's conventional existence.

33. Śāntideva, *Bodhicaryāvatāra*, 2:7.

34. Śāntideva, *Bodhicaryāvatāra*, 2:26.

35. Śāntideva, *Guide to the Bodhisattva Way of Life*, 24.

36. Śāntideva, *Bodhicaryāvatāra*, 2:43

37. Śāntideva, *Bodhicaryāvatāra*, 2:44.

38. Śāntideva, *Bodhicaryāvatāra*, 2:43–44.

39. See Śāntideva, *Bodhicaryāvatāra*, 6:120.

40. Śāntideva, *Bodhicaryāvatāra*, 3:5.

41. Śāntideva, *Bodhicaryāvatāra*, 3:6.

42. Śāntideva, *Bodhicaryāvatāra*, 3:17–18; Śāntideva, *Guide to the Bodhisattva Way of Life*, 35.

43. See Bstan- 'dzin rgya-mtsho, *For the Benefit*, 32–33.

44. Śāntideva, *Bodhicaryāvatāra*, 4:8–9. Similarly, even a single impure thought directed at a genuine bodhisattva will generate an eon in hell (Śāntideva, *Bodhicaryāvatāra*, 1.34).

45. Śāntideva, *Bodhicaryāvatāra*, 4:21

46. Śāntideva, *Bodhicaryāvatāra*, 4:17

47. Śāntideva, *Bodhicaryāvatāra*, 4:13

48. Śāntideva, *Bodhicaryāvatāra*, 4:41–42; Śāntideva, *Guide to the Bodhisattva Way of Life*, 43–44.

49. Śāntideva, *Bodhicaryāvatāra*, 4:38.

50. Śāntideva, *Bodhicaryāvatāra*, 4:43 (see the variant reading from the Tibetan text compared to the Sanskrit one).

51. Śāntideva, *Bodhicaryāvatāra*, 4:47.

52. Śāntideva, *Bodhicaryāvatāra*, 5:10–11.

53. Śāntideva, *Bodhicaryāvatāra*, 5:24.

54. Śāntideva, *Bodhicaryāvatāra*, 5:29

55. Śāntideva, *Bodhicaryāvatāra*, 5:47

56. Śāntideva, *Bodhicaryāvatāra*, 5:69.

57. Śāntideva, *Bodhicaryāvatāra*, 5:80.

58. Specifics are in fact provided in Śāntideva, *Bodhicaryāvatāra*, 5:85–98, but these verses are not found in the Dunhuang texts and so arguably are later expansions. They include a string of more mundane instructions, including that one should not teach the profound *dharma* to certain kinds of people, including those with an umbrella or weapon, or a woman in the absence of a man; urinate in potable water; or chew with one's mouth full. These are a firm part of the canonical text and are drawn from the sources Śāntideva commends. The *Śikṣā Samuccaya* collects quotations from various Buddhist sources, portions of which show up in the *Bodhicaryāvatāra* without specific attribution.

59. Śāntideva, *Bodhicaryāvatāra*, 5:83.

60. Tobden, *Way of Awakening*, 126.

61. Śāntideva, *Bodhicaryāvatāra*, 5:84.

62. Tobden, *Way of Awakening*, 125. See also Ze-chen rgyal-tshab padma-'gyur-med-rnam-rgyal, *Path of Heroes: Birth of Enlightenment*, Tibetan Translation Series, vol. 1, (Berkeley, Calif.: Dharma Publishing, 1995), 112–16.

63. But we will have reason to revisit this question: as part of her compassion, can a bodhisattva actually entertain wrong views, such as those that attribute reality to beings and their sufferings?

64. See the example from the Upāyakauśalya Sutra, as described in Williams, *Mahāyāna Buddhism*, 152. Also discussed in Rupert Gethin, "Can Killing a Living Being Ever Be an Act of Compassion? The Analysis of the Act of Killing in the Abhidhamma and Pali Commentaries," *Journal of Buddhist Ethics* 11 (2004): 188–89. In the sutra, the five hundred who are to be killed are all bodhisattvas, and this emphasizes the gravity of the act, given the weight of interfering with those who are benefiting all beings.

65. Commentaries point out that merits generated in higher realms are not subject to degradation by anger. See Bstan- 'dzin rgya-mtsho, *For the Benefit*, 52–53.

66. Śāntideva, *Bodhicaryāvatāra*, 6:2.

67. Śāntideva, *Bodhicaryāvatāra*, 6:21.

68. Śāntideva, *Bodhicaryāvatāra*, 6:22.

69. Śāntideva, *Bodhicaryāvatāra*, 6:31.

70. Śāntideva takes a brief detour in verses 27–30 to argue that those Hindus or others who believe in an eternal being or some primal matter—something that could be regarded as a real actor and object for our response—are involved in self-contradiction.

71. Śāntideva, *Bodhicaryāvatāra*, 6:32.

72. Bstan- 'dzin rgya-mtsho, *For the Benefit*, 62.

73. Śāntideva, *Bodhicaryāvatāra*, 6:35, 39.

74. Śāntideva, *Bodhicaryāvatāra*, 6:40.

75. Śāntideva, *Bodhicaryāvatāra*, 6:41.

76. Śāntideva, *Bodhicaryāvatāra*, 6:43.

77. Śāntideva, *Bodhicaryāvatāra*, 6:72.

78. Śāntideva, *Bodhicaryāvatāra*, 6:75.

79. Bstan- 'dzin rgya-mtsho, *For the Benefit*, 64.

80. Śāntideva, *Bodhicaryāvatāra*, 6:102.

81. Śāntideva, *Bodhicaryāvatāra*, 6:106.

82. Śāntideva, *Bodhicaryāvatāra*, 6:107.

83. Śāntideva, *Bodhicaryāvatāra*, 6:111.

84. Śāntideva, *Bodhicaryāvatāra*, 6:109.

85. Śāntideva, *Bodhicaryāvatāra*, 6:113. Śāntideva goes on to explain that no ordinary beings are *fully* equal to the Buddhas.

86. Śāntideva, *Bodhicaryāvatāra*, 6:120.

87. Śāntideva, *Bodhicaryāvatāra*, 6:124.

88. Śāntideva, *Bodhicaryāvatāra*, 6:126. Pelden, in his commentary, explains this by saying that the Buddha developed this identification precisely through the practices of equalizing and exchanging self and others that will be expounded in Chapter 8. This is another example of the internal cross-references in Śāntideva's presentation. See Pelden, *Nectar*, 228–29.

89. Śāntideva, *Bodhicaryāvatāra*, 6:125

90. Śāntideva, *Bodhicaryāvatāra*, 6:133–34.

91. Bstan- 'dzin rgya-mtsho, *For the Benefit*. 76.

92. Śāntideva, *Way of the Bodhisattva*, 7:8.

93. Śāntideva, *Bodhicaryāvatāra*, 7:10.

94. Śāntideva, *Way of the Bodhisattva*, 7:14.

95. Śāntideva, *Way of the Bodhisattva*, 7:17.

96. See Bstan- 'dzin rgya-mtsho, *For the Benefit*, 81.

97. Bstan- 'dzin rgya-mtsho, *For the Benefit*, 81.

98. Śāntideva, *Bodhicaryāvatāra*, 7:18. According to Crosby and Skilton, the source of this quotation is unknown. See Śāntideva, *Bodhicaryāvatāra*, 171. In Chapter 6, Śāntideva explained how ordinary beings function as Buddhas for us. He also indicated that the basic nature of humans is good, that defilements are like smoke in an otherwise clear sky. Here, even insects and worms are destined for enlightenment. There could be no stronger encouragement in the face of despair than the intimation that we already have a Buddha nature. This becomes a large issue in the tradition generally.

99. Śāntideva, *Bodhicaryāvatāra*, 7:25–26.

100. Śāntideva, *Bodhicaryāvatāra*, 7:44–45.

101. See for instance Bstan- 'dzin rgya-mtsho, *For the Benefit*; Pelden, *Nectar*; and Tobden, *Way of Awakening*.

102. Pelden, *Nectar*, 188.

103. Śāntideva, *Bodhicaryāvatāra*, 7:49–50.

3. *Extreme Wisdom, Groundless Compassion*

1. Introduction to Chapter 8, in Śāntideva, *Bodhicaryāvatāra*, trans. Kate Crosby and Andrew Skilton, Oxford World's Classics (Oxford: Oxford University Press, 1996), 75–76.

2. See Kunzang Pelden, *Nectar of Manjushri's Speech: A Detailed Commentary on Shantideva's Way of the Bodhisattva*, trans. the Padmakara Translation Group (Boston: Shambhala, 2007), 282.

3. Crosby and Skilton point out that this chapter exhibits the most dramatic divergence between the canonical text and the presumably earlier Duhuang manuscript. The older text has only 58 verses of the 186 in the canonical version. See the Introduction to Chapter 8, in Śāntideva, *Bodhicaryāvatāra*, 77.

4. Śāntideva, *Bodhicaryāvatāra*, 8:4.

5. Śāntideva, *Bodhicaryāvatāra*, 8:22.

6. Śāntideva, *Bodhicaryāvatāra*, 8:14a.

7. Śāntideva, *Bodhicaryāvatāra*, 8:14b–15a.

8. Śāntideva, *Bodhicaryāvatāra*, 8:33.

9. Śāntideva, *Bodhicaryāvatāra*, 8:35.

10. Śāntideva, *Bodhicaryāvatāra*, 8:39.

11. Śāntideva, *Bodhicaryāvatāra*, 8:49.

12. Śāntideva, *Bodhicaryāvatāra*, 8:53.

13. Śāntideva, *Bodhicaryāvatāra*, 8:71, 81.

14. See Paul Griffiths, "Indian Buddhist Meditation" in *Buddhist Spirituality*, ed. Yoshinori Takeuchi (New York: Crossroad, 1993), 52–53.

15. Śāntideva, *Bodhicaryāvatāra*, 8:85.

16. See the Introduction to Chapter 8 in Śāntideva, *Bodhicaryāvatāra*, 78. The traditional biographies of Śāntideva did attribute to him periods of forest meditation when he was not at Nalanda.

17. Śāntideva, *Bodhicaryāvatāra*, 8:89.

18. Bstan- 'dzin rgya-mtsho, *For the Benefit of All Beings: A Commentary on the Way of the Bodhisattva*, Shambhala Classics (Boston: Shambhala, 2009), 99.

19. Pelden, *Nectar*, 282.

20. Śāntideva, *Bodhicaryāvatāra*, 8:96.

21. Śāntideva, *Bodhicaryāvatāra*, 8:98.

22. This seems to cast in doubt the bedrock conviction that karmic causes are connected to their effects. One reason to care about the future "me" is that it is the only future state of affairs to which my actions are causally related. But if my current "self" is illusory, then so, too, is a future one. Insofar as I see through the first, I will be less invested in the second. Pelden raises the point about karma in his commentary and says that the assertion that karmic effects are not lost rests upon exclusive appeal to deliverances of an omniscient mind and thus "is to be accepted through reliance on the word of the Conqueror." Pelden, *Nectar*, 287–88.

23. Śāntideva, *Bodhicaryāvatāra*, 8:102.

24. Śāntideva, *Bodhicaryāvatāra*, 8:104.

25. Śāntideva, *Bodhicaryāvatāra*, 8:104–05.

26. See Pelden, *Nectar*, 290. The story is also described by Crosby and Skilton in their commentary on this part of the text. They refer there to an interesting variation on this story, in which it is the evil king—the repentant bad guy—who is said to have been the prior-life Buddha. See Śāntideva, *Bodhicaryāvatāra*, 177.

27. Śāntideva, *Bodhicaryāvatāra*, 8:107.

28. Śāntideva, *Bodhicaryāvatāra*, 8:108.

29. Bstan- 'dzin rgya-mtsho, *For the Benefit*, 98.

30. Pelden, *Nectar*, 282.

31. Susanne Mrozik, *Virtuous Bodies: The Physical Dimensions of Morality in Buddhist Ethics* (New York: Oxford University Press, 2007), 38–39.

32. We can think about skillful means as a hierarchy of conventional truths. We could picture this in an ascending order in which a more adequate but imperfect account of

things is given at each step. Śāntideva gives us an even more dynamic perspective. The exchange of different selves (a lower kind of truth) must be deferred until a higher truth about nonduality or nonself can be grasped in some preliminary way. Otherwise, the qualities involved in putting one's self in differentiated positions will lead to the negative emotions and distinctions that undermine wisdom. We could actually see this as a kind of circle, given the coextensiveness of *saṃsāra* and *nirvāṇa*. That is, belief in conventional selves gives way to the conventional truth of "no self" and that in turn gives way to a return, so to speak, of conditioned selves, which are now viewed in the clear light of emptiness.

33. See Geshe Yeshe Tobden, *Way of Awakening: A Commentary on Shantideva's Bodhicharyavatara*, ed. Fiorella Rizzi, trans. Manu Bazzano and Sarita Doveton (Boston: Wisdom Publications, 2005), 222. See also Pelden, *Nectar*, 292.

34. See Śāntideva, *Bodhicaryāvatāra*, 8:121.

35. Śāntideva, *Bodhicaryāvatāra*, 8:127.

36. Śāntideva, *Bodhicaryāvatāra*, 8:129.

37. Śāntideva, *Way of the Bodhisattva: A Translation of the Bodhicaryāvatāra*, trans. the Padmakara Translation Group, 2nd ed. (Boston: Shambhala, 2006), 8:140.

38. Śāntideva, *Bodhicaryāvatāra*.

39. Śāntideva, *Way of the Bodhisattva*, 8:141–42.

40. Śāntideva, *Bodhicaryāvatāra*, 8:146.

41. Śāntideva, *Way of the Bodhisattva*, 8:147a, 8:148.

42. Śāntideva, *Way of the Bodhisattva*, 8:150.

43. Śāntideva, *Way of the Bodhisattva*, 8:151.

44. Śāntideva, *Way of the Bodhisattva*, 8:153–54.

45. This was a tack already developed in Chapter 6 on patience, in which Śāntideva studiously avoided going into the inner lives of our enemies or opponents, but made a case that they are in fact benefactors and Buddhas to us by giving us the opportunity to develop the good qualities that will deliver us from suffering while their sins will land them in hell.

46. See for instance Pelden, *Nectar*, 298–304.

47. Bstan-'dzin rgya-mtsho. *For the Benefit*, 111.

48. Śāntideva, *Bodhicaryāvatāra*, 8:158.

49. Śāntideva, *Way of the Bodhisattva*, 8:160.

50. Śāntideva, *Way of the Bodhisattva*, 8:150.

51. Śāntideva, *Bodhicaryāvatāra*, 8:157.

52. See for instance Tobden, *Way of Awakening*, 225–27.

53. Śāntideva, *Way of the Bodhisattva*, 8:162–63, 8:165.

54. Śāntideva, *Bodhicaryāvatāra*, 8:166. This was and is a notoriously difficult position in Indian culture.

55. Pelden, *Nectar*, 306.

56. Śāntideva, *Bodhicaryāvatāra*, 8:165. The point is made much more extensively in Śāntideva. *Śikṣā Samuccaya: A Compendium of Buddhist Doctrine*, trans. Cecil Bendall and W. H. D. Rouse (Delhi, India: Motilal Banarsidass, 1971), 256. Śāntideva quotes from the *Vajradhvaja Sūtra*: "Certainly, the burden or all creatures must be borne by me."

57. Tobden, *Way of Awakening*, 229.
58. Śāntideva, *Bodhicaryāvatāra*, 10:56.
59. Śāntideva, *Bodhicaryāvatāra*, 8:170.
60. Śāntideva, *Bodhicaryāvatāra*, 8:172.
61. Śāntideva, *Bodhicaryāvatāra*, 8:179.
62. Śāntideva, *Bodhicaryāvatāra*, 8:184.
63. See the Introduction to Chapter 9 in Śāntideva, *Bodhicaryāvatāra*, 108–11. The canonical text has 167 verses, while the Dunhuang text has only 62.
64. Śāntideva, *Bodhicaryāvatāra*, 9:1–3.
65. See the discussion in Pelden, *Nectar*, 317–19.
66. Paul Williams, *Mahāyāna Buddhism: The Doctrinal Foundations*, 2nd ed. (London: Routledge, 2009), 2.
67. Bstan-'dzin rgya-mtsho, *For the Benefit*, 120.
68. Ultimate truth is "defined as what is realized explicitly by a direct, valid perceiver without dualistic appearances" (Tobden, *Way of Awakening*, 244).
69. There is some disagreement about whether some of these verses address realists or Yogācāra, which can be seen as realist in comparison with Madhyamaka but as stressing emptiness more than earlier realist schools. Crosby and Skilton and the Wallaces associate most of these verses with Yogācāra. Pelden and the Dalai Lama do not. See Śāntideva, *Bodhicaryāvatāra*; and Śāntideva, *Guide to the Bodhisattva Way of Life*, trans. Vensa A. Wallace and B. Alan Wallace (Ithaca, N.Y.: Snow Lion Publications, 1997).
70. Bstan-'dzin rgya-mtsho, *Practicing Wisdom: The Perfection of Shantideva's Bodhisattva Way*, ed. and trans. Thupten Jinpa (Boston: Wisdom Publications, 2004), 42.
71. Pelden, *Nectar*, 317.
72. Bstan-'dzin rgya-mtsho, *Practicing Wisdom*, 87.
73. Bstan-'dzin rgya-mtsho, *For the Benefit*, 120.
74. Bstan-'dzin rgya-mtsho, *For the Benefit*, 118–19.
75. Pelden, *Nectar*, 367.
76. Williams, *Mahāyāna Buddhism*, 79.
77. Also called Cittamara.
78. This discussion of Yogācāra is drawn largely from Williams, *Mahāyāna Buddhism*, 89–91.
79. Bstan-'dzin rgya-mtsho, *Practicing Wisdom*, 87.
80. Though the Yogācāra and Madhyamaka views are so finely honed that they can be hard to distinguish, they see each other as falling respectively into the "extreme of existence" and the "extreme of nonexistence." See the quotation attributed to Saraha: "To hold on to things as real is to be stupid like a cow. To hold on to things as unreal is to be even more stupid!" Douglas S. Duckworth, "Onto-Theology and Emptiness: The Nature of Buddha Nature," *Journal of the American Academy of Religion* 82, no. 4 (2014): 1075.
81. Mirages are not real even in conventional terms. The ordinary objects of our perception, including our own "selves" are real in a conventional sense, but not an ultimate one. Yogācāra and Madhyamaka agree on the status of these three things: mirages, objects of perception and selves. All of these are empty. But when we come to mind itself, they diverge. Mind is empty in the sense that it does not have the kind of con-

tinuous self-existence we project on it when we attribute a "self" (so far both agree again). But, as we have noted, Yogācāra holds that the mind is not empty because there is an actual basis for it, the nondual flow of experience.

82. See the different ways that Crosby and Skilton and the Wallaces parse 9:16 for example. Śāntideva, *Bodhicaryāvatāra*; Śāntideva, *Guide to the Bodhisattva Way of Life*.

83. Śāntideva, *Bodhicaryāvatāra*, 9:17.

84. This point is related to but distinct from the Yogācāra belief in a store consciousness in which karmic seeds are planted. The store consciousness has primarily to do with the process of transmigration, whereas the issue here is the nature of the mind's insight into wisdom.

85. Śāntideva, *Bodhicaryāvatāra*, 9:23.

86. Tobden, *Way of Awakening*, 296.

87. Śāntideva, *Bodhicaryāvatāra*, 9:29.

88. Bstan-'dzin rgya-mtsho, *Transcendent Wisdom*, ed. and trans. B. Alan Wallace, 2nd ed. (Ithaca, N.Y.: Snow Lion Publications, 1994), 139.

89. See Duckworth's explanation of what he calls implicative negation and nonimplicative negation in Duckworth, "Onto-Theology," 1075–76.

90. Bstan-'dzin rgya-mtsho, *Transcendent Wisdom*, 100.

91. Bstan-'dzin rgya-mtsho, *Practicing Wisdom*, 59.

92. Śāntideva, *Way of the Bodhisattva*, 9:32b.

93. Śāntideva, *Bodhicaryāvatāra*, 9:34.

94. Pelden, *Nectar*, 336.

95. Śāntideva, *Bodhicaryāvatāra*, 9:40a.

96. Śāntideva, *Bodhicaryāvatāra*, 9:40b.

97. Tobden, *Way of Awakening*, 339.

98. Bstan-'dzin rgya-mtsho, *Transcendent Wisdom*, 45.

99. See Bstan-'dzin rgya-mtsho, *Practicing Wisdom*, 76.

100. Śāntideva, *Way of the Bodhisattva*, 9:48.

101. Tobden, *Way of Awakening*, 342.

102. Tobden, *Way of Awakening*, 342.

103. The Dalai Lama speaks of some contemporary figures widely regarded as *arhat*s. His opinion is that they are only "Arhats as described in the Abidharma [i.e., classic Buddhist texts]" who "have temporarily suppressed the active mental distortions that are explained" in those texts, but are not "actual Arhats." Bstan-'dzin rgya-mtsho, *Transcendent Wisdom*, 46.

104. The Dalai Lama says that "most ordinary beings are unable to perceive this clearly, just as one might not feel a hair on the palm of one's hand. But in the same way as a hair in the eye causes intense irritation and pain, realized beings experience this all-pervading suffering acutely." Bstan-'dzin rgya-mtsho, *For the Benefit*, 130. See also Tobden, *Way of Awakening*, 309–11.

105. Bstan-'dzin rgya-mtsho, *Practicing Wisdom*, 76.

106. Śāntideva, *Way of the Bodhisattva*, 9:52.

107. Bstan-'dzin rgya-mtsho, *Practicing Wisdom*, 83.

108. Śāntideva, *Bodhicaryāvatāra*, 9:75–76. I have changed the terms in brackets for clarity.

109. Pelden, *Nectar*, 355.

110. Introduction to Chapter 8 in Śāntideva, *Bodhicaryāvatāra*, 86–87.

111. See Stephen Batchelor's interpretation in Śāntideva, *Guide to the Bodhisattva's Way of Life*, trans. Stephen Batchelor (Dharamsala, India: Library of Tibetan Works & Archives, 1979), 159.

112. Bstan-'dzin rgya-mtsho, *Practicing Wisdom*, 49.

113. Bstan-'dzin rgya-mtsho, *Practicing Wisdom*, 154.

114. Ze-chen rgyal-tshab padma-'gyur-med-rnam-rgyal, *Path of Heroes: Birth of Enlightenment*, Tibetan Translation Series, vol. 1 (Berkeley, Calif.: Dharma Publishing, 1995), xxi.

115. Bstan-'dzin rgya-mtsho, *Practicing Wisdom*, 85.

116. Bstan-'dzin rgya-mtsho, *Practicing Wisdom*, 86.

117. The argument comes from Nagarjuna and was later referred to as the "diamond splinters" argument because it is thought to cut like a diamond, making the finest distinctions possible. Williams, *Mahāyāna Buddhism*, 73.

118. Williams, *Mahāyāna Buddhism*, 73. This passage is a quotation of Nagarjuna that is found in the *Madhyamakakārikā*.

119. Bstan-'dzin rgya-mtsho, *Practicing Wisdom*, 146.

120. This is the Dalai Lama's suggestion, at least, as he notes that there are two kinds of causation, natural and karmic. The effects of "natural law" are not the products of karma, he says. Bstan-'dzin rgya-mtsho, *Practicing Wisdom*, 148.

121. Bstan-'dzin rgya-mtsho, *Practicing Wisdom*, 114–15.

122. 9:140 in Śāntideva, *Way of the Bodhisattva*.

123. Bstan-'dzin rgya-mtsho, *Practicing Wisdom*, 154.

124. Śāntideva, *Bodhicaryāvatāra*, 9:149.

125. Tobden, *Way of Awakening*, 326

126. Tobden, *Way of Awakening*, 345. Paul Williams says that Tibetan commentaries on the *Bodhicaryāvatāra* are rich in this kind of allusion to Buddha nature while such are not found in Indian Sanskrit commentaries and may not be intended by Śāntideva. The word for "emptiness" in Sanskrit carries a neutral sense of absence of inherent existence—"this is the nature of things whether there are Buddhas or not"—while the word typically used in Tibetan carries strong additional positive connotations relating to *nirvāṇa*: radiant by nature or purified. See Williams, *Altruism and Reality: Studies in the Philosophy of the Bodhicaryāvatāra* (Surrey, U.K.: Curzon Press, 1998), 2–3.

127. Tobden, *Way of Awakening*, 345.

128. See Chapter 5, titled "Absence of Self and the Removal of Pain: How Śāntideva Destroyed the Bodhisattva Path," in Williams, *Altruism and Reality*, 104–63.

129. Bstan-'dzin rgya-mtsho, *Practicing Wisdom*, 90.

130. Makransky, *Buddhahood Embodied*, 346–47.

131. Bstan-'dzin rgya-mtsho, *Practicing Wisdom*, 69.

132. Śāntideva, *Bodhicaryāvatāra*, 10:1–2. The Tibetan version of the first verse puts this in Śāntideva's first person: "Due to the virtue of my composing *A Guide to the Bodhisattva Way of Life* . . ."

133. One discordant note from our perspective is Śāntideva, *Bodhicaryāvatāra*, 10:30: "May the women in the world become men."

134. Śāntideva, *Bodhicaryāvatāra*, 10:10.

135. Śāntideva, *Bodhicaryāvatāra*, 10:47.

136. Śāntideva, *Bodhicaryāvatāra*, 10:55–56.
137. Makransky says that postponement imagery was an early experiment in formulating the reality of a nonabiding *nirvāṇa*. It remained embedded as a feature in older rituals, like the plea to bodhisattvas to remain in *saṃsāra* that Śāntideva includes in 3:5, while being reinterpreted in later tradition in terms like those of Buddha nature and Buddha bodies. See Makransky, *Buddhahood Embodied*, 336–37.
138. Duckworth. "Onto-Theology," 1074.
139. Duckworth. "Onto-Theology," 1074–75.
140. This obviously has some connections with the Yogācāra position discussed in Śāntideva's Chapter 9.
141. See Lama Thubten Yeshe, *Introduction to Tantra: The Transformation of Desire* (Somerville, Maine: Wisdom Publications 2014).
142. The number of bodies of the Buddha, and their related terminology and definition, are not settled issues even within Tibetan Buddhism. See Makransky, *Buddhahood Embodied*, 4–6.
143. Williams, *Mahāyāna Buddhism*, 181.
144. Williams, *Mahāyāna Buddhism*, 180–91.
145. See Makransky, *Buddhahood Embodied*, 97–104.
146. Makransky, *Buddhahood Embodied*, 100.
147. Makransky describes these two in the context of Tibetan tradition by examining the views of two eighth century writers, Ye shes sde and Haribhadra. See Makransky, *Buddhahood Embodied*, 348–62.
148. Makransky, *Buddhahood Embodied*, 361.
149. Makransky, *Buddhahood Embodied*, 361.
150. Quoted in Malcolm David Eckel, "Perspectives on the Buddhist-Christian Dialogue," in *Christ and the Bodhisattva*, ed. Donald S. Lopez and Steven C. Rockefeller (Albany: State University of New York Press, 1987), 57–58.
151. Eckel, "Perspectives," 58.
152. See the discussion by Crosby and Skilton in Śāntideva, *Bodhicaryāvatāra*, 85–87.
153. Makransky, *Buddhahood Embodied*, 244.
154. Makransky, *Buddhahood Embodied*, 356.
155. Makransky, *Buddhahood Embodied*, 245.
156. By some accounts the phenomena of both *saṃsāra* and *nirvāṇa* can appear under two modes, an "appearance mode" and an "abiding mode." So, the appearance modes of *saṃsāra* and enlightenment are both part of conventional truth, while the abiding modes of each are part of ultimate truth. See Pelden, *Nectar*, 315.
157. Williams, *Mahāyāna Buddhism*, 215.
158. Williams, *Mahāyāna Buddhism*, 240–41.
159. Williams, *Mahāyāna Buddhism*, 240–41. The math here seems quite daunting, as presumably all beings are on their way to becoming Buddhas, and this would seem to require a universe for each to set up a Buddha field, each of those universes being full of beings who are on their way to the same. These mind-blowing extrapolations are an index of the distance between truth and our limited imagination, or are an indication that such literalism is beside the point.
160. Williams, *Mahāyāna Buddhism*, 217.

161. See Williams, *Mahāyāna Buddhism*, 245.

162. Williams, *Mahāyāna Buddhism*, 249.

163. William Empson, *Face of the Buddha*, ed. Rupert Richard Arrowsmith with Partha Mitter (Oxford; Oxford University Press, 2016), 81.

164. Empson, *Face*. He illustrated his point by comparing photographic images in which complete faces were produced by mirroring the left side on itself and then doing the same with the right side. See figures 61 through 63 for his prime example. Empson, *Face*, 89–91.

165. Empson, *Face*, 92.

4. *The Bodhisattva as Aspirant: Creatures and No-Self*

1. These three chapters explore the spectrum of Christian nondualisms in conversation with the Buddhist nondualism expressed as emptiness/no-self, as Buddha nature, and as the bodhisattva's activity for all beings. This perspective was outlined in the Introduction.

2. Śāntideva, *Bodhicaryāvatāra*, trans. Kate Crosby and Andrew Skilton, Oxford World's Classics (Oxford: Oxford University Press, 1996), 8:102.

3. Terrence Tilley, unpublished manuscript.

4. Similarly, Aquinas accepts Aristotle's philosophy as an account of our humanity in its natural state, derived from analysis of the teleology of our life in the world. To Aquinas, Aristotle had the nearly last word on what it was to be a creature and know one's self as a creature, based on nature and reason.

5. Buddhist interpretations of *anattā* are very nuanced about just what sort of self is denied, reflected in different schools of thought in the tradition. And Christian understanding has engaged in a long interaction with other sources to shape the way the self has been understood, a process addressed in different ways in John Zizioulis' contention that Trinitarian thought reshaped the understanding of the human person, Krister Stendahl's famous essay on Paul and the introspective conscience of the West, and Charles Taylor's magisterial study *Sources of the Self*. See Stendahl, "Apostle Paul and the Introspective Consciousness of the West," in *Paul among Jews and Gentiles, and Other Essays* (London: SCM Press, 1976); Charles Taylor, *Sources of the Self: The Making of the Modern Identity* (Cambridge, Mass.: Harvard University Press, 1989); Zizioulas, *Being as Communion: Studies in Personhood and the Church*, Contemporary Greek Theologians No. 4 (Crestwood, N.Y.: St. Vladimir's Seminary Press, 1985).

6. Luke 9:24.

7. Niebuhr's somewhat misleading term for the second was "sensuality." See Reinhold Niebuhr, *Nature and Destiny of Man: A Christian Interpretation*, Gifford Lectures vol. 1, (New York: Scribner, 1964). The distortion in his nearly exclusive focus on pride was recognized by later feminist theologians, beginning with Valerie Saiving, "Human Situation: A Feminine View," *Journal of Religion* 40, no. 2 (1960).

8. This example is taken from a teaching of Lama John Makransky.

9. In our exposition of the *Bodhicaryāvatāra*, we already encountered the various schools of Buddhist thought on the vexed question of how to treat the special case of minds, which is so closely tied to the question of selves: according to realist views, the

mind is empty but the elements that make it up are real, phenomenal awareness is real but a subject of awareness is not, and the mind is as empty as everything else. These are sophisticated nuances in the views of Madhyamaka and Yogācāra perspectives.

10. Indeed, for a full-scale argument about this, one would have to turn to Zoroastrians, Manichaeans, or Gnostics, who would hold that there are human souls that are in fact uncreated pieces of eternal spirit, an ontological essence incompatible with matter.

11. God at first appears an obvious instance of *svabhāva* existence. But we will see in the next chapter that a Trinitarian God, a coinherent communion, is resistant to that characterization, as well.

12. One area where the question is asked is in the monastic dialogue between Buddhists and Christians, and the similarities in contemplative experience described there would seem to support this perspective. See Donald W. Mitchell and James Wiseman, *Gethsemani Encounter: A Dialogue on the Spiritual Life by Buddhist and Christian Monastics* (New York: Continuum, 1997).

13. Athanasius and John Behr, *On the Incarnation*, Popular Patristics Series (Yonkers, N.Y.: St. Vladimir's Seminary Press, 2011), 52.

14. Karl Barth, *Church Dogmatics*, ed. Geoffrey William Bromiley, trans. Thomas F. Torrance, vol. 3, part 2 (London: T. & T. Clark International, 2004), 345.

15. Barth, *Church Dogmatics*.

16. Barth, *Church Dogmatics*, vol. 3, pt. 3, 310.

17. See Thomas Merton, *Conjectures of a Guilty Bystander* (Garden City, N.Y.: Doubleday, 1966).

18. Quoted from Merton's private journal on June 22, 1966, in Williams, Rowan, "Not Being Serious: Thomas Merton and Karl Barth." Accessed March 11, 2017. http://rowanwilliams .archbishopofcanterbury.org/articles.php/1205/not-being-serious-thomas-merton-and -karl-barth.

19. This is Williams' summary statement of Merton's text. Williams, Rowan, "Not Being Serious: Thomas Merton and Karl Barth." Accessed March 11, 2017. http://rowanwilliams .archbishopofcanterbury.org/articles.php/1205/not-being-serious-thomas-merton-and -karl-barth.

20. Ecclesiastes 3:20.

21. Orthodox writer Pavel Florensky describes original sin as the failure to recognize the self's identity in the "participatory nexus" set by the Trinity and the construction of a static self. See Donald W. Mitchell, *Spirituality and Emptiness: The Dynamics of Spiritual Life in Buddhism and Christianity* (New York: Paulist Press, 1991), 47.

22. See B. Alan Wallace's note in mtsho Bstan 'dzin rgya, *Transcendent Wisdom*, ed. and trans. B. Alan Wallace, 2nd ed. (Ithaca, N.Y.: Snow Lion Publications, 1994), 140.

23. See Leo D. Lefebure's fine discussion of Augustine and Buddhist emptiness in Lefebure. *Buddha and the Christ: Explorations in Buddhist and Christian Dialogue*, Faith Meets Faith (Maryknoll, N.Y.: Orbis Books, 1993), 115–42.

24. Since I used Reinhold Niebuhr as our earlier example, I should note that Niebuhr was well aware of this, as reflected in his discussion of anxiety, the blameless precondition or occasion of sin. Anxiety is the implicit awareness of creaturely no-self, which leads to various forms of pride or self-denial unless met with faith (in the Christian view) or which leads to suffering, unless it is met with awakening (in the Buddhist view).

25. One can see why the Dalai Lama says that the hardest thing for Madhyamaka was making a case for conventional truth. Once one has a vivid sense of no-self, one may be tempted not to credit the deliverances of such a self on any level.

26. Williams, *Mahāyāna Buddhism,* 71–72.

27. In some of its Western forms, Buddhist practice and especially mindfulness meditation may be applied in a manner that reverses this principle: the effects on health, productivity, and creativity are the primary purpose for the practice. See for instance Donald S. Lopez's critique of this from a Buddhist perspective in Lopez, *Buddhism & Science: A Guide for the Perplexed,* Buddhism and Modernity (Chicago: University of Chicago Press, 2008).

28. We will say a great deal more about this in the next chapter, in discussing Buddha nature.

29. See Ruben L. F. Habito, *Zen and the Spiritual Exercises: Paths of Awakening and Transformation* (Maryknoll, N.Y.: Orbis Books, 2013).

30. They can also demonstrably have negative effects. Negative states can be seen as normal stages in meditation progress but may also be dangerous to people who already have emotional or mental difficulties. See Ron Crouch, "Refugees of Mindfulness: Rethinking Psychology's Experiment with Meditation," https://alohadharma.com /2013/07/23the-refugees-of-mindfulness-rethinking-psychologys-experiment-with -meditation. Note particularly the "dark night" research project at Brown University and forthcoming publications from scholars there.

31. Paul F. Knitter writes affectingly of the way this approach freed his own thinking about the plausibility of life after death and mooted his discomfort with the presumptive self-ishness of an interest in individual continuation. See Paul F. Knitter, *Without Buddha I Could Not Be a Christian* (Oxford, U.K.: Oneworld, 2009), 74–91.

32. This is part of the obvious affinity for Buddhist teachings in the West among psychologists, therapists, and other caring professionals, both as a source of practical technique in counseling others and as an antidote to the burnout that comes from being party themselves to so much painful experience.

33. See for instance a recent study in Allen Verhey, *Christian Art of Dying: Learning from Jesus* (Grand Rapids: Eerdmans, 2011).

34. S. L. Hurley and Nick Chater, *Perspectives on Imitation: From Neuroscience to Social Science,* vol. 1 (Cambridge, Mass.: MIT Press, 2005), 1.

35. Vittorio Gallese, "Two Sides of Mimesis: Mimetic Theory, Embodied Simulation, and Social Identification," in *Mimesis and Science: Empirical Research on Imitation and the Mimetic Theory of Culture and Religion,* ed. Scott R. Garrels (East Lansing: Michigan State University Press, 2011), 103

36. See Vittorio Gallese, "Being Like Me: Self-Other Identity, Mirror Neurons and Empathy," in *Perspectives on Imitation: From Neuroscience to Social Science,* ed. S. L. Hurley and Nick Chater (Cambridge: MIT Press, 2005).

37. Robert N. Bellah, *Religion in Human Evolution: From the Paleolithic to the Axial Age* (Cambridge, Mass.: Belknap Press, 2011), 131. The extent to which other higher mammals share this theory-of-mind mimetic capacity is debated. See F. B. M. de Waal, et al., *Primates and Philosophers: How Morality Evolved,* University Center for Human Values Series (Princeton: Princeton University Press, 2006).

38. P. Ekman, "Cross-Cultural Studies of Facial Expression," in *Darwin and Facial Expression: A Century of Research in Review*, ed. P. Ekman (New York: Academic Press, 1973); P. Ekman, W. V. Friesen, and P. Ellsworth, *Emotion in the Human Face: Guidelines for Research and an Integration of Findings* (New York: Pergamon, 1972); C. E. Izard, *Face of Emotion* (New York: Appleton-Century-Crofts, 1971).

39. For many researchers, developments in the study of imitation throw new light on the question of autism. It is precisely what is known as the mindreading basis for developing empathy that appears to be diminished in autistic children. As one study put it, it is not so much that autistic children can't imitate actions, as that they can't imitate *persons*. See R. Peter Hobson and Anthony Lee, "Imitation and Identification in Autism," *Journal of Child Psychology and Psychiatry* 40, no. 4 (1999): 649–59.

40. More of the data relating to this perspective will be developed in the next chapter.

41. On the scientific end, Merlin Donald has correlated much of the research data in his constructive overview. See Donald, *Mind So Rare: The Evolution of Human Consciousness* (New York: W.W. Norton, 2001). On the cultural end, mimetic theory is most identified with the work of René Girard. See for instance Girard, *Girard Reader*, ed. James G. Williams (New York: Crossroad, 1996).

42. See for instance Girard and Yvonne Freccero, *Deceit, Desire, and the Novel: Self and Other in Literary Structure* (Baltimore: Johns Hopkins University Press, 1976).

43. See Book 3 on intervidual psychology in Girard, Jean-Michel Oughourlian, and Guy Lefort, *Things Hidden since the Foundation of the World* (London: Continuum, 1987 [2003 printing]). See also Eugene Webb, *Self Between: From Freud to the New Social Psychology of France* (Seattle: University of Washington Press, 1993).

44. For a helpful discussion see Lefebure, "Mimesis, Violence and Socially Engaged Buddhism: Overture to a Dialogue," *Contagion: Journal of Violence, Mimesis, and Culture* 3 (1996): 121–40.

45. Joseph Stephen O'Leary, *Buddhist Nonduality, Paschal Paradox: A Christian Commentary on the Teaching of Vimalakirti*, ed. Catherine Cornille. Christian Commentaries on Non-Christian Sacred Texts (Grand Rapids: Eerdmans, 2017), 234.

46. Both face questions of identity or continuity. For Buddhists, it is the question of in what sense even instant to instant any consciousness can be the same one, as well as for purposes of karma and rebirth. For Christians, it is the question of how the same one as a participant in relations can go beyond the dissolution or recombination of all its conditioned elements—death and resurrection.

47. John P. Keenan, *Emptied Christ of Philippians: Mahayana Meditations* (Eugene, Ore.: Wipf and Stock, 2016), 248. In another work, Keenan quotes Wayne Meeks: "Some of the most provocative thinkers of our time—Mead, Piaget, Bakhtin—have argued that a person's identity is not a given essence with which one begins, but an open-ended and continuous transaction between self and others, between self and community." John P. Keenan and Linda Klepinger Keenan, *I Am/No Self: A Christian Commentary on the Heart Sutra*, Christian Commentaries on Non-Christian Sacred Texts (Grand Rapids: Eerdmans, 2011), 299.

48. Some forms of Christian theology, however, would object to the idea that there is no essential desire in the self, contending that love of God is natural to our created nature. This could mean either that it is essential, an inbuilt part of our nature, or that it

is a potential, whose fulfillment is necessary for the full good of our nature. The latter would be the case if we are made with a mimetic nature. We cannot but form our desires on the model of others. God is our good model, though not by nature our only one. In such a situation, it is entirely natural (i.e., usual) to develop the love of God and it is objectively necessary for our fulfillment. But it is not inevitable: "This rejection of the language of natural desire opens to us, instead, the truth that we are creatures—inchoate, unformed, and hovering over the void from which we were made—who must seek either to return to that void or to find happiness in the arms of the one who brought us forth from it. There is no glassy essence to discover; there is nothing but an unformed gaze that receives form only by looking away from itself and receiving the gift of being looked at by God." Paul J. Griffiths, "Nature of Desire," *First Things* 198 (December 2009): 30.

49. "Cool Arhat and Hot God," in Kosuke Koyama, *Water Buffalo Theology: A Thailand Theological Notebook*, rev. ed. (Maryknoll, N.Y.: Orbis Books, 1999), 96–117.

50. Luke 18:19

51. These are often compared to the temptations experienced by the Buddha during his time under the bodhi tree.

52. John P. Keenan has devoted an entire book to the letter to the Philippians, centered on this passage. He sees Paul's ultimate message here to be in line with Śāntideva's Madhyamaka philosophy. The teaching and example of Jesus show how us to live without absolutes and without captivity to any penultimate identities. Keenan, "Prospects for a Mahāyāna Theology of Emptiness," *Buddhist-Christian Studies*, no. 30 (2010): 3–27.

53. A majority of scholars probably still incline to this reading. See Larry W. Hurtado, *How on Earth Did Jesus Become a God?: Historical Questions about Earliest Devotion to Jesus* (Grand Rapids: Eerdmans, 2005), 88–90.

54. See James D. G. Dunn, "Christ, Adam and Preexistence," in *Where Christology Began: Essays on Philippians*, ed. Ralph P. Martin and Brian J. Dodd (Louisville: Westminster John Knox Press, 1998).

55. Thich Nhat Hanh, "Fullness of Emptiness," Lion's Roar, last modified August 6, 2012, accessed April 28, 2018, https://www.lionsroar.com/the-fullness-of-emptiness. He reports placing on the altar in his hermitage images of both Buddha and Jesus as his spiritual ancestors. Hạnh, *Living Buddha, Living Christ* (New York: Riverhead Books, 1995), 6.

56. This is formally reminiscent of the Manichean reading discussed in the Introduction, in which the death of Jesus is taken as a sign of the universal condition of suffering for spirit so long as it was tied to the material world of the body.

57. Pan-chiu Lai and So Yuen-tai, "*Mahāyāna* Interpretation of Christianity: A Case Study of Zhang Chunyi (1871–1955)," *Buddhist-Christian Studies*, no. 27 (2007): 77.

58. These views are consistent with allegorical or practical spiritual applications of the cross (seeing it as modeling the overcoming of bodily desires for instance) that are widespread in Christian tradition. In this connection, see early Christian use of Plato's observation that humans are "fixed to the body by desire as by a nail." Donald Senior, *Why the Cross?*, Reframing New Testament Theology (Nashville: Abingdon Press, 2014), 7.

59. John B. Cobb and Christopher Ives, eds., *Emptying God: A Buddhist-Jewish-Christian Conversation* (Maryknoll, N.Y.: Orbis Books, 1990), 13.

60. Thich Nhat Hanh, "Suffering Can Teach Us," Plum Village Mindfulness Practice Centre, last modified August 11, 2013, accessed April 28, 2018, http://plumvillage.org/transcriptions/suffering-can-teach-us.

61. See Chapter 3 in Peter Feldmeier, *Christianity Looks East: Comparing the Spiritualities of John of the Cross and Buddhaghosa* (New York: Paulist Press, 2006).

62. Thich Nhat Hanh, *Going Home: Jesus and Buddha as Brothers* (New York: Riverhead Books, 1999), 46–47.

63. See for instance works of the Indian artist Jyoti Sahi, including those on Christ as the good shepherd and the ascension. Jyoti Sahi Art Ashram, "Mandala of the Good Shepherd, "*Jyoti Art Ashram* (blog), October 1, 2007, accessed 28 April 2018, http://jyotiartashram.blogspot.com/2007/10/mandala-of-good-shepherd.html; Markraja, "Jyoti Sahi," *Integrated Arts Movement* (blog), September 30, 2015, accessed April 28, 2018, https://indiaartsmovement.wordpress.com/2015/09/30/jyoti-sahi.

64. Notto R. Thelle, "What Do I as a Christian Expect Buddhists to Discover in Jesus?," in *Buddhist Perceptions of Jesus*, ed. Perry Schmidt-Leukel, (St. Ottilien, Ger.: EOS-Verlag, 2001), 146.

65. Daisetz Teitaro Suzuki, *Mysticism, Christian and Buddhist* (London: Unwin Paperbacks, 1979).

66. James A. Benn, *Burning for the Buddha: Self-Immolation in Chinese Buddhism*, Kuroda Institute Studies in East Asian Buddhism (Honolulu: University of Hawai'i Press, 2007), 15.

67. This is similar to another analogy that might occur: there are relatively rare images of the Buddha as an emaciated, corpselike figure, representing his pursuit of the radical asceticism of renouncers, before finding the truth of the middle way between hedonism and asceticism. The moral is that no one went further in mortifying the body than the Buddha did, only to discover that this was not the path to wisdom. So the extremity of Jesus's physical trial can be seen as admirable efforts in a lesser vehicle.

68. In many *Mahāyāna* traditions, the administering of a small, ritual skin burn is a part of the ordination ceremony for monks.

69. An extensive discussion of these sources can be found in Benn, *Burning*. See especially Chapter 4.

70. The stress on spontaneous combustion also distanced the act from suicide, from which it was strenuously distinguished. Benn, *Burning*, 148.

71. Benn, *Burning*, 121.

72. Benn, *Burning*, 106.

73. From the *Śūraṃgama* Sutra, quoted in Benn, *Burning*, 130.

74. See Soho Machida, "Jesus, Man of Sin: Toward a New Christology in the Global Era," *Buddhist-Christian Studies* 19, no. 1 (1999): 81–91.

75. Since Buddhist insight breaks down the distinction between selves, it seems that there would be no reason that a bodhisattva could not regard all karmic burdens as her own, and that Jesus's taking on the sins of the world would be intelligible in those terms. But this is a rather complicated question, as we will see in further discussion of how bodhisattvas help, in Chapter 6.

76. We will discuss this further in the next chapter, contrasting an emergent person with no-self.

77. See for instance Machida, "Jesus, Man of Sin."

78. Wonhee Ann Joh, "Authoring a Multiplicity of Selves and No-Self." *Journal of Feminist Studies in Religion* 24, no. 2 (2008), 171.

79. See Christopher S. Queen and Sallie B. King, *Engaged Buddhism: Buddhist Liberation Movements in Asia* (Albany: State University of New York Press, 1996).

80. Thich Nhat Hanh, "Letter to Martin Luther King Jr.," accessed March 12, 2017, http://www.aavw.org/special_features/letters_thich_abstracto2.html.

81. Hanh stresses that the act aimed not to fight against any human enemy but only the defilements of mind (e.g., hatred, intolerance, and dictatorship) that led to suffering. Such would be the universal message of a bodhisattva's self-immolation as an offering to the Buddha. But to direct it at a specific human conflict is a distinct step in the direction of "passion." Hanh, "Letter."

82. Hanh, "Letter."

83. There have been a significant number of self-immolations by Tibetans (monks and lay people) over recent years, relating to Chinese occupation of Tibet. The Dalai Lama's nuanced response to these events is discussed by several observers. See Zara Ramsay, "Religion, Politics, and the Meaning of Self-Sacrifice for Tibet," *Contemporary South Asia* 24, no. 1 (2016): 75–93.

5. The Bodhisattva as Buddha: Immanence and Emptiness

1. Some Buddhists contest the *tathāgatagarbha* teaching and regard it as perilously close to violating the very no-self insights just discussed. *Mahāyāna* and *Theravāda* traditions typically differed on this point. The most dramatic recent expression of this disagreement within the broad *Mahāyāna* world is the critical-Buddhism controversy. See Jamie Hubbard and Paul L. Swanson, *Pruning the Bodhi Tree: The Storm over Critical Buddhism*, Nanzan Library of Asian Religion and Culture (Honolulu: University of Hawai'i Press, 1997).

2. Kunzang Pelden, *Nectar of Manjushri's Speech: A Detailed Commentary on Shantideva's Way of the Bodhisattva*, trans. the Padmakara Translation Group (Boston: Shambhala, 2007), 88.

3. Pelden, *Nectar*, 88.

4. Pelden, *Nectar*, 226.

5. Pelden, *Nectar*, 229.

6. This paragraph is summarized from Pelden, *Nectar*, 228–29.

7. Pelden, *Nectar*, 229.

8. A noted Buddhist artist showed his students a single, winged line in the middle of a white canvas and asked them "What is this?" "A bird," they immediately responded. "No," he said. "It is the sky with a bird in it." In other words, the consciousness of Buddha nature is not just the emptying of the mind's contents, but this reversal of fields.

9. It is interesting to reflect that this universal awareness is the imagined reference point behind philosophies of realism—an objective, nonrelative God's-eye view. But this is a God's-eye view with no "I" consciousness. It has immediacy but no content.

10. "Consciousness" may be a misleading term. In Buddhist studies, it is often used to translate the Sanskrit term *vijñāna* that specifically refers to dualistic, conventional mind. A different term, *jnana* or *nirvikalpa-jñāna*, designates enlightened, nonconceptual awareness.

11. The comparable Christian formulation would be that no single view can be absolute because truth is relational and no one perspective can capture or contain it. Even God's view of the world, being Trinitarian in its nature, conforms to this truth.

12. See for instance Chapter 6 in John J. Makransky and Philip Osgood, *Awakening through Love: Unveiling Your Deepest Goodness* (Boston: Wisdom Publications, 2007), 157–200.

13. From the Pātaligama Vagga of the *Khuddaka Nikāya*, quoted in Lynn A. De Silva, *Problem of the Self in Buddhism and Christianity*, Library of Philosophy and Religion (London; New York: Macmillan Press, 1979), 139.

14. Śāntideva, *Bodhicaryāvatāra*, trans. Kate Crosby and Andrew Skilton, Oxford World's Classics (Oxford: Oxford University Press, 1996), 10:55.

15. See Roger Corless and Paul F. Knitter, *Buddhist Emptiness and Christian Trinity: Essays and Explorations* (New York: Paulist Press, 1990).

16. See Keith Ward, "Cosmos as Kenosis" in *Work of Love: Creation as Kenosis*, ed. John Polkinghorne (Grand Rapids: Eerdmans 2001).

17. On relational ontology, see Wesley Wildman, "An Introduction to Relational Ontology" in *The Trinity and an Entangled World: Relationality in Physical Science and Theology*, ed. J. C. Polkingnorne (Grand Rapids: Eerdmans, 2010).

18. Ward, "Cosmos."

19. Quoted in R. Kendall Soulen, *Divine Name(s) and the Holy Trinity* (Louisville: Westminster John Knox Press, 2011), 59.

20. In many cases, the word "glory" carries these overtones. For instance, in Romans 6:4 Jesus is said to have been raised from the dead through "the glory of the Father." This can be taken to mean by the power of God, but it also connotes a concrete medium for action by sharing the radiance or energies of God.

21. The fourteenth-century theological controversy over *hesychasm*, mystical practices associated with the divine energies in the form of light, were as formative in Eastern Christianity as the Reformation in the West. See John Meyendorff, *Byzantine Theology: Historical Trends and Doctrinal Themes* (New York: Fordham University Press, 1974), 76–77. In this connection, it is interesting that the Chinese Christian church of the Tang dynasty adopted the self-designation "luminous religion," and one of its key surviving texts is the sutra of "returning to original nature." In that Buddhist and Taoist context, Christian thinkers appear to have explored the same themes of divine immanence that our contemporary dialogue with Buddhism calls forth. See Martin Palmer and Eva Wong, *Jesus Sutras: Rediscovering the Lost Scrolls of Taoist Christianity* (New York: Ballantine, 2001), Chapters Seven and Eight, 169–232.

22. Bishop of Diokleia Kallistos, *Orthodox Way* (Crestwood, N.Y.: St. Vladimir's Seminary Press, 1995), 118.

23. As a concrete expression of this, see the photography of Christopher Burkett, "Welcome," West Wind Arts Inc., 2018, accessed April 28, 2018, http://christopherburkett .com. Burkett believes that as these divine energies manifest with the qualities of light, it should be possible under the right circumstances to capture something of them in photography. In his Artist's Statement, he writes, "The world untouched and

undefiled by man is one of indescribable beauty and wonder. All of our world, each living cell, every stone and drop of water, even the air and light around us, reflects and mirrors the glory and presence of the Creator and calls us to respond with wonder and praise. . . . The purpose of my photography is to provide a brief, if somewhat veiled glimpse into that clear and brilliant world of light and power." Burkett, "About the Artist," West Wind Arts Inc., 2018, accessed April 28, 2018, http://christopherburkett.com /about.

24. "Creativity" here is meant to align with Gordon Kaufman's use of "serendipitous creativity." See Kaufman, "On Thinking of God as Serendipitous Creativity," *Journal of the American Academy of Religion* 69, no. 2 (2001): 409–25.

25. See Kallistos Ware, "God Immanent, yet Transcendent: The Divine Energies According to Saint Gregory Palamas," in *In Whom We Live and Move and Have Our Being*, ed. Philip Clayton and A. R. Peacocke (Grand Rapids: Eerdmans 2004), 164.

26. Vladimir Lossky, *Mystical Theology of the Eastern Church* (Crestwood, N.Y.: St. Vladimir's Seminary Press, 1976), 87.

27. For a sophisticated exploration of this question, including elements in Tibetan Buddhist tradition that could draw the parallel more deeply, see Thomas Cattoi, "What Has Chalcedon to Do with Lhasa? John Keenan's and Lai Pai-Chiu's Reflections on Classical Christology and the Possible Shape of a Tibetan Theology of Incarnation," *Buddhist-Christian Studies* 28 (2008).

28. Dionysius the Areopagite, quoted in Lossky, *Mystical Theology*, 89.

29. Here is an avenue where Buddhism is an occasion for Christian theology to reflect upon the various kinds of divine presence in nature, an issue that Buddhism has addressed more extensively as regards sentient beings by virtue of its teaching of transmigration.

30. The term "big history" comes from the movement to expand the discipline of world history to embed it within the wider cosmological and biological chronology of nature and life. See David Christian and William H. McNeill, *Maps of Time: An Introduction to Big History* (Oakland: University of California Press, 2011).

31. See the brief summary in Robert N. Bellah, *Religion in Human Evolution: From the Paleolithic to the Axial Age* (Cambridge, Mass.: Belknap Press, 2011), xviii.

32. Bellah notes in *Religion in Human Evolution* that argument continues over which came first, language or ritual, but he comes down firmly on the side of ritual, as an achievement made possible first by humans' basic mimetic access to the contents of each other's subjectivity.

33. Jean-Jacques Rousseau, "Discourse on the Arts and Sciences," in *Essential Rousseau: The Social Contract, Discourse on the Origins of Inequality, Discourse on the Arts and Sciences, the Creed of a Savoyard Priest*, ed. Lowell Blair (New York: Mentor New American Library, 1975), 216

34. See M. A. Nowak and Sarah Coakley, *Evolution, Games, and God: The Principle of Cooperation* (Cambridge, Mass.: Harvard University Press, 2013); and David Sloan Wilson, *Darwin's Cathedral: Evolution, Religion, and the Nature of Society* (Chicago: University of Chicago Press, 2002).

35. There is an interesting discussion of Buddhist and Christian views of evolution in Rose Drew, *Buddhist and Christian?: An Exploration of Dual Belonging*, Routledge Critical Studies in Buddhism (New York: Routledge, 2011), 118–19.

36. Rick Hanson and Richard Mendius, *Buddha's Brain: The Practical Neuroscience of Happiness, Love & Wisdom* (Oakland, Calif.: New Harbinger Publications, 2009), 26.

37. Hanson and Mendius, *Buddha's Brain*, 27.

38. Hanson and Mendius, *Buddha's Brain*, 27.

39. Hanson and Mendius, *Buddha's Brain*, 52.

40. Hanson and Mendius present the Buddhist teachings as a kind of balancing force in order to avoid the gratuitous pain that comes from overactive adherence to separation, stability, and vigilance in situations in which they are counterproductive. This seems to understate greatly the nature of the bodhisattva attainment, which is precisely to disregard any survival strategy when it conflicts with the good of others. Buddhist wisdom has almost become solely conventional truth—useful for practical ends but not the highest end.

41. Norman Doidge, *Brain That Changes Itself: Stories of Personal Triumph from the Frontiers of Brain Science* (New York: Viking, 2007). It has long been known that human infants exhibit great brain plasticity and, so, great learning capacity. In many regions of the brain and many functions, this window has been shown to remain dramatically open in adults.

42. This was famously William James's definition of human freedom—the capacity to allot attention.

43. See for instance the prior treatment in Chapter 2 of Śāntideva's emphasis on this in Chapter 5 of Śāntideva, *Bodhicaryāvatāra*.

44. See David Galin, "Concepts of 'Self,' 'Person,' and 'I' in Western Psychology and Buddhism," in *Buddhism and Science: Breaking New Ground*, ed. B. Alan Wallace (New York Columbia University Press, 2003).

45. See the most comprehensive review of studies in this area, which specifies conditions for which well-documented positive effects are known, reviews limitations on many existing studies and suggests that overall claims about benefits are often inflated. M. Goyal, et al., "Meditation Programs for Psychological Stress and Well-Being: A Systematic Review and Meta-Analysis," *JAMA Internal Medicine* 174, no. 3 (2014).

46. There are disagreements among Buddhists over how far a focus on cognitive science and the practical health or mental benefits of Buddhist practice may reduce it merely to an instrumental tool rather than the path to the thorough transformation it is intended to be. See Lopez, *Buddhism & Science: A Guide for the Perplexed*, Buddhism and Modernity (Chicago: University of Chicago Press, 2008).

47. See Andrew B. Newberg, et al., *Why God Won't Go Away: Brain Science and the Biology of Belief* (New York: Ballantine Books, 2001).

48. Newberg, et al., *Why God Won't Go*, 4–5.

49. Newberg, et al., *Why God Won't Go*, 6.

50. Eric Bergemann, et al., "Neuroscience and Spirituality," in *In Search of Self: Interdisciplinary Perspectives on Personhood*, ed. J. Wentzel Van Huyssteen and Erik P. Wiebe (Grand Rapids: Eerdmans, 2011), 90.

51. And other cognitive states, more characteristic of interaction with other minds, would be the type of states associated with personal or communion religious experience. See S. Mark Heim, "Diverse Religious Experiences and First Order Religious

Beliefs: A Response to Branden Thornhill-Miller, Peter Millican and Janusz Salamon," *European Journal for Philosophy of Religion* 8 no. 3 (2016): 237–55.

52. Hanson and Mendius, *Buddha's Brain*, 256.

53. Hanson and Mendius, *Buddha's Brain*, 260.

54. This is something like the case with split-brain patients, for whom communication between the hemispheres of the brain has been severed and one side invents explanations for the behavior of the other. See Michael S. Gazzaniga, *Tales from Both Sides of the Brain: A Life in Neuroscience* (New York: Ecco, 2015).

55. Hanson and Mendius, *Buddha's Brain,* 212.

56. A similar idea is expressed by the philosopher Nicholas Rescher, quoted in James W. Haag, Terrence W. Deacon, and Jay Ogilvy, "Emergence of Self," in *In Search of Self: Interdisciplinary Perspectives on Personhood,* ed. J. Wentzel Van Huyssteen and Erik P. Wiebe (Cambridge, Mass.: MIT Press, 2005), 197.

57. Antonio R. Damasio, *Self Comes to Mind: Constructing the Conscious Brain* (New York: Pantheon Books, 2010), 25.

58. Damasio, *Self,* 286. This has interesting relevance to theological discussions of the bondage of the will.

59. Damasio, *Self,* 285.

60. See Terrence William Deacon, *Incomplete Nature: How Mind Emerged from Matter* (New York: W.W. Norton & Co., 2012).

61. Perhaps the most famous example is the work of Lynn Margulis in making the case that this is the origin of mitochondria and that cells can be viewed as tightly knit communities as much as solitary individuals. See Lynn Margulis and René Fester, *Symbiosis as a Source of Evolutionary Innovation: Speciation and Morphogenesis* (Cambridge, Mass.: MIT Press, 1991).

62. This points to a wider discussion of Buddhist and Christian views on the relation of humans to the rest of nature/creation. In Buddhist terms, human life is a unique opportunity, the only realm in which karmic futures can be affected. It remains unclear to me whether, from Buddhist perspectives, the human world exists solely by the circular logic of the need to remedy what has gone wrong in the same human world (and that much of the rest of nature—the animal world, the realm of hungry spirits, etc.—exists as an adjunct to play out the effects of lives in the human realm) or whether this world (enabling the bodhisattvas whose existence depends on the suffering in it) is integral to the good of Buddha nature. Is human life the only state in which things can go astray? Can preconscious "selves" not mistake their own identity, or can only conscious selves can do this? There would seem to be no path to Buddhahood without the field of suffering beings.

63. Damasio, *Self,* 24.

64. Haag, Deacon, and Ogilvy, "Emergence of Self," 336.

65. Andrew N. Meltzoff, "Imitation and Other Minds: The 'Like Me' Hypothesis," in *Perspectives on Imitation: From Neuroscience to Social Science,* ed. S. L. Hurley and Nick Chater, vol. 1 (Cambridge, Mass.: MIT Press, 2005).

66. Meltzoff, "Imitation," 63.

67. Galin, "Concepts," 136.

68. Galin, "Concepts," 118.

69. For one of the most well-known statements, see Thich Nhat Hanh, "Fullness of Emptiness," Lion's Roar, last modified August 6, 2012, accessed April 28, 2018, https://www.lionsroar.com.the-fullness-of-emptiness.

70. This is the title of a chapter in Thich Nhat Hanh and Peter Levitt, *Heart of Understanding: Commentaries on the Prajnaparamita Heart Sutra* (Berkeley, Calif.: Parallax Press, 1988).

71. Christian theologies of religion have built on this basis, whether in terms of knowledge of God given in creation or of contact with God's will through conscience. See S. Mark Heim, ed. *Grounds for Understanding: Ecumenical Resources for Responses to Religious Pluralism* (Grand Rapids: Eerdmans, 1998).

72. Roberta C. Bondi, *To Love as God Loves: Conversations with the Early Church* (Philadelphia: Fortress Press, 1987), 86.

73. Romans 8:26.

74. And for this purpose, Buddhists are correct that the difference over whether they had an origin in the past is irrelevant. They are changelessly going forward.

75. Nonconceptual and nondual do not equate to more absolute. However unrestricted the subjective qualities of experiences of these sorts, they are experienced and reported by beings who are every bit as limited and conditioned as the concepts and individuals that figure in other kinds of experience.

76. Seiichi Yagi, "'I' in the Words of Jesus," in *Myth of Christian Uniqueness: Toward a Pluralistic Theology of Religions*, ed. John Hick and Paul F. Knitter, Faith Meets Faith (Maryknoll, N.Y.: Orbis Books, 1987), 128.

77. John P. Keenan, *Emptied Christ of Philippians: Mahayana Meditations* (Eugene, Ore.: Wipf and Stock, 2016), 176. Keenan himself rejects the Buddha nature strand in Buddhist thinking, but this is not relevant to my immediate point.

78. Yagi associates such "spiritually presumptuous" statements by Jesus with those of famous Buddhist figures such as Dogen. See Seiichi Yagi and Leonard J. Swidler, *Bridge to Buddhist-Christian Dialogue* (New York: Paulist Press, 1990), 57.

79. This is the point of Keenan's commendation of Buddhist categories as alternatives or correctives for the Hellenistic philosophical categories in which this question is traditionally addressed.

80. Drew notes that many of her dual-belonging subjects like to stress that we are already saved/liberated, that we are living in paradise and don't know it. Drew, *Buddhist*, 120.

81. Raimundo Panikkar has effectively expounded this point in various writings. See for instance Panikkar, *Silence of God: The Answer of the Buddha*, Faith Meets Faith (Maryknoll, N.Y.: Orbis Books, 1989).

82. I see no value in the speculative attempts to fill in the lost years before Jesus's public ministry with journeys to India or study with Buddhist teachers, where the identity realizations become the precondition of all of Jesus's known life and ministry. These appear to reduce Jesus's Jewish faith and identity to a kind of skillful-means mask for the *dharma,* and Buddhist-Christian dialogue simply to a misunderstanding among Buddhists.

83. Netland and Yandell frame the matter this way as Christians. See Harold A. Netland and Keith E. Yandell, *Buddhism: A Christian Exploration and Appraisal* (Downers

Grove, Ill.: IVP Academic, 2009). José Cabezón does the same from a Buddhist perspective. See his essay in José Ignacio Cabezón, "Buddhist Response to Paul Williams' *The Unexpected Way*," in *Converging Ways? Conversation and Belonging in Buddhism and Christianity*, ed. John D'Arcy May (Sankt Ottilien, Ger.: EOS-Verlag, 2007).

84. Along these lines, even God is not a Buddha, and Buddhas are not God.

85. Sallie B. King, "Mommy and the Yogi," in *Beside Still Waters: Jews, Christians and the Way of the Buddha*, ed. Harold Kasimow, John P. Keenan, and Linda Keenan Klepinger (Boston: Wisdom 2003).

86. King, "Mommy," 163.

87. King, "Mommy," 168

88. Cabezón, in a thoughtful response to Paul Williams's account of his conversion from Buddhism to Christianity, argues powerfully for the centrality of love in *Mahāyāna* Buddhism. He affirms both that nondual experience is one form of love and that bodhisattvas are able to move in and out of dualistic forms of other-love as part of their (from a conventional view) supernatural abilities to inhabit wisdom and conventional worlds at the same time. If this is so, then such behavior seems to strain the category of skillful means and become intrinsic to the very realization-nature of the Buddha, though he himself does not extend this to the *dharmakāya* itself. This is relevant to the concerns that King raises and leads into discussion in Chapter 6. See Cabezón, "Buddhist Response."

6. How Do Buddhas Help? Bodhisattva as Benefactor and Christ as Savior

1. The religious setting for Avalokiteśvara's origins seems to involve the example of Hindu gods. See Taigen Daniel Leighton, *Faces of Compassion: Classic Bodhisattva Archetypes and Their Modern Expression—an Introduction to Mahayana Buddhism*, rev. ed. (Boston: Wisdom Publications, 2012), 169.

2. Gene Reeves, *Lotus Sutra: A Contemporary Translation of a Buddhist Classic* (Boston: Wisdom Publications, 2008), 371.

3. Reeves, *Lotus Sutra*, 372.

4. Leighton, *Faces*, 167

5. The example of the Virgin Mary, known in these areas in advance of this time, possibly played a role in this transition. See Martin Palmer, Jay Ramsay, and Man-Ho Kwok, *Kuan Yin Chronicles: The Myths and Prophecies of the Chinese Goddess of Compassion* (Charlottesville, Va.: Hampton Roads, 2009), xix.

6. Leighton, *Faces*, 167–210.

7. There are many versions of this tale. This summary comes from Palmer, Ramsay, and Kwok, *Kuan Yin Chronicles*, 77–97.

8. Palmer, Ramsay, and Kwok, *Kuan Yin Chronicles*, 97.

9. Palmer, Ramsay, and Kwok, *Kuan Yin Chronicles*, 97.

10. See for instance Śāntideva, *Bodhicaryāvatāra*, trans. Kate Crosby and Andrew Skilton, Oxford World's Classics (Oxford: Oxford University Press, 1996), 6:48: "Because of them, and through my patience, all my many sins are cleansed and purified. But they will be the ones who, thanks to me, will have the long-drawn agonies of hell."

11. Quoted in Rose Drew, *Buddhist and Christian?: An Exploration of Dual Belonging*, Routledge Critical Studies in Buddhism (New York: Routledge, 2011), 122.

12. Śāntideva, *Bodhicaryāvatāra*, 6:115.

13. As in the structure of the early chapters of the *Bodhicaryāvatāra* around the seven-part ritual with its offerings to the Buddha.

14. Kunzang Pelden, *Nectar of Manjushri's Speech: A Detailed Commentary on Shantideva's Way of the Bodhisattva*, trans. the Padmakara Translation Group (Boston: Shambhala, 2007), 452n140.

15. Pelden, *Nectar*, 226.

16. Aspirant bodhisattvas continue to take rebirth because they still have a karmic necessity to do so and are cultivating the perfections. "Descending" bodhisattvas are those whose rebirth is more in the nature of a *nirmāṇakāya*, a manifestation produced by their prior vow and the spiritual readiness of some to receive it. These are hard to tell apart, and perhaps there is no need to do so.

17. See Śāntideva, *Bodhicaryāvatāra*, 9:35: "Just as a wish-fulfilling gem or a wish-granting tree satisfies desires, so the image of the Jina is seen, because of his vow and his disciples."

18. Arya Maitreya, with Jamgön Kongtrül Lodrö Thayé and Khenpo Tsultrim Gyamtso Rinpoche, *Buddha Nature: The Mahayana Uttaratantra Shastra*, trans. Rosemarie Fuchs (Ithaca, N.Y.: Snow Lion Publications, 2000), 354.

19. This helps to understand what Śāntideva means when he says that from the moment of the vow, an "uninterrupted stream of merit, equal to the sky, constantly arises even when one is asleep or distracted." Śāntideva, *Bodhicaryāvatāra*, 1:19. The vow becomes a kind of operative force.

20. Buddhists almost universally attribute such omniscience to Buddhas in principle. But when viewed from the perspective of Buddhahood itself rather than from the point of view of the effects of the conditioned acts of bodhisattvas, it presents problems. How can the perfect awareness of a Buddha include constructed appearances? This recalls the observation made in Chapter 3 that there are some Buddhists who maintain that there is a conditioned dimension, even to a Buddha's consciousness, for the purposes of this kind of activity. On omniscience, see also Paul J. Griffiths, *On Being Buddha: The Classical Doctrine of Buddhahood*, SUNY Series toward a Comparative Philosophy of Religions (Albany: State University of New York Press, 1994), 161–73.

21. Maitreya, *Buddha Nature*, 264. From the commentary text by Jamgön Kongtrül Lodrö Thayé.

22. Maitreya, *Buddha Nature*, 354. From the Explanations by Khenpo Tsultrim Gyamtso Rinpoche.

23. Maitreya, 248. From the commentary text by Jamgön Kongtrül Lodrö Thayé.

24. Maitreya, 260. From the Mahayana Uttaratantra translation.

25. Maitreya, 260. From the commentary text by Jamgön Kongtrül Lodrö Thayé.

26. Maitreya, 256. From the commentary text by Jamgön Kongtrül Lodrö Thayé.

27. Maitreya, 258. From the commentary text by Jamgön Kongtrül Lodrö Thayé.

28. This also helps explain why Buddhists are generally undisturbed if such activities are in large measure farmed out to other spirits or gods. This is the lower register of

bodhisattva manifestations. Such worldly benefits can be ceded to the realm of penultimate powers, gods, or spirits who may be effective in such relative causes but are no less lost than humans in regard to suffering and enlightenment.

29. Śāntideva, *Bodhicaryāvatāra*, 3:17–18.

30. The Pure Land tradition elevates this element in its specification of what could be expected from simple repetition of the Buddha's name, but the element is present in other traditions, as well.

31. What I am calling "benefactor practice" is more commonly called "Innate Compassion Training" or "Sustainable Compassion Training" by its adherents. For an explanation and invitation for such practice from its key teacher, see John J. Makransky and Philip Osgood, *Awakening through Love: Unveiling Your Deepest Goodness* (Boston: Wisdom Publications, 2007).

32. In many respects, this resembles the approach found in internal family systems theory in psychology, in which various parts of the self are identified with generation of specific emotions. See Richard C. Schwartz, *Internal Family Systems Therapy*, Guilford Family Therapy Series (New York: Guilford Press, 1995).

33. See the brief, clear description of *tonglen* in Paul F. Knitter, *Without Buddha I Could Not Be a Christian* (Oxford, U.K.: Oneworld, 2009), 150–51. One of the most influential current teachers in the West is Pema Chödrön. See for instance Chapter 15 in Chödrön, *When Things Fall Apart: Heart Advice for Difficult Times*, Shambhala Library (Boston: Shambhala, 2002).

34. We reviewed above, in Chapter 3, ways in which a Buddha mind is held to have knowledge of all phenomena, consistent with a nondual awareness.

35. Luke 7:23.

36. A related instruction comes to Christians from the Jewish custom of treating Torah study as itself not only a beneficial act, an obligation of the faithful Jew, and a loving conversation with God, but also an activity dedicated to the good of others as well as of the student.

37. Schubert Miles Ogden, *Is There Only One True Religion or Are There Many?* (Dallas: Southern Methodist University Press, 1992), 98.

38. For a discussion of bodhisattvas as responsive to different personality types and human conditions, see Leighton, *Faces*.

39. Buddhist interreligious and intra-Buddhist tolerance is based on the long time horizon (within which the superior vehicles can sort themselves out) and the unerring equity in karmic causality. Christian interreligious and intra-Christian tolerance is based on the limitation and corruption of our perspectives, the diversity that must characterize salvation itself and the depth of divine mercy and providence.

40. Makransky, the central teacher in this regard, has long taught in a Roman-Catholic setting, engaging appreciatively with Christian traditions. His innate compassion training, including benefactor practice, stems directly from the root of Tibetan patterns of practice, informed by analogies he has observed in a Catholic context and in other contemplative traditions. See Makransky, "Buddha and Christ as Mediations of Ultimate Reality: A Mahayana Buddhist Perspective," in *Buddhism and Christianity in Dialogue*, ed. Perry Schmidt-Leukel (Norfolk, Eng.: SCM Press, 2005).

41. It is no accident that a primary audience for the teachings discussed here are those in caring professions struggling with compassion fatigue and burnout.

42. I John 4:12b.

43. This indicates the great significance of substituting ordinary people in this role.

44. This is true even among the biblical traditions. See Solomon Schimmel, *Wounds Not Healed by Time: The Power of Repentance and Forgiveness* (Oxford: Oxford University Press, 2002).

45. See Sallie B. King's very interesting discussion of justice and reconciliation in Buddhist perspective, in connection with the idea of forgiveness in King, *Being Benevolence: The Social Ethics of Engaged Buddhism*, Topics in Contemporary Buddhism (Honolulu: University of Hawai'i Press, 2005), 216–18.

46. Thich Nhat Hanh, "Please Call Me by My True Names," in *Call Me by My True Names: The Collected Poems of Thich Nhat Hanh* (Berkeley, Calif.: Parallax Press, 1993), 72.

47. One area where Buddhism is of particular help is in recognizing that our anger and resentment can be misplaced. Based on our misperceptions and limited knowledge, for instance, we may feel betrayed by someone who neither intended to act nor acted in a way that merits that reaction. Since we are so profoundly shaped by our internalization of other people's attitudes, we can be profoundly affected by internalizing mistaken projections of others' inner lives. This illustrates the fact that forgiveness is often not a one-way street.

48. See the classic discussion by Aloysius Pieris, *Love Meets Wisdom: A Christian Experience of Buddhism*, Faith Meets Faith (Maryknoll, N.Y.: Orbis Books, 1988). See also Christopher S. Queen, *Engaged Buddhism in the West* (Boston: Wisdom Publications, 2000).

49. See for instance our discussion of this in Section 2 of this chapter.

50. On haecceity, see John Hare's description in J. E. Hare, *God's Command*, Oxford Studies in Theological Ethics (Oxford: Oxford University Press, 2015), 145–47.

51. I draw on information from this source in the balance of this paragraph. See Sarah Coakley and Kay Kaufman Shelemay, *Pain and Its Transformations: The Interface of Biology and Culture* (Cambridge, Mass.: Harvard University Press, 2007), 98.

52. The pioneering work in this area is Herbert Benson, *Relaxation Response* (New York: Morrow, 1975).

53. The former would be the case for those who hold to universalism or to the literal cessation of those who are separated from God. Christians might adapt from Buddhists a new way to conceive of hell, one that is more or less coincident with the Buddhist view of normal *saṃsāra*, minus rebirth. In such a world, there are sufferings with no actual owners or subjects, only the misapprehension of such, but nothing inflicted and no one to be afflicted. Such might be the state of creaturely no-selves if they were or could be severed from their relational connection with God and others, the isolation that Christians view as hell.

54. Sallie B. King, *Buddha Nature*, SUNY Series in Buddhist Studies (Albany: State University of New York Press, 1991), 208. King remembered this intervention, in that context, as "the starkest example of incommensurability that I have ever witnessed." King, *Buddha Nature*, 209.

55. Iso Kern, *Buddhistische Kritik Am Christentum Im China Des 17. Jahrhunderts: Texte Von Yu Shunxi (?-1621), Zhuhong (1535–1615), Yuanwu (1566–1642), Tongrong (1593–1679), Xingyuan (1611–1662), Zhixu (1599–1655)* (Bern: Peter Lang, 1992), 230.

56. José Ignacio Cabezón, "Buddhist Views of Jesus," in *Buddhism and Religious Diversity Volume II: Christianity,* ed. Perry Schmidt-Leukel, Critical Concepts in Religious Studies (London: Routledge, 2013), 211. The abbot of a Zen monastery in China made a similar point to me. He stated unequivocally that it is impossible for anyone's spiritual attainment to take the place of another's or for the benefit of one's practice or decision to accrue to another.

57. Śāntideva, *Bodhicaryāvatāra,* 10:56.

58. Chödrön and Helen Berliner, *No Time to Lose: A Timely Guide to the Way of the Bodhisattva* (Boston: Shambhala Publications, 2005), 237.

59. Tenzin Gyatso, "Practices of Bodhisattvas," in *Christ and the Bodhisattva,* ed. Donald S. Lopez Jr. and Steven C. Rockefeller (Albany: State University of New York Press, 1987), 218.

60. Donald S. Lopez Jr. and Thupten Jinpa, *Dispelling the Darkness: A Jesuit's Quest for the Soul of Tibet* (Cambridge, Mass.: Harvard University Press, 2017), 237. The translator underlines that Desideri clearly had Śāntideva in mind in this phrasing. See Lopez and Jinpa, *Dispelling,* 237. Lopez's commentary can be found at Lopez and Jinpa, *Dispelling,* 184–85.

61. For a fuller exposition of the way in which this mode of suffering solidarity is also a transformative cause in the social-historical order, see S. Mark Heim, *Saved from Sacrifice: A Theology of the Cross* (Grand Rapids: Eerdmans, 2006).

62. 2 Corinthians 5:21.

63. Christians have long argued over whether God can suffer. Such a possibility has been denied on the grounds that the human Jesus suffered while the divine logos did not, or that God knows what suffering is but does not actually experience it. I think that careful study of the Buddhist understanding of the conditioned and the unconditioned, and the clarity of the causal distinction between them, points toward the conclusion that Christian beliefs necessarily involve crossing that line. Certainly, when defined in the precise and rarified ways in which Buddhism conceives it, it is plain that suffering does attach to God.

64. John 15:15.

65. This is true whether one holds, with most Christian traditions, that Christ is totally without sin from the beginning or whether the overcoming of sin requires some subjection to its power prior to that overcoming, as would be true of the bodhisattva in the case of suffering.

66. Recalling Dietrich Bonhoeffer's famous phrase from his prison letters, "Only the suffering God can help." Bonhoeffer, *Letters and Papers from Prison,* (New York: Macmillan, 1972), 361.

WORKS CITED

Athanasius. *On the Incarnation*. Translated by John Behr. Popular Patristics Series. Yonkers, N.Y.: St. Vladimir's Seminary Press, 2011.

Barth, Karl. *Church Dogmatics*. Edited by Geoffrey William Bromiley. Translated by Thomas F. Torrance. Vol. 3. Pt. 2. London: T. & T. Clark International, 2004.

Basham, A. L. "The Evolution of the Concept of the Bodhisattva." In *The Bodhisattva Doctrine in Buddhism*, edited by Leslie S. Kawamura, 19–60. Waterloo, ON: Wilfrid Laurier University Press, 1986.

Batchelor, Stephen. *After Buddhism: Rethinking the Dharma for a Secular Age*. New Haven: Yale University Press, 2015.

Bellah, Robert N. *Religion in Human Evolution: From the Paleolithic to the Axial Age*. Cambridge, Mass.: Belknap Press, 2011.

Benn, James A. *Burning for the Buddha: Self-Immolation in Chinese Buddhism*. Kuroda Institute Studies in East Asian Buddhism. Honolulu: University of Hawai'i Press, 2007.

Benson, Herbert. *The Relaxation Response*. New York: Morrow, 1975.

Bergemann, Eric, Daniel J. Siegel, Deanie Eichenstein, and Ellen Streit. "Neuroscience and Spirituality." In *In Search of Self: Interdisciplinary Perspectives on Personhood*, edited by J. Wentzel Van Huyssteen and Erik P. Wiebe, 83–103. Grand Rapids: Eerdmans, 2011.

Bondi, Roberta C. *To Love as God Loves: Conversations with the Early Church*. Philadelphia: Fortress Press, 1987.

Bonhoeffer, Dietrich. *Letters and Papers from Prison*. New York: Macmillan, 1972.

Brassard, Francis. *The Concept of Bodhicitta in Śāntideva's Bodhicaryāvatāra*. McGill Studies in the History of Religions. Albany: State University of New York Press, 2000.

Bstan- 'dzin rgya-mtsho. *For the Benefit of All Beings: A Commentary on the Way of the Bodhisattva*. Shambhala Classics. Boston: Shambhala, 2009.

———. *Practicing Wisdom: The Perfection of Shantideva's Bodhisattva Way*. Edited and translated by Thupten Jinpa. Boston: Wisdom Publications, 2004.

———. *Transcendent Wisdom*. Edited and translated by B. Alan Wallace. 2nd ed. Ithaca, N.Y.: Snow Lion Publications, 1994.

Burkett, Christopher. "About the Artist." West Wind Arts Inc. 2018. Accessed April 28, 2018. http://christopherburkett.com/about.

——. "Welcome." West Wind Arts Inc. 2018. Accessed April 28, 2018, http://christopher burkett.com.

Cabezón, José Ignacio. "A Buddhist Response to Paul Williams' *The Unexpected Way*." In *Converging Ways? Conversation and Belonging in Buddhism and Christianity*, edited by John D'Arcy. May, 89–116. Sankt Ottilien, Ger.: EOS-Verlag, 2007.

——. "Buddhist Views of Jesus." In *Buddhism and Religious Diversity Volume II: Christianity*, edited by Perry Schmidt-Leukel. Critical Concepts in Religious Studies, 205–13. London: Routledge, 2013.

Cattoi, Thomas. "What Has Chalcedon to Do with Lhasa? John Keenan's and Lai Pai-Chiu's Reflections on Classical Christology and the Possible Shape of a Tibetan Theology of Incarnation." *Buddhist-Christian Studies* 28 (2008): 13–25.

Chappell, David Wellington. "Early Forebodings of the Death of Buddhism." *Numen* 27, no. 1 (1980): 122–54.

Chödrön, Pema. *When Things Fall Apart: Heart Advice for Difficult Times*. Shambhala Library. Boston: Shambhala, 2002.

Chödrön, Pema, and Helen Berliner. *No Time to Lose: A Timely Guide to the Way of the Bodhisattva*. Boston: Shambhala Publications, 2005.

Christian, David, and William H. McNeill. *Maps of Time: An Introduction to Big History*. Oakland: University of California Press, 2011.

Clooney S.J, Francis X. *Hindu God, Christian God: Faith, Reason, and Argument in a World of Many Religions*. New York: Oxford University Press, 1999.

Coakley, Sarah, and Kay Kaufman Shelemay. *Pain and Its Transformations: The Interface of Biology and Culture*. Cambridge, Mass.: Harvard University Press, 2007.

Cobb, John B., and Christopher Ives, eds. *The Emptying God: A Buddhist-Jewish-Christian Conversation*. Maryknoll, N.Y.: Orbis Books, 1990.

Corless, Roger, and Paul F. Knitter. *Buddhist Emptiness and Christian Trinity: Essays and Explorations*. New York: Paulist Press, 1990.

Cornille, Catherine. "Discipleship in Hindu-Christian Comparative Theology." *Theological Studies* 77, no. 4 (2016): 869–85.

Cowell, E. B., ed. "Sasa-Jataka." In *The Jataka: Or Stories of the Buddha's Former Births*, translated by H. T. Francis and R. A. Neil. Vol. 3. 34–37.Cambridge: Cambridge University Press, 1897.

Crouch, Ron. "The Refugees of Mindfulness: Rethinking Psychology's Experiment with Meditation." Aloha Dharma. July 23, 2013. Accessed May 4, 2017. https://alohadharma .com/2013/07/23the-refugees-of-mindfulness-rethinking-psychologys-experiment-with -meditation.

Dalai Lama, His Holiness the. "The Problem of Exclusivism." In *Buddhism and Religious Diversity*, Vol. 4, *Religious Pluralism*, edited by Perry Schmidt-Leukel, 241–51. New York: Routledge, 2013.

Damasio, Antonio R. *Self Comes to Mind: Constructing the Conscious Brain*. New York: Pantheon Books, 2010.

Dayal, Har. *The Bodhisattva Doctrine in Buddhist Sanskrit Literature*. Delhi, India: Motilal Banarsidass, 1970.

De Silva, Lynn A. *The Problem of the Self in Buddhism and Christianity*. Library of Philosophy and Religion. London: Macmillan Press, 1979.

Deacon, Terrence William. *Incomplete Nature: How Mind Emerged from Matter.* New York: W.W. Norton & Co., 2012.

Deeg, Max. "Towards a New Translation of the Chinese Nestorian Documents from the Tang Dynasty." In *Jingjiao: The Church of the East in China and Central Asia*, edited by Roman Malek, Peter Hofrichter, and the Monumenta Serica Institute. Collectanea Serica, 115–32. Sankt Augustin, Ger.: Institut Monumenta Serica, 2006.

Dharmasiri, Gunapala. *A Buddhist Critique of the Christian Concept of God.* Antioch, Calif.: Golden Leaves, 1988.

Doidge, Norman. *The Brain That Changes Itself: Stories of Personal Triumph from the Frontiers of Brain Science.* New York: Viking, 2007.

Donald, Merlin. *A Mind So Rare: The Evolution of Human Consciousness.* New York: W.W. Norton, 2001.

Drew, Rose. *Buddhist and Christian?: An Exploration of Dual Belonging.* Routledge Critical Studies in Buddhism. New York: Routledge, 2011.

Duckworth, Douglas S. "Onto-Theology and Emptiness: The Nature of Buddha Nature." *Journal of the American Academy of Religion* 82, no. 4 (2014): 1070–90.

Dunn, James D. G. "Christ, Adam and Preexistence." In *Where Christology Began: Essays on Philippians* 2, edited by Ralph P. Martin and Brian J. Dodd, 74–83. Louisville: Westminster John Knox Press, 1998.

Eckel, Malcolm David "Perspectives on the Buddhist-Christian Dialogue." In *The Christ and the Bodhisattva*, edited by Donald S. Lopez and Steven C. Rockefeller, 43–62. Albany: State University of New York Press, 1987.

Ekman, P. "Cross-Cultural Studies of Facial Expression." In *Darwin and Facial Expression: A Century of Research in Review*, edited by P. Ekman, 169–222. New York: Academic Press, 1973.

Ekman, P., W. V. Friesen, and P. Ellsworth. *Emotion in the Human Face: Guidelines for Research and an Integration of Findings.* New York: Pergamon, 1972.

Empson, William. *The Face of the Buddha.* Edited by Rupert Richard Arrowsmith with Partha Mitter. Oxford; Oxford University Press, 2016.

Farley, Wendy. "Duality and Non-Duality in Christian Practice Reflections on the Benefits of Buddhist-Christian Dialogue for Constructive Theology." *Buddhist-Christian Studies*, no. 31 (2011): 135–46.

———. *The Thirst of God: Contemplating God's Love with Three Women Mystics.* Louisville: Westminster John Knox Press, 2015.

Feldmeier, Peter. *Christianity Looks East: Comparing the Spiritualties of John of the Cross and Buddhaghosa.* New York: Paulist Press, 2006.

Galin, David "The Concepts of 'Self,' 'Person,' and 'I' in Western Psychology and Buddhism." In *Buddhism and Science: Breaking New Ground*, edited by B. Alan Wallace, 107–44. New York Columbia University Press, 2003.

Gallese, Vittorio. "Being Like Me: Self-Other Identity, Mirror Neurons, and Empathy." In *Perspectives on Imitation: From Neuroscience to Social Science*, edited by S. L. Hurley and Nick Chater, vol. 1, 101–18. Cambridge, Mass.: MIT Press, 2005.

———. "The Two Sides of Mimesis: Mimetic Theory, Embodied Simulation, and Social Identification." In *Mimesis and Science: Empirical Research on Imitation and the*

Mimetic Theory of Culture and Religion, edited by Scott R. Garrels, 87–108. East Lansing: Michigan State University Press, 2011.

Gazzaniga, Michael S. *Tales from Both Sides of the Brain: A Life in Neuroscience*. New York: Ecco, 2015.

Gethin, Rupert. "Can Killing a Living Being Ever Be an Act of Compassion? The Analysis of the Act of Killing in the Abhidhamma and Pali Commentaries." *Journal of Buddhist Ethics* 11 (2004): 167–202.

Girard, René. *Deceit, Desire, and the Novel: Self and Other in Literary Structure*. Translated by Yvonne Freccero. Baltimore: Johns Hopkins University Press, 1976.

———. *The Girard Reader*. Edited by James G. Williams. New York: Crossroad, 1996.

Girard, René, with Jean-Michel Oughourlian and Guy Lefort. *Things Hidden since the Foundation of the World*. London: Continuum, 1987.

Goyal, M., S. Singh, E. M. Sibinga, N. F. Gould, A. Rowland-Seymour, R. Sharma, Z. Berger, D. Sleicher, D. D. Maron, H. M. Shihab, P. D. Ranasinghe, S. Linn, S. Saha, E. B. Bass, and J .A. Haythornthwaite. "Meditation Programs for Psychological Stress and Well-Being: A Systematic Review and Meta-Analysis." *JAMA Internal Medicine* 174, no. 3 (2014): 357–68.

Griffiths, Paul. "Indian Buddhist Meditation." In *Buddhist Spirituality*, edited by Yoshinori Takeuchi, 34–66. New York: Crossroad, 1993.

Griffiths, Paul J. "Concentration or Insight: The Problematic of Theravāda Buddhist Meditation-Theory." *Journal of the American Academy of Religion* 49, no. 4 (1981): 605–24.

———. "The Nature of Desire." *First Things* 198 (December 2009): 27–30.

———. *On Being Buddha: The Classical Doctrine of Buddhahood*. SUNY Series, toward a Comparative Philosophy of Religions. Albany: State University of New York Press, 1994.

Gyatso, Tenzin. "Practices of Bodhisattvas." In *Christ and the Bodhisattva*, edited by Donald S. Lopez Jr. and Steven C. Rockefeller, 217–27. Albany: State University of New York Press, 1987.

Haag, James W., Terrence W. Deacon, and Jay Ogilvy. "The Emergence of Self." In *In Search of Self: Interdisciplinary Perspectives on Personhood*, edited by J. Wentzel Van Huyssteen and Erik P. Wiebe, 319–37. Grand Rapids: Eerdmans, 2011.

Habito, Ruben L. F. *Healing Breath: Zen for Christians and Buddhists in a Wounded World*. Rev. and updated ed. Boston: Wisdom Publications, 2006.

———. *Zen and the Spiritual Exercises: Paths of Awakening and Transformation*. Maryknoll, N.Y.: Orbis Books, 2013.

Hanh, Thich Naht. *Call Me by My True Names: The Collected Poems of Thich Nhat Hanh*. Berkeley, Calif.: Parallax Press, 1993.

———. "The Fullness of Emptiness." *Lion's Roar*. August 6, 2012. Accessed April 28, 2018. https://www.lionsroar.com/the-fullness-of-emptiness.

———. *Going Home: Jesus and Buddha as Brothers*. New York: Riverhead Books, 1999.

———. "Letter to Martin Luther King Jr." African-American Involvement in the Vietnam War. Accessed March 12, 2017. http://aavw.org/special_features/letters_thich _abstract02.html.

———. *Living Buddha, Living Christ*. New York: Riverhead Books, 1995.

———. "Suffering Can Teach Us." Plum Village Mindfulness Practice Centre. August 11, 2013. Accessed April 28, 2018. http://plumvillage.org/transcriptions/suffering-can-teach-us.

Hanh, Thich Nhat, and Peter Levitt. *The Heart of Understanding: Commentaries on the Prajnaparamita Heart Sutra*. Berkeley, Calif.: Parallax Press, 1988.

Hanson, Rick, and Richard Mendius. *Buddha's Brain: The Practical Neuroscience of Happiness, Love & Wisdom*. Oakland, Calif.: New Harbinger Publications, 2009.

Hare, J. E. *God's Command*. Oxford Studies in Theological Ethics. Oxford: Oxford University Press, 2015.

Harvey, Peter. *An Introduction to Buddhism: Teachings, History, and Practices*. 2nd ed. New York: Cambridge University Press, 2013.

Heim, S. Mark. *The Depth of the Riches: A Trinitarian Theology of Religious Ends*. Sacra Doctrina. Grand Rapids: Eerdmans, 2001.

———. "Diverse Religious Experiences and First Order Religious Beliefs: A Response to Branden Thornhill-Miller, Peter Millican, and Janusz Salamon." *European Journal for Philosophy of Religion* 8 no. 3 (2016): 237–55.

———. *Salvations: Truth and Difference in Religion*. Faith Meets Faith. Maryknoll, N.Y.: Orbis Books, 1995.

———. *Saved from Sacrifice: A Theology of the Cross*. Grand Rapids: Eerdmans, 2006.

———. "The Shifting Significance of Theologies of Religious Pluralism." In *Understanding Religious Pluralism: Perspectives from Religious Studies and Theology*, edited by Peter C. Phan and Jonathan S. Ray, 242–59. Eugene, Ore.: Pickwick Publications, 2014.

Heim, S. Mark, ed. *Grounds for Understanding: Ecumenical Resources for Responses to Religious Pluralism*. Grand Rapids: Eerdmans, 1998.

Hobson, R. Peter, and Anthony Lee. "Imitation and Identification in Autism." *Journal of Child Psychology and Psychiatry* 40, no. 4 (1999): 649–59.

Hubbard, Jamie, and Paul L. Swanson. *Pruning the Bodhi Tree: The Storm over Critical Buddhism*. Nanzan Library of Asian Religion and Culture. Honolulu: University of Hawai'i Press, 1997.

Hurley, S. L., and Nick Chater. *Perspectives on Imitation: From Neuroscience to Social Science*. Vol. 1. Cambridge, Mass.: MIT Press, 2005.

Hurtado, Larry W. *How on Earth Did Jesus Become a God?: Historical Questions about Earliest Devotion to Jesus*. Grand Rapids: Eerdmans, 2005.

Izard, C. E. *The Face of Emotion*. New York: Appleton-Century-Crofts, 1971.

Jonas, Hans. *The Gnostic Religion; the Message of the Alien God and the Beginnings of Christianity*. 2nd ed. Boston: Beacon Press, 1963.

Jyoti Sahi Art Ashram. "Mandala of the Good Shepherd." *Jyoti Art Ashram* (blog), October 1, 2007. Accessed 28 April 2018. http://jyotiartashram.blogspot.com/2007/10/mandala-of-good-shepherd.html.

Kallistos, Bishop of Diokleia. *The Orthodox Way* Crestwood, N.Y.: St. Vladimir's Seminary Press, 1995.

Kaufman, Gordon. "On Thinking of God as Serendipitous Creativity." *Journal of the American Academy of Religion* 69, no. 2 (2001): 409–25.

Keenan, John P. *The Emptied Christ of Philippians: Mahayana Meditations* Eugene, Ore.: Wipf and Stock, 2016.

———. *The Gospel of Mark: A Mahayana Reading.* Faith Meets Faith. Maryknoll, N.Y.: Orbis Books, 1995.

———. *The Meaning of Christ: A Mahayana Theology.* Faith Meets Faith. Maryknoll, N.Y.: Orbis Books, 1989.

———. "The Prospects for a Mahāyāna Theology of Emptiness." *Buddhist-Christian Studies,* no. 30 (2010): 3–27.

Keenan, John P., and Linda Klepinger Keenan. *I Am / No Self: A Christian Commentary on the Heart Sutra.* Christian Commentaries on Non-Christian Sacred Texts. Grand Rapids: Eerdmans, 2011.

Kelsang, Gyatso. *Meaningful to Behold: Becoming a Friend of the World.* 5th ed. Ulverston: Tharpa, 2008.

Kern, Iso. *Buddhistische Kritik Am Christentum Im China Des 17. Jahrhunderts: Texte Von Yu Shunxi (?-1621), Zhuhong (1535-1615), Yuanwu (1566-1642), Tongrong (1593-1679), Xingyuan (1611-1662), Zhixu (1599-1655).* Bern: Peter Lang, 1992.

King, Sallie B. *Being Benevolence: The Social Ethics of Engaged Buddhism.* Topics in Contemporary Buddhism. Honolulu: University of Hawai'i Press, 2005.

———. *Buddha Nature.* SUNY Series in Buddhist Studies. Albany: State University of New York Press, 1991.

———. "The Mommy and the Yogi." In *Beside Still Waters: Jews, Christians and the Way of the Buddha,* edited by Harold Kasimow, John P. Keenan, and Linda Keenan Klepinger, 157–70. Boston: Wisdom 2003.

Klimkeit, Hans-Joachim. "Adaptations to Buddhism in East Iranian and Central Asian Manichaeism." In *Studies in Manichaean Literature and Art,* edited by Manfred Heuser and Hans-Joachim Klimkeit, 237–53. Leiden, Neth.: Brill, 1998.

———. "Apocryphal Gospels in Central and East Asia." In *Studies in Manichaean Literature and Art,* edited by Manfred Heuser and Hans-Joachim Klimkeit, 189–211. Leiden, Neth.: Brill, 1998.

———. *Gnosis on the Silk Road: Gnostic Texts from Central Asia.* [San Francisco]: HarperSanFrancisco, 1993.

———. "Jesus' Entry into Parinirvana: Manichean Identity in Buddhist Central Asia." In *Studies in Manichaean Literature and Art,* edited by Manfred Heuser and Hans-Joachim Klimkeit, 254–69. Leiden, Neth.: Brill, 1998.

Knitter, Paul F. *Without Buddha I Could Not Be a Christian.* Oxford, U.K.: Oneworld, 2009.

Koyama, Kosuke. *Water Buffalo Theology: A Thailand Theological Notebook.* Rev. ed. Maryknoll, N.Y.: Orbis Books, 1999.

Lai, Whalen, and Michael von Brück. *Christianity and Buddhism: A Multicultural History of Their Dialogue.* Faith Meets Faith. Maryknoll, N.Y.: Orbis Books, 2001.

Lefebure, Leo D. *The Buddha and the Christ: Explorations in Buddhist and Christian Dialogue.* Faith Meets Faith. Maryknoll, N.Y.: Orbis Books, 1993.

———. "Mimesis, Violence, and Socially Engaged Buddhism: Overture to a Dialogue." *Contagion: Journal of Violence, Mimesis, and Culture* 3 (1996): 121–40.

Lefebure, Leo D., and Peter Feldmeier. *The Path of Wisdom: A Christian Commentary of the Dhammapada.* Christian Commentaries on Non-Christian Sacred Texts. Grand Rapids: Eerdmans, 2011.

Leighton, Taigen Dan. *Faces of Compassion: Classic Bodhisattva Archetypes and Their Modern Expression—an Introduction to Mahayana Buddhism*. Rev. ed. Boston: Wisdom Publications, 2012.

Lopez, Donald S. *Buddhism & Science: A Guide for the Perplexed*. Buddhism and Modernity. Chicago: University of Chicago Press, 2008.

Lopez, Donald S., Jr., and Peggy McCracken. *In Search of the Christian Buddha: How an Asian Sage Became a Medieval Saint*. New York: W.W. Norton & Company, 2014.

Lopez, Donald S., Jr., and Thupten Jinpa. *Dispelling the Darkness: A Jesuit's Quest for the Soul of Tibet*. Cambridge, Mass.: Harvard University Press, 2017.

Lopez, Donald S., Jr., and Steven C. Rockefeller. *The Christ and the Bodhisattva*. SUNY Series in Buddhist Studies. Albany: State University of New York Press, 1987.

Lossky, Vladimir. *The Mystical Theology of the Eastern Church*. Crestwood, N.Y.: St. Vladimir's Seminary Press, 1976.

Loy, David. *Nonduality: A Study in Comparative Philosophy*. New Haven: Yale University Press, 1988.

Lubac, Henri de. *Aspects of Buddhism*. New York: Sheed and Ward, 1954.

Lybarger, Loren D. "How Far Is Too Far? Defining Self and Other in Religious Studies and Christian Missiology." *Journal of the American Academy of Religion* 84, no. 1 (2016): 127–56.

Machida, Soho. "Jesus, Man of Sin: Toward a New Christology in the Global Era." *Buddhist-Christian Studies* 19, no. 1 (1999): 81–91.

Maitreya, Arya, with Jamgön Kongtrül Lodrö Thayé and Khenpo Tsultrim Gyamtso Rinpoche. *Buddha Nature: The Mahayana Uttaratantra Shastra*. Translated by Rosemarie Fuchs. Ithaca, N.Y.: Snow Lion Publications, 2000.

Makransky, John J. "Buddha and Christ as Mediations of Ultimate Reality: A Mahayana Buddhist Perspective." In *Buddhism and Christianity in Dialogue*, edited by Perry Schmidt-Leukel, 176–99. Norfolk, U.K.: SCM Press, 2005.

———. *Buddhahood Embodied: Sources of Controversy in India and Tibet*. SUNY Series in Buddhist Studies. Albany: State University of New York Press, 1997.

Makransky, John J., and Philip Osgood. *Awakening through Love: Unveiling Your Deepest Goodness*. Boston: Wisdom Publications, 2007.

Margulis, Lynn, and René Fester. *Symbiosis as a Source of Evolutionary Innovation: Speciation and Morphogenesis*. Cambridge, Mass.: MIT Press, 1991.

Markraja. "Jyoti Sahi." *Integrated Arts Movement* (blog). September 30, 2015. Accessed April 28, 2018. https://indiaartsmovement.wordpress.com/2015/09/30/jyoti-sahi.

Meltzoff, Andrew N. "Imitation and Other Minds: The 'Like Me' Hypothesis." In *Perspectives on Imitation: From Neuroscience to Social Science*, edited by S. L. Hurley and Nick Chater, vol. 1, 55–78. Cambridge, Mass.: MIT Press, 2005.

Merton, Thomas. *Conjectures of a Guilty Bystander*. Garden City, N.Y.: Doubleday, 1966.

Meyendorff, John. *Byzantine Theology: Historical Trends and Doctrinal Themes*. New York: Fordham University Press, 1974.

Mitchell, Donald W. *Spirituality and Emptiness: The Dynamics of Spiritual Life in Buddhism and Christianity*. New York: Paulist Press, 1991.

Mitchell, Donald W., and James Wiseman. *The Gethsemani Encounter: A Dialogue on the Spiritual Life by Buddhist and Christian Monastics*. New York: Continuum, 1997.

Mrozik, Susanne. *Virtuous Bodies: The Physical Dimensions of Morality in Buddhist Ethics*. New York: Oxford University Press, 2007.

Murphy, Nancey C., and Christopher C. Knight. *Human Identity at the Intersection of Science, Technology, and Religion*. Ashgate Science and Religion Series. Burlington, Vt.: Ashgate, 2010.

Nagao, Gadjin. "The Bodhisattva Returns to This World." In *The Bodhisattva Doctrine in Buddhism*, edited by Leslie S. Kawamura, 61–80. Waterloo, ON: Wilfrid Laurier University Press, 1981.

——. *The Foundational Standpoint of Madhyamika Philosophy*. Edited by Kenneth Inada. Translated by John P. Keenan. SUNY Series in Buddhist Studies, edited by Kenneth Inada. Albany: State University of New York Press, 1989.

Netland, Harold A., and Keith E. Yandell. *Buddhism: A Christian Exploration and Appraisal*. Downers Grove, Ill.: IVP Academic, 2009.

Newberg, Andrew B., Eugene G. D'Aquili, Vince Rause, and Judith Cummings. *Why God Won't Go Away: Brain Science and the Biology of Belief*. New York: Ballantine Books, 2001.

Niebuhr, Reinhold. *The Nature and Destiny of Man: A Christian Interpretation*. Gifford Lectures. 2 vols. New York: Scribner, 1964.

Nowak, M. A., and Sarah Coakley. *Evolution, Games, and God: The Principle of Cooperation*. Cambridge, Mass.: Harvard University Press, 2013.

O'Leary, Joseph Stephen. *Buddhist Nonduality, Paschal Paradox: A Christian Commentary on the Teaching of Vimalakirti*. Edited by Catherine Cornille. Christian Commentaries on Non-Christian Sacred Texts. Grand Rapids: Eerdmans, 2017.

Ogden, Schubert Miles. *Is There Only One True Religion or Are There Many?* Dallas: Southern Methodist University Press, 1992.

Palmer, Martin, Jay Ramsay, and Man-Ho Kwok. *The Kuan Yin Chronicles: The Myths and Prophecies of the Chinese Goddess of Compassion*. Charlottesville, Va.: Hampton Roads, 2009.

Palmer, Martin, and Eva Wong. *The Jesus Sutras: Rediscovering the Lost Scrolls of Taoist Christianity*. New York: Ballantine, 2001.

Pan-chiu, Lai, and So Yuen-tai. "Mahāyāna Interpretation of Christianity: A Case Study of Zhang Chunyi (1871–1955)." *Buddhist-Christian Studies*, no. 27 (2007): 67–87.

Panikkar, Raimundo. *The Intrareligious Dialogue*. Rev. ed. New York: Paulist Press, 1999.

——. *The Silence of God: The Answer of the Buddha*. Faith Meets Faith. Maryknoll, N.Y.: Orbis Books, 1989.

Pelden, Kunzang. *The Nectar of Manjushri's Speech: A Detailed Commentary on Shantideva's Way of the Bodhisattva*. Translated by the Padmakara Translation Group. Boston: Shambhala, 2007.

Pieris, Aloysius. *Love Meets Wisdom: A Christian Experience of Buddhism*. Faith Meets Faith. Maryknoll, N.Y.: Orbis Books, 1988.

Pomplun, Trent. *Jesuit on the Roof of the World: Ippolito Desideri's Mission to Eighteenth-Century Tibet*. Oxford: Oxford University Press, 2010.

Queen, Christopher S. *Engaged Buddhism in the West*. Boston: Wisdom Publications, 2000.

Queen, Christopher S., and Sallie B. King. *Engaged Buddhism: Buddhist Liberation Movements in Asia*. Albany: State University of New York Press, 1996.

Rahula, Walpola. *What the Buddha Taught*. Rev. ed. New York: Grove Press, 1974.

Ramsay, Zara. "Religion, Politics, and the Meaning of Self-Sacrifice for Tibet." *Contemporary South Asia* 24, no. 1 (2016): 75–93.

Reeves, Gene. *The Lotus Sutra: A Contemporary Translation of a Buddhist Classic*. Boston: Wisdom Publications, 2008.

Rousseau, Jean-Jacques. "Discourse on the Arts and Sciences." In *The Essential Rousseau: The Social Contract, Discourse on the Origins of Inequality, Discourse on the Arts and Sciences, the Creed of a Savoyard Priest*, edited by Lowell Blair, 203–30. New York: Mentor New American Library, 1975.

Saeki, Yoshirō. *The Nestorian Documents and Relics in China*. Tokyo: Toho Bunkwa Gakuin: Academy of Oriental Culture, Tokyo Institute, 1951.

Saiving, Valerie. "The Human Situation: A Feminine View." *Journal of Religion* 40, no. 2 (1960): 100–12.

Salomon, Richard. *Ancient Buddhist Scrolls from Gandhāra: The British Library Kharoṣṭhī Fragments*. Gandhāran Buddhist Texts. Seattle: University of Washington Press, 1999.

Samuel, Geoffrey. *Civilized Shamans: Buddhism in Tibetan Societies*. Washington, D.C.: Smithsonian Institution Press, 1993.

Śāntideva. *The Bodhicaryāvatāra*. Translated by Kate Crosby and Andrew Skilton. Oxford World's Classics. Oxford: Oxford University Press, 1996.

———. *A Guide to the Bodhisattva's Way of Life*. Translated by Stephen Batchelor. Dharamsala, India: Library of Tibetan Works & Archives, 1979.

———. *A Guide to the Bodhisattva Way of Life*. Translated by Vensa A. Wallace and B. Alan Wallace. Ithaca, N.Y.: Snow Lion Publications, 1997.

———. *Śikṣā Samuccaya: A Compendium of Buddhist Doctrine*. Translated by Cecil Bendall and W. H. D. Rouse. Delhi, India: Motilal Banarsidass, 1971.

———. *The Way of the Bodhisattva: A Translation of the Bodhicaryāvatāra*. Translated by the Padmakara Translation Group. 2nd ed. Boston: Shambhala, 2006.

Schimmel, Solomon. *Wounds Not Healed by Time: The Power of Repentance and Forgiveness*. Oxford: Oxford University Press, 2002.

Schmidt-Leukel, Perry. "Finding God in the Bodhicaryāvatāra: An Interim Report on as 'Christian Commentary to the Bodhicaryāvatāra.'" *Journal of Comparative Scripture*, no. 6 (2015): 9–35.

Schmied, K. "Jesus in Recent Buddhist Writings Published in the West." In *Buddhist Perceptions of Jesus: Papers of the Third Conference of the European Network of Buddhist-Christian Studies*, edited by Perry Schmidt-Leukel, 130–39. St. Ottilien, Ger.: EOS-Verlag, 2001.

Schwartz, Richard C. *Internal Family Systems Therapy*. Guilford Family Therapy Series. New York: Guilford Press, 1995.

Senior, Donald. *Why the Cross? Reframing New Testament Theology*. Nashville: Abingdon Press, 2014.

Sheridan, Daniel P. *Loving God: Kṛṣṇa and Christ: A Christian Commentary on the Nārada Sūtras*. Christian Commentaries on Non-Christian Sacred Texts. Grand Rapids: Eerdmans, 2007.

Smart, Ninian. *Buddhism and Christianity: Rivals and Allies*. Honolulu: University of Hawai'i Press, 1993.

Soulen, R. Kendall. *The Divine Name(s) and the Holy Trinity*. Louisville: Westminster John Knox Press, 2011.

Stendahl, Krister. "The Apostle Paul and the Introspective Consciousness of the West." In *Paul among Jews and Gentiles, and Other Essays*, 78–96. London: SCM Press, 1976.

Studholme, Alexander. *The Origins of Oṃ Manipadme Hūṃ: A Study of Kāraṇḍavyūha Sūtra*. Albany: State University of New York Press, 2002.

Suzuki, Daisetz Teitaro. *Mysticism, Christian and Buddhist*. London: Unwin Paperbacks, 1979.

Tanner, Kathryn. *Economy of Grace*. Minneapolis: Fortress Press, 2005.

Taylor, Charles. *Sources of the Self: The Making of the Modern Identity*. Cambridge, Mass.: Harvard University Press, 1989.

Thatamanil, John J. *The Immanent Divine: God, Creation, and the Human Predicament*. Minneapolis: Fortress Press, 2006.

Thelle, Notto R. "What Do I as a Christian Expect Buddhists to Discover in Jesus?" In *Buddhist Perceptions of Jesus*, edited by Perry Schmidt-Leukel, 142–57. St. Ottilien, Ger.: EOS-Verlag, 2001.

Thubten Yeshe, Lama. *Introduction to Tantra: The Transformation of Desire*. Somerville, Maine: Wisdom Publications 2014.

Thurman, Robert A. F. "The Buddhist Messiahs: The Magnificent Deeds of the Bodhisattvas." In *The Christ and the Bodhisattva*, edited by Donald S. Lopez and Steven C. Rockefeller, 65–98. Albany: State University of New York Press, 1987.

Thurston, Bonnie. "The Buddha Offered Me a Raft." In *Buddhists Talk about Jesus, Christians Talk about the Buddha*, edited by Rita M. Gross and Terry C. Muck, 118–28. New York: Continuum, 2000.

Tillich, Paul, and Tomoaki Fukai. *Paul Tillich—Journey to Japan in 1960*. Boston: De Gruyter, 2013.

Tobden, Geshe Yeshe. *The Way of Awakening: A Commentary on Shantideva's Bodhicharyavatara*. Edited by Fiorella Rizzi. Translated by Manu Bazzano and Sarita Doveton. Boston: Wisdom Publications, 2005.

Trelstad, Marit. *Cross Examinations: Readings on the Meaning of the Cross*. Minneapolis: Fortress Press, 2006.

Varma, C. B. "Story of a Tigress from the Illustrated Jataka and Other Stories of the Buddha." *Illustrated Jataka: Other Stories of the Buddha*. Indira Gandhi National Centre for the Arts. Accessed June 9, 2018. http://ignca.nic.in/jatako25.htm.

Verhey, Allen. *The Christian Art of Dying: Learning from Jesus*. Grand Rapids: Eerdmans, 2011.

Von Glasenapp, Helmuth. *Von Buddha Zu Gandhi*. Wiesbaden: Harrassowitz, 1962.

de Waal, F. B. M., Stephen Macedo, Josiah Ober, and Robert Wright. *Primates and Philosophers: How Morality Evolved*. University Center for Human Values Series. Princeton: Princeton University Press, 2006.

Ward, Keith. "Cosmos as Kenosis." In *The Work of Love: Creation as Kenosis*, edited by John Polkinghorne, 152–66. Grand Rapids: Eerdmans, 2001.

Ware, Kallistos. "God Immanent, yet Transcendent: The Divine Energies According to Saint Gregory Palamas." In *In Whom We Live and Move and Have Our Being*, edited by Philip Clayton and A. R. Peacocke, 157–68. Grand Rapids: Eerdmans, 2004.

Webb, Eugene. *The Self Between: From Freud to the New Social Psychology of France.* Seattle: University of Washington Press, 1993.

Whelan, Christal. *The Beginning of Heaven and Earth: The Sacred Book of Japan's Hidden Christians.* Honolulu: University of Hawai'i Press, 1996.

Wildman, Wesley. "An Introduction to Relational Ontology." In *Trinity and an Entangled World: Relationality in Physical Science and Theology* edited by J. C. Polkingnorne, 55–73. Grand Rapids: Eerdmans, 2010.

Williams, Paul. *Altruism and Reality: Studies in the Philosophy of the Bodhicaryāvatāra.* Surrey, U.K.: Curzon Press, 1998.

———. *Mahāyāna Buddhism: The Doctrinal Foundations.* 2nd ed. London: Routledge, 2009.

Williams, Rowan, "Not Being Serious: Thomas Merton and Karl Barth." Accessed March 11, 2017. http://rowanwilliams.archbishopofcanterbury.org/articles.php/1205/not-being-serious-thomas-merton-and-karl-barth.

Wilson, David Sloan. *Darwin's Cathedral: Evolution, Religion, and the Nature of Society.* Chicago: University of Chicago Press, 2002.

Wriggins, Sally Hovey. *The Silk Road Journey with Xuanzang.* Boulder, Colo.: Westview Press, 2004.

Yagi, Seiichi. "'I' in the Words of Jesus." In *The Myth of Christian Uniqueness: Toward a Pluralistic Theology of Religions,* edited by John Hick and Paul F. Knitter. Faith Meets Faith, 117–36. Maryknoll, N.Y: Orbis Books, 1987.

Yagi, Seiichi, and Leonard J. Swidler. *A Bridge to Buddhist-Christian Dialogue.* New York: Paulist Press, 1990.

Yong, Amos. "On Doing Theology and Buddhology: A Spectrum of Christian Proposals." *Buddhist-Christian Studies,* no. 31 (2011): 103–18.

Ze-chen rgyal-tshab padma-'gyur-med-rnam-rgyal. *Path of Heroes: Birth of Enlightenment.* Tibetan Translation Series. Vol. 1. Berkeley, Calif.: Dharma Publishing, 1995.

Zizioulas, John. *Being as Communion: Studies in Personhood and the Church.* Contemporary Greek Theologians No. 4. Crestwood, N.Y.: St. Vladimir's Seminary Press, 1985.

INDEX

Comparative / Thinking Across
Theology / Traditions

SERIES EDITORS

Loye Ashton and John Thatamanil

Hyo-Dong Lee, *Spirit, Qi, and the Multitude: A Comparative Theology for the Democracy of Creation*

Michelle Voss Roberts, *Tastes of the Divine: Hindu and Christian Theologies of Emotion*

Michelle Voss Roberts (ed.), *Comparing Faithfully: Insights for Systematic Theological Reflection*

F. Dominic Longo, *Spiritual Grammar: Genre and the Saintly Subject in Islam and Christianity*

S. Mark Heim, *Crucified Wisdom: Theological Reflection on Christ and the Bodhisattva*